REVISED EDITION

2015

GUIDE TO
SELF-PUBLISHING

Robert Lee Brewer, Editor

WD
WRITER'S DIGEST
BOOKS

WritersDigest.*com*
Cincinnati, Ohio

Publisher & Editorial Director, Writing Community: Phil Sexton

Writer's Market website: www.writersmarket.com
Writer's Digest website: www.writersdigest.com
Writer's Digest Bookstore: www.writersdigestshop.com

Distributed in Canada by Fraser Direct
100 Armstrong Avenue
Georgetown, Ontario, Canada L7G 5S4
Tel: (905) 877-4411

Distributed in the U.K. and Europe by F&W Media International
Brunel House, Newton Abbot, Devon, TQ12 4PU, England
Tel: (+44) 1626-323200, Fax: (+44) 1626-323319
E-mail: postmaster@davidandcharles.co.uk

Distributed in Australia by Capricorn Link
P.O. Box 704, Windsor, NSW 2756 Australia
Tel: (02) 4577-3555

ISSN: 2330-281X
ISBN-13: 978-1-59963-847-8
ISBN-10: 1-59963-847-9

Attention Booksellers: This is an annual directory of F+W Media, Inc. Return deadline for this edition is December 31, 2015.

Edited by: Robert Lee Brewer
Cover designed by: Claudean Wheeler
Interior designed by: Claudean Wheeler
Page layout by: Geoff Raker
Production coordinated by: Greg Nock

CONTENTS

FROM THE EDITOR

When it comes to self-publishing, there's so much writers can (and should) tackle on their own. It's the liberating DIY aspect of self-publishing—and higher profit margins—that draws in so many writer-publishers. But few people are capable of pulling off everything.

For instance, cover design is something most writers might be able to "kind of" handle, but the cover is often an element of self-publishing in which authors are best served to call in a professional. The words are super important to any book, but the cover is the first impression for readers that can either excite them or temper their expectations.

Before readers can check out your words, they need to feel compelled to crack the spine. Once they do open the book, the words better be top notch. For this reason, all authors— even indie authors—need editors. In fact, even editors need editors for their own writing.

If you're not receiving free editing and design services already, then this book offers listings for hundreds of freelancers who are ready to help your book have the same polished feel of traditional publishers. Plus, there are articles to help guide indie authors through the design, management, and promotion processes—not to mention interviews with indie authors who've found success with their self-publishing efforts.

You can make this happen and reap the rewards of self-publishing, but it doesn't mean you have to do it all on your own. By enlisting help, you'll be able to stay independent and professional at the same time to increase your chances of success.

Speaking of help, access your webinar at www.writersmarket.com/gsp15-webinar.

Until next time, keep publishing!

Robert Lee Brewer
Senior Content Editor, *Guide to Self-Publishing*
http://blog.writersmarket.com
http://twitter.com/robertleebrewer

GETTING STARTED

Guide to Self-Publishing is here to help you navigate the world of self-publishing your work. This article includes information about using this book, but it also covers some of the basics of creating your own books. In fact, this section of the book is labeled Production, because it covers the production of your indie products and services.

Other sections include Management, Promotion, and Interviews. In the Management section, there are articles covering topics like record keeping, self-publishing contracts, pay rates for freelancers you may wish to use, and even handling sales tax. The Promotion section is geared toward reaching your target audience and spreading the gospel about your indie books. Finally, the Interviews section shares stories from indie publishers who have found success self-publishing in a variety of genres.

Beyond the articles, there are plenty of listings for self-publishing companies, freelance editors, freelance designers, independent publicists, and conferences. Each listing section includes an introduction and overview about those specific listings, and the listings include contact information, rates, specialties, and more.

WHERE TO BEGIN

Any project, whether creating books or putting on an event, has to start somewhere—and usually that's with an idea. In book publishing, that idea hopefully turns into a manuscript and eventually a book. That's the simple explanation. Of course, book publishing, whether indie or traditional, is anything but simple.

Here's a better breakdown of what happens:

- **Writer gets idea.** The idea might start as the line in a poem or scene in a novel. But it starts as a spark, and that spark begins to catch other words and ideas on fire.
- **Writer pushes through a first draft.** For some writers, this might be a month-long novel writing challenge or years of research on a nonfiction book. It might even be collecting blog content to package and sell. Anyway, the writer gets from beginning to end.
- **Writer revises the first draft.** Well, writers who are serious about putting out a good product will revise their first drafts. Many books that fail can point to a lack of editing and production value as the main reason the book didn't catch on with readers. In traditional publishing, an editor and agent will work with a writer at this point.
- **Writer turns in final draft.** In traditional publishing, the writer is now pretty much done with creating the book. However, the indie publisher/writer still has plenty left to do in creating the book.
- **Designer lays out book.** Fonts are chosen (and licensed in some cases). Front matter, including title and copyright pages, and back matter, including glossaries and indexes, are designed. And don't forget the covers.
- **Publisher files a lot of paperwork.** Copyright is registered. ISBNs are secured (for print books, digital books—various versions). Budgets and marketing plans are set. Records are kept. Eventually, the book is sent to the printer.
- **Printer prints books.** For indie authors, this might mean sending to printer, or it could mean getting it loaded with a POD company. Also, it could mean loading a compatible electronic file for the digital platform of your choice (Kindle, Nook, iPad, etc.).
- **Publisher handles distribution.** For the indie publisher, distribution is going to be an uphill battle. But it's not impossible. Plus, successful indie publishers are good about getting creative with distribution and finding alternative routes to connecting with their target audience.
- **Publisher and writer promote the books.** Sometimes, the publisher does more; usually, the writer does more. In indie publishing, there's no question as to who shoulders most—if not all—of the work. That's right, the indie publisher/writer has to roll up her sleeves, make connections, and get her book in front of potential readers.
- **Next idea.** Successful writers and publishers are never finished with one book. If anything, they feel an even greater urge to figure out the next great idea and successful project. And so, the cycle continues.

KNOW YOUR OPTIONS

Indie publishers have more publishing options than ever. That can be a blessing and a curse. Do writers publish in print or electronic? Print-on-demand (POD) or print run? Local printer or self-publishing company? Writers have a lot of options to weigh.

Here are a few:

Vanity Publishing

Vanity publishers used to be the main game in town for self-publishing, and they accepted any project regardless of its quality. In fact, the quality was often so bad that many contemporary indie publishers are still working their way out of that shadow.

....

For some writers, these services are exactly what they're looking to find, and they're happy to pay a premium to receive them. However, many writers looking to 'make it' in indie publishing find vanity publishers are not the best (or most cost-effective) fit.

....

There's nothing wrong with vanity publishing if you know what you're getting into, but it's often not the most profitable enterprise. Vanity publishers often offer bundled services that might include producing a small print run of books, editing services, promotional services, ISBN registration, and more.

For some writers, these services are exactly what they're looking to find, and they're happy to pay a premium to receive them. However, many writers looking to "make it" in indie publishing find vanity publishers are not the best (or most cost-effective) fit.

Subsidy Publishing

Subsidy publishers are supposedly more selective than vanity publishers, but writers really need to do their homework to make sure this is the case. After all, subsidy publishing contracts and bundled offers are often nearly identical to vanity publishers. With the same money at stake, it's no secret that some subsidy publishers make more money from writers than readers.

Printers

Printing services don't typically screen writers at all and will print to order, but they are focused more on excellent printing than on upselling authors to bundled services. For ambitious indie publishers who aren't afraid to roll up their sleeves and handle everything from design to promotion, these are the folks that will help them get their words into print most effectively.

Some printing services will print a run of books all at once. Others offer POD options.

E-book Conversion Services

More than 20% of traditional book sales in 2012 were e-books. Many in the industry suspect that the ratio is much higher among indie authors. As a result of e-book success stories and multiple platforms, e-book conversion services have sprung up to service writers who need help getting their books digitally ready.

However, as with print publishing, the most ambitious indie publishers learn how to effectively convert their files without paying big fees to adapt to each new platform.

BOOK COVER, COVER TEXT, INTERIOR

by Leslie Lee Sanders

A book is typically judged by its cover, its back cover description, and the quality of its interior text. Some readers still hold on to the once popular belief that all self-published books are of poor quality, filled with spelling and grammatical errors, and are no competition for the traditionally published books it shares the marketplace with. Here's how to self-publish with affordable traditionally published quality inside and out, so readers won't second guess taking a chance on your book.

WHAT YOU NEED

The first thing readers see when deciding to purchase a book is the cover. If the book's cover intrigues them, they move onto the back cover description. If the back cover description is well written and engaging, a skim of the interior pages will follow. Being in the digital age "skimming pages" can also refer to reading online excerpts and sample pages.

So it makes sense to appropriately implement these three suggestions when trying to self-publish a book with traditionally published quality:

- Professional-looking book cover
- Engaging back cover description
- Well-edited interior text

THE PERFECT BOOK COVER

When hiring a professional book cover designer there are certain things you need to look for. This will increase the likelihood you'll be happy with the final product.

Before hiring a cover artist, review their online portfolio for samples of past work. The best cover artists are those who are familiar with your particular genre, know exactly what book covers should look like for that genre, and possess the ability to create original art. Veteran cover artist, Mina Carter, advises to, "Always ask for a draft and whether alterations to the cover, and how many, are included in the price."

Book cover prices vary greatly depending on how detailed the design is, but a basic digital front cover design can start at $100.

- **Request high-resolution stock photos.** Using high-resolution photos and images can help you avoid a final product where the images are distorted, pixilated, or blurred. A professional cover artist is responsible for acquiring the photo art and usage license, and considers the price of the stock photos when providing you with a quote.
- **Make sure the typography on the cover matches the overall tone of the book and is legible.** Play around with different fonts and colors. The title of your book should be in a font that reflects the story's mood and should be easy to read on a thumbnail sized cover.

....

Use a compelling tagline that asks a question, or include a memorable line of the book that persuades the reader to find out more. Good shout lines are original, short, and are linked to the story's major conflict.

....

- **Add a one-line quote** from a respectable reader such as a top blogger, a bestselling author, or a well-known name or reviewer.
- **Add a shout line.** No quote? Use a compelling tagline that asks a question, or include a memorable line of the book that persuades the reader to find out more. Good shout lines are original, short, and are linked to the story's major conflict, i.e., *Fighting to live is easier when you have someone to live for.*
- **Add your credentials in a sentence or two.** Have you made it on a reputable bestsellers list? Have you won a prestigious literary award? A potential reader who sees this on your self-published book cover may be more likely to purchase.

PROFESSIONAL COVER ARTISTS

Here are some important things to know when looking for a cover artist.

According to veteran cover artist Mina Carter, "A cover artist should always be able to give you a quote and an idea of their workflow, as well as a lead time on the cover."

Cover artists also ask plenty of questions and require detailed answers regarding the look and feel you want to portray for your cover. Sometimes they ask you to fill out a cover art form, which is your chance to provide as much detail about the cover as you can. Details can range from a character's eye color to the exact name of the font for the title text.

The more in depth you are about what you want, the happier you'll be with the results.

- Get quotes and lead times from a few cover artists before getting too close to a deadline.
- Know the difference between print quality covers and sizes and e-covers and ensure you know what you're paying for (i.e., most cover artists charge more for a full cover, which includes the front and back covers and the spine).
- Cover artists may not purchase stock until the author gives the go ahead, so the draft may have stock site watermarks on them. However, the final cover should be free of watermarks.

THE PERFECT BACK COVER DESCRIPTION (BLURB)

After capturing the reader's attention with a great book cover, you need to hook them with an engaging back cover description also known as a "blurb." Here's how:

- **Restrict your blurb to around 200 words.** An average back cover description is about two or three paragraphs and around 200 words in length. You want to grab your reader quickly, using as few words as possible. Two hundred words broken into a couple paragraphs are easier to read. It's always best to write your blurb without word count in mind and edit later to tighten up the text.

Get to the meat of the story without giving too much away. What are the characters working, fighting, and striving for? Don't include twists and surprises, but hint at them.

- **Select the proper words.** Focus on the overall plot of the story while emphasizing the mood readers should expect from the book. To accomplish this, use certain words that convey the tone of the book. For example, if your book is a thriller, use words like: haunt, escape, and catch. If it's a romance, use words like: soul, warmth, longing, etc.

- **Introduce the main characters immediately**. The characters are the vehicles in which the reader travels through the conflict and experience the overall theme or message of the story. By introducing the main characters in the first few lines of your blurb, the reader quickly builds an interest in that character and their quest through conflict.
- **Indicate the major conflict**. Get to the meat of the story without giving too much away. What are the characters working, fighting and striving for? Don't include twists and surprises, but hint at them. Show them what they should expect from reading the book by enticing them with your blurb.

Entice readers by using the who-what-where-why-how system. This structure is similar to the Five Ws of journalism and could be used in a similar way to create an appealing book blurb.

Hook: Every great piece of writing should have a hook to reel the reader in. The hook should be something shocking, funny, or interesting enough to keep the reader engaged, and should tie into the overall tone of the story.

Construct your blurb by answering the five Ws and one H.

Who: Introduce the main characters.

What: What are the characters fighting for? What is the major conflict of the story?

Where: Provide a brief description of the story's setting. Include a sentence describing the location, i.e., outer space, college, a battlefield, etc.

When: When does the story take place and during what time? Here is a chance to mention the unique time period of your story, i.e., nineteenth century, medieval times, post-apocalypse, etc.

Why: Dedicate a sentence or a paragraph to answering or asking "why" in regards to the conflict or character's motives. Why are the characters in conflict? Why should the readers care? Tie in the conflict with what makes the situation relatable to your readers in order to make it more appealing. Use the very things that attract us to good storytelling, i.e., loss of something important, fighting for justice, finding courage, seeking understanding, or whatever makes your story's conflict relatable to your audience.

How: Always leave the reader wondering how the characters will get through the conflict. You can accomplish this by simply asking a question the reader would most likely ask. Or leave them with some sort of cliff hanger, e.g., *"How will they make it out and still stay strong?"* Or *"They must fight their way through the unknown, only then they'll know if it was worth it."*

MORE EXAMPLES OF WORD USAGE BY GENRE:

Use words to excite a mood or portray an idea that's related to your book's genre. Just like tropes in genres where the reader expects certain things to take place (i.e. wandering a wasteland in most post-apocalyptic fiction), certain words can set the mood or setting in specific genres. Examples are below. You would probably be able to guess the genre just by reading the list of words.

Thrillers: Tension, uncertainty, gritty, rousing, anticipate.

Romance: Emotional, ripen, satisfy, commitment, rouse.

Horror: Dark, haunt, startle, induce, eerie, thrill, chill, presence.

Science Fiction: Imagine, alternate, worldly, elements, speculate.

Humor: Amuse, appeal, wit, absurd, wild.

Erotica: Heat, moist, rushes, stir, indulge, desire, affair, indecent, stimulate, provoke.

Fantasy: Phenomena, vibrant, super, imagery, fantastic, elements, grand.

Western: Portray, desolate, settle, native, conquest, civil, honor, justice.

Historical: Period, depict, record, regard, deviate, present, adhere.

WELL-EDITED INTERIOR TEXT

Well-edited interior text is important when making book samples and excerpts available to readers. This helps with a consumer's book-buying decision. Every good piece of writing has one thing in common. It is well edited. If you want interior text that is edited like a traditionally published book you can hire a freelance editor. If you decide not to hire an editor, here are ways to polish your interior text at little or no cost:

- **Red Ink.** Space your lines at 1.5 or 2.0, print out the pages of your manuscript, and mark revisions with a red ink pen. Editing on printed paper could give your eyes a much-needed break from staring at a computer screen for hours. Using red ink over black printed text can help you spot your revisions easier than black or blue ink which tends to get lost among all the dark print.
- **Get it critiqued**. Have someone else look over it. Get an author friend to critique it as well. Enlist as many people as possible to look over the final draft, fix errors and then have another person look over it again. Request honest comments and

embrace criticism about the book's content. Try not to focus only on typos but on characterization, dialogue, motive, etc.

When red ink and several critiques are not enough, here are some tips for finding an editor.

- **Hire an editor.** Look for referrals and testimonials before committing, and ask for a test edit. An editor will usually edit the first few pages or up to a certain word count for free to give you an idea of what she can do for your entire manuscript. Keep in mind, many editors charge per word, per page, or per hour.
- **Know what kind of editing your story needs.** There are a few types of editors to choose from. Make sure you choose the ones you need for your story. *Copyeditors and Line Editors* look for errors in spelling and grammar, small inconsistencies, and factual errors, etc. *Content Editors* edit the content for consistent characterization, point of view errors, plot issues, authentic-sounding dialogue, etc.

Utilize these tips and make your book shine among the average traditionally published books and even among the rare self-published gems.

LESLIE LEE SANDERS has self-published over a dozen erotic romance titles since 2005. She multi-published with romance publishers in 2011. Her blog was a finalist in the Goodreads' 2012 Independent Blogger Awards in the publishing category. Her website/blog (www.leslieleesanders.com) provides tips, advice, and information on writing and publishing for novice and indie authors..

TOP THREE TOOLS FOR PRODUCING GREAT BOOK COVERS

by Peggy DeKay

In the age of online book sites like Amazon.com and Barnes and Noble's online store, bn.com, the book cover has taken on a new significance. The burgeoning e-book market has created more stringent requirements and expectations for every book cover.

The growth of online book sales, and that 600-pound gorilla in the room, Amazon, demand that your book cover not only look great on a bookshelf, but also be enticing to online buyers in the form of a one-inch-by-one-inch icon displayed on a computer screen, an e-reader, or on a smart phone.

> The burgeoning e-book market has created more stringent requirements and expectations for every book cover.

For indie authors who hear the siren's call of DIY, there are some great resources available for creating your own book covers. Keep in mind that the best book covers are those that follow the P-A-R-C-S principle:

- P – Proper placement of graphics and text in a pleasing, uncluttered design
- A – Artistic in that you make sure your graphic symbolizes your story
- R – Readable fonts large enough to read on a book shelf or in a small icon online
- C – Contrast and clarity of each element
- S – Simplicity of design to engage online buyers

Since the graphic element is so important to creating a great book cover, obtaining great pictures that are properly licensed, or that you as the author own, is important. My top three favorite sites for graphics are:

- www.dreamstime.com
- www.istockphoto.com
- www.bigstockphoto.com

While there are hundreds of other sites out there, these three are easy to use, reasonably priced, and have a large inventory of photos, and graphics. Always make sure that you have properly licensed your graphics since most downloadable graphics are licensed for use on websites, not book covers. Most copyright holders license their photographs or graphic designs according to the number of anticipated "views."

Make sure that your license is adequate for use as a book cover. If you are using clipart as an element in your book cover, be sure you have proper licensing.

Book covers, especially when sold online, can have hundreds of thousands of views. Read the fine print on these sites before you purchase and download the photo. Make sure that your license is adequate for use as a book cover. If you are using clipart as an element in your book cover, be sure that you have proper licensing.

Now that you have purchased and properly licensed your graphic element, it is time to design the cover. There are lots of tool out there to design book covers. They range from simple e-book cover creator programs to top of the line applications like Photoshop CS6 by Adobe, which retails for a whooping $689. You can purchase it online for less.

If you are not a professional designer, an application like Photoshop CS6 can be daunting and come with an extended learning curve. Don't lose heart. There are three great alternatives to blowing up your book marketing budget while spending the next six months of your life learning Photoshop.

COVER CREATOR BY CREATESPACE.COM

If you are on a tight budget and need to design a great cover without spending *any* money…the answer is Cover Creator by Createspace. Cover Creator is a free online tool for designing a professional book cover using your own photos, text, and logos. Cover Creator automatically formats and sizes your cover based on your book's trim size and page count. You can choose between a limited set of templates and fonts. Once you have set-up your book title in CreateSpace.com, you can access Cover Creator from within their site.

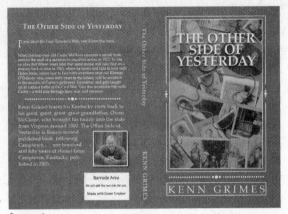

figure 1

I recently did a book cover for a client using Cover Creator with great results. Because you can upload your own photographs or artwork as the background, two book covers using the same template can look very different.

Figures 1 and 2 are samples of two templates I used for the book *The Other Side of Yesterday* by Kenn Grimes.

Figure 1 is the book cover we ultimately choose for Kenn's book. Figure 2 is the first template we tried. The photo on the front cover was taken by Kenn on his coffee table, using some old photographs and a

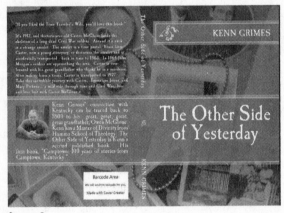

figure 2

pendent, arranged in a collage. Save your photograph or graphic as a jpeg. High-resolution photographs work best.

Figure 2 is a different template. Notice that the photograph on this template covers both the front and back cover of the book. The color behind the text was changed. On most CreateSpace templates, you can change the background color, fonts, and the background photograph or graphic.

You can also add or delete the author photo and publisher's logo. The white block at the bottom of the back cover labeled "barcode area" is where the bar code and ISBN for your book will appear when the book is printed.

ADOBE PHOTOSHOP ELEMENTS 11

My second book cover tool of choice is a lighter version of Photoshop CS6 called Photoshop Elements 11. This is a great little program, and one that you can learn in less than an afternoon.

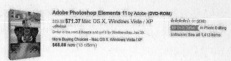

If you are stuck on a command, go to Youtube.com and watch a tutorial online. There are hundreds if not thousands of helpful videos on how to use Photoshop Elements 11 on Youtube.com.

Suggested retail for this product is $99. If you are into video editing, you can purchase a bundled package with Photoshop Elements 11 and Photoshop Premier for a suggested retail of $149.00. Again, both Photoshop Elements 11 and the bundle can be purchased online at a discount.

I like this software because it is versatile, and you can create a full-blown book cover or e-book cover in an afternoon. Fair warning; for best results download a free book cover template from CreateSpace.com. You can do that for any book by clicking on this link: https://www.createspace.com/Help/Book/Artwork.do.

You will need to know your trim size (the dimensions of your book), and the total number of pages including the front and back matter.

Open Photoshop Elements 11 and then open the template that you just downloaded from CreateSpace. It should look like Figure 3. This will allow you to create a second layer and insert the background and graphic elements into the template.

BOOKCOVERPRO

The third tool for creating e-book and print book covers is BookCoverPro at www.bookcoverpro.com. BookCoverPro Standard retails for $97 and BookCoverPro Deluxe retails for $187. With this software, you can create any size book cover using a template from the galley or you can design your cover from scratch. It will work in either RGB or CMYK color mode.

figure 3

BookCoverPro also comes with an add-on for $59 that will allow you to turn your book cover art into brochures, postcards, fliers, mailers, bookmarks, bumper stickers, and more. This is a great feature for building your own promo kit. The software is easy to learn and with some experimentation, you should be creating exciting book covers in no time.

Now that you have the tools, go out and experiment. I am confident that you can, with tenacity, trial and error, and patience, create your own smashing book cover.

BONUS TOOL

For those of you who want to go it alone, without spending money, there is a bonus option. If you love all the features of Photoshop CS6 but hate the price, try www.gimp.org. Gimp is the free alternative to Adobe Photoshop CS6 with about as steep a learning curve. If you are serious about graphics and creating book covers from scratch, Gimp is a great choice.

PEGGY DEKAY is an author, blogger, podcaster, and book coach. She is a frequent speaker at writer's conferences, book fairs, and civic groups and is an adjunct instructor for the University of Louisville, Carnegie Center for Literacy, and Bellarmine University. She is a past director of Women Who Write, Inc., and the former editor of Writer's Wire. DeKay is the author of *Self-Publishing for Virgins: The first time author's guide to self-publishing.* Her podcast, The Business of Writing Today can be downloaded on iTunes or from her website at http://tbowt.com. DeKay is the co-organizer of The Business of Writing Today International Summit held annually in Louisville, Kentucky. E-mail her at peggy@tbowt.com.

10 KEYS TO STANDOUT COVERS

....

by Alicia Kat Vancil

There are bad covers out there—we have all seen them. The ones with the glaring, eye-searing colors, painful design, and horrid photoshopping that should be a crime against humanity. I could go on for days about the horrors I have seen lurking in the dark corners of bookshops, but I'm sure you'd rather I talk about what makes a good cover. The kind that stands out on a crowded shelf and demands you buy it. So here are 10 key ways you can make your covers stand out without falling prey to the aforementioned pitfalls of bad design.

Don't Panic! Some of you may find the technical aspects of this a little over your head. Don't worry, number 10 was written especially for you.

1. Braving the Bookshelf Jungle

The first thing you should do when sitting down to create or commission a cover for your latest novel is assess your playing field. What's currently trending? What catches your eye? What makes you cringe? About half of great design comes down to good observation. There are a lot of good design ideas out there that could be used in new and interesting ways. That being said, don't blatantly copy a bestseller's style either. Remember we're trying to stand out in the crowd, not blend in as a pale comparison to a currently trendy book.

Exercise: Make a design board or project folder of covers you like. (Pinterest is really handy for this.) Study these covers and assess why you were attracted to them. Then develop some ideas about what to use for your own cover.

2. What's in a Name?

Unlike traditionally published authors, you, as an independent author, have control of your book titles. The thing to keep in mind when crafting a book title is to keep it short and to the point. Make the title easy for a potential book buyer to remember, and make sure it has at least some relevance to the content of your book.

Exercise: Come up with 5 potential titles for your book. Ask members of your inner circle—whose opinion you trust—what they think a story with each of the titles might be about. Then select the one you think best fits your book, or the one with the most favorable response.

3. Well, It's About...

You need to think of your cover like a billboard for your book. A really small billboard. Why? Because your cover has to convey what the book is about in a matter of seconds and usually from only an inch or two in height. So a quick, clear visual read is important. That being said, don't go for clichéd designs (i.e. hearts for romance, or light breaking through the clouds for spiritual). This is also not to say your cover has to be flat and plain, just that you shouldn't have too much going on. Movie posters are a very good example of concise, yet detailed designs, and in essence aren't so different from book covers.

Exercise: Sit down and think about your book. What is your story about? Can you boil the book down into a sentence or two? How would you express that visually? Take the answers to these questions and add them to your project board, folder, or notebook, you will need them for the rest of the exercises.

4. Exploring the Unexpected

As I mentioned in the previous point, avoid selecting overused, clichéd, or symbolic images for your cover unless you have a *really* creative twist on them. Instead pick elements that convey the story without resorting to overused visual shorthand (i.e. space ships and planets for science fiction books or romance novels with bare chested men). Some truly extraordinary designs have come from just exploring the visual aspects of a story just one step farther than most. And remember the point is to make someone stop and go, "What is *that* story about?" And not, "Oh look, another romance book."

Exercise: Make a visual board of imagery that reflects your book. (Again, Pinterest is a great tool for this.) Select 3-5 of those items and explore cover ideas focused around them.

5. Lights, Camera, Action!

As a good friend pointed out to me recently: Nobody wants to read a book about a bunch of people just standing around. The same can be said for cover design. The elements on your cover should be seemingly in motion as if you are capturing a single moment instead of staging a formal photograph. Blurred images, fluttering hair, debris in the air, and sweeping clouds can all lend movement to a static image. If you've decided not to feature people on your cover, a lot can still be done to make the elements interesting, eye-catching, and dynamic.

Exercise: Take a look at the elements you have chosen for your cover. Are they interesting? Do they capture a moment in time instead of a static idealized portrait? Do the elements lead your eye around the cover? If your cover feels lifeless, what can be done to revive it? Take the answers to these questions and add them to your project board, folder, or notebook.

6. It's More than Just Cut and Paste

Due to easy access as well as affordable pricing, the popularity of stock imagery has risen greatly in recent years. This is fantastic really, since stock photography can really save you time and resources. However, without customization, your cover could fall flat or *worse*, be mistaken for another book using the same stock. So this may be why with the rise of stock imagery, we're also seeing the rise of new art forms like Photomanipulation and Enhanced Photo Imagery. And of artists, like yours truly, that specialize in the customization of stock imagery. So if you don't possess the tools or ability to customize your stock imagery yourself, there are plenty of professionals out there that can lend a hand.

Exercise: Take a look at the stock photography you have chosen for your cover. What creative ways could your chosen stock be altered? Come up with 3-5 different ways you could make the stock unique. (Hint: Image blending, color isolation, and creative cropping are all ways to change up great but overused stock.)

7. Technicolor Dream Cover

Colors are arguably the most important ingredient in a cover design. It's the first thing the potential reader sees in the pursuit of a new read. Limited palettes, contrasting color combinations, or color selections that evoke a mood can go a long way in conveying the tone, setting, or content of your story.

Exercise: Look at the color scheme of your cover. Is it vivid? Engaging? Evocative? *No*? How can you improve it? Test out a few color variations on your design and see if it improves your cover's impact.

8. For the Love of Fonts, Anything but Papyrus!

Your font selections should reflect the genre and design of the book cover while also being clearly readable. If every book in your book's genre is using the same font, don't use it! Remember the goal here is to stand out from the crowd. Also remember you don't have to use a font straight out of the box. Modern computer programs allow for a lot of customization when it comes to fonts. Bolding the font, or adjusting the tracking, and vertical scaling can go a long way in making a font look unique.

Exercise: Pick 5 potential title fonts and secondary fonts for your cover and play around with the various font settings in your program of choice. Who knows, it might yield something original and unexpected.

9. Look Me in the Eye

I've noticed in the last few years that a lot of book covers have cropped out heads, covered up eyes, or characters with their backs to us. Which is odd, seeing as magazines and movie posters tend to do the exact opposite. It's been said that eyes are the windows to the soul, and to an extent they are. You can learn a vast amount about someone's personality and mood just looking into their eyes. With that in mind, your cover should be catching the eyes of the potential buyer. Daring them to pick up your book instead of shyly hiding away. That being said, if cropped-head covers don't unnerve you, feel free to skip this one.

Exercise: Search for compelling stock images and models that fit not only the physical description, but the personality of your character(s).

10. Trust Me, I'm the Designer

For those of you hiring out for your cover design, remember that you've hired them for a reason and this is their job. If you have not spent some years studying the ins and outs of design, thinking you know more about design than a trained professional will only set you up for failure. Likewise, trusting the opinion of someone with no professional design training over your designer never ends well either. These warnings aside, completing the exercises above with help you deliver a clear and concise project brief to your designer that will aid them in arriving at the perfect cover in no time.

Exercise: Find 5 cover designers of other indie books you like and explore their work. Are they within your budget? Do they produce the type of cover you're looking for? Having a hard time finding what the right designer? Ask your fellow indie authors for recommendations.

Alicia Kat Vancil lives in the San Francisco Bay Area with her husband, two very crazy studio cats, and nine overfull bookcases. When not running amuck in the imaginary worlds within her head, Kat can usually be found performing, watching anime, or hanging out in Twitter chats.

WHY AND HOW TO HIRE A FREELANCE EDITOR

....

by Kit Cooley

Many writers don't feel they need to have a professional editor look at their work before they begin sending it out to an agent, a publisher, or to the printer. Even a well-written piece can contain some errors. As the author, you are quite intimate with your own work. You have read it so many times that you may not see the mistakes. You may not be aware of standards of usage and style.

An editor can help you to polish your manuscript no matter how you decide to publish, whether through traditional publishing or by self-publishing. An edited manuscript, free of typos, looks better to publishers and readers.

First impressions are important. When I worked on staff as an assistant editor for an independent publisher, I had the task of wading through the slush pile. The cover letter scribbled in red marker pen, the smudged copy, and the manuscripts full of typos were some of the first submissions to be discarded. I'm sure you've heard it said before: Most editors are busy people. Your story is much less likely to get a chance at publication if an editor can't read it. With two manuscripts in front of me, one polished and clean, and one full of errors in punctuation and grammar, I would be inclined to reject the sloppy one no matter how good the underlying story might be.

It is true that a publisher's staff editors will edit your manuscript once it is accepted for publication, but if you submit work riddled with errors, then it is unlikely to make it to a manuscript editor's desk. There certainly have been exceptions, and pieces have been accepted because the strength of the story shone through the mess, but with so much competition in the market today, it is worth the extra investment of hiring an editor to give your work the best chance to get published.

If you take the self-publishing route, please don't scrimp on editing. Writers who decide to self-publish often do so to retain more control over a manuscript. This independence also means that there will be no publisher or editorial staff behind you to clean up, so it is even more important that you enlist the support and expertise of an editor to help you apply the high standards needed to produce a quality publication.

A finished book or e-book with misspelled words, typos, and confusing sentence structure gives the impression that you don't care about what you have written. It lacks professionalism, and can cost you potential readers. You are paying to publish your hard work, so don't waste money on something that is not quite finished. A professional editor can help you to make your book a success. You should also be aware that there are print-on-demand publishers who are concerned with producing quality work, and who will not process a manuscript full of errors.

Writers who decide to self-publish often do so to retain control over a manuscript. This independence also means that there will be no publisher or editorial staff behind you to clean up.

I was recently given a self-published novel to read. The flow of the story was interrupted with sections of text repeated word-for-word throughout the book. It seemed more like a rough draft than a finished piece. There were additional issues with the story, but for me, the disjointed scenes made the book unreadable. The author had gotten "good feedback" for the original stories from friends, family and writers' groups, and so these shorter vignettes (apparently unedited) were what became the published novel.

Writing groups and writing workshops are great venues for building your confidence as a writer. Working with other writers can offer a place to hone your skills, get constructive criticism for your work, and provide an opportunity to receive advice from others in your craft, including editors who also write. As beneficial as these activities are to your writing practice, none of them can replace what the undivided attention of a good editor can do for your manuscript.

WHAT AN EDITOR CAN DO FOR YOU

You can use the editing functions of word processing software programs to check spelling and grammar, but it is not sufficient, as computer programs cannot provide a careful reading of your work. A good editor will pick up on nuance in your writing, as well as pay attention to the mechanics of grammar, punctuation, syntax, usage, and style. The editor can also give an objective opinion, and point out parts of the text that may not make sense to a reader.

Professional editors will usually read through the entire manuscript first to get a sense of what the author is attempting to convey. The next step in the editing process is giving attention to the details of grammar and punctuation. Skillful application of the appropriate editorial style and determining if the text adheres to current usage is also part of what an editor can do for you. (For more information on the publishing process an excellent source is *The Chicago Manual of Style*. It also has a section describing editorial functions in detail.)

The best time to hire an editor is when you have completed your manuscript, ... and when you feel it is ready to send to a publisher, agent or printer. The closer to finished the writing work is, the more thorough and cost-effective the editing process will be.

A good editor is not going to make heavy-handed changes to an author's work. During a close reading of your manuscript, he or she will point out inconsistencies and problem areas in the text, and make suggestions for additions, subtractions, or other changes. Some suggested changes may include alternative word usage, fixing problems in tense and person, advice on how to make seamless transitions from scene to scene, and rearranging sections of text to tighten narrative to help you improve the flow of the story. An editor with some publishing house experience can also bring a knowledge of book layout to your project that can be especially helpful to the author who is going the self-publishing route.

The best time to hire an editor is when you have completed your manuscript, whether it is a book, essay, short story, or group of poems, and when you feel it is ready to send to a publisher, agent or printer. The closer to finished the writing work is, the more thorough and cost-effective the editing process will be. There are reasons to hire an editor earlier in the writing process, but only if you require help in the development of the entire manuscript or project. (See a definition of developmental editing below.)

HOW TO CHOOSE AN EDITOR

When you are ready to have your manuscript polished and perfected, you want to make sure the editor that you hire for the job is a good match. How will you know if an editor is right for you? Here are some questions to ask potential manuscript editors and some guidelines to help you choose.

When you first interview an editor, find out what kind of experience he or she has had. If you are writing a novel, you want an editor who has worked with fiction writers. Are you writing a memoir? A technical manual? Make sure that the editor you hire has experience in your genre and has worked on similar projects. If the editing is to be done electronically, ask about software programs and platforms to confirm that these are compatible with what you are using. Most editors today must have some level of experience with electronic editing. Check to see if the editor's experience applies by being specific in describing the final format of your project.

Can you communicate with the editor that you choose? Your relationship with an editor is a professional partnership, and it is necessary to have clear communication. You must feel comfortable with discussing your work with the editor. Ask about expectations and what the editor needs from you. You will need to supply a word or page count and a printed paper manuscript or the electronic file. Ask for references from former clients or a list of completed projects to give you an idea of how the editor collaborates and what kind and quality of work she or he produces.

When you first interview an editor, find out what kind of experience he or she has had. If you are writing a novel, you want an editor who has worked with fiction writers. Are you writing a memoir? A technical manual? Make sure that the editor you hire has experience in your genre and worked on similar projects.

What style guides does the editor use (*The Chicago Manual of Style, AP Style Manual*)? Here is where knowledge of the guide used in your genre is helpful. If you don't know, a professional editor will be able to help you in that regard. The editor should also provide you with a style sheet (an alphabetical list designating unique usage of words in a particular manuscript) when the editing is complete.

What will it cost and what is included in the cost? What are the payment terms? Common arrangements are half of the money at the start of the project and the other half on completion, or a third paid at the start, middle and end of the project. A professional editor can provide you with an estimate of cost once you provide information on word count and subject matter. You get what you pay for, so be wary of low quotes. To determine a reasonable cost for your project, you can check the rates in the "How Much Should I Charge" section of this book.

Professional editing takes time. Discuss your desired submission or publication schedule to be sure the editor can fit you into the calendar.

Will the editor sign a letter of agreement or contract? A professional editor will have a standard form of one or the other (or both). Insist on memorializing the terms of your relationship with the editor you choose to hire. It can be as basic as a description of the scope of the project, when and in what format you will get your manuscript to the editor, and when and in what format you will get it back again.

Other important items to include are costs and payment terms, whether the author or the editor will be inserting changes into the text (this applies to both paper and electronic editing), and how to end the relationship in an equitable way if it is not working for either party.

KNOW WHAT KIND OF EDITOR YOU NEED

In these fluid days of change in the publishing world, editorial job functions can flow into one another. Job descriptions change. The flexible freelance editor will often be skilled in a variety of roles in the editorial process. The following definitions can help you in discussing your needs with a potential editor.

Copyediting (also called manuscript editing or line editing) involves reading a manuscript to correct spelling, punctuation, grammar, and syntax, improve style, and clarify inconsistencies or rearrange text for clarity and consistency of voice. Your finished novel or nonfiction manuscript will most likely require copyediting.

Developmental editing entails working with an author to develop a manuscript for submission and publication, deciding how material will be presented, and commenting on the content of the work, character flaws, or plot inconsistencies. This can include providing direction and helping to reorganize whole chapters, paragraphs or sections of the manuscript.

Your finished novel or nonfiction manuscript will most likely require copyediting.

Proofreading includes checking spelling, punctuation and formatting. Proofreading can also involve reading typeset galleys for typographical errors and inconsistencies against a copy of the final manuscript. This is usually the final step before a manuscript goes to the printer.

Substantive editing deals with the organization and presentation of content and can involve much rewriting and reorganizing. It is usually done through a combined effort of a publisher, an editor, and the author to improve the style of a book after it has been accepted for publication and before manuscript editing.

WHERE DO YOU FIND AN EDITOR?

By far the best way to find a good editor is through a recommendation from another writer. Ask at your writers' group meetings or at conferences and workshops for referrals. Classified ads in trusted writing publications, like *Writer's Digest*, are also a good place to look. Many editors have websites, so search online for someone in your area. If you are on LinkedIn or Facebook try making connections with other professionals in writing and editing groups.

As a writer you dig deep to bring raw ideas to the page. Using these guidelines will help you to find the right editor to work with you to make your words shine.

KIT COOLEY is a freelance editor and writer, who has been "making words shine" since 1999, and whose current business, Dream Lizard Creations, provides excellent service from research to ghostwriting, proofreading to content editing, and anything in between. Her freelance experience includes CNET, the *San Francisco Bay Guardian*, and Barrera Reporting, to name a few.

HOW TO HIRE A FREELANCE DESIGNER

....

by Thursday Bram

As a writer, you've built up certain skills: you can craft a story that will keep readers engaged and choose the right words to make your writing ring true. But you may not have the same level of skill in design, which can make getting your book ready for readers harder. Whether you're planning to sell your book electronically or in print, readers will judge your book by its cover. That means you need an experienced designer who can ensure your book looks its best.

Finding a freelancer designer is not actually all that difficult: there are numerous websites where designers offer their services on a per project basis, sometimes very inexpensively. Finding a designer who is experienced in working on book projects, however, is harder. You need to focus your search on finding designers who the right experience to make your book a polished product.

Your book also has to be ready for a designer's attention. Charlie Pabst specializes in designing book covers and formatting his clients' books at Charfish Design. Before he'll work with a client, he requires a manuscript to be completely ready. Pabst says, "I let clients know that their book should be entirely and 100 percent ready to go. It needs to be proofread, edited, fact-checked, and whatever else needs to happen to it content-wise. Anything that happens to the content after the book has been designed might actually alter the design. Page breaks move. Table of contents need to be regenerated. Images get cut off. All sorts of odd things happen, so the design stage shouldn't commence until the document is ready to go."

That readiness includes knowing what constraints you have in choosing a designer: if you have a limitless budget and an endless timeline for bringing your book to market, you're firmly in the minority. As you're beginning the search process, you should consider your budget for your book's design. Design can include a few different expenses:

Cover design

Perhaps the most important design expense you'll face, your cover can cost as much as $3,500 (a number cited by book design expert Joel Friedlander in a interview on JaneFriedman.com) or as little as $5 on Fiverr.com (a site that specializes in providing creative services for just $5 a piece).

Formatting for print

Similarly, you can have a book manuscript formatted for print for just $5 (though you many not get fully prepared reproduction files that a printer will expect at that point). Friedlander has seen prices closer to $1,500 at the higher end of the spectrum for book interiors that don't require extensive design, such as novels. For books with lots of diagrams or other visual elements, the price can be harder to cap.

Formatting for digital conversion

Technically, you can format your manuscript for certain types of e-readers for free. Amazon, for instance, allows writers to upload Word files and automatically generate Kindle files. However, that approach can result in unexpected glitches. You can see similar price ranges for digital conversion as for print formatting.

DESIGN IS AN INVESTMENT

Especially with the lower end of the pricing spectrum, it's important to remember that you get what you pay for. While you can find freelancers ready to transform your manuscript into an e-book for a few dollars, at that price point, they'll just be running your file through an automated converter for you.

Just looking at a portfolio is not enough to make a final decision on whether to sign a contract with a given designer.

Pabst has seen some of the low-quality books that can result: ranging from whole chapters vanishing during the conversion process to missing page breaks and headings. He notes, "A good book designer knows how to automate some of the design process (which is a benefit as it keeps the process quicker and prices down). But even these automated processes are done with a keen eye towards the overall effect it has on the book and any related issues that might creep up. A computer doesn't think this way."

Even an online search for book designers will turn up numerous options, but consider starting your search with writers who you know: ask who designed their books, even if they went through a traditional publisher (many of the book designers who work for publishing houses are actually freelancers). As you're looking through potential book designers, focus on examining their portfolios. Freelance designers, as a rule, have portfolios that they will make available to prospective customers—though you may have to ask them to send you a copy, depending on whether they've posted their work online. You're looking for signs that this designer's work has a similar feel to what you hope to see on your book's design. You're also looking for professionalism and polish.

> Especially if you're facing a resource crunch, the more you can do to make your manuscript easy for your designer to work with, the better.

Just looking at a portfolio is not enough to make a final decision on whether to sign a contract with a given designer. With a little more time spent searching online, you can get a good idea of what a designer has been able to do for his past clients. Look for where the books in his portfolio are sold, along with whether they've won awards. You might also consider looking for some of the authors who have worked with a given designer to ask how they felt about the project process. Since you're paying for a book design, you have the right to make sure your money will be well spent.

MOVING FORWARD WITH A DESIGNER

Once you've finalized your choice of designer, you'll need to make sure he's on board for the process. Particularly good book designers often have to book projects several months in advance, because their work is in demand. If you have a given date you absolutely need your book out by, you may be able to negotiate a rush fee; however, you may also need to revisit other designers you considered if your first choice isn't available on your schedule.

Especially if you're facing a resource crunch, the more you can do to make your manuscript easy for your designer to work with, the better. Taking even basic steps can ensure that you're the type of client a book designer is happy to work with. Pabst suggests focusing on making your manuscript as easy for your designer to understand as possible: "In a best-case scenario, the original manuscript from the author should already show the main title headers as bigger than everything else. Subheaders will be a notch down, and sub-subheaders smaller yet. Unordered and ordered lists should already be bulleted or numbered respectively. Anything intended to be bolded or italicized should be shown as such."

The process, once the book designer you've chosen has your manuscript in hand, can depend on the workflow of the designer. In general, you can expect that a good designer will discuss your expectations with you, as well as your design preferences—though you should trust your designer to make design-related decisions. Pabst says, "The shortcut to that is asking the author straight out what they feel would be appropriate for the book. You'll note that's a different question from 'What colors do you like?' and 'What fonts are your favorites?'"

From there, the designer will create a sample or a mockup to help you get a feel for what the final design will look like. You'll be asked to approve those samples, but after that point the designer will be able to complete the layout and cover for your book. Soon you'll have your final product ready to sell.

THURSDAY BRAM has self-published seven e-books and provided consulting services for a variety of clients publishing their own content. My writing has appeared on FreelanceSwitch, OpenForum and a variety of other websites, as well as in *Entrepreneur Magazine* and other print publications. I've even had an article in another F+W Media book, the *2010 Novel & Short Story Writer's Market*. Samples of my writing are available at thursdaybram.contently.com.

SELF-PUBLISHING CHECKLIST

Below is a checklist of essential hurdles to clear when self-publishing your book. This list makes the assumption that you've already completed and polished your manuscript. For even more information on self-publishing, check out *The Complete Guide to Self-Publishing*, by Tom and Marilyn Ross (Writer's Digest).

- ❏ **CREATE PRODUCTION SCHEDULE.** Put a deadline for every step of the process of self-publishing your book. A good rule of thumb is to double your estimates on how long each step will take. It's better to have too much time and hit your dates than constantly have to extend deadlines.

- ❏ **FIND EDITOR.** Don't skimp on your project and do all the editing yourself. Even editors need editors. Try to find an editor you trust, whether through a recommendation or a search online. Ask for references if the editor is new to you.

- ❏ **FIND DESIGNER.** Same goes here. Find a good designer to at least handle the cover. If you can have a designer lay out the interior pages too, that's even better.

- ❏ **DEFINE THE TARGET AUDIENCE.** In nonfiction this is an important step, because knowing the needs of the audience can help with the editing process. Even if you're writing fiction or poetry, it's a good idea to figure out who your audience is, because this will help you with the next few steps.

- ❏ **FIGURE OUT A PRINT AND DISTRIBUTION PLAN.** This plan should first figure out what the end product will be: printed book, e-book, app, or a combination of options. Then, the plan will define how the products will be created and distributed to readers.

☐ **SET PUBLICATION DATE.** The publication date should be set on your production schedule above. Respect this deadline more than all the others, because the marketing and distribution plans will most likely hinge on this deadline being met.

☐ **PLOT OUT YOUR MARKETING PLAN.** The smartest plan is to have a soft launch date of a week or two (just in case). Then, hard launch into your marketing campaign, which could be as simple as a book release party and social networking mentions, or as involved as a guest blog tour and paid advertising. With self-publishing, it's usually more prudent to spend energy and ideas than money on marketing—at least in the beginning.

☐ **HAVE AN EXCELLENT TITLE.** For nonfiction, titles are easy. Describe what your book is covering in a way that is interesting to your target audience. For fiction and poetry, titles can be a little trickier, but attempt to make your title easy to remember and refer.

☐ **GET ENDORSEMENT.** Time for this should be factored into the production schedule. Contact some authors or experts in a field related to your title and send them a copy of your manuscript to review. Ask them to consider endorsing your book, and if they do, put that endorsement on the cover. Loop in your designer to make this look good.

☐ **REGISTER COPYRIGHT.** Protect your work. Go to http://copyright.gov for more information on how to register your book.

☐ **SECURE ISBN.** An ISBN code helps booksellers track and sell your book. To learn more about securing an ISBN, go to www.isbn.org.

☐ **CREATE TABLE OF CONTENTS AND INDEX (FOR NONFICTION).** The table of contents (TOC) helps organize a nonfiction title and give structure for both the author and the reader. An index serves a similar function for readers, making it easier for them to find the information they want to find. While an index is usually not necessary for fiction or poetry, most poetry collections do use a table of contents to make it easy to locate individual poems.

☐ **INCLUDE AUTHOR BIO.** Readers want to know about the authors of the books they read. Make this information easy to find in the back of the book.

☐ **INCLUDE CONTACT INFORMATION.** In the front of the book, preferably on the copyright and ISBN page, include all contact information, including mailing address and website. E-mail address is optional, but the more options you give the better chance you'll be contacted.

❏ **EXECUTE MARKETING PLAN.** Planning is important, but execution is critical to achieving success. If you're guest posting, finish posts on time and participate in comments section of your blog post. If you're making bookstore appearances, confirm dates and show up a little early—plus invite friends and family to attend.

❏ **KEEP DETAILED ACCOUNTING RECORDS.** For tax purposes, you'll need to keep records of how much money you invest in your project, as well as how much you receive back. Keep accurate and comprehensive records from day one, and you'll be a much happier self-published author.

HOW TO SWING BOTH WAYS

Writers who publish indie & traditional

by C. Hope Clark

Indie publishing is roaring and strong. Don't you love that name—Indie? It beats the worn-out, stigmatized *self-publishing*, as if producing our own books ranks with hand sewing clothes from burlap instead of buying them from the high-falutin department store catalog.

Traditional is no longer the kingpin. We do not need a publisher and do not have to give up the lion's share of royalties. We are no longer at the mercy of houses that move on only six weeks after the books hit the shelf. We have a louder voice. We call our own shots! Power to the people!

Some indie authors even proclaim New York dead. Some traditionals, holding tight to, um, tradition, still look down on the indies, gripping hard to a manifesto claiming a need for gatekeepers.

The squabbling reminds us of politics, with the left leading for a term, then the right, then the left again, leaving us craving a middle ground that could make everybody happy and put 24-hour cable news out of business.

Truth is authors can swing both ways. Many authors successfully use both publishing methods. Some enter the old-fashioned way first while some start with indie. Some use traditional for one series and indie with another. Our options are many.

C. HOPE CLARK: FICTION ONE WAY, NONFICTION ANOTHER

When I could not sell my mystery 15 years ago back when I entered the profession, I turned to nonfiction for my living. My platform grew through FundsforWriters.com, and I soon learned of the need for *The Shy Writer*, a guide for introverted writers in their painful efforts to earn an income. Needing the book quickly for conference appearances pushed me to self-publish in 2004 with a company called Booklocker, back when made-from-scratch self-publishing almost didn't exist, way before e-books were taken seriously.

But I continued with the mystery. A decade later I landed an agent and publisher for my novel *Lowcountry Bribe*, then a year later its sequel, *Tidewater Murder*. In my work promoting The Carolina Slade Mystery Series, however, I kept hearing accolades about *The Shy Writer*, a book now nine years old. I sold out of every one I had.

The interest prompted me to pen a sequel, *The Shy Writer Reborn*. When a conference asked me to teach a half-day class on the subject, I realized I needed this book in the hands of readers sooner than a traditional publisher could make it happen.

I now self-pub nonfiction in between my mystery books that take a year each to release. The more I promote one book, regardless the genre, regardless how it was printed, the more the others sell.

....

When a conference asked me to teach a half-day class on the subject, I realized I needed this book in the hands of readers sooner than a traditional publisher could make it happen.

....

Authors debate continuously about which method rules, which makes more sense, and which writers deserve the most respect. Why argue? The two worlds can co-exist. Readers don't care how a book comes to be, as long as it's a quality read.

J.A. KONRATH: TRADITIONAL SPRINGBOARD INTO INDIE HEAVEN

J.A. Konrath could be labeled the poster child for indie publishing. He began his career through Hyperion, with his Lt. Jacqueline "Jack" Daniels series. However, along the way he discovered a hunger for having more control over his books. He entered the indie arena back when the stigma was intense, and he excelled at cranking out more books, more series, more often, making much more money than he did as a conventional author.

He jumped into electronic publishing in its infancy and hit the ground running. His must-read blog is called A Newbie's Guide to Publishing, www.jakonrath.blogspot.com, and at the end of 2011 he announced he made $22,000 for the month of December from e-book sales. His success has only risen since then, not only due to a spiraling word-of-mouth platform, but also from his prolific production.

Konrath loves indie work and is an iron-clad indie author now. "I've worked with three major publishers. If the price was right, I'd work with them again. That said, I see no advantage to sending out queries and waiting to get an agent or a pub deal when it's possible to self-publish. If you do well self-publishing, you'll get offers, if that's your goal. But I believe holding out for a legacy publisher is silly when Kindle, Kobo, Apple, B&N, and Smashwords make self-pubbing so easy. Unless I was given a giant advance, I wouldn't give up the larger royalty and total control that self-pubbing offers. Writers should experiment, share information, and do a lot of research to figure out which path is best for them."

DEB STOVER: FROM DINOSAUR TO E-BOOK MAVEN

Digital rights weren't even mentioned in Deb Stover's first 11 contracts. She sold her initial book in December 1993 to Kensington, subsequently adding nine more single titles, plus one novella. Then she wrote a two-book series for Penguin's Jove imprint, and one book for Dorchester. In those days, *self-publishing* was a dirty word synonymous with vanity publishing, with stories of sub-standard product and stealing from authors. Still, she forecasted then that digital publishing could turn into a remarkable force in the industry.

And she found being a dinosaur has its advantages. In recent years she requested the reversion on all her books that went out of print. With the flourish of Kindle and iBooks, then the improvement of Nook, she saw her future. At first, she contracted a service that formatted and distributed her works for a percentage of her royalties. Now she produces the e-books herself.

In those days, self-publishing was a dirty word synonymous with vanity publishing, with stories of sub-standard product and stealing from authors.

She was asked whether she'd self-publish a new work. "I have never self-published a new project. These (her e-books) are novels and novellas that have been vetted and edited by a traditional publisher in the past. I have no plans to self-publish a new project. I actually prefer to work with traditional presses, even though I don't make as much money."

LISA SCOTT: TRADITIONAL FOR LONG WORKS AND INDIE FOR SHORTS

Lisa Scott had a bumpy start. She wrote women's fiction and a middle grade novel, but couldn't find an agent, a route she felt was her only choice at the time. So she turned to romance, but then couldn't find a publisher. So she uploaded her romance *No Foolin'* to Amazon, only for Harlequin to ask for the full manuscript for consideration. Harlequin ultimately said no, so she uploaded it again to Amazon.

Then Belle Books asked for the manuscript, and she landed a two-book deal to include *No Foolin'*, the first in her Willowdale Romance series. Having learned enough about self-publishing to feel cozy with it, she chose to write and upload collections of romantic short stories she called *Flirts!* since regular presses rarely show interest in collections.

When asked why she kept hoping for a traditional contract, she replied: "I'm definitely a believer in the 'more eggs in more baskets' theory. I felt they could offer some promotional opportunities for the books that I could not. And I felt that promotion in turn could help my self-published titles. So while I waited for *No Foolin's* release, I put out more *Flirts!* collections. Then a funny thing happened: My agent ended up selling my middle grade novel, *School of Charm* to HarperCollins for 2014 publication."

Scott admits the biggest obstacle for authors these days is getting noticed. The more avenues she uses, the better her chances of being seen by readers and industry professionals. But then she professes she has no backlist, so the power of a press empowers her a bit. "I might have a different opinion if I had already made a name for myself. I have a few writing friends who no longer feel they need the support of their traditional publisher and are self-publishing from here on out because they've got the fan base to support it. It's an exciting time to be a writer. I bring in a nice monthly four-figure income from my self-publishing that will help support me between royalty and advance checks from the traditional deals."

PUBLISHING IS WHAT WE MAKE IT

Finally, publishing has grown up to the point authors can dabble in and master both sides of the line that once divided the industry. Our indie books can establish our names while we seek representation, or our traditional image can sell our self-pubbed works. No longer an either/or dilemma, publishing is what we make it, however method we choose, with the grandest result often involving both.

C. HOPE CLARK is editor of FundsforWriters.com, chosen by *Writer's Digest* for its 101 Best Websites for Writers for over a dozen years. Hope also adores mysteries and is author of The Carolina Slade Mystery Series (Bell Bridge Books). She speaks often at events across the United States. www.fundsforwriters.com | www.chopeclark.com

WE LOVE SALES, BUT NOT SALES TAX

When and How to Charge Sales Tax

by Carol Topp, CPA

As indie publishers, we love sales and seeing our bank deposits grow, but with sales comes the challenge of understanding sales tax. The rules surrounding sales tax are changing and can be quite complex. Keeping records and paying sales tax are burdens we shoulder as a result of doing what we love—selling books.

WHEN TO CHARGE SALES TAX

The rules that govern when you must charge sales tax vary by state, but most depend on two important concepts:

Nexus means a connection or presence in a state, such as a physical location, property, employees, and sometimes affiliates. Attorney Martin I. Eisenstein explains, "Many publishers do business with third parties such as sales representatives, fulfillment houses, and platforms for the sale of e-books. Each of these relationships can create nexus for state tax purposes." If an indie publisher has nexus in a particular state, the publisher must collect and remit sales taxes in that state.

For example, Janice Campbell of Everyday Education based in Virginia sells and mails a copy of her book, *Get a Jump Start on College*, to a customer in Virginia. She must collect and remit sales tax to Virginia, where she has nexus. Campbell also sells and mails a book to a customer in Michigan. She does not have to collect Michigan sales tax because she does not have nexus in Michigan. Campbell travels to Pennsylvania and sells her books there. She created nexus (a physical presence, although temporary) and must collect sales tax and remit it to Pennsylvania.

Tangible personal property usually means physical property, other than real estate, that can be felt, touched, and moved, such as paperback books. Most sales of tangible personal property to the final purchaser are sales-taxable. However, some states have begun to tax the sale of electronic books and music downloads, even though they cannot be felt or touched. (See **Sales Tax on E-Books**.)

These concepts of nexus and tangible personal property will be important as you begin to understand your obligation to collect sales tax. Surprisingly, how you sell your books—in person, by mail, or over the Internet—is not as important as you might think when it comes to sales tax.

SALES TAX ON E-BOOKS

Most states charge sales tax on tangible personal property. What about digital items such as e-books? E-books are not tangible, but many states have expanded the definition of tangible goods to include anything that holds value. So far 23 states have enacted laws that charge sales tax on digital goods.

Michael Mazerov, a senior fellow at the Center on Budget and Public Policy Priorities, explains that digital goods can include computer software, games, music, video, and e-books. Research your state laws carefully. For example, North Dakota and Ohio tax software and games, but (so far) e-books, music, and film are exempt from sales tax there. A list of current state taxation of digital goods is available from CBPP.org here: http://www.cbpp.org/files/12-13-12sfp.pdf

---

SALES TAX AND THE INTERNET

Some people mistakenly believe that sales over the Internet are sales-tax-free, but this is not so. In 1998, President Clinton signed into law the Internet Tax Freedom Act (ITFA). Its purpose was to prevent state and local governments from imposing new taxes on Internet transactions and access. Contrary to popular belief, ITFA did not create a sales tax exemption for sales made over the Internet.

As SalesTaxSupport.com points out, "Sellers of items via the Internet must collect and remit applicable sales tax if the seller has nexus in the state of the destination of the sale. If the seller does not have nexus, the seller is not yet required to collect and remit the tax."

....

Some people mistakenly believe that sales over the Internet are sales-tax-free, but this is not so.

....

For an indie publisher, the method of conducting the sale (online, face-to-face, or catalog order) is not a determining factor for sales tax. Nexus is. If you have nexus in the destination state, you have to collect sales tax for that state. If not, then you do not have to collect sales tax for that state.

For example, I sell books on my website and ship them from my office in Ohio, so I have nexus in Ohio. When a buyer's destination address is in Ohio, my electronic shopping cart (Paypal) adds sales tax to that sale. I do not collect sales tax from purchasers in other states. Every six months, I remit the sales tax collected to the state of Ohio.

WHEN YOU DO NOT HAVE TO CHARGE SALES TAX

Sales tax is a record-keeping challenge for indie publishers, so it is important to understand when you do *not* have to collect sales tax. States vary in offering sales tax exemptions, but here are some common exemptions:

- Sales to a buyer who is not the final purchaser are exempt. If you sell your books to a bookstore, catalog, or other reseller, they collect the sales tax from the final purchaser. For example, Hal and Melanie Young sell their book, *Raising Real Men*, to Christian Book Distributors (CBD), an online bookseller. CBD collects sales tax on orders shipped to addresses where they have nexus (Massachusetts and Colorado). The Youngs neither collect nor pay sales tax on the books they sell to CBD.
- Sales to government agencies, nonprofit organizations, schools, and churches are frequently tax exempt. The exemption varies by state, but most states allow government agencies, especially public schools, to be exempt from paying sales tax. Many charities, which may include private schools and churches, may also receive sales tax exemption from their states. If you sell to a school, church, or charity, you should request a copy of their sales tax exemption certificate to keep in your files.
- Sales to out-of-state customers are exempt (for now). Typically, the seller does not have to collect sales tax on remote sales to out-of-state customers. This ruling was last clarified in 1992 under the landmark case *Quill v. North Dakota*. The Supreme Court ruled that no state may require a seller to collect tax on sales if the seller lacks a physical presence (nexus) in the state. The case left the door open for Congress to address the issue, particularly the burden on sellers to comply with over 6,000 taxing jurisdictions in the United States. Congress has been considering legislation to simplify sales tax collection and may allow states to require sales tax collection across state borders in the future. (See **Recent Legislation.**)

RECENT LEGISLATION

State governments are losing sales tax revenue as online shopping becomes more popular. Consumers who are not charged sales tax when purchasing online are supposed to report the sale and pay a use tax to their state but often do not. Because states found it difficult to obtain compliance from individuals, they turned to the federal government. Governors have been putting pressure on the federal government to allow the states to force remote sellers to collect and pay sales tax.

A number of recent federal bills like The Marketplace Equity Act, The Main Street Fairness Act, and The Marketplace Fairness Act promote simplification and fairness in collecting sales tax. These bills outline a centralized, one-stop, multistate registration system and uniform definitions of products and exemptions. The bills establish a small seller exemption, with a threshold of $500,000 or less in annual sales being exempt from mandatory collection of tax on remote sales.

If Congress passes sales tax legislation, many indie publishers will qualify as small sellers and be exempt from collecting sales tax on remote sales. For in-state sales, business would continue as usual: indie publishers would continue to collect sales tax in states where they have nexus. The proposed legislation could also benefit small sellers with a simplified, uniform system to manage sales tax obligations.

You can stay up to date on the status of sales tax legislation with the news feed at MarketplaceFairness.org/.

HOW TO COLLECT AND REMIT SALES TAX

All states except Alaska, Delaware, Montana, New Hampshire, and Oregon collect sales tax. When collecting and remitting sales tax, indie publishers should follow these steps:

1. Apply for a vendor's license (sometimes called a reseller registration or resale permit) from your state. Also apply for a temporary or transient vendors license if you travel and sell books in another state. Outright.com, an online accounting software program, provides sales tax information for each state at http://outright.com/blog/sales-tax-resources-for-online-sellers-in-every-state/
2. Research exemptions if your customers include schools, churches, or charities.

....

Some states allow each city or county to set its own sales tax rate in addition to the state sales tax rate. Accounting software such as QuickBooks allows you to set up several tax rates.

....

3. Set a reminder to remit the sales tax. It might be quarterly, biannually, or annually. If you reach a large dollar threshold, you may need to remit monthly.
4. Keep records of each sale and the applicable tax rate. Some states allow each city or county to set its own sales tax rate in addition to the state sales tax rate. Accounting software such as QuickBooks allows you to set up several tax rates.

5. Consider keeping the sales tax collected in a separate bank account so you will have the entire amount needed to remit to the state when it is due.

6. Determine if your state requires you to file a return even if you made no sales or owe no tax. For example, Ohio requires a report even if no sales were made. My client Alice received a $50 fine for failing to file a sales tax return even though she did not have any taxable sales for the period.

I tested how long would it take for me to gather information about sales tax in the state of Wisconsin. I researched answers to these specific questions:

- What is the sales tax rate? Can counties add onto the state rate? (The state sales tax rate is 5%, and counties can add up to .5% more.)
- Are e-book sales taxable? (Yes.)
- How frequently must I report and pay sales tax? (Report every quarter unless told by the state to submit monthly or annually.)
- How do I obtain a seller's permit? (Complete Wisconsin Form BTR-101 online. The fee is $20.)
- Am I required to file even if no sales tax is due? (Yes. Wisconsin requires reporting every quarter.)

I estimate it would take about two hours to research these questions and register my business in Wisconsin. I thought Wisconsin's information was fairly easy to follow. I considered myself a resident of Wisconsin for this example; finding information for a transient or temporary vendor may take more time.

For more help in collecting and remitting sales tax, visit The Sales Tax Institute's website SalesTaxInstitute.com. They offer helpful FAQs and links to more resources including sales tax software.

HOW TO SIMPLIFY YOUR SALES TAX

Sales tax involves tedious record keeping with little reward, so most indie publishers find legal ways to avoid the paperwork. Any or all of these suggestions might work to make sales tax compliance easier:

- Sell only to resellers, not to the final purchaser.
- If you live in a state that does not tax digital products, consider selling only e-books.
- Consider nontraditional sales avenues. Brian Jud, author of *How to Make Real Money Selling Books*, encourages sales to nonbookstore buyers. He explains, "One author sold over 5,000 copies of her dog care book to a dog food company. Not only did she make a bulk sale of books, but this smart author avoided collecting sales tax as well."

- Sell only online and let your merchant service provider (Paypal or Amazon, for example) collect the sales tax. Nina Roesner, author of *The Respect Dare*, does not directly sell her own books, even when she speaks. Buyers must purchase her book from a bookstore or online. Roesner admits that she may lose sales this way, but the simplicity appeals to her.
- Avoid traveling out of state to sell books. This limits your sales tax collection to only your home state, where you have nexus.
- If federal legislation is passed, keep sales below the $500 million threshold to be considered a small seller.
- If none of these options is viable, use software like QuickBooks to record all sales and the sales tax payable.

Sales tax is a complex and ever-changing topic. Indie publishers should stay abreast of their states' laws and the status of federal sales tax legislation. The concepts of nexus and tangible property are changing and will affect indie publishers in the future. Keeping detailed records and remitting sales tax are necessary, although unwelcome, burdens for everyone who loves to sell books.

CAROL TOPP, CPA is a Certified Public Accountant and author of *Business Tips and Taxes for Writers* (Media Angels). She has authored 10 books, both as an indie publisher and author for a small press. Learn more at CarolToppCPA.com and TaxesForWriters.com.

DISSECTING THE SELF-PUBLISHING CONTRACT

5 Key Issues for Authors

by Aimee Bissonette

Self-publishing can be a huge undertaking. There are so many issues to weigh. Different self-publishing service providers have different strengths and it can be hard to know which to use. Is your book primarily text or images? Do you plan to publish your book as an e-book, in print, or both? Do you need assistance with the entire self-publishing process or are you able to do some of the work yourself?

All of these are important considerations. But these aren't the only considerations. The contract terms offered by the Providers you are considering are important, as well. Provider contracts (often referred to as "Terms of Use" by online Providers) vary widely and some are more fair than others. Authors need to protect their creative works and their investment in the self-publishing process. Understanding the terms that govern the Author/Provider relationship is essential.

The following are 5 key contract issues for Authors evaluating self-publishing providers:

RIGHTS OWNERSHIP

Who "owns" the book and who controls its distribution and sale are key issues in all publishing contracts. Provider contracts should clearly state the Author is the sole owner of the text of the self-published book. In addition, the Author should own the book design, cover art, and formatting of the self-published book—even when these are created by the Provider. Plainly said, self-publishing should mean that you, the Author, own 100% of the rights to your book.

Instead of talking in terms of ownership, a Provider's contract language should discuss licensing of rights. The contract should enumerate the rights licensed, most commonly, the right to print, publish, distribute, and sell the book. The Author may also license the right to convert the book to one or more e-book formats and the right to house an electronic copy of the book on the Provider's server.

The Provider's contract should state whether the licenses are "exclusive" or "non-exclusive." If an Author grants an exclusive license to a Provider, the Provider is the only person or entity that may exercise that right while the contract is in place. The licensed right may not even be exercised by the Author during that time, so Authors should be careful about granting exclusive licenses. Exclusive licenses are appropriate when a Provider agrees to significant obligations beyond merely publishing and selling (e.g. warehousing, order fulfillment, marketing, publicity, catalog and website presence) but then only if the contract is easily terminated by the Author.

....

If an Author grants an exclusive license to a Provider, the Provider is the only person or entity that may exercise that right while the contract is in place. The licensed right may not even be exercised by the Author during that time, so Authors should be careful about granting exclusive licenses.

....

Licensed rights should be limited only to those that are necessary for the Provider to fulfill the self-publishing services and the length of time those licenses remain in place should also be limited (licenses should either be for a specific period of time or terminable at will by the Author). Some Provider contracts require Authors to grant very expansive licenses that allow the Provider tremendous control. These Providers also may try to include "out of print" clauses, non-compete clauses, and option clauses in their contracts—none of which is appropriate in a self-publishing scenario. Steer clear of these Providers.

DESIGN SERVICES

Providers of self-publishing services offer a range of packages and services. Authors engage these Providers for their expertise in editing and design, as well as distribution and e-book conversion. It is important to compare and contrast these offerings to determine exactly what the various Providers include in terms of cover art, interior design, fonts, placement of bar codes, etc.

Provider contracts should be clear about the services offered and when additional fees will be charged. For instance, the contract should state whether an Author must pay additional fees for revisions of the designs created and whether the Provider will refund an Author's money should the Provider and the Author fail to see eye to eye on production issues.

When evaluating the many additional services offered by various Providers (and the attendant fees), Authors should consider what, if anything, they can do themselves. There is no need to buy what you don't need. For instance, many Providers will procure ISBNs as part of their services. Because it is expensive for an individual to purchase a single ISBN, it may make sense for the Author to have the Provider do so, unless the Author intends to issue the self-published book in multiple formats or editions. (Each version and format of a book requires a separate ISBN. If you anticipate that you will be issuing the book in multiple formats or that you may reissue your book in the future through someone other than your current provider, you may be better off purchasing a block of 10 ISBNs.)

By comparison, copyright registration is easily done online and requires payment only of a nominal filing fee to the US Copyright Office (the current fee is $35). Registering your copyright yourself is preferable to paying your provider a marked up fee to do so.

....

Because it is expensive for an individual to purchase a single ISBN, it may make sense for the Author to have the Provider do so, unless the Author intends to issue the self-published book in multiple formats or editions.

....

As was noted above, ownership issues can arise with regard to design aspects of self-published books. Authors who engage Providers to design and format their books are encouraged to look for contract language along the lines of "Author owns 100% of the book cover, design and layout." If Authors supply their own images for their self-published books, they must be sure first to clear the rights to use those images.

Authors own the rights to images they create themselves (e.g. photos they take), but they are not free to use images pulled from the Internet without first obtaining permission. Even stock images obtained via Internet or subscription services are subject to restrictions. Authors must abide by the licensing terms and pay the appropriate fees to such services before including images on or in their self-published books.

If an Author retains a freelancer (an independent contractor) to provide cover art or other book design services, an agreement between the Author and freelancer should be crafted that specifically states, in writing, that the freelancer's work is a "work for hire" under US Copyright law and that the freelancer makes no claim of ownership in the Author's book. This will allow the Author to use the book's cover and design aspects in other ways as well, for example, on the Author's website, in print materials, and on social media.

HOW THE MONEY FLOWS

Providers take different approaches to pricing. Some dictate pricing and royalty terms, while others allow Authors to set their own retail price, author discount, and wholesale price (although sometimes subject to a minimum dollar amount to ensure the Provider can cover its administrative and credit card costs). Authors should seek arrangements that provide the Author with 100% of book royalties after deduction of production costs and third party service provider costs.

When it comes to tracking and getting paid for sales, self-publishing service Providers offer an advantage over traditional publishers. A number offer easily accessible sales information online and pay royalties on a monthly or quarterly basis, as opposed to the annual or semiannual payments provided by traditional publishers.

Compare Provider contracts based on how Providers track sales, how frequently they pay royalties, and the manner in which they pay. Many Providers set up Author accounts and establish a threshold amount above which funds are made available for electronic transfer. (If an Author prefers a physical check, a processing fee may be charged.) Look for contract language that establishes definite parameters and procedures for payment and provides a mechanism by which Authors can track sales and thus, judge the accuracy of payments made.

If funds owing the Author for book sales are not remitted to the Provider, the Provider has no obligation to pay the Author. The Author must undertake collection efforts agains the third party in such an instance.

With regard to payments, be aware that, as with traditional publishers, Providers will declare the right to withhold payments as an offset against any money the Author owes the Provider (e.g. payment for services, returns, refunds, customer credits). Providers will withhold payments if a claim is made against an Author for copyright infringement, defamation, or other violation of a third party's rights. Some Providers will also withhold payments for a period of time after termination of the contract (e.g. Amazon will hold funds for 3 months) so they are sure to have funds on hand to process refunds, credits, and returns accruing after the contract has ended.

In addition, be aware that the risk of non-payment of sales proceeds by a third party is borne solely by the Author. If funds owing the Author for book sales are not remitted to the Provider, the Provider has no obligation to pay the Author. The Author must undertake collection efforts against the third party in such an instance.

Lastly, Authors are responsible for paying income tax on the revenue they derive from book sales. Most Providers will require, at a minimum, that you provide them with a Social Security or Tax Identification number so they may fulfill their reporting obligations to the taxing authorities.

ENDING THE RELATIONSHIP

Self-publishing is changing rapidly. The services offered by Providers this year may be radically different from the services offered in the years to come. For that reason, it is important to have flexibility when it comes to terminating a contract with a Provider. Ideally, an Author should be able to terminate a Provider contract (in legal terms, "rescind" the Author's grant of rights) at any time. Provider contracts may require advance notice of termination, but such notice should not exceed 30 days.

Most Provider contracts allow for immediate termination followed by a short period within which the Provider may alert third party sellers and fulfill sales pending at the time of termination. Authors who have purchased additional services from their Providers (e.g. inclusion in an online or print catalog, premium distribution services) may have separate contracts for those services and may need to take additional steps to terminate those contracts.

> Provider contracts may require advance notice of termination, but such notice should not exceed 30 days.

Be aware that Providers also have termination rights. Many Providers include contract language that allows the Provider to suspend an Author's access to its services, particularly if an Author engages in illegal or unethical behavior, or otherwise violates the rights of others. Authors are counseled to keep backup copies of their books and other content as protection in the unlikely event they are denied access to their Providers' services.

RESOLVING DISPUTES

As with any business relationship, the possibility exists for a dispute between Authors and Providers. Sometimes these disputes are about money, which highlights the importance of reviewing/auditing royalty statements, as mentioned above. Sometimes the disputes occur pre-publication and are resolved by a refund of some or all of the Author's money. Regardless of the dispute, Provider contracts will include dispute resolution provisions, which generally benefit the Provider.

Some provider contracts set a discrete and usually short (e.g. 6 months, 12 months) period of time within which an Author may bring a claim against the Provider for breach of contract. Authors are contractually bound by these time periods, even if state law provides a longer period of time within which a claim may be brought.

Providers also often include language that limits the issues on which an Author may base a claim, limits the Author's recovery to unpaid royalties only, or requires the Author to use arbitration rather than the courts to resolve disputes. These dispute resolution provisions are not likely to be negotiable but, because they dictate how and when an Author may bring legal claims against a Provider, they should not be disregarded.

BE A SMART CONSUMER

In conclusion, there are a multitude of issues for Authors to consider when evaluating self-publishing Provider contracts. The issues outlined above are particularly important, however, because they affect an author's ability to control the self-published work. There are many reputable Providers whose contracts offer even-handed terms.

In comparing provider contracts, trust your gut. Ask yourself: Does the contract seem fair? Is it written in language that is easy to understand? Am I able to negotiate any terms (or, at least, choose from a variety of packages)?

Be a smart consumer. Talk to others who have used the self-publishing Provider you are considering. And, above all, review contract terms so you can minimize the risk of problems and maximize all the benefits that can accrue from self-publishing.

AIMEE BISSONETTE has worked as a lawyer, teacher, and writer since 1987. Through Little Buffalo Law & Consulting, she helps her clients make smart decisions about licensing their creative works. She has negotiated publishing contracts with all of the major publishing houses and many small and medium size presses, as well. Aimée holds a J.D. from the University of Minnesota. She is the author of *Cyber Law: Maximizing Safety and Minimizing Risk in Classrooms* (Corwin Press 2009).

HOW MUCH SHOULD I CHARGE?

by Aaron Belz

The first question most aspiring freelance writers ask themselves is, "Where do I find paying gigs?" But once a writer finds that first freelance gig, they often ask, "How much should I charge?"

They ask this question, because often their clients ask them. In the beginning, this can be one of the most stressful parts of the freelancing process: Trying to set rates that don't scare away clients, but that also help put dinner on the table.

Maybe that's why the "How Much Should I Charge?" pay rate chart is one of the most popular and useful pieces of the *Writer's Market*. Freelancers use the rates to justify their worth on the market to potential clients, and clients use the chart as an objective third party authority on what the current market is paying.

Use the following chart to help you get started in figuring out your freelance rates. If you're a beginner, it makes sense to price yourself closer to the lower end of the spectrum, but always use your gut in negotiating rates. The rate on that first assignment often helps set the expectations for future rates.

As you find success in securing work, your rates should naturally increase. If not, consider whether you're building relationships with clients that lead to multiple assignments. Also, take into account whether you're negotiating for higher rates on new assignments with familiar and newer clients.

Remember that smarter freelancers work toward the goal of higher rates, because better rates mean one of two things for writers: Either they're able to earn money, or they're able to earn the same money in less time. For some freelancers, having that extra time is worth more than anything money can buy.

Use the listings in Writer's Market to find freelance work for magazines, book publishers, and other traditional publishing markets. But don't restrict your search to the traditional markets if you want to make a serious living as a freelance writer.

As the pay rate chart shows, there are an incredible number of opportunities for writers to make a living doing what they love: writing. Maybe that writing critiques, editing anthologies, blogging, or something else entirely.

While this pay rate chart covers a wide variety of freelance writing gigs, there are some that are just too unique to get a going rate. If you can't find a specific job listed here, try to find something that is similar to use as a guide for figuring out a rate. There are times when you just have to create the going rate yourself.

Thank you, Aaron Belz, for assembling this pay rate chart and sharing your sources in the sidebar below. I know it will help more than one freelance writer negotiate the freelance rates they deserve.

—*Robert Lee Brewer*

PARTICIPATING ORGANIZATIONS

Here are the organizations surveyed to compile the "How Much Should I Charge?" pay rate chart. You can also find Professional Organizations in the Resources.

- American Medical Writers Association (AMWA), (301)294-5303. Website: www.amwa.org.
- American Society of Journalists & Authors (ASJA), (212)997-0947. Website: www.asja.org.
- American Society of Media Photographers (ASMP), (215)451-2767. Website: www.asmp.org.
- American Society of Picture Professionals (ASPP), (703)299-0219. Website: www.aspp.com.
- American Translators Association (ATA), (703)683-6100. Website: www.atanet.org.
- Association of Independents in Radio (AIR), (617)825-4400. Website: www.airmedia.org.
- Educational Freelancers Association (EFA), (212)929-5400. Website: www.the-efa.org.
- Freelance Success (FLX), (877) 731-5411. Website: www.freelancesucess.com.
- Investigative Reporters & Editors (IRE), (573)882-2042. Website: www.ire.org.
- Media Communicators Association International (MCA-I), (888)899-6224. Website: www.mca-i.org.
- National Cartoonists Society (NCS), (407)647-8839. Website: www.reuben.org/main.asp.

- National Writers Union (NWU), (212)254-0279. Website: www.nwu.org.
- National Association of Science Writers (NASW), (510)647-9500. Website: www.nasw.org.
- Society of Professional Journalists (SPJ), (317)927-8000. Website: www.spj.org.
- Women in Film (WIF). Website: www.wif.org.
- Writer's Guild of America East (WGAE), (212)767-7800. Website: www.wgaeast.org.
- Writer's Guild of America West (WGA), (323)951-4000. Website: www.wga.org.

AARON BELZ is a freelance writer, poet, and the author of Lovely, Raspberry and Glitter Bomb. Learn more about him at belz.net.

	PER HOUR			PER PROJECT			OTHER		
	HIGH	LOW	AVG	HIGH	LOW	AVG	HIGH	LOW	AVG
ADVERTISING & PUBLIC RELATIONS									
Advertising copywriting	$156	$36	$84	$9,000	$160	$2,760	$3/word	30¢/word	$1.57/word
Advertising editing	$125	$20	$65	n/a	n/a	n/a	$1/word	30¢/word	66¢/word
Advertorials	$182	$51	$93	$1,890	$205	$285	$3/word	85¢/word	$1.58/word
Business public relations	$182	$30	$85	n/a	n/a	n/a	$500/day	$200/day	$356/day
Campaign development or product launch	$156	$36	$100	$8,755	$1,550	$4,545	n/a	n/a	n/a
Catalog copywriting	$156	$25	$71	n/a	n/a	n/a	$350/item	$30/item	$116/item
Corporate spokesperson role	$182	$72	$107	n/a	n/a	n/a	$1,200/day	$500/day	$740/day
Direct-mail copywriting	$156	$36	$85	$8,248	$500	$2,839	$4/word $400/page	$1/word $200/page	$2.17/word $315/page
Event promotions/publicity	$126	$30	$76	n/a	n/a	n/a	n/a	n/a	$500/day
Press kits	$182	$31	$81	n/a	n/a	n/a	$850/60sec	$120/60sec	$458/60sec
Press/news release	$182	$30	$80	$1,500	$125	$700	$2/word $750/page	50¢/word $150/page	$1.20/word $348/page
Radio commercials	$102	$30	$74	n/a	n/a	n/a	$850/60sec	$120/60sec	$456/60sec

	PER HOUR			PER PROJECT			OTHER		
	HIGH	LOW	AVG	HIGH	LOW	AVG	HIGH	LOW	AVG
Speech writing/editing for individuals or corporations	$168	$36	$92	$10,000	$2,700	$5,036	$355/minute	$105/minute	$208/minute
BOOK PUBLISHING									
Abstracting and abridging	$125	$30	$74	n/a	n/a	n/a	$2/word	$1/word	$1.48/word
Anthology editing	$80	$23	$51	$7,900	$1,200	$4,588	n/a	n/a	n/a
Book chapter	$100	$35	$60	$2,500	$1,200	$1,758	20¢/word	8¢/word	14¢/word
Book production for clients	$100	$40	$67	n/a	n/a	n/a	$17.50/page	$5/page	$10/page
Book proposal consultation	$125	$25	$66	$1,500	$250	$788	n/a	n/a	n/a
Book publicity for clients	n/a	n/a	n/a	$10,000	$500	$2,000	n/a	n/a	n/a
Book query critique	$100	$50	$72	$500	$75	$202	n/a	n/a	n/a
Children's book writing	$75	$35	$50	n/a	n/a	n/a	$5/word $5,000/adv	$1/word $450/adv	$2.75/word $2,286/adv
Content editing (scholarly/textbook)	$125	$20	$51	$15,000	$500	$4,477	$20/page	$3/page	$6.89/page
Content editing (trade)	$125	$19	$54	$20,000	$1,000	$6,538	$20/page	$3.75/page	$8/page
Copyediting (trade)	$100	$16	$46	$5,500	$2,000	$2,892	$6/page	$1/page	$4.22/page

	PER HOUR			PER PROJECT			OTHER		
	HIGH	LOW	AVG	HIGH	LOW	AVG	HIGH	LOW	AVG
Encyclopedia articles	n/a	n/a	n/a	n/a	n/a	n/a	50¢/word $3,000/item	15¢/word $50/item	35¢/word $933/item
Fiction book writing (own)	n/a	n/a	n/a	n/a	n/a	n/a	$40,000/adv	$525/adv	$14,193/adv
Ghostwriting, as told to	$125	$35	$67	$47,000	$5,500	$22,892	$100/page	$50/page	$87/page
Ghostwriting, no credit	$125	$30	$73	n/a	n/a		$3/word $500/page	50¢/word $50/page	$1.79/word $206/page
Guidebook writing/editing	n/a	n/a		n/a	n/a	n/a	$14,000/adv	$10,000/adv	$12,000/adv
Indexing	$60	$22	$35	n/a	n/a	n/a	$12/page	$2/page	$4.72/page
Manuscript evaluation and critique	$150	$23	$66	$2,000	$150	$663	n/a	n/a	n/a
Manuscript typing	n/a	n/a	$20	n/a	n/a	n/a	$3/page	95¢/page	$1.67/page
Movie novelizations	n/a	n/a	$80	$15,000	$5,000	$9,159	n/a	n/a	n/a
Nonfiction book writing (collaborative)	$125	$40	$80	n/a	n/a	n/a	$110/page $75,000/adv	$50/page $1,300/adv	$80/page $22,684/adv
Nonfiction book writing (own)	$125	$40	$72	n/a	n/a	n/a	$110/page $50,000/adv	$50/page $1,300/adv	$80/page $14,057/adv
Novel synopsis (general)	$60	$30	$45	$450	$150	$292	$100/page	$10/page	$37/page

	PER HOUR			PER PROJECT			OTHER		
	HIGH	LOW	AVG	HIGH	LOW	AVG	HIGH	LOW	AVG
Personal history writing/editing (for clients)	$125	$30	$60	$40,000	$750	$15,038	n/a	n/a	n/a
Proofreading	$75	$15	$31	n/a	n/a	n/a	$5/page	$2/page	$3.26/page
Research for writers or book publishers	$150	$15	$52	n/a	n/a	n/a	$600/day	$400/day	$525/day
Rewriting/structural editing	$120	$25	$67	$50,000	$2,500	$13,929	14¢/word	5¢/word	10¢/word
Translation—literary	n/a	n/a	n/a	$95,000	$6,500	$8,000	17¢/target word	4¢/target word	8¢/target word
Translation—nonfiction/technical	n/a	n/a	n/a	n/a	n/a	n/a	30¢/target word	5¢/target word	12¢/target word
BUSINESS									
Annual reports	$185	$60	$102	$15,000	$500	$5,850	$600	$100	$349
Brochures, booklets, flyers	$150	$45	$91	$15,000	$300	$4,230	$2.50/word $800/page	35¢/word $50/page	$1.21/word $341/page
Business editing (general)	$155	$40	$80	n/a	n/a	n/a	n/a	n/a	n/a
Business letters	$155	$40	$79	n/a	n/a	n/a	$2/word	$1/word	$1.47/word
Business plan	$155	$40	$87	$15,000	$200	$4,115	n/a	n/a	n/a

	PER HOUR			PER PROJECT			OTHER		
	HIGH	LOW	AVG	HIGH	LOW	AVG	HIGH	LOW	AVG
Business writing seminars	$155	$70	$112	$8,600	$550	$2,919	n/a	n/a	n/a
Consultation on communications	$155	$50	$80	n/a	n/a	n/a	$1,300/day	$530/day	$830/day
Copyediting for business	$155	$35	$65	n/a	n/a	n/a	$4/page	$2/page	$3/page
Corporate histories	$155	$45	$91	160,000	$5,000	$54,525	$2/word	$1/word	$1.50/word
Corporate periodicals, editing	$155	$45	$74	n/a	n/a	n/a	$2.50/word	75¢/word	$1.42/word
Corporate periodicals, writing	$155	$45	$83	n/a	n/a	n/a	$3/word	$1/word	$1.71/word
Corporate profiles	$155	$45	$93	n/a	n/a	$3,000	$2/word	$1/word	$1.50/word
Ghostwriting for business execs	$155	$45	$89	$3,000	$500	$1,400	$2.50/word	50¢/word	$2/word
Ghostwriting for businesses	$155	$45	$114	$3,000	$500	$1,790	n/a	n/a	n/a
Newsletters, desktop publishing/production	$155	$45	$75	$6,600	$1,000	$3,490	$750/page	$150/page	$429/page
Newsletters, editing	$155	$35	$72	n/a	n/a	$3,615	$230/page	$150/page	$185/page
Newsletters, writing	$155	$35	$82	$6,600	$800	$3,581	$5/word $1,250/page	$1/word $150/page	$2.31/word $514/page

	PER HOUR			PER PROJECT			OTHER		
	HIGH	LOW	AVG	HIGH	LOW	AVG	HIGH	LOW	AVG
Translation services for business use	$80	$45	$57	n/a	n/a	n/a	$35/ target word $1.41/ target line	7¢/ target word $1/ target line	$2.31/ target word $1.21/ target line
Resume writing	$105	$70	$77	$500	$150	$295	n/a	n/a	n/a
COMPUTER, INTERNET & TECHNICAL									
Blogging—paid	$150	$35	$100	$2,000	$500	$1,250	$500/post	$6/post	$49/post
E-mail copywriting	$135	$30	$85	n/a	n/a	$300	$2/word	30¢/word	91¢/word
Educational webinars	$500	$0	$195	n/a	n/a	n/a	n/a	n/a	n/a
Hardware/Software help screen writing	$95	$60	$81	$6,000	$1,000	$4,000	n/a	n/a	n/a
Hardware/Software manual writing	$165	$30	$80	$23,500	$5,000	$11,500	n/a	n/a	n/a
Internet research	$95	$25	$55	n/a	n/a	n/a	n/a	n/a	n/a
Keyword descriptions	n/a	n/a	n/a	n/a	n/a	n/a	$200/page	$130/page	$165/page
Online videos for clients	$95	$60	$76	n/a	n/a	n/a	n/a	n/a	n/a

	PER HOUR			PER PROJECT			OTHER		
	HIGH	LOW	AVG	HIGH	LOW	AVG	HIGH	LOW	AVG
Social media postings for clients	$95	$25	$62	n/a	n/a	$500	n/a	n/a	$10/word
Technical editing	$150	$30	$65	n/a	n/a	n/a	n/a	n/a	n/a
Technical writing	$160	$30	$80	n/a	n/a	n/a	n/a	n/a	n/a
Web editing	$100	$25	$57	n/a	n/a	n/a	$10/page	$4/page	$5.67/page
Webpage design	$150	$25	$80	$4,000	$200	$1,278	n/a	n/a	n/a
Website or blog promotion	n/a	$30	n/a	$650	$195	$335	n/a	n/a	n/a
Website reviews	n/a	$30	n/a	$900	$50	$300	n/a	n/a	n/a
Website search engine optimization	$89	$30	$76	$50,000	$8,000	$12,000	n/a	n/a	n/a
White papers	$135	$30	$82	$10,000	$2,500	$4,927	n/a	n/a	n/a
EDITORIAL/DESIGN PACKAGES									
Desktop publishing	$150	$18	$67	n/a	n/a	n/a	$750/page	$30/page	$202/page
Photo brochures	$125	$60	$87	$15,000	$400	$3,869	$65/picture	$30/picture	$48/picture
Photography	$100	$45	$71	$10,500	$50	$2,100	$2,500/day	$500/day	$1,340/day

	PER HOUR			PER PROJECT			OTHER		
	HIGH	LOW	AVG	HIGH	LOW	AVG	HIGH	LOW	AVG
Photo research	$75	$45	$49	n/a	n/a	n/a	n/a	n/a	n/a
Picture editing	$100	$45	$64	n/a	n/a	n/a	$65/picture	$30/picture	$53/picture
EDUCATIONAL & LITERARY SERVICES									
Author appearances at national events	n/a	n/a	n/a	n/a	n/a	n/a	$500/hour $30,000/event	$100/hour $500/event	$285/hour $5,000/event
Author appearances at regional events	n/a	n/a	n/a	n/a	n/a	n/a	$1,500/event	$50/event	$615/event
Author appearances at local groups	$63	$40	$47	n/a	n/a	n/a	$400/event	$75/event	$219/event
Authors presenting in schools	$125	$25	$78	n/a	n/a	n/a	$350/class	$50/class	$183/class
Educational grant and proposal writing	$100	$35	$67	n/a	n/a	n/a	n/a	n/a	n/a
Manuscript evaluation for theses/dissertations	$100	$15	$53	$1,550	$200	$783	n/a	n/a	n/a
Poetry manuscript critique	$100	$25	$62	n/a	n/a	n/a	n/a	n/a	n/a
Private writing instruction	$60	$50	$57	n/a	n/a	n/a	n/a	n/a	n/a

	PER HOUR			PER PROJECT			OTHER		
	HIGH	LOW	AVG	HIGH	LOW	AVG	HIGH	LOW	AVG
Readings by poets, fiction writers	n/a	n/a	n/a	n/a	n/a	n/a	$3,000/event	$50/event	$225/event
Short story manuscript critique	$150	$30	$75	$175	$50	$112	n/a	n/a	n/a
Teaching adult writing classes	$125	$30	$82	n/a	n/a	n/a	$800/class $5,000/course	$115/class $500/course	$450/class $2,667/course
Writer's workshop panel or class	$220	$30	$92	n/a	n/a	n/a	$5,000/day	$60/day	$1,186/day
Writing for scholarly journals	$100	$40	$63	$450	$100	$285	n/a	n/a	n/a
FILM, VIDEO, TV, RADIO, STAGE									
Book/novel summaries for film producers	n/a	n/a	n/a	n/a	n/a	n/a	$34/page	$15/page	$23/page $120/book
Business film/video scriptwriting	$150	$50	$97	n/a	n/a	$600	$1,000/run min	$50/run min	$334/run min $500/day
Comedy writing for entertainers	n/a	n/a	n/a	n/a	n/a	n/a	$150/joke $500/group	$5/joke $100/group	$50/joke $283/group
Copyediting audiovisuals	$90	$22	$53	n/a	n/a	n/a	n/a	n/a	n/a
Educational or training film/video scriptwriting	$125	$35	$81	n/a	n/a	n/a	$500/run min	$100/run min	$245/run min

	PER HOUR			PER PROJECT			OTHER		
	HIGH	LOW	AVG	HIGH	LOW	AVG	HIGH	LOW	AVG
Feature film options	First 18 months, 10% WGA minimum; 10% minimum each 18-month period thereafter.								
TV options	First 180 days, 5% WGA minimum; 10% minimum each 180-day period thereafter.								
Industrial product film/video scriptwriting	$150	$30	$99	n/a	n/a	n/a	$500/run min	$100/run min	$300/run min
Playwriting for the stage	5-10% box office/Broadway, 6-7% box office/off-Broadway, 10% box office/regional theatre.								
Radio editorials	$70	$50	$60	n/a	n/a	n/a	$200/run min $400/day	$45/run min $250/day	$124/run min $325/day
Radio interviews	n/a	n/a	n/a	$1,500	$110	$645	n/a	n/a	n/a
Screenwriting (original screenplay-including treatment)	n/a	n/a	n/a	n/a	n/a	n/a	$118,745	$63,526	$92,153
Script synopsis for agent or film	$2,344/30 min, $4,441/60 min, $6,564/90 min								
Script synopsis for business	$75	$45	$62	n/a	n/a	n/a	n/a		
TV commercials	$99	$60	$81	n/a	n/a	n/a	$2,500/30 sec	$150/30 sec	$1,204/30 sec
TV news story/feature	$1,550/5 min, $3,000/10 min, $4,200/15 min								
TV scripts (non-theatrical)	Prime Time: $33,700/60 min, $47,500/90 min Not Prime Time: $12,900/30 min, $23,500/60 min, $35,300/90 min								

	PER HOUR			PER PROJECT			OTHER		
	HIGH	LOW	AVG	HIGH	LOW	AVG	HIGH	LOW	AVG
TV scripts (teleplay/MOW)	$70,000/120 min								
MAGAZINES & TRADE JOURNALS									
Article manuscript critique	$130	$25	$69	n/a	n/a	n/a	n/a	n/a	n/a
Arts query critique	$105	$50	$80	n/a	n/a	n/a	n/a	n/a	n/a
Arts reviewing	$100	$65	$84	$335	$95	$194	$1.25/word	12¢/word	63¢/word
Book reviews	n/a	n/a	n/a	$900	$12	$348	$1.50/word	20¢/word	73¢/word
City magazine calendar	n/a	n/a	n/a	$250	$45	$135	$1/word	35¢/word	75¢/word
Comic book/strip writing				$225 original story, $525 existing story, $50 short script.					
Consultation on magazine editorial	$155	$35	$86	n/a	n/a	n/a	n/a	n/a	$100/page
Consumer magazine column	n/a	n/a	n/a	$2,500	$70	$898	$2.50/word	37¢/word	$1.13/word
Consumer front-of-book	n/a	n/a	n/a	$850	$320	$550	n/a	n/a	n/a
Content editing	$130	$30	$62	$6,500	$2,000	$3,700	15¢/word	6¢/word	11¢/word
Contributing editor	n/a	n/a	n/a	n/a	n/a	n/a	$160,000/ contract	$22,000/ contract	$53,000/ contract

	PER HOUR			PER PROJECT			OTHER		
	HIGH	LOW	AVG	HIGH	LOW	AVG	HIGH	LOW	AVG
Copyediting magazines	$105	$18	$55	n/a	n/a	n/a	$10/page	$2.90/page	$5.78/page
Fact checking	$130	$15	$46	n/a	n/a	n/a	n/a	n/a	n/a
Gag writing for cartoonists	$35/gag; 25% sale on spec.								
Ghostwriting articles (general)	$225	$30	$107	$3,500	$1,100	$2,200	$10/word	65¢/word	$2.50/word
Magazine research	$125	$20	$53	n/a	n/a	n/a	$500/item	$100/item	$200/item
Proofreading	$80	$20	$40	n/a	n/a	n/a	n/a	n/a	n/a
Reprint fees	n/a	n/a	n/a	$1,500	$20	$439	$1.50/word	10¢/word	76¢/word
Rewriting	$130	$25	$74	n/a	n/a	n/a	n/a	n/a	$50/page
Trade journal feature article	$128	$45	$80	$4,950	$150	$1,412	$3/word	20¢/word	$1.20/word
Transcribing interviews	$185	$95	$55	n/a	n/a	n/a	$3/min	$1/min	$2/min
MEDICAL/SCIENCE									
Medical/scientific conference coverage	$125	$50	$85	n/a	n/a	n/a	$800/day	$300/day	$600/day
Medical/scientific editing	$96	$15	$33	n/a	n/a	n/a	$12.50/page $600/day	$3/page $500/day	$4.40/page $550/day

	PER HOUR			PER PROJECT			OTHER		
	HIGH	LOW	AVG	HIGH	LOW	AVG	HIGH	LOW	AVG
Medical/scientific writing	$91	$20	$46	$4,000	$500	$2,500	$2/word	25¢/word	$1.12/word
Medical/scientific multimedia presentations	$100	$50	$75	n/a	n/a	n/a	$100/slide	$50/slide	$77/slide
Medical/scientific proofreading	$80	$18	$50	n/a	n/a	$500	$3/page	$2.50/page	$2.75/page
Pharmaceutical writing	$125	$100	$50	n/a	n/a	n/a	n/a	n/a	n/a
NEWSPAPERS									
Arts reviewing	$69	$30	$53	$200	$15	$101	60¢/word	6¢/word	36¢/word
Book reviews	$69	$45	$58	$350	$15	$140	60¢/word	25¢/word	44¢/word
Column, local	n/a	n/a	n/a	$600	$25	$206	$1/word	38¢/word	50¢/word
Column, self-syndicated	n/a	n/a	n/a	n/a	n/a	n/a	$35/insertion	$4/insertion	$16/insertion
Copyediting	$35	$15	$27	n/a	n/a	n/a	n/a	n/a	n/a
Editing/manuscript evaluation	$75	$25	$35	n/a	n/a	n/a	n/a	n/a	n/a
Feature writing	$79	$40	$63	$1,040	$85	$478	$1.60/word	10¢/word	59¢/word
Investigative reporting	n/a	n/a	n/a	n/a	n/a	n/a	$10,000/grant	$250/grant	$2,250/grant

	PER HOUR			PER PROJECT			OTHER		
	HIGH	LOW	AVG	HIGH	LOW	AVG	HIGH	LOW	AVG
Obituary copy	n/a	n/a	n/a	$225	$35	$124	n/a	n/a	n/a
Proofreading	$45	$15	$23	n/a	n/a	n/a	n/a	n/a	n/a
Stringing	n/a	n/a	n/a	$2,400	$40	$525	n/a	n/a	n/a
NONPROFIT									
Grant writing for nonprofits	$150	$12	$75	$3,000	$400	$1,852	n/a	n/a	n/a
Nonprofit annual reports	$100	$28	$60	n/a	n/a	n/a	n/a	n/a	n/a
Nonprofit writing	$150	$17	$65	$17,600	$100	$4,706	n/a	n/a	n/a
Nonprofit editing	$125	$16	$50	n/a	n/a	n/a	n/a	n/a	n/a
Nonprofit fundraising literature	$110	$35	$74	$3,500	$200	$1,597	$1,000/day	$300/day	$767/day
Nonprofit presentations	$100	$40	$73	n/a	n/a	n/a	n/a	n/a	n/a
Nonprofit public relations	$100	$30	$60	n/a	n/a	n/a	n/a	n/a	n/a
POLITICS/GOVERNMENT									
Government agency writing/editing	$110	$25	$64	n/a	n/a	n/a	$1.25/word	25¢/word	75¢/word

	PER HOUR			PER PROJECT			OTHER		
	HIGH	LOW	AVG	HIGH	LOW	AVG	HIGH	LOW	AVG
Government grant writing/editing	$150	$19	$72	n/a	n/a	n/a	n/a	n/a	n/a
Government-sponsored research	$110	$35	$66	n/a	n/a	n/a	n/a	n/a	$600/day
Public relations for political campaigns	$150	$40	$86	n/a	n/a	n/a	n/a	n/a	n/a
Speechwriting for government officials	$200	$40	$96	$4,550	$1,015	$2,755	$200/run min	$110/run min	$155/run min
Speechwriting for political campaigns	$155	$65	$101	n/a	n/a	n/a	$200/run min	$100/run min	$162/run min

RECORDKEEPING 101

Keep Records to Save on Your Taxes

....

by Joanne E. McFadden

Few people enjoy preparing their tax returns. For the self-employed, which many writers are, this means extra work, namely the Schedule C, Profit or Loss From Business. The extra work, though, results in tax savings, making it worth the time and effort.

I didn't get really serious about my record keeping until a few years ago when I decided to give myself the gift of thorough, stress-free tax preparation. I set up a system that made everything all ready to go at tax time, thus saving me valuable time that I could be writing or researching. I eliminated tax time procrastination and the anxiety of collecting, organizing and adding up my business expenses the night before meeting with my accountant.

In addition to eliminating the stress of filing my tax return, developing a system that made me already prepared at tax time with minimal effort also reduced the amount of taxes I paid because I maintained an extremely thorough accounting of the expenses I could deduct from the amount of my freelance income.

GET MOTIVATED

Being self-employed means that one pays the employer's share as well as the employee's of Social Security and Medicare, which is 7.65 percent twice, for a total of 15.3 percent. Like a regular employer, you get a deduction for the employer's half, points out Internal Revenue Service (IRS) spokesperson Eric Smith. Nevertheless, the better a person keeps track of legitimate, tax-deductible business expenses, the less self-employment *and* federal taxes he pays, legally. This seems to be reason enough to take the time to set up a system that allows you to do just that, without a last-minute scramble before April 15.

Yet, the most common mistake that people make is simply failing to keep adequate records or any records at all, according to Ronald R. Mueller, author of *Home Business Tax*

Savings, Made Easy! who has dedicated a whole career to helping and instructing people with home-based businesses about their taxes. "Paperwork is part of running a business," Mueller said. "People don't recognize the importance of it until they're audited," he said. If a person doesn't have adequate records to prove his expenses at an audit, he could end up having to pay up, with interest.

For me, tax time used to mean facing a hanging file folder full of crumpled up, disorganized receipts that I had to spend hours organizing and tallying. It also meant finding caches of receipts that I had failed to throw in the file folder long after I had filed my tax return, so I paid more taxes than I owed because of my sloppy record-keeping. (If the amount of excluded expenses is significant enough, one can file an amended return, but keeping good records in the first place is far more efficient.)

If this sounds familiar, read on to find out how to keep complete, organized records that will be ready to go at tax time, thus maximizing your income and time, all in alignment with Internal Revenue Service (IRS) regulations.

DO YOUR HOMEWORK

Make some time in your schedule for becoming really familiar with the expenses that you can deduct on your tax return. Employ the same sound research skills that you use for writing an article to finding out about the expenses and what records you are required to keep to document them. In addition to the IRS website, the internet abounds with information for small business owners, and there are also entire books and websites dedicated to just this topic. Familiarize yourself with the eligible expenses; you might even find that there are some you have overlooked.

For the official word and to double-check your research, a good reference is IRS Publication 583, Starting A Business and Keeping Records. It provides an overview and refers the reader to other publications with more detail, said Smith. In addition, it includes some sample record-keeping systems.

SET UP YOUR STRUCTURE

The first critical step in easy record keeping is setting up a system for filing the records of your business expenses. Don't be put off; it's easier and less time consuming than you might think.

Any organizer will tell you it's important to set up a style that fits your personality, which is key to following through with the actual filing of receipts and other supporting documentation of business expenses. This may be hanging file folders, an accordion style file, a day planner, a 3-ring binder, or for the techie-type, a software program on the computer or even an app on a smart phone. (Smith points out that the IRS website has a list of vendors who sell tax preparation software.) If you choose either of the electronic options, be sure to back up files regularly, and know that you also must retain receipts and other documentation that prove those expenses you recorded electronically. It's critical to be honest with yourself and choose the system that you are most likely to use.

USE THE SCHEDULE C FORM

Once you've chosen how to set up your files, decide on the categories for each file. If you're using an electronic system, the program will already have these set up for you. If you're using paper, the Schedule C form, available at www.irs.gov can help with this. Part II of the form lists the different categories of business expenses as they have to be recorded on the tax return. Since each person's expenses are different, make a study of the form to determine which files will be useful to you. For example, if you make business use of your home and take a deduction for that (Line 18), you'll want a file for records related to this expense. If your home office doubles as a guest room making you ineligible to take that deduction, you don't need a tab for that category. If you paid an independent contractor for business-related services, you will want a file for "Contract labor" (Line 11). If you didn't, you don't need this file. (Note that there is a separate line for "Legal and professional services," i.e., attorneys and accountants.)

If it sounds complicated to know what expense goes where, consult the "Instructions for Schedule C" booklet available online that provides details about these expenses as well as other publications to consult for further clarification.

Here are some of the categories that most all writers will have.

- **Vehicle expenses (Line 9).** There is a standard deduction for mileage (the amount changes every year and sometimes even in the middle of the year, so check the IRS website for the most up-to-date figure). This means that you need to document the business-related miles that you drive, and not just the date and mileage, but where you traveled and for what purpose. The simplest way to do this is to keep a mileage log right in your car to write down the date, place you traveled, the business purpose, and number of miles, the four requirements to satisfy an allowable business expense. Mueller, who has a free downloadable Vehicle Use Log on his website, said that mileage is an expense that people often forget to record. He suggests putting the mileage log right on the driver's seat so that you have to move it when you sit down, or to put it on the dashboard where you'll see it. If you do not want to use the standard deduction for mileage, there are additional records that you need to keep about your gas purchases and vehicle maintenance expenses.
- **Depreciation (Line 13).** This can look confusing, but it simply refers to equipment that you put into service in a given year whose life will extend beyond that year. (For writers, this most likely includes their computers and printers.) Reading the

Schedule C Instruction booklet can give you a better idea of what is included in this category and the receipts and records that you need to keep on file for this expense. Since the IRS requires paper (or scanned) receipts for expenses in excess of $75, it is important to keep these. If the receipt is printed on electrostatic paper, make a copy or scan it, Mueller said, because the print will fade over time.

- **Supplies (Line 22).** This is what it sounds like–paper clips, toner cartridges, paper, USB drives, file folders, etc.
- **Travel, meals and entertainment (Line 24).** The IRS asks that the travel costs (like airfare to a writer's conference and hotel expenses) be separated from meals and entertainment (for example, the bill for when you took a source to lunch for an interview, or the meals you incurred while attending the writers' conference). The IRS has very specific rules about which expenses are deductible and which are not, which it spells out in the Schedule C Instruction booklet. Mueller said that in order to claim entertainment expenses, there are five pieces of information that must be recorded: where, when, how much, the name of the person you entertained and the business objective.

> **INFO BOX**
>
> Some recordkeeping resources:
>
> At www.irs.gov:
>
> Publication 583, Starting A Business and Keeping Records
>
> Publication 463, Travel, Entertainment, Gift and Car Expenses
>
> Instructions for Schedule C
>
> For the latest changes to the Schedule C, visit www.irs.gov/schedulec

- **Utilities (Line 25).** This can include your telephone if you have a separate line.
- **Other.** This is for expenses that don't fit into other categories, such as postage, photocopying fees, books and your *Writer's Digest* subscription.
- **Income.** This is where you can keep check stubs, invoices, and other records of payments you receive. When you're paid $600 or more in a year, you should receive a 1099-MISC, but for amounts under that, you might not receive this documentation at the end of the year.

THE SECRET: DO IT NOW, NEVER LATER

Once you've taken the time to set up your filing system, whether it be folders, a notebook, or whatever works best for you, you need to get into the habit of filing receipts there. "Records are your friends," said Smith. "The best records are those that you keep at the time that you're doing whatever it is. A lot of people know to keep a log book to write things down when they pay the expense. It helps them to really keep track of the expenses that they're legitimately entitled to," he said.

ANOTHER RESOURCE

Ron Mueller's website is www.home-businesstaxsavings.com. There you'll find free and low-cost downloads, including a vehicle use log and year-end tax deduction memory jogger, as well as a newsletter with tax savings tips and the latest updates about changes to the tax law, among other information relating to home-based businesses

Your filing system won't serve you if you don't utilize it. The trick is to do it right away, whether it be recording that trip downtown to do an interview or printing a receipt for something ordered online and tucking it into the right file. If you wait to record a trip, for example, with our lives as busy as they are, you're likely to forget by the end of the week. If you receive an e-mail receipt, if you don't print it out and file it right away, you might forget about it come tax time and lose that deduction. I keep my notebook right on the bookshelf in the kitchen so that it's easily accessible for me to use.

Setting up a time daily to record business expenses and file any receipts you gather while you're out is a good idea. Go through your pocketbook or wallet and pull out any receipts you've acquired and file them. The longer you wait, the bigger the chance that those receipts will be lost or misplaced. Train yourself to get in the habit of recording and filing frequently. When tax time comes, all the receipts you need will be neatly filed away.

A trick that Mueller uses is to write in his day planner in pencil. At the end of each day, he goes through and erases what he didn't get done and writes in what he did do. Then he takes a moment to ask himself if he spent money on anything that might be deductible, and he writes those items in. If items are over $75, he files the receipts for those. "It's a discipline," Mueller said, noting that it only takes three to four minutes a day—the time you would take to brush your teeth—to keep good records.

Maintaining thorough records of your writing expenses can help you to keep more of the income you earn.

SCHEDULE C EXPENSE DOCUMENTATION:

Why (business purpose):

What (description, including itemized accounting of cost):

When (date):

Where (location):

Who (names of those for whom the expense was incurred; e.g., meals and entertainment):

JOANNE E. MCFADDEN has been a freelance writer for 21 years, although she admits it took her almost two decades to get so serious and organized about her bookkeeping. She's worked for three daily newspapers and has published articles in many more publications.

HOW TO KEEP YOUR MANUSCRIPT SAFE

....

by Peggy DeKay

On February 13, 1991, Sotheby's announced the discovery of a long lost manuscript of *Huckleberry Finn* by Mark Twain. The manuscript was the first half of Twain's original heavily corrected in his hand. It had been missing for more than a century and was discovered when a 62-year-old librarian in Los Angeles got around to opening six trunks full of old papers which were sent to her when her aunt died.

Bestselling author James Michener said that he had a dream about writing a novel about Mexico. He researched the ideas after the dream, wrote the novel, and then lost it. Thirty years later, he discovered it, finished the novel and published it.

Dylan Thomas lost the manuscript to *Under Milk Wood* three times: first in London, then in American and then again in London. The third time it was lost it was discovered in a pub by Thomas' friend Doug Cleversdon.

James Faulkner lost his fourth novel on a train between Durham and New Castle. Robert Ludlum, the famous thriller writer lost his first novel which he called a "literary effort" while he was serving in the Marine Corp. The manuscript was lost after a long drinking session while on leave in San Francisco.

Losing manuscripts is so prolific in the world of writing that even Hollywood has gotten into the act. In the hilarious movie, *The Wonder Boys*, Michael Douglas plays Prof. Tripp, a college professor who has published one bestselling novel but can't seem to complete his second novel. In the course of the movie, Prof. Tripp puts his 2,000 plus-page manuscript into his car only to have the car door thrown open after a wreck and the pages scattered into the bay, lost forever.

In the movie *Love Actually*, Colin Firth plays "Jamie" a writer who has broken up with his fiancée and goes to Europe to write his next novel. He rents a house in the countryside complete with a gazebo and pond in his backyard. As he sits in a gazebo typing on a manual typewriter, the loose pages of his manuscript precariously piled beside him are held down by the weight of his cup of tea. When his housekeeper comes out to give him a fresh cup of tea, she lifts the cup from the loose pile, releasing a flurry of flying pages driven by a sudden gust of wind. The pages of the manuscript flutter silently into the pond.

So what is a writer to do to make sure his or her manuscript is safe from harm? I think the first thing is too look seriously at your body of work and make the determination: This is my livelihood. I have hours, weeks, months and years of my life invested in these documents. It is my responsibility to keep them safe.

SAVING PAPER MANUSCRIPTS

Although in this article our focus is on electronic backups from your laptop or PC it is important to keep substantive edited versions of your work as well. If the editing is done on paper than keep the paper copy with hand-written corrections in an acid free storage box, clearly marked with the name of the manuscript, author and date. If you edit on the computer using the "tracker" feature in Word, save a markup version in addition to the finished manuscript.

SAVING MANUSCRIPTS ELECTRONICALLY

When making electronic backups we must decide what types of files we want backed up. There are two types of backup programs: Ghost drive backups which backup not just file folders on your hard drive but programs as well. Backups are stored in the cloud and they usually keep at least one prior version from the current backup. Ghost drive programs create a "recovery disk" which, in the case of a catastrophic hard drive failure can restore the old drive's programs and data to a newly installed hard drive on your PC or laptop.

I have hours, weeks, months and years of my life invested in these documents. It is my responsibility to keep them safe.

File folder and document backup software does not backup your computer program files but only the files and folders that you specify. For example if you designate the "document" folder as a folder to be backed up then the program will back up all sub-folders and files within the document folder which would include videos, music, pictures and documents.

Most backup software is fee-based but there are some free tools available online that can help you backup selected files without investing in a backup program.

FEE-BASED BACKUP PROGRAMS

Carbonite.com

Cost: Starting at $59.95 a year

I have used Carbonite.com for my own backups and find it easy to install from a simple download from their website, with good customer support.

Backup Genie

http://www.backupgenie.com/

Cost: $4.49 per month basic plan

Easy to use software that is straightforward and reliable. It can create backups in the form of executable files that can run on any Windows machine. Genie has many advanced options as well but these may be beyond the average user.

Rebit

http://rebit.com

Cost: $34.95

Cheap and easy to setup. Offers automatic continuous backup.

Norton Ghost

http://us.norton.com

Cost: $35

Norton Ghost 15.0 has been around a long time. I used it back in the 90s when I ran my own computer network design firm. It does file and image drive backups. For most writers ghost imaging is overkill and isn't necessary. It also includes Norton anti-virus software, which you may not want or need.

FREE BACKUP TOOL ALTERNATIVES

Dropbox.com

A cloud based backup and file sharing system. The beauty of using a cloud-based backup system is that you can access your Dropbox files and folders from anywhere—your cell phone, your iPad, tablet, or another PC.

To use Dropbox.com go to the website and sign up. Once Dropbox is downloaded onto the hard drive on your PC, you will see the Dropbox folder appear in your file folders. Once you see the Dropbox icon in your folders directory you can copy, save, or move files to the Dropbox folder.

The five icons with arrow are for Upload, New Folder, Share Folder, Share Link, and Delete. To use Dropbox as a backup for you manuscripts, I recommend creating a file folder for each manuscript. Once you have created the folder, you can save as many versions of your manuscript as you like to that Dropbox folder. You can also share that folder with an editor if you choose to. If you don't want to share the entire folder, you can share a link to one file. Dropbox is easy to use. There is no online support but you can print off a comprehensive guide to using Dropbox from the their website. You can store your book cover graphics, completed book cover designs, and photos and any other files related to publishing your book.

Dropbox provides new users with 2 GB of data at sign-up. Additional storage is available for $99 or you can earn free storage upgrades by recommending Dropbox to a friend.

A writer's document files are his life as a writer. Protect yours.

The strength of Dropbox is its limited functionality. Because it only does two things: (1) store your files in the cloud and (2) allow you to share files and/or folders; it is simple and easy for most people to master in one day.

Google Drive

Google drive allows you to backup documents to their cloud-based server. You create an account with a login and password. Once you have created your account you can access Google Drive through your Gmail account. Google Drive comes with convenient applications, which allow you to create simple documents, spreadsheets, and tables that you can share with others. (www.google.com/drive/)

Google Drive gives you 15 GB of storage free and you can purchase additional storage, as you need it. I find Google Drive not as easy to learn as Dropbox but more useful once you have mastered the program.

In summary, there are many ways to keep your manuscript safe. The first thing that must happen is for you to decide that keeping your manuscript safe is not just an option but good business. You have hours of work that could be difficult or impossible to recreate if it were lost. A writer's document files are his life as a writer. Protect yours.

PEGGY DEKAY is an author, blogger, podcaster, and book coach. She is the author of *Self-Publishing for Virgins*. Her podcast, The Business of Writing Today can be downloaded on iTunes or from her website at http://tbowt.com. DeKay is the co-organizer of The Business of Writing Today International Summit held annually in Louisville, Kentucky. E-mail her at peggy@tbowt.com..

MAKING THE MOST OF THE MONEY YOU EARN

....

by Sage Cohen

Writers who manage money well can establish a prosperous writing life that meets their short-term needs and long-term goals. This article will introduce the key financial systems, strategies, attitudes and practices that will help you cultivate a writing life that makes the most of your resources and sustains you over time.

DIVIDING BUSINESS AND PERSONAL EXPENSES

If you are reporting your writing business to the IRS, it is important that you keep the money that flows from this source entirely separate from your personal finances. Here's what you'll need to accomplish this:

- **BUSINESS CHECKING ACCOUNT:** Only two types of money go into this account: money you have been paid for your writing and/or "capital investments" you make by depositing your own money to invest in the business. And only two types of payments are made from this account: business-related expenses (such as: subscriptions, marketing and advertisement, professional development, fax or phone service, postage, computer software and supplies), and "capital draws" which you make to pay yourself.
- **BUSINESS SAVINGS ACCOUNT OR MONEY MARKET ACCOUNT:** This account is the holding pen where your quarterly tax payments will accumulate and earn interest. Money put aside for your retirement account(s) can also be held here.
- **BUSINESS CREDIT CARD:** It's a good idea to have a credit card for your business as a means of emergency preparedness. Pay off the card responsibly every month and this will help you establish a good business credit record, which can be useful down the line should you need a loan for any reason.

When establishing your business banking and credit, shop around for the best deals, such as highest interest rates, lowest (or no) monthly service fees, and free checking. Mint.com is a good source for researching your options.

EXPENSE TRACKING AND RECONCILING

Once your bank accounts are set up, it's time to start tracking and categorizing what you earn and spend. This will ensure that you can accurately report your income and itemize your deductions when tax time rolls around every quarter. Whether you intend to prepare your taxes yourself or have an accountant help you, immaculate financial records will be the key to speed and success in filing your taxes.

For the most effective and consistent expense tracking, I highly recommend that you use a computer program such as QuickBooks. While it may seem simpler to do accounting by hand, I assure you that it isn't. Even a luddite such as I, who can't comprehend the most basic principles of accounting, can use QuickBooks with great aplomb to plug in the proper categories for income and expenses, easily reconcile bank statements, and with a few clicks prepare all of the requisite reports that make it easy to prepare taxes.

PAYING BILLS ONLINE

While it's certainly not imperative, you might want to check out your bank's online bill pay option if you're not using this already. Once you've set up the payee list, you can make payments in a few seconds every month or set up auto payments for expenses that are recurring. Having a digital history of bills paid can also come in handy with your accounting.

MANAGING TAXES

Self-employed people need to pay quarterly taxes. A quick, online search will reveal a variety of tax calculators and other online tools that can help you estimate what your payments should be. Programs such as TurboTax are popular and useful tools for automating and guiding you step-by-step through tax preparation. An accountant can also be helpful in understanding your unique tax picture, identifying and saving the right amount for taxes each quarter, and even determining SEP IRA contribution amounts (described later in this article). The more complex your finances (or antediluvian your accounting skills), the more likely that you'll benefit from this kind of personalized expertise.

Once you have forecasted your taxes either with the help of a specialized, tax-planning program or an accountant, you can establish a plan toward saving the right amount for quarterly payments. For example, once I figured out what my tax bracket was and the approximate percentage of income that needed to be set aside as taxes, I would immediately transfer a percentage of every deposit to my savings account, where it would sit and grow a little interest until quarterly tax time came around. When I could afford to do so, I would also set aside the appropriate percentage of SEP IRA contribution from each deposit so that I'd be ready at end-of-year to deposit as much as I possibly could for retirement.

THE PRINCIPLE TO COMMIT TO IS THIS: Get that tax-earmarked cash out of your hot little hands (i.e., checking account) as soon as you can, and create whatever deterrents you need to leave the money in savings so you'll have it when you need it.

INTELLIGENT INVESTING FOR YOUR CAREER

Your writing business will require not only the investment of your time but also the investment of money. When deciding what to spend and how, consider your values and your budget in these three, key areas:

EDUCATION	MARKETING AND PROMOTION	KEEPING THE WHEELS TURNING
Subscriptions to publications in your field	URL registration and hosting for blogs and websites	Technology and application purchase, servicing and back-up
Memberships to organizations in your field	Contact database subscription (such as Constant Contact) for communicating with your audiences	Office supplies and furniture
Books: on topics you want to learn, or in genres you are cultivating	Business cards and stationery	Insurances for you and/or your business
Conferences and seminars	Print promotions (such as direct mail), giveaways and schwag	Travel, gas, parking
Classes and workshops	Online or print ad placement costs	Phone, fax and e-mail

This is not an absolute formula for spending, by any means—just a snapshot of the types of expenses you may be considering and negotiating over time. My general rule would be: start small and modest with the one or two most urgent and/or inexpensive items in each list, and grow slowly over time as your income grows.

The good news is that these legitimate business expenses may all be deducted from your income—making your net income and tax burden less. Please keep in mind that the IRS allows losses as long as you make a profit for at least three of the first five years you are in business. Otherwise, the IRS will consider your writing a non-deductible hobby.

PREPARATION AND PROTECTION FOR THE FUTURE

As a self-employed writer, in many ways your future is in your hands. Following are some of the health and financial investments that I'd recommend you consider as you build and nurture The Enterprise of You. Please understand that these are a layperson's suggestions. I am by no means an accountant, tax advisor or financial planning guru. I am simply a person who has educated herself on these topics for the sake of her own writing business, made the choices I am recommending and benefited from them. I'd like you to benefit from them, too.

SEP IRAS

Individual Retirement Accounts (IRAs) are investment accounts designed to help individuals save for retirement. But I do recommend that you educate yourself about the Simplified Employee Pension Individual Retirement Account (SEP IRA) and consider opening one if you don't have one already.

A SEP IRA is a special type of IRA that is particularly beneficial to self-employed people. Whereas a Roth IRA has a contribution cap of $5,000 or $6,000, depending on your age, the contribution limit for self-employed people in 2011 is approximately 20% of adjusted earned income, with a maximum contribution of $49,000. Contributions for a SEP IRA are generally 100% tax deductible and investments grow tax deferred. Let's say your adjusted earned income this year is $50,000. This means you'd be able to contribute $10,000 to your retirement account. I encourage you to do some research online or ask your accountant if a SEP IRA makes sense for you.

CREATING A 9-MONTH SAVINGS BUFFER

When you're living month-to-month, you are extremely vulnerable to fluctuation in the economy, client budget changes, life emergencies and every other wrench that could turn a good working groove into a frightening financial rut. The best way to prepare for the unexpected is to start (or continue) developing a savings buffer. The experts these days are suggesting that we accumulate nine months of living expenses to help us navigate transition in a way that we feel empowered rather than scared and desperate to take the next thing that comes along.

When I paid off one of my credit cards in full, I added that monthly payment to the monthly savings transfer.

I started creating my savings buffer by opening the highest-interest money market account I could find and setting up a modest, monthly automatic transfer from my checking account. Then, when I paid off my car after five years of monthly payments, I added my car payment amount to the monthly transfer. (I'd been paying that amount for five years, so I was pretty sure I could continue to pay it to myself.) When I paid off one of my credit cards in full, I added that monthly payment to the monthly savings transfer. Within a year, I had a hefty sum going to savings every month before I had time to think about it, all based on expenses I was accustomed to paying, with money that had never been anticipated in the monthly cash flow.

What can you do today—and tomorrow—to put your money to work for your life, and start being as creative with your savings as you are with language?

DISABILITY INSURANCE

If writing is your livelihood, what happens if you become unable to write? I have writing friends who have become incapacitated and unable to work due to injuries to their brains, backs, hands and eyes. Disability insurance is one way to protect against such emergencies and ensure that you have an income in the unlikely event that you're not physically able to earn one yourself.

Depending on your health, age and budget, monthly disability insurance payments may or may not be within your means or priorities. But you won't know until you learn more about your coverage options. I encourage you to investigate this possibility with several highly rated insurance companies to get the lay of the land for your unique, personal profile and then make an informed decision.

HEALTH INSURANCE

Self-employed writers face tough decisions about health insurance. If you are lucky, there is someone in your family with great health coverage that is also available to you. Without the benefit of group health insurance, chances are that self-insuring costs are high and coverage is low. Just as in disability insurance, age and health status are significant variables in costs and availability of coverage. (Once again, I am no expert on this topic; only a novice who has had to figure things out for myself along the way, sharing the little I know with you.)

Ideally, of course, you'll have reasonably-priced health insurance that helps make preventive care and health maintenance more accessible and protects you in case of a major medical emergency. The following are a few possibilities to check out that could reduce costs and improve access to health coverage:

- Join a group that aggregates its members for group coverage, such as a Chamber of Commerce or AARP. Ask an insurance agent in your area if there are any other group coverage options available to you.

- Consider a high-deductible health plan paired with a Health Savings Account (HSA). Because the deductible is so high, these plans are generally thought to be most useful for a major medical emergency. But an HSA paired with such a plan allows you to put aside a chunk of pre-tax change every year that can be spent on medical expenses or remain in the account where it can be invested and grow. 2011 HSA investment limits, for example, are: $3,050 for individual coverage and $6,150 for family coverage.

Establishing effective financial systems for your writing business will take some time and energy at the front end. I suggest that you pace yourself by taking an achievable step or two each week until you have a baseline of financial management that works for you. Then, you can start moving toward some of your bigger, longer-term goals. Once it's established, your solid financial foundation will pay you in dividends of greater efficiency, insight and peace of mind for the rest of your writing career.

SAGE COHEN is the author of *The Productive Writer* and *Writing the Life Poetic*, both from Writer's Digest Books. She's been nominated for a Pushcart Prize, won first prize in the Ghost Road Press Poetry contest and published dozens of poems, essays and articles on the writing life. Sage holds an MFA in creative writing from New York University and a BA from Brown University. Since 1997, she has been a freelance writer serving clients including Intuit, Blue Shield, Adobe, and Kaiser Permanente.

PHOTO © Nyla Alisia

SHOULD YOUR WRITING BUSINESS BE AN LLC?

Business Structures Explained

by Carol Topp, CPA

A new member to my writers group told us her writing business was structured as a corporation. As a certified public accountant, I found that a little odd. I didn't know Connie well, but she had told us she had just written her first book, a self-published memoir. *Why would a brand new author want corporate status for her business?* I wondered. It seemed overly complex to me, so I asked her why she had formed a corporation. "I don't know," she said, "it's what my lawyer and CPA set up." Now I was really concerned. She'd had two professionals set her up in a complex business structure when she hadn't yet sold one copy of her book!

What was going on?

SOLE PROPRIETORSHIP

Most authors prefer the simplest business structure possible—what the IRS calls a sole proprietorship, meaning a business with one owner.

Sole proprietors may go by many names including:

- freelancer
- independent contractor
- self-employed writer
- independent publisher
- self-published or traditionally published author

During a consultation with a new author, I explained the advantages of sole proprietorship. She asked me, "Why would I want to be a sole proprietor? Why not just be a freelancer?" I explained that "sole proprietor" is a tax-related term to describe her profession as a freelance writer.

Sole proprietorships are easy and quick to start. You are in business as soon as you say that you are! Or at least when you are paid for your writing. I became a professional writer when I received $50 for writing a magazine article. A business had been born. Sole proprietorships have minimal government filings and licenses, if any. Usually a writer can use his or her own name as the business name, so business name filing is needed. Best of all, sole proprietorships have the simplest tax structure. Sole proprietors use a two-page form (Schedule C Business Income or Loss) and attach it to their Form 1040 tax return.

I would have thought that Connie's writing business would be structured as a sole proprietorship. Why then was she saying that her writing business was a corporation? I asked her a few more questions.

LIMITED LIABILITY STATUS

"Oh, they set up an LLC," she explained. Now I understood. Connie was talking about limited liability company (LLC) status. She had mistakenly thought that the "C" in LLC meant "corporation," but it means "company." They are quite different. LLC status is a legal standing granted by your state (not the IRS), and it offers limited liability to protect your personal assets from any business liabilities.

It's easy to get confused as Connie did; some advertising adds to the confusion. I've seen one ad that says "Get incorporated today" while showing a smiling woman holding a business card with "Your Business, LLC" circled in red. The ad confused incorporation with LLC status. Incorporating involves forming your business as a corporation for tax purposes; LLC status is a legal standing that limits liability.

LLCs are not one of the three business structures that the IRS recognizes for tax purposes. As a matter of fact, the IRS calls LLCs "disregarded entities." (We all wish the IRS would disregard us a little more!) Certainly, the IRS knows that LLCs exist, but for tax purposes, the LLC status is disregarded, and the business owner must choose one of three structures: sole proprietorship, partnership or corporation.

What LLC status will do for you

So why had Connie's lawyer and CPA set up her sole proprietorship with LLC status? Probably because they wanted to protect her personal assets from any business debts.

LLC status offers limited liability protection. When you read "liability," think "lawsuit" or, more specifically, the money you might owe if sued. LLC status cannot stop a lawsuit, but your liabilities may be limited to your business assets. As a writer, your business assets might include your laptop computer and the cash in your business checking account. The advantage of protecting your personal assets is the main reason why authors and other small business owners obtain LLC status for their businesses.

An example of how LLC status can help involved a ghostwriter who was sued for breach of contract. He was a sole proprietor with LLC status for his business. If he had lost, the lawsuit damages would have been limited to his business assets and could not have touched his personal assets, such as his house or savings. Fortunately, he won his case.

What LLC status won't do for you

Limited Liability Company status will not reduce your taxes. Your business files the same tax forms it did before having LLC status. "If an expense is business related, it's tax deductible, no matter what business structure you use," says tax attorney Julian Block, author of *Easy Tax Guide for Writers, Photographers and Other Freelancers.*

My tax client Russ showed me a handout from a seminar that claimed one of the benefits of LLC status was a health insurance tax deduction, leading Russ to believe he needed LLC status to receive this tax break. This health insurance deduction is available to all sole proprietorships, whether they have LLC status or not. The seminar handout had inadvertently confused him.

LLC STATUS IS NOT BULLETPROOF

For years the bulletproof vest of limited liability was only available to corporations. In the 1980s, LLC status became popular and sole proprietors signed up in droves. Finally, they could receive limited liability protection without the complexities of corporate status. It all seemed too good to be true, and perhaps it was.

Lately, limited liability status has been challenged in court, and several business owners found that their personal assets were at risk. The bulletproof vest has some cracks. "If an author were driving a car while on business and injured someone, he or she could still be sued," explains attorney Julian Block. "It's not a magic bullet."

To avoid piercing your limited liability, you must keep your business separate from your personal life. Mixing assets may lead a court to determine that your LLC status is weak and therefore hold you personally liable. "It isn't enough for business people merely to carry a liability shield; they must also take reasonable measures to this shield," cautions New Hampshire attorney John Cunningham.

There are several ways to protect your shield of limited liability:

- Don't commit fraud. Even LLC status can't protect you if you're a crook!
- Set up a separate checking account for your business.
- Avoid treating business assets as your own.
- Avoid personal guarantees on business loans.
- Purchase professional liability insurance.
- Sign contracts in the name of your LLC.
- Consider placing your home or investments into a trust to further protect your assets.

Disadvantages to LLC status

To obtain LLC status from your state, you file paperwork with an accompanying fee. Often, the paperwork is fairly straightforward, especially for single-member LLCs. Some individuals file for LLC status without assistance, but I recommend you seek professional advice to understand the pros and cons of LLC status for your business. If your LLC has multiple members or is a complex arrangement, you should hire a business attorney to assist you in establishing your LLC.

When should you consider LLC status for your writing business?

Consider LLC status when you wish to protect your personal assets. In Connie's case, her lawyer and CPA were possibly being overly cautious because she had no business income or assets yet.

I operated my accounting business as a sole proprietorship for its first six years. After that, I was attracting more clients and generating more income. I already had professional liability insurance, but I decided it was time to add limited liability status to my sole proprietorship. I applied to be a single member LLC in my state by filing the paperwork and paying a $125 fee. My business name is now Carol Topp, CPA, LLC (are you impressed?) but I still file the same tax forms I did before obtaining LLC status. I hope my limited liability status is never challenged in court, but I have it (and insurance) just in case I am ever sued.

PARTNERSHIPS ARE LIKE MARRIAGE

A second business structure is a partnership with two or more other people. Occasionally, a writer may co-author a book, but these are usually collaborations, not formal business partnerships

I usually discourage co-authors from forming a business partnership, warning them that a partnership is like being married but not being in love. You may be responsible for debts the other person can take on. Partnerships have complex tax situations necessitating professional expertise, and they may require a lawyer to draft the partnership agreement.

"Forming a business partnership really isn't necessary, and that is especially true when it is a one-shot deal," explains Dr. Dennis Hensley, coauthor of more than six titles. Quite frequently a publisher will hire the coauthors and make all the business arrangements. "When I was teamed with Stanley Field to write *The Freelancer: A Writer's Guide to Success*, we signed an agreement defining our writing responsibilities, how we would share earnings, who would serve as lead writer for the project, and how we would communicate during the writing of the manuscript. The publisher was putting us together because we had separate areas of expertise that were needed for the book the publisher wanted to release."

Alternatively, you may come up with a book idea of your own. Dauna and Marcie, long-time friends, decided to write a book together, but they did not form a business partnership. Both women maintained separate sole proprietorships, agreeing on how to split expenses and share the royalties. This kept each of their businesses separate and made the book project easier to operate.

"Before jumping into a business partnership with your life partner, friend, family member or an entrepreneur you know, sit down and talk over expectations with each other,'" advises James Chartrand of Men With Pens. "Create an agreement for sharing work and profits. Decide who does what and when, and how to split up the money—or else you'll be splitting up, period."

WRITER, INC.

The third and most complex business structure is a corporation. There are two types of corporations, S corporations and C corporations. An S corporation has a limited number of shareholders and may have only one shareholder, the owner, while C corporations can have an unlimited number of shareholders and are typically run by a board of directors. If a writer forms a corporation, it is typically an S corporation.

S corporation status may be a desirable business structure for authors who form a publishing company. Felice Gerwitz self-published her books as a sole proprietor for many years. She started publishing other authors and found that forming an S corporation could save on taxes, particularly self-employment tax. "Self-employment taxes as a sole proprietor were killing me," says Gerwitz. "Fortunately, my CPA advised me to form an S corporation, and I saw my self-employment tax drop."

As an S corporation, Gerwitz takes some of her profit as wages and some as ordinary income, which is not subject to self-employment tax. An S corporation has more complex tax preparation than a sole proprietorship, so you should seek professional accounting advice for your record keeping and tax preparation.

CONCLUSION

A writer has three business structures from which to choose: sole proprietorship, partnership or corporate status (S or C). In addition, a writer may obtain limited liability company status to limit his or her liability. Each business structure has advantages and increasing complexity. For most writers, the sole proprietorship with LLC status will serve their needs well.

BUSINESS STRUCTURES

Word pictures can explain the different business structures an author might choose.

Picture a sole proprietorship as a single-family house. Single-family homes are very common, as is the sole proprietorship form of business (78 percent of all businesses are sole proprietorships).

A partnership is like a duplex with two families living in one house. Living that close together can bring benefits but can also create friction, just like a business partnership.

A corporation is like an apartment building with many tenants in one building. In the same way, a corporation can have many owners called shareholders. Apartment buildings are expensive to start and can be difficult to maintain, just like a corporation.

A limited liability company (LLC) is not any of these. It is a legal status granted by your state, not a business structure in the eyes of the IRS. It is similar to a fence surrounding a building, providing protection. Picture the single family home with a fence protecting it. That would be a sole proprietorship with LLC status. A partnership or corporation can also have LLC protection, just as duplexes and apartment buildings may also have fences.

CAROL TOPP, CPA is a Certified Public Accountant and author of *Business Tips and Taxes for Writers* (Media Angels). She has authored 10 books, both as an indie publisher and author for a small press. Learn more at CarolToppCPA.com and TaxesForWriters.com.

30-DAY PLATFORM CHALLENGE

Build Your Writer Platform in a Month

....

by Robert Lee Brewer

Whether writers are looking to find success through traditional publication or the self-publishing route, they'll find a strong writer platform will help them in their efforts. A platform is not marketing; it's the actual and quantifiable reach writers have to their target audience.

Here is a 30-day platform challenge I've developed to help writers get started in their own platform-building activities without getting overwhelmed. By accomplishing one task for one day, writers can feel a sense of accomplishment and still handle their normal daily activities. By the end of the month, writers should have a handle on what they need to do to keep growing their platform into the future.

DAY 1: DEFINE YOURSELF

For Day 1, define yourself. Don't worry about where you'd like to be in the future. Instead, take a look at who you are today, what you've already accomplished, what you're currently doing, etc.

EXAMPLE DEFINE YOURSELF WORKSHEET

Here is a chart I'm using (with my own answers). Your worksheet can ask even more questions. The more specific you can be the better for this exercise.

Name (as used in byline): Robert Lee Brewer

Position(s): Senior Content Editor - Writer's Digest Writing Community; Author; Freelance Writer; Blogger; Event Speaker; Den Leader - Cub Scouts; Curator of Insta-poetry Series

Skill(s): Editing, creative writing (poetry and fiction), technical writing, copywriting, database management, SEO, blogging, newsletter writing, problem solving, idea generation, public speaking, willingness to try new things, community building.

Social media platforms: Facebook, LinkedIn, Google+, Twitter, Tumblr, Blogger.

URLs: www.writersmarket.com; www.writersdigest.com/editor-blogs/poetic-asides; http://robertleebrewer.blogspot.com/; www.robertleebrewer.com

Accomplishments: Named 2010 Poet Laureate of Blogosphere; spoken at several events, including Writer's Digest Conference, AWP, Austin International Poetry Festival, Houston Poetry Fest, and more; author of Solving the World's Problems (Press 53); published and sold out of two limited edition poetry chapbooks, **ENTER** and **ESCAPE**; edited several editions of **Writer's Market** and **Poet's Market**; former GMVC conference champion in the 800-meter run and MVP of WCHS cross country and track teams; undergraduate award-winner in several writing disciplines at University of Cincinnati, including Journalism, Fiction, and Technical Writing; BA in English Literature from University of Cincinnati with certificates in writing for Creative Writing-Fiction and Professional and Technical Writing.

Interests: Writing (all genres), family (being a good husband and father), faith, fitness (especially running and disc golf), fantasy football, reading.

In one sentence, who am I? Robert Lee Brewer is a married Methodist father of five children (four sons and one daughter) who works as an editor but plays as a writer, specializing in poetry and blogging.

As long as you're being specific and honest, there are no wrong answers when it comes to defining yourself. However, you may realize that you have more to offer than you think. Or you may see an opportunity that you didn't realize even existed.

DAY 2: SET YOUR GOALS

For today's platform-building task, set your goals. Include short-term goals and long-term goals. In fact, make a list of goals you can accomplish by the end of this year; then, make a list of goals you'd like to accomplish before you die.

EXAMPLE GOALS

Here are some of examples from my short-term and long-term goal lists:

SHORT-TERM GOALS:

- Promote new book, Solving the World's Problems.
- In April, complete April PAD Challenge on Poetic Asides blog.

- Get 2015 Writer's Market to printer ahead of schedule.
- Get 2015 Poet's Market to printer ahead of schedule.
- Lead workshop at Poetry Hickory event in April.
- Etc.

LONG-TERM GOALS:

- Publish book on platform development for small businesses.
- Raise 5 happy and healthy children into 5 happy, healthy, caring, and self-sufficient adults.
- Continue to learn how to be a better husband and human being.
- Become a bestselling novelist.
- Win Poet Laureate of the Universe honors.
- Etc.

Some writers may ask what defining yourself and creating goals has to do with platform development. I maintain that these are two of the most basic and important steps in the platform-building process, because they define who you are and where you want to be.

A successful platform strategy should communicate who you are and help you get where you'd like to be (or provide you with a completely new opportunity). If you can't communicate who you are to strangers, then they won't realize how you might be able to help them or why you're important to them. If you don't have any goals, then you don't have any direction or purpose for your platform.

A successful platform strategy should communicate who you are and help you get where you'd like to be (or provide you with a completely new opportunity).

By defining who you are and what you want to accomplish, you're taking a huge step in establishing a successful writing and publishing career.

DAY 3: JOIN FACEBOOK

For today's task, create a profile on Facebook. Simple as that. If you don't have one, it's as easy as going to www.facebook.com and signing up. It takes maybe 5 or 10 minutes. If that.

10 FACEBOOK TIPS FOR WRITERS

Many readers probably already have a Facebook profile, and that's fine. If you have already created a profile (or are doing so today), here are some tips for handling your profile:

- Complete your profile. The most checked page on most profiles is the About page. The more you share the better.
- Make everything public. Like it or not, writers are public figures. If you try to hide, it will limit the potential platform.
- Think about your audience in everything you do. When your social media profiles are public, anyone can view what you post. Keep this in mind at all times.
- Include a profile pic of yourself. Avoid setting your avatar as anything but a headshot of yourself. Many people don't like befriending a family pet or cartoon image.
- Update your status regularly. If you can update your status once per day, that's perfect. At the very least, update your status weekly. If your profile is a ghost town, people will treat it like one.
- Communicate with friends on Facebook. Facebook is a social networking site, but networking happens when you communicate. So communicate.
- Be selective about friends. Find people who share your interests. Accept friends who share your interests. Other folks may be fake or inappropriate connections trying to build their "friend" totals.
- Be selective about adding apps. If you're not sure, it's probably best to avoid. Many users have wasted days, weeks, and even months playing silly games on Facebook.
- Join relevant groups. The emphasis should be placed on relevancy. For instance, I'm a poet, so I join poetry groups.
- Follow relevant fan pages. As with groups, the emphasis is placed on relevancy. In my case, I'm a fan of several poetry publications.

In addition to the tips above, be sure to always use your name as it appears in your byline. If you're not consistent in how you list your name in your byline, it's time to pick a name and stick with it. For instance, my byline name is Robert Lee Brewer—not Robbie Brewer, Bob Brewer, or even just Robert Brewer.

There are times when I absolutely can't throw the "Lee" in there, but the rest of the time it is Robert Lee Brewer. And the reasoning behind this is that it makes it easier for people who know me elsewhere to find and follow me on Facebook (or whichever social media site). Name recognition is super important when you're building your writer platform.

DAY 4: JOIN TWITTER

For today's task, create a Twitter account. That's right. Go to www.twitter.com and sign up—if you're not already. This task will definitely take less than 5 minutes.

As with Facebook, I would not be surprised to learn that most readers already have a Twitter account. Here are three important things to keep in mind:

- **Make your profile bio relevant.** You might want to use a version of the sentence you wrote for Day 1's task. Look at my profile (twitter.com/robertleebrewer) if you need an example.
- **Use an image of yourself.** One thing about social media (and online networking) is that people love to connect with other people. So use an image of yourself—not of your pet, a cute comic strip, a new age image, flowers, robots, etc.
- **Make your Twitter handle your byline—if possible.** For instance, I am known as @RobertLeeBrewer on Twitter, because I use Robert Lee Brewer as my byline on articles, in interviews, at speaking events, on books, etc. Be as consistent with your byline as humanly possible.

Once you're in Twitter, try finding some worthwhile tweeps to follow. Also, be sure to make a tweet or two. As with Facebook, people will only interact with your profile if it looks like you're actually there and using your account.

SOME BASIC TWITTER TERMINOLOGY

Twitter has a language all its own. Here are some of the basics:

- **Tweet.** This is what folks call the 140-character messages that can be sent on the site. Anyone who follows you can access your tweets.
- **RT.** RT stands for re-tweet. This is what happens when someone shares your tweet, usually character for character. It's usually good form to show attribution for the author of the original tweet.
- **DM.** DM stands for direct message. This is a good way to communicate with someone on Twitter privately. I've actually had a few opportunities come my way through DMs on Twitter.
- **#.** The #-sign stands for hashtag. Hashtags are used to organize group conversations. For instance, Writer's Digest uses the #wdc to coordinate messages for their Writer's Digest Conferences. Anyone can start a hashtag, and they're sometimes used to add humor or emphasis to a tweet.
- **FF.** FF stands for follow Friday—a day typically set asides to highlight follow-worthy tweeps (or folks who use Twitter). There's also a WW that stands for writer Wednesday.

DAY 5: START A BLOG

For today's task, create a blog. You can use Blogger (www.blogger.com), WordPress (www.wordpress.com), or Tumblr (www.tumblr.com). In fact, you can use another blogging platform if you wish. To complete today's challenge, do the following:

- **Create a blog.** That is, sign up (if you don't already have a blog), pick a design (these can usually be altered later if needed), and complete your profile.
- **Write a post for today.** If you're not sure what to cover, you can just introduce yourself and share a brief explanation of how your blog got started. Don't make it too complicated.

If you already have a blog, excellent! You don't need to create a new one, but you might want to check out some ways to optimize what you have.

OPTIMIZE YOUR BLOG

Here are some tips for making your blog rock:

- Use images in your posts. Images are eye candy for readers, help with search engine optimization, and can even improve clicks when shared on social media sites, such as Facebook and Google+.
- Use headers in posts. Creating and bolding little headlines in your posts will go a long way toward making your posts easier to read and scan. Plus, they'll just look more professional.
- Write short. Short sentences (fewer than 10 words). Short paragraphs (fewer than five sentences). Concision is precision in online composition.
- Allow comments. Most bloggers receive very few (or absolutely zero) comments in the beginning, but it pays to allow comments, because this gives your audience a way to interact with you. For my personal blog, I allow anyone to comment on new posts, but those that are more than a week old require my approval.

DAY 6: READ AND COMMENT ON A POST

For today's task, read at least one blog post and comment on it (linking back to your blog). And the comment should not be something along the lines of, "Hey, cool post. Come check out my blog." Instead, you need to find a blog post that really speaks to you and then make a thoughtful comment.

Here are a few possible ways to respond:

- **Share your own experience.** If you've experienced something similar to what's covered in the post, share your own story. You don't have to write a book or anything, but maybe a paragraph or two.
- **Add another perspective.** Maybe the post was great, but there's another angle that should be considered. Don't be afraid to point that angle out.
- **Ask a question.** A great post usually will prompt new thoughts and ideas—and questions. Ask them.

As far as linking back to your blog, you could include your blog's URL in the comment, but also, most blogs have a field in their comments that allow you to share your URL. Usually, your name will link to that URL, which should either be your blog or your author website (if it offers regularly updated content).

It might seem like a lot of work to check out other blogs and comment on them, but this is an incredible way to make real connections with super users. These connections can lead to guest post and interview opportunities. In fact, they could even lead to speaking opportunities too.

DAY 7: ADD SHARE BUTTONS TO YOUR BLOG

For today's challenge, add share buttons to your blog and/or website.

The easiest way to do this is to go to www.addthis.com and click on the Get AddThis button. It's big, bright, and orange. You can't miss it.

Here's the thing about social sharing buttons: They make it very easy for people visiting your site to share your content with their social networks... The more your content is shared the wider your writer platform.

Basically, the site will give you button options, and you select the one you like best. The AddThis site will then provide you with HTML code that you can place into your site and/or blog posts. Plus, it provides analytics for bloggers who like to see how much the buttons are boosting traffic.

If you want customized buttons, you could enlist the help of a programmer friend or try playing with the code yourself. I recently learned that some really cool buttons on one friend's blog were created by her husband (yes, she married a programmer, though I don't think she had her blog in mind when she did so).

Plus, most blogging platforms are constantly adding new tools. By the time you read this article, there are sure to be plenty of fun new buttons, apps, and widgets available.

Here's the thing about social sharing buttons: They make it very easy for people visiting your site to share your content with their social networks via Facebook, Twitter, LinkedIn, Google+, Pinterest, and other sites. The more your content is shared the wider your writer platform.

DAY 8: JOIN LINKEDIN

For today's challenge, create a LinkedIn profile. Go to www.linkedin.com and set it up in a matter of minutes. After creating profiles for Facebook and Twitter, this task should be easy.

LINKEDIN TIPS FOR WRITERS

In many ways, LinkedIn looks the same as the other social networks, but it does have its own quirks. Here are a few tips for writers:

- Use your own head shot. You've heard this advice before. People want to connect with people, not family pets and/or inanimate objects.
- Complete your profile. The more complete your profile the better. It makes you look more human.
- Give thoughtful recommendations to receive them. Find people likely to give you recommendations and recommend them first. This will prompt them to return the favor.
- Search for connections you already have. This is applicable to all social networks. Find people you know to help you connect with those you don't.
- Make meaningful connections with others. Remember: It's not about how many connections you make; it's about how many meaningful connections you make.
- Make your profile easy to find. You can do this by using your byline name. (For instance, I use linkedin.com/in/robertleebrewer.)
- Tailor your profile to your visitor. Don't fill out your profile thinking only about yourself; instead, think about what your target audience might want to learn about you.

LinkedIn is often considered a more "professional" site than the other social networks like Facebook, Google+, and Twitter. For one thing, users are prompted to share their work experience and request recommendations from past employers and current co-workers.

However, this site still offers plenty of social networking opportunities for people who can hook up with the right people and groups.

DAY 9: RESPOND TO AT LEAST THREE TWEETS

For today's task, respond to at least three tweets from other tweeps on Twitter.

Since Day 4's assignment was to sign up for Twitter, you should have a Twitter account—and you're hopefully following some other Twitter users. Just respond to at least three tweets today.

As far as your responses, it's not rocket science. You can respond with a "great article" or "cool quote." A great way to spread the wealth on Twitter is to RT (retweet) the original tweet with a little note. This accomplishes two things:

- One, it lets the tweep know that you appreciated their tweet (and helps build a bond with that person); and
- Two, it brings attention to that person for their cool tweet.

Plus, it helps show that you know how to pick great resources on Twitter, which automatically improves your credibility as a resource on Twitter.

DAY 10: DO A GOOGLE SEARCH ON YOURSELF

For today's task, do a search on your name.

First, see what results appear when you search your name on Google (google.com). Then, try searching on Bing (bing.com). Finally, give Yahoo (yahoo.com) a try.

By searching your name, you'll receive insights into what others will find (and are already finding) when they do a search specifically for you. Of course, you'll want to make sure your blog and/or website is number one in the search results. If it isn't, we'll be covering SEO (or search engine optimization) topics later in this challenge.

OTHER SEARCH ENGINES

For those who want extra credit, here are some other search engines to try searching (for yourself):

- DuckDuckGo.com
- Ask.com
- Dogpile.com
- Yippy.com
- YouTube.com

(Note: It's worth checking out which images are related to your name as well. You may be surprised to find which images are connected to you.)

DAY 11: FIND A HELPFUL ARTICLE AND LINK TO IT

For today's task, find a helpful article (or blog post) and share it with your social network—and by social network, I mean that you should share it on Facebook, Twitter, and LinkedIn at a minimum. If you participate on message boards or on other social networks, share in those places as well.

Before linking to an article on fantasy baseball or celebrity news, however, make sure your article (or blog post) aligns with your author platform goals. You should have an idea of who you are and who you want to be as a writer, and your helpful article (or blog post) should line up with those values.

> Before linking to an article on fantasy baseball or celebrity news, however, make sure your article (or blog post) aligns with your author platform goals.

Of course, you may not want to share articles for writers if your platform is based on parenting tips or vampires or whatever. In such cases, you'll want to check out other resources online. Don't be afraid to use a search engine.

For Twitter, you may wish to use a URL shortener to help you keep under the 140-character limit. Here are five popular URL shorteners:

- bit.ly. This is my favorite.
- goo.gl. Google's URL shortener.
- owl.ly. Hootsuite's URL shortener.
- deck.ly. TweetDeck's URL shortener.
- su.pr. StumbleUpon's URL shortener.

By the way, here's an extra Twitter tip. Leave enough room in your tweets to allow space for people to attribute your Twitter handle if they decide to RT you. For instance, I always leave at least 20 characters to allow people space to tweet "RT @robertleebrewer" when retweeting me.

DAY 12: WRITE A BLOG POST AND INCLUDE CALL TO ACTION

For today's task, write a new blog post for your blog. In the blog post, include a call to action at the end of the post.

What's a call to action?

I include calls to action at the end of all my posts. Sometimes, they are links to products and services offered by my employer (F+W Media) or some other entity. Often, I include links to other posts and ways to follow me on other sites. Even the share buttons are a call to action of sorts.

Why include a call to action?

A call to action is good for giving readers direction and a way to engage more with you. Links to previous posts provide readers with more helpful or interesting information. Links to your social media profiles give readers a way to connect with you on those sites. These calls to action are beneficial to you and your readers when they are relevant.

What if I'm just getting started?

Even if you are completely new to everything, you should have an earlier blog post from last week, a Twitter account, a Facebook account, and a LinkedIn account. Link to these at the end of your blog post today. It's a proper starting place.

And that's all you need to do today. Write a new blog post with a call to action at the end. (By the way, if you're at a loss and need something to blog about, you can always comment on that article you shared yesterday.)

DAY 13: LINK TO POST ON SOCIAL MEDIA PROFILES

For today's challenge, link your blog post from yesterday to your social networks.

At a minimum, these social networks should include Facebook, Twitter, and LinkedIn. However, if you frequent message boards related to your blog post or other social networks (like Google+, Pinterest, etc.), then link your blog post there as well.

I understand many of you may have already completed today's challenge. If so, hooray! It's important to link your blog to your social media accounts and vice versa. When they work together, they grow together.

Is it appropriate to link to my blog post multiple times?

All writers develop their own strategies for linking to their articles and blog posts, but here's my rule. I will usually link to each blog post on every one of my social networks at least once. Since I have a regular profile and a fan page on Facebook, I link to each of those profiles once—and I only link to posts once each on Google+ and LinkedIn. But Twitter is a special case.

The way Twitter works, tweets usually only have a few minutes of visibility for tweeps with an active stream. Even tweeps with at least 100 follows may only have a 30-minute to hour window of opportunity to see your tweet. So for really popular and timely blog posts, I will tweet them more often than once on Twitter.

> The way Twitter works, tweets usually only have a few minutes of visibility of tweeps with an active stream.

That said, I'm always aware of how I'm linking and don't want to become that annoying spammer that I typically avoid following in my own social networking efforts.

LINKING TIPS

Some tips on linking to your post:

- Use a URL shortener. These are discussed above.
- Apply title + link formula. For instance, I might Tweet this post as: Platform Challenge: Day 13: (link). It's simple and to the point. Plus, it's really effective if you have a great blog post title.
- Frame the link with context. Using this post as an example, I might Tweet: Take advantage of social media by linking to your blog posts: (link). Pretty simple, and it's an easy way to link to the same post without making your Twitter feed look loaded with the same content.
- Quote from post + link formula. Another tactic is to take a funny or thought-provoking quote from the post and combine that with a link. Example Tweet: "I will usually link to each blog post on every one of my social networks at least once." (link). Again, easy stuff.

DAY 14: JOIN GOOGLE+

For today's task, create a Google+ (plus.google.com) profile.

Many of you may already have G+ profiles, but this social networking site is still rather new compared to Facebook and Twitter. Plus, Google+ status updates often show up in search results on Google's search engine.

I've heard people describe Google+ as a mix between Facebook and Twitter, and I don't think that's too far off the mark. Personally, I think it's still growing, which can be a good and bad thing.

The good news is that you could still be one of the first G+-users on the block; bad news is that you have to wait (and hope) for other people to migrate over to the block. Of course, Google has a huge reach online, so there's no reason to doubt that people will migrate...eventually.

One tool I've really learned to appreciate on Google+ is the Hangouts feature, which makes it easy to record video chats with other people, including experts in your field on Google+ and then share permanently on YouTube.

One tool I've really learned to appreciate on Google+ is the Hangouts feature, which makes it easy to record video chats with other people, including experts in your field on Google+ and then share permanently on YouTube. Since I feel video is the future of online, I think this is really cool.

As with Facebook and LinkedIn, keep these tips in mind:

- Complete your profile completely. Use your name. Provide easy to find contact information. Describe who you are.
- Use an image of yourself. Not a cartoon. Not an animal. Not a piece of art. Remember that people like to connect with other people.
- Post new content regularly. Let people know you are using your account. That means connecting with other G+'ers as well.

DAY 15: MAKE THREE NEW CONNECTIONS

For today's task, make an attempt to connect with at least three new people on one of your social networks.

Doesn't matter if it's Facebook, Twitter, LinkedIn, or Google+. The important thing is that you find three new people who appear to share your interests and that you try to friend, follow, or connect to them.

As a person who has limited wiggle room for approving new friends on Facebook, I'd like to share what approach tends to work the best with me for approving new friend requests. Basically, send your request and include a brief message introducing yourself and why you want to connect with me.

That's right. The best way to win me over is to basically introduce yourself. Something along the lines of, "Hello. My name is Robert Lee Brewer, and I write poetry. I read a poem of yours in *XYZ Literary Journal* that I totally loved and have sent you a friend request. I hope you'll accept it." Easy as that.

Notice that I did not mention anything about checking out my blog or reading my poems. How would you like it if someone introduced themselves and then told you to buy their stuff? It sounds a bit telemarketer-ish to me.

While it's important to cultivate the relationships you already have, avoid getting stuck in a rut when it comes to making connections. Always be on the lookout for new connections who can offer new opportunities and spark new ideas. Your writing and your career will benefit.

DAY 16: ADD E-MAIL FEED TO BLOG

For today's challenge, add an e-mail feed to your blog.

There are many ways to increase traffic to your blog, but one that has paid huge dividends for me is adding Feedblitz to my blog. As the subscribers to my e-mail feed have increased, my blog traffic has increased as well. In fact, after great content, I'd say that adding share buttons (mentioned above) and an e-mail feed are the top two ways to build traffic.

Though I have an account on Tumblr, I'm just not sure if it offers some kind of e-mail/RSS feed service.

> In fact, after great content, I'd say that adding share buttons and an e-mail feed are the top two ways to build traffic.

The reason I think e-mail feeds are so useful is that they pop into my inbox whenever a new post is up, which means I can check it very easily on my phone when I'm waiting somewhere. In fact, this is how I keep up with several of my favorite blogs. It's just one more way to make your blog content accessible to readers in a variety of formats.

If I remember, this task didn't take me long to add, but I've been grateful for finally getting around to adding it ever since.

DAY 17: TAKE PART IN A TWITTER CONVERSATION

For today's task, take part in a Twitter conversation.

Depending upon the time of month or day of week, there are bound to be any number of conversations happening around a hashtag (mentioned above). For instance, various conferences and expos have hashtag conversations that build around their panels and presentations.

Poets will often meet using the #poetparty hashtag. Other writers use #amwriting to communicate about their writing goals. Click on the hashtag to see what others are saying, and then, jump in to join the conversation and make new connection on Twitter.

DAY 18: THINK ABOUT SEO

For today's task, I want you to slow down and think a little about SEO (which is tech-speak for search engine optimization, which is itself an intelligent way of saying "what gets your website to display at or near the top of a search on Google, Bing, Yahoo, etc.").

So this task is actually multi-pronged:

- Make a list of keywords that you want your website or blog to be known for. For instance, I want my blog to be known for terms like "Robert Lee Brewer," "Writing Tips," "Parenting Tips," "Platform Tips," "Living Tips," etc. Think big here and don't limit yourself to what you think you can actually achieve in the short term.
- Compare your website or blog's current content to your keywords. Are you lining up your actual content with how you want your audience to view you and your online presence? If not, it's time to think about how you can start offering content that lines up with your goals. If so, then move on to the next step, which is...
- Evaluate your current approach to making your content super SEO-friendly. If you need some guidance, check out my SEO Tips for Writers below. There are very simple things you can do with your titles, subheads, and images to really improve SEO. Heck, I get a certain bit of traffic every single day just from my own SEO approach to content—sometimes on surprising posts.
- Research keywords for your next post. When deciding on a title for your post and subheads within the content, try researching keywords. You can do this using Google's free keyword tool (googlekeywordtool.com). When possible, you want to use keywords that are searched a lot but that have low competition. These are the low-hanging fruit that can help you build strong SEO for your website or blog.

A note on SEO: It's easy to fall in love with finding keywords and changing your content to be keyword-loaded and blah-blah-blah. But resist making your website or blog a place that is keyword-loaded and blah-blah-blah. Because readers don't stick around for too much keyword-loaded blah-blah-blah. It's kind of blah. And bleck. Instead, use SEO and keyword research as a way to optimize great content and to take advantage of opportunities as they arise.

SEO TIPS FOR WRITERS

Here are a few SEO tips for writers:

- Use keywords naturally. That is, make sure your keywords match the content of the post. If they don't match up, people will abandon your page fast, which will hurt your search rankings.
- Use keywords appropriately. Include your keywords in the blog post title, opening paragraph, file name for images, headers, etc. Anywhere early and relevant should include your keyword to help place emphasis on that search term, especially if it's relevant to the content.
- Deliver quality content. Of course, search rankings are helped when people click on your content and spend time reading your content. So provide quality content, and people will visit your site frequently and help search engines list you higher in their rankings.
- Update content regularly. Sites that are updated more with relevant content rank higher in search engines. Simple as that.
- Link often to relevant content. Link to your own posts; link to content on other sites. Just make sure the links are relevant and of high interest to your audience.
- Use images. Images help from a design perspective, but they also help with SEO, especially when you use your main keywords in the image file name.
- Link to your content on social media sites. These outside links will help increase your ranking on search engines.
- Guest post on other sites/blogs. Guest posts on other blogs are a great way to provide traffic from other relevant sites that increase the search engine rankings on your site.

DAY 19: WRITE A BLOG POST

For today's task, write a new blog post.

Include a call to action (for instance, encourage readers to sign up for your e-mail feed and to share the post with others using your share buttons) and link to it on your social networks. Also, don't forget to incorporate SEO.

I think it's imperative that you post at least once a week.

One of the top rules of finding success with online tools is applying consistency. While it's definitely a great thing if you share a blog post more than once a week, I think it's imperative that you post at least once a week.

The main reason? It builds trust with your readers that you'll have something to share regularly and gives them a reason to visit regularly.

So today's task is not about making things complicated; it's just about keeping it real.

DAY 20: CREATE EDITORIAL CALENDAR

For today's task, I want you to create an editorial calendar for your blog (or website). Before you start to panic, read on.

First, here's how I define an editorial calendar: A list of content with dates attached to when the content goes live. For instance, I created an editorial calendar specifically for my Platform Challenge and "Platform Challenge: Day 20" was scheduled to go live on day 20.

It's really simple. In fact, I keep track of my editorial calendar with a paper notebook, which gives me plenty of space for crossing things out, jotting down ideas, and attaching Post-It notes.

EDITORIAL CALENDAR IDEAS

Here are tips for different blogging frequencies:

- Post once per week. If you post once a week, pick a day of the week for that post to happen each week. Then, write down the date for each post. Beside each date, write down ideas for that post ahead of time. There will be times when the ideas are humming and you get ahead on your schedule, but there may also be times when the ideas are slow. So don't wait, write down ideas as they come.
- Post more than once per week. Try identifying which days you'll usually post (for some, that may be daily). Then, for each of those days, think of a theme for that day. For instance, my 2012 schedule offered Life Changing Moments on Wednesdays and Poetic Saturdays on Saturdays.

You can always change plans and move posts to different days, but the editorial calendar is an effective way to set very clear goals with deadlines for accomplishing them. Having that kind of structure will improve your content—even if your blog is personal, fictional, poetic, etc. Believe me, I used to be a skeptic before diving in, and the results on my personal blog speak for themselves.

One more benefit of editorial calendars

There are times when I feel less than inspired. There are times when life throws me several elbows as if trying to prevent me from blogging. That's when I am the most thankful for maintaining an editorial calendar, because I don't have to think of a new idea on the spot; it's already there in my editorial calendar.

Plus, as I said earlier, you can always change plans. I can alter the plan to accommodate changes in my schedule. So I don't want to hear that an editorial calendar limits spontaneity or inspiration; if anything, having an editorial calendar enhances it.

One last thing on today's assignment

Don't stress yourself out that you have to create a complete editorial calendar for the year or even the month. I just want you to take some time out today to think about it, sketch some ideas, and get the ball rolling. I'm 100% confident that you'll be glad you did.

DAY 21: SIGN UP FOR SOCIAL MEDIA TOOL

For today's task, try joining one of the social media management tools, such as Tweetdeck, Hootsuite, or Seesmic.

Social media management tools are popular among social media users for one reason: They help save time and effort in managing multiple social media platforms. For instance, they make following specific threads in Twitter a snap.

I know many social media super users who swear by these tools, but I actually have tried them and decided to put in the extra effort to log in to my separate social media accounts manually each day.

Here's my reasoning: I like to feel connected to my profile and understand how it looks and feels on a day-to-day basis. Often, the design and feel of social media sites will change without notice, and I like to know what it feels like at ground zero.

DAY 22: PITCH GUEST BLOG POST

For today's task, pitch a guest blog post to another blogger.

Writing guest posts is an incredible way to improve your exposure and expertise on a subject, while also making a deeper connection with the blogger who is hosting your guest post. It's a win for everyone involved.

In a recent interview with super blogger Jeff Goins, he revealed that most of his blog traffic came as a result of his guest posting on other blogs. Some of these blogs were directly related to his content, but he said many were in completely different fields.

GUEST POST PITCHING TIPS

After you know where you want to guest blog, here are some tips for pitching your guest blog post:

- Let the blogger know you're familiar with the blog. You should do this in one sentence (two sentences max) and be specific. For instance, a MNINB reader could say, "I've been reading your Not Bob blog for months, but I really love this Platform Challenge." Simple as that. It lets me know you're not a spammer, but it doesn't take me a long time to figure out what you're trying to say.
- Propose an idea or two. Each idea should have its own paragraph. This makes it easy for the blogger to know where one idea ends and the next one begins. In a pitch, you don't have to lay out all the details, but you do want to be specific. Try to limit the pitch to 2-4 sentences.
- Share a little about yourself. Emphasis on "a little." If you have previous publications or accomplishments that line up with the blog, share those. If you have expertise that lines up with the post you're pitching, share those. Plus, include any details about your online platform that might show you can help bring traffic to the post. But include all this information in 1-4 sentences.
- Include your information. When you close the pitch, include your name, e-mail, blog (or website) URL, and other contact information you feel comfortable sharing. There's nothing more awkward for me than to have a great pitch that doesn't include the person's name. Or a way to learn more about the person.

What do I do after the pitch is accepted?

First off, congratulations! This is a great opportunity to show off your writing skills. Here's how to take advantage of your guest post assignment:

- **Write an exceptional post.** Don't hold back your best stuff for your blog. Write a post that will make people want to find more of your writing.
- **Turn in your post on deadline.** If there's a deadline, hit it. If there's not a deadline, try to turn around the well-written post in a timely manner.
- **Promote the guest post.** Once your guest post has gone live, promote it like crazy by linking to your post on your blog, social networks, message boards, and wherever else makes sense for you. By sending your own connections to this guest post, you're establishing your own expertise—not only through your post but also your connections.

DAY 23: CREATE A TIME MANAGEMENT PLAN

For today's task, create a time management plan.

You may be wondering why I didn't start out the challenge with a time management plan, and here's the reason: I don't think some people would've had any idea how long it takes them to write a blog post, share a link on Twitter and Facebook, respond to social media messages, etc. Now, many of you probably have a basic idea—even if you're still getting the hang of your new-fangled social media tools.

Soooo... the next step is to create a time management plan that enables you to be "active" socially and connect with other writers and potential readers while also spending a majority of your time writing and publishing.

> I use social media as a break, which I consider more productive than watching TV or playing Angry Birds.

As with any plan, you can make this as simple or complicated as you wish. For instance, my plan is to do 15 minutes or less of social media after completing each decent-sized task on my daily task list. I use social media time as a break, which I consider more productive than watching TV or playing Angry Birds.

I put my writing first and carve out time in the mornings and evenings to work on poetry and fiction. Plus, I consider my blogging efforts part of my writing too. So there you go.

My plan is simple and flexible, but if you want to get hardcore, break down your time into 15-minute increments. Then, test out your time management plan to see if it works for you. If not, then make minor changes to the plan until it has you feeling somewhat comfortable with the ratio of time you spend writing and time you spend building your platform.

Remember: A platform is a life-long investment in your career. It's not a sprint, so you have to pace yourself. Also, it's not something that happens overnight, so you can't wait until you need a platform to start building one. Begin today and build over time—so that it's there when you need it.

DAY 24: TAKE PART IN A FACEBOOK CONVERSATION

For today's task, take part in a conversation on Facebook.

You should've already participated in a Twitter conversation, so this should be somewhat similar—except you don't have to play with hashtags and 140-character restrictions. In fact, you just need to find a group conversation or status update that speaks to you and chime in with your thoughts.

Don't try to sell or push anything when you join a conversation. If you say interesting things, people will check out your profile, which if filled out will lead them to more information about you (including your website, blog, any books, etc.).

Goal one of social media is making connections. If you have everything else optimized, sales and opportunities will take care of themselves.

DAY 25: CONTACT AN EXPERT FOR AN INTERVIEW POST

For today's task, find an expert in your field and ask if that expert would like to be interviewed.

If you can secure the interview, this will make for a great blog post. Or it may help you secure a freelance assignment with a publication in your field. Or both, and possibly more.

How to Ask for an Interview

Believe it or not, asking for an interview with an expert is easy. I do it all the time, and these are the steps I take.

- **Find an expert on a topic.** This is sometimes the hardest part: figuring out who I want to interview. But I never kill myself trying to think of the perfect person, and here's why: I can always ask for more interviews. Sometimes, it's just more productive to get the ball rolling than come up with excuses to not get started.
- **Locate an e-mail for the expert.** This can often be difficult, but a lot of experts have websites that share either e-mail addresses or have online contact forms. Many experts can also be reached via social media sites, such as Facebook, Twitter, LinkedIn, Google+, etc. Or they can be contacted through company websites. And so on.
- **Send an e-mail asking for an e-mail interview.** Of course, you can do this via an online contact form too. If the expert says no, that's fine. Respond with a "Thank you for considering and maybe we can make it work sometime in the future." If the expert says yes, then it's time to send along the questions.

How to Handle an E-mail Interview

Once you've secured your expert, it's time to compose and send the questions. Here are some of my tips.

- **Always start off by asking questions about the expert.** This might seem obvious to some, but you'd be surprised how many people start off asking "big questions" right out of the gate. Always start off by giving the expert a chance to talk about what he or she is doing, has recently done, etc.

- **Limit questions to 10 or fewer.** The reason for this is that you don't want to over-whelm your expert. In fact, I usually ask around eight questions in my e-mail interviews. If I need to, I'll send along some follow-up questions, though I try to limit those as well. I want the expert to have an enjoyable experience, not a horrible experience. After all, I want the expert to be a connection going forward.
- **Try not to get too personal.** If experts want to get personal in their answers, that's great. But try to avoid getting too personal in the questions you ask, because you may offend your expert or make them feel uncomfortable. Remember: You're interviewing the expert, not leading an interrogation.
- **Request additional information.** By additional information, I mean that you should request a headshot and a preferred bio—along with any links. To make the interview worth the expert's time, you should afford them an opportunity to promote themselves and their projects in their bios.

Once the Interview Goes Live...

Link to it on your social networks and let your expert know it is up (and include the specific link to the interview). If you're not already searching for your next expert to interview, be sure to get on it.

DAY 26: WRITE A BLOG POST AND LINK TO SOCIAL PROFILES

For today's task, write a new blog post.

In your blog post, include a call to action and link it on your social networks. Also, don't forget SEO.

Remember: One of the top rules of finding success with online tools is applying consistency. While it's definitely a great thing if you share a blog post more than once a week, I think it's imperative that you post at least once a week.

The main reason? It builds trust with your readers that you'll have something to share regularly and gives them a reason to visit regularly.

....

Remember: One of the top rules of finding success with online tools is applying consistency.

....

If this sounds repetitive, good; it means my message on consistency is starting to take root.

DAY 27: JOIN ANOTHER SOCIAL MEDIA SITE

For today's task, join one new social media site. I will leave it up to you to decide which new social media site it will be.

Maybe you'll join Pinterest. Maybe you'll choose Goodreads. Heck, you might go with RedRoom or some social media site that's not even on my radar at the time of this article. Everything is constantly evolving, which is why it's good to always try new things.

To everyone who doesn't want another site to join...

I understand your frustration and exhaustion. During a normal month, I'd never suggest someone sign up for so many social media sites in such a short period of time, but this isn't a normal month. We're in the midst of a challenge!

And no, I don't expect you to spend a lot of time on every social media site you join. That's not always the point when you first sign up. No, you sign up to poke around and see if the site interests you at all. See if you have any natural connections. Try mingling a little bit.

If the site doesn't appeal to you, feel free to let it be for a while. Let me share a story with you.

How I Came to Rock Facebook and Twitter

My Facebook and Twitter accounts both boast more than 5,000 followers (or friends/subscribers) today. But both accounts were originally created and abandoned, because they just weren't right for me at the time that I signed up.

For Facebook, I just didn't understand why I would abandon a perfectly good MySpace account to play around on a site that didn't feature the same level of music and personal blogging that MySpace did. But then, MySpace turned into Spam-opolis, and the rest is history.

> For Facebook, I just didn't understand why I would abandon a perfectly good MySpace account to play around on a site that didn't feature the same level of music and personal blogging that MySpace did.

For Twitter, I just didn't get the whole tweet concept, because Facebook already had status updates. Why tweet when I could update my status on Facebook?

But I've gained a lot professionally and personally from Facebook and Twitter—even though they weren't the right sites for me initially. In fact, Google+ is sort of in that area for me right now. I don't use it near enough, but I started an account, because it just feels like a place that will explode sooner or later. It's not like Facebook is going to be around forever.

The Importance of Experimentation

Or as I prefer to think of it: The importance of play. You should constantly try new things, whether in your writing, your social media networks, or the places you eat food. Not only does it make life more exciting and provide you with new experiences and perspective, but it also helps make you a more well-rounded human being.

So don't complain about joining a new social media site. Instead, embrace the excuse to try something new, especially when there are only three more tasks left this month (and I promise no more new sites after today).

DAY 28: READ POST AND COMMENT ON IT

For today's task, read and comment on a blog post, making sure that your comment links back to your blog or website.

If you remember, this was the same task required way back on Day 6. How far we've come, though it's still a good idea to stay connected and engaged with other bloggers. I know I find that sometimes I start to insulate myself in my own little blogging communities and worlds—when it's good to get out and read what others are doing. In fact, that's what helped inspire my Monday Advice for Writers posts—it gives me motivation to read what others are writing (on writing, of course).

DAY 29: MAKE A TASK LIST

For today's task, make a task list of things you are going to do on each day next month. That's right, I want you to break down 31 days with 31 tasks for each day—similar to what we've done this month.

You see, I don't want you to quit challenging yourself once this challenge is over. Of course, you get to decide what the tasks will be. So if you aren't into new social media sites, don't put them on your list. Instead, focus on blog posts, commenting on other sites, linking to articles, contacting experts, or whatever it is that you are going to do next month to keep momentum building toward an incredible author platform.

....

Keep it going, keep it rolling, and your efforts will continue to gain momentum and speed. I promise.

....

Somewhere near the end of the month, you should have a day set aside with one task: Make a task list of things to do on each day of the next month. And so on and so forth. Keep it going, keep it rolling, and your efforts will continue to gain momentum and speed. I promise.

DAY 30: ENGAGE THE WORLD

For today's task, engage the world.

By this, I mean that you should comment on status updates, ask questions, share answers, start debates, continue debates, and listen—that's right, don't be that person who dominates a conversation and makes it completely one-sided.

Engage the world by entering the conversation. Engage the world by having the courage to take risks and share things of consequence. Engage the world by having the courage to make mistakes and fail and learn from those mistakes and failures.

The only people who never fail are those who never try, and those people never succeed at anything except avoiding failure and success. Don't be that person. Engage the world and let the world engage you.

ROBERT LEE BREWER is Senior Content Editor for the Writer's Digest Writing Community. This challenge was originally on his personal blog (http://robertleebrewer.blogspot.com) My Name Is Not Bob. Named Poet Laureate of the Blogosphere in 2010, his debut full-length poetry collection, *Solving the World's Problems*, was recently published by Press 53. For more information, engage Brewer via e-mail at robertleebrewer@gmail.com.

BUILD PLATFORM AS AN INTERNET RADIO SHOW HOST

by Dorit Sasson

In today's digital age, promotion means online promotion, having a social media presence, a website, followers and fans. A platform is a tool used for promotion. It's a way to sell yourself as an expert and to sell the products, books or services that you have to offer. It's a method for publicity and can be a way of branding yourself. According to Dr. Deborah Siegel, a writing coach and co-founder of SheWrites.com, the editor's definition of a writer's platform is "qualifiable proof that you're the person to write this book and quantifiable proof that you have the ability to promote it."

At the end of the day, authors want to know how they can succeed in doing what they love for a living. In today's world of self-publishing, an author's author is based on how many fans they have, how much publicity they can garner and what kind of network they're tapped into. Similarly, acquisition editors at many publishing houses are placing extraordinary emphasis on platform and are actually no longer the deciders of what makes a good book.

Since this phenomenon has been true for several years and authors can't make it go away, authors need to be their best promoters and platform builders regardless of the format of how they are publishing.

WHY HOST YOUR RADIO SHOW?

Most self-published authors reach other authors either through their websites or ezines. Not many self-published authors have maximized the "real estate" of the web by hosting their own radio show in order to spread their message. This is where hosting a radio show can be very powerful platform-building. Internet radio is quickly becoming one of the fastest and most popular ways to get the story and the message of your book out even before it is published. Expanding your online author "voice" and persona through Internet radio is one of more savvy marketing moves a self-published author can make.

Having a radio show allows people to hear and "feel" you more deeply than they could with a newsletter. An author's influence is a lot stronger than with text-based methods. Because a radio show can be highly interactive and user-friendly, people are more likely to be drawn to your voice which makes it easier for them afterwards to read your blog or e-zine. Today's web radio hosting interface is also social media friendly which makes it even easier to embed Facebook and Twitter platforms. Having your own radio show also integrates the key elements of public speaking and media appearances as part of building an author's platform.

KNOW YOUR LIMITS

If the idea of spreading your message via a radio show channel wildly appeals to you, but having your own weekly show is daunting and time consuming, consider the other side of the extrovert-introvert writer spectrum. Start small by being a guest on various radio shows which allows you to target specific niches while still building your platform.

The nice thing about this option is that it gives you the flexibility of doing the research, and then picking and choosing those radio show hostings that speak to you. Regardless of the route you choose, you still have to do a modicum of planning and promotion regardless whether you are a host or a guest.

HARNESS THE POWER OF CONNECTION AND CREDIBILITY

Hosting your own radio show is a great way to get your name in front of a target audience. One of the best ways to build this connection is by bringing on popular guest experts in your industry or niche in the earlier stages of programming. One possibility is to ask your listeners who they would like to see on your show as a featured guest. Take any questions before the live show and encourage people to attend the live show.

....

Start small by being a guest on various radio shows which allows you to target specific niches while still building your platform.

....

Another way is to approach literary agencies and request to interview their authors who publish similar material. When you associate yourself with people of influence, your credibility and expert status as an author are enhanced. These literary agencies are hungry to secure media requests and are usually open to any type of online interview so long as it's not too complicated for their authors to call-in.

IDEAS FOR AUTHOR PLATFORM ON INTERNET RADIO

When building a platform, authors have to think about the readers' perspectives. There are many alternatives to engaging a target audience than just reading chapters from a book.

Readers are probably a lot less interested in an author's stories than they are in the lessons they can learn from them. In this way, self-published authors can talk about the life lessons and then allude to their self-published book or upcoming book and then create Tweets and Facebook posts from different points in the radio show.

It's never too soon to start building your platform. Begin working on it as you write your first book. A strong platform will make your dive into writing more successful.

Authors can also talk about the writing process itself in terms of how to work with different point of views, how to write about challenging emotions or painful parts of life, or how to write about uncomfortable issues in such a way that the reader is engaged. For example, many readers of memoir are also other memoir writers and they would get value from this kind of information. All these kinds of strategies can be used to build an author platform on Internet radio way before a book is self-published whether it is a memoir or not.

BEGINNING STEPS: DEFINE YOUR TARGET AUDIENCE

When you know your target audience, it will be easier for you to market your radio show specifically for these people. These two main steps should help:

- **Define your niche.** Who is your "specific" target audience? The better you can define this, the better your chances are at marketing your show. For example, if you are a writer of mysteries, it might be easier to market to this specific group of readers.
- **Find out what this audience needs and how your book can help them.** Do online surveys, teleconferences, forums with your target audience and find out what they need, want and what they are willing to buy to get the answers they're looking for. This is particularly true for all writers of fiction or non-fiction but is particularly crucial for memoir writers.

FINAL WORDS

It's never too soon to start building your platform. Begin working on it as you write your first book. A strong platform will make your dive into writing more successful. Platform building of any kind is not for the faint hearted. It's an exercise in discipline and self-validation. There will be many days when no one pays attention to the work you're putting out there despite your long hours without pay. Building an author's platform is a multi-legged stool. Having your own radio show brings the written and spoken worlds together.

Dorit Sasson, creator of Giving Voice to Your Story, www.givingavoicetothevoicelessbook.com, is also a radio show host of "Giving Voice to Your Story" over at Blog Talk Radio. She is currently writing a memoir of her years serving in the Israeli Defense Forces. She won first place in the MidlifeCollage.com weekly contest with her winning story, "Life After Birth." She's a featured author in the bestselling series, *Pebbles in the Pond: Transforming the World One Person at a Time* alongside *New York Times* bestselling authors such as Sonia Choquette and Arielle Ford.

IT TAKES A VILLAGE

Book Marketing Begins at Home

....

by Mary Shafer

Self-published authors and other indie publishers quickly learn they must work for every sale. Most effective is a grassroots campaign beginning with a thorough marketing plan that includes starting local, building regional buzz, then moving out to larger national and global audiences. No one does it alone—it truly takes the efforts of an extended metaphorical village to successfully launch and sustain a book.

When my first book was published in 1993, I was woefully unprepared to effectively promote it. With no author experience, I fell back on my marketing background and treated my book as I would one of my clients' projects. I began promoting locally, took advantage of every opportunity to build wider buzz by following up on each success, then moved out to a wider audience. I leveraged all my personal and professional networks and gladly allowed the enthusiasm of family, friends, neighbors and colleagues to propel my book to respectable sales. I knew from the start it would take a village to make my book a success.

Though there are more robust promotional tools today, the basis of this success remains the same: Every author and indie publisher needs to enlist the power of their respective "villages" through a five-step book promotion formula:

1. Plan
2. Start local
3. Build buzz
4. Widen reach
5. Be consistent

PLAN

Planning any kind of marketing provides guidelines to keep you on budget, from going off on unproductive tangents and spending too many of your resources for too little return. Things change so rapidly these days that it makes sense to plan the book's launch and first year of marketing, then a year at a time after that. You'll learn as you go, but there are many great books and online resources to help you understand the key components of a sound book marketing plan.

Ideally, you'll begin this plan before you even start writing your book, since there are things you can build into your book to make it more marketable. But whenever you start, there's always something you can do as soon as your plan is written.

START LOCAL

"My advice for newly self-published authors or those published with indie presses is to start locally in person, while embracing the promotional power of Facebook and Twitter," says Barbara Techel, award-winning author and publisher of Joyful Paw Prints Press, LLC (joyfulpaws.com).

"Starting local is so important to building a brand and confidence, then enhancing that with social media avenues. In fact, combining the two right out of the gate is the ideal thing to do." She began talking to local teachers and librarians about her first children's book, *Frankie the Walk 'N Roll Dog*, before it came out. This created awareness and anticipation. When her books were printed, she contacted those same people to schedule the presentations, where she built visibility, credibility, and book sales.

....

You can include a brief introduction to your release, suggesting local story angles or tie-ins to topic-related current events. Anything you can do to make editors' and journalists' jobs easier increases your possibilities of coverage.

....

Create news releases and e-mail them to your local newspapers, magazines and any online local news outlets such as AOL Patch®. You should have a website about you and your book, so post high resolution photos of yourself and your book's cover there, where they can be downloaded at news reporters' convenience, to illustrate any features they may write based on your release. You can include a brief introduction to your release, suggesting local story angles or tie-ins to topic-related current events. Anything you can do to make editors' and journalists' jobs easier increases your possibilities of coverage.

"The first tool I developed was a press kit, which served as an introduction to me and my book," recalls Erika Liodice, self-published author and publisher of Dreamspire Press (erikaliodice.com). "It contained a press release about the launch of my book, *Empty Arms;* my author bio; a professional headshot; early reviews from book bloggers; and media interviews with me. I sent them to local newspapers, magazines, and bookstores, along with a personal letter.

"A few days later, I received my first invitation to do a book signing at the local bookshop, which not only connected me with readers, but scored me valuable shelf space. The event garnered free advertising in area newspapers—space that would've cost me a fortune—and convinced the region's premier lifestyle magazine to review my book."

BUILD BUZZ

Once you've established recognition for your author "brand" and your book, it's time to widen your horizons to include state and national markets. Online, follow other authors in your genre, says Techel. Learn where your readers congregate—whether that's Facebook, Twitter, discussion forums or related blogs. Those places are where you want to hang out, too, and actively participate. Interaction with your audience is key to building credibility, trust and relationships.

"One of the best and easiest ways to build an author brand or platform is through blogging," says Amy Shojai, award-winning author of 26 pet books, who features pet-centric topics on her "Bling, Bitches and Blood" blog (AmyShojai.com). "Blogs draw a following, offer new writers a venue to experiment and find their voice, and provide discipline for getting ass-ets in the chair and WRITING on a schedule." This works even for fiction, and is quite effective if you develop a targeted following.

Learn where your readers congregate—whether that's Facebook, Twitter, discussion forums or related blogs. Those places are where you want to hang out, too, and actively participate.

Research other blogs about your book's topic, find other author blogs in your genre and start hanging out there. "Lurk" quietly for a week or two to get a feel for the conversation, then jump right in! Just remember the first rule of social media: *Give before you get.* On average, out of ten comments you make on anyone else's blog or on other social outlets, nine should give pertinent, valuable information others there can use and enjoy. The tenth comment can be about your book, but use a soft approach. No one likes a blatant self-promoter, and that approach will backfire badly. Promotional comments should contain a link back to your website or blog.

LOCATE RELATED BLOGS

Use these online tools to find blogs related to your book and writing:

- Google Blogs - http://www.google.com/blogsearch
- Best of the Web - http://search.botw.org/
- Your Version - http://www.yourversion.com/
- Technorati - http://technorati.com/
- Alltop - http://alltop.com/

"Pair your blog with another venue such as Facebook or Twitter (or if very visual, Pinterest)," Shojai advises. "That way, you can share your blog posts on these other venues, and your 'friends, likes, fans' and 'followers' can more easily find you throughout the Internet. Choose social network options you enjoy using. It's all about networking, connecting and building relationships, and *not, not, NOT* about selling your book. Get folks to engage and get to know you first. You become a friend, then they're more interested in checking out what that friend is doing: "Wow, my friend wrote a book? I've got to read that, and tell all MY friends!"

WIDEN YOUR HORIZONS

Techel remembers, "As I built confidence, requested and received wonderful testimonials, I decided to expand my outreach to other states. Not really wanting to travel, I wholeheartedly embraced the free audio and video conferencing technology of Skype. I knew I could do in front of my computer's webcam the same classroom presentation I did locally in person. It allowed me to reach out to schools across the United States and Canada.

"Skype and Facebook have been essential to building my author platform and for creating buzz about my appearances. I've met teachers, librarians and others via Facebook that I would not have otherwise met, and they've helped spread the word about my work."

Liodice says, "As *Empty Arms* gained visibility, I began receiving invitations to exhibit at book festivals and speak at events. Whenever I have the chance to speak publicly about my book, I come prepared with a few key items to maximize the experience for potential buyers:

- a ten-second elevator speech that gets people interested in reading my book
- pocket-size brochures that remind them what it's about and where they can buy it
- folded business cards that look like my book, so people remember me long after our conversation has ended.

BE CONSISTENT

Though you're only planning a year at a time, it's critical to have an "in it for the long haul" attitude and to continue developing strategies to promote your book in creative and outstanding ways. One tactic is to find ways to build credibility and visibility for authors as experts in their chosen subjects.

As a nano-publisher of topical nonfiction on business, finance, and cultural subjects, longtime author Foster Winans of Winans Kuenstler Publishing, LLC (WKPublishing.com) encourages authors to write guest columns and other content for relevant websites, trade and general interest outlets. He says this should ideally begin long before the book is published. That way, when people search the Web for the author or the book, results return more than just an Amazon listing.

> Though you're only planning a year at a time, it's critical to have an 'in it for the long haul' attitude and to continue developing strategies to promote your book in creative and outstanding ways.

"Authoring a book makes one an expert," Winans explains. "In the area of personal finance and investing, I have ghostwritten more than three dozen guest columns and blog posts that have been effective in getting our authors visibility. Most effective so far has been a relationship I developed with Forbes.com. Sites like this and others are hungry for free content from experts. Forbes builds their database of material, and the experts get to hitch their wagons to a trusted brand name. The bigger bang, however, is in tearsheets. Authors can reprint their columns with the Forbes logo and use them as handouts to burnish their credibility."

The key to this tactic is creating material that relates to current events and hot news topics, so it's a good idea to establish Google Alerts to anticipate when related topics are beginning to trend.

QUICK TIP

Each author's topic will determine a different group of potential outlets for contributed material. A general outlet is Quora.com, where people with knowledge in just about any field can answer questions about most any topic.

Free subscription services Help A Reporter Out (HARO.com) and Reporter Connection (ReporterConnection.com) provide daily leads to journalists looking for expert interview subjects.

Then just remember to keep up the effort on an ongoing basis. You don't have to go for broke with every campaign. Ultimately, small efforts done consistently will always be more effective than splashy events done in an unplanned, "shotgun" manner.

"It's important to remember this all takes time, so be patient and commit yourself for the long haul," Techel adds. "Be consistent, build slowly and be authentic — that's what will attract your audience and keep it with you for a long time to come."

MARY SHAFER (maryshafer.com) is an award-winning author, and an independent publisher who served as president of the MidAtlantic Book Publishers Association from 2010-2012. As an unkown author, she promoted her debut regional nonfiction title that wasn't even expected to earn out (make back the author advance), into three printings that sold 15,000 copies and generated royalty checks for five years before it was allowed to go out of print.

HOW TO USE PUBLIC RELATIONS TO PROMOTE YOUR BOOK AND CAREER

by Lorena Beniquez

The beauty of executing your own public relations campaign as a writer is you already possess the crucial skill to be a successful publicist: writing. I know what you are thinking. "I've just poured my heart and soul into writing a book and now you want me to write more?!"

Yes, because your words may not reach a wide enough audience, if you don't use words further to promote yourself. Whether you want to reach a local or national audience, a public relations plan can get you exposure as an author and for your work.

The first thing to ignore when approaching publicity is that little voice in your head that asks, "Why would anyone care about my book?" That voice is just tired from already writing a book and would much rather go play a video game. Ignore it and become your own publicist.

Coffee House Press Publicist Kelsey Shanesy offers, "Being a good publicist is really being a good journalist." Like a journalist, ask, "Who, what, when, where, why and how. These questions will serve as guideposts for your public relations strategy.

Before answering those questions, examine what "public relations" means. It is part of your marketing strategy like advertising. However, unlike advertising you do not pay for placement. Public relations is anything that gets your name out to the public via traditional media, social media or even word of mouth. It can be an article in your local newspaper, a tweet about your upcoming stint at an open mic night or your Aunt Angie telling her bridge club about your book signing (never, never underestimate the power of Aunt Angie). If things go really well, it could be the Associated Press disseminating your story nationwide.

Now that writers have been employing social media, some think they are covered when it comes to publicity. Unless all your friends are editors or talk show producers, you need to go beyond social media. While it is crucial, there are other elements that are just as crucial.

HOW?

Let's start with the last question of "How?". How will you reach out to your public? Pitch letters and press releases will do some of that work for you. Luckily, you just happen to be a writer so these will be a no-brainer.

The "pitch" is really just a public relations term for "query". The same rules apply for both. Like a query letter, it has to be attention grabbing. Shanesy advises that it should be a two to three paragraph e-mail.

The first sentence of your pitch will include your angle. This is what captures the gate-keeper's attention. Again, very much like a query letter.

Take a look at the day's headlines, study what's trending, and monitor what stories are getting play on national shows. One of the easiest ways to grab exposure is to develop an angle tied to a national story. For example, if a story breaks on how donuts are the new health food craze and you just wrote "The Hole Truth about Donuts" offer yourself to media outlets to comment on the craze.

Of course, your angle may have no current event tie-in and that is just fine. Anything about you or your book can help spur an angle. The setting of the book, the subject matter and your background as a writer (and human) are just some things to consider. Have you written a sci-fi graphic novel and happen to be a rocket scientist? The angles are endless with the most obvious being, "Rocket scientist gains lift-off with first book." Have fun with the angles and use your creativity.

> Take a look at the day's headlines, study what's trending, and monitor what stories are getting play on national shows. One of the easiest ways to grab exposure is to develop an angle tied to a national story.

Another tool to employ is the press release. It is a more formal way of communicating. It is best used when you have really big news and need to reach multiple outlets at once. Do an Internet search to learn how a press release is properly constructed by looking at ones that are already out there. Many times, a pitch will also accompany the press release. Include the press release in the body of your e-mail rather than attaching it.

WHO?

Who do you pitch? Just like selecting the proper publisher or editor to approach, know the outlet you are pitching and make sure their target market is your target market. Study the target to see what has been covered in the past and what they are focusing on now. Also, get a feel for their work timelines. Talk show producers prepare for segments about a month in advance, while monthly and regional magazine editors need to be pitched up to six months in advance. Outlets with shorter lead times include wire services, daily newspapers, radio, television news and blogs. Following is partial list of outlets to consider pitching.

Locally: Newsletters, television news, local news websites, daily newspapers, free weeklies, college newspapers and regional magazines.

Nationally: Yahoo News, wire services, metropolitan newspapers, national newspapers (i.e. USA Today), daily talk shows, magazines (just peruse your *Writer's Market*), radio syndicates, trade publications, journals, news websites and blogs.

When pitching to television, keep this in mind. Some assignment desk editors and television producers shy away from covering books and authors because they aren't always visually enticing. They think a writer writing or a book just sitting there isn't spirited enough for video. However, if you give them something exciting to shoot, they will be more willing to offer coverage.

Say you just penned a children's book about a lunatic Siamese cat and you are inviting local news crew to interview you. Give them the option of interviewing you beside a lunatic Siamese cat. This gives them a visual other than a talking head (and maybe that lunatic cat will go viral which would be PR gold).

....

When pitching to television, keep this in mind. Some assignment desk editors and television producers shy away from covering books and authors because they aren't always visually enticing. ... However, if you give them something exciting to shoot, they will be more willing to offer coverage.

....

After sending out your pitch, follow-up via email. Shanesy says that it is best not to call when doing so. "It is rare when I actually talk to editors on the phone. If I have heard there is interest, or I know it is a great fit, then I will follow up on the phone," she says.

WHAT?

What are you pitching? It could be you as an author, your book or a million other reasons. Whenever there is a new development in your writing life, ask yourself if it is something that merits pitching. Got an assignment as a contributor to a book? Crow about it on Linked-In!

Did you just win a book award? Time for a press release. Did your research uncover Jimmy Hoffa's final resting place? You better hold a press conference.

Here are some reasons to crank up the publicity machine: book signing, new writing assignment, book reviews, spoken word readings, speaking engagements, blog updates, new website, securing a publisher, awards, conference participation and volunteer work. Also, always publicize any media coverage you have already received on social sites and websites.

WHEN?

When should you launch your public relations assault? Don't wait to begin your publicity until after you have penned your tome. If you are just now reading this, and have already completed said tome, do not fret. You can still publicize away!

Novelist Dennis R. Miller's day job is in public relations which he has done for over forty years. He says that when he puts aside three hours to write, he uses one of those hours to do his public relations outreach. Shanesy agrees. "Put yourself on a schedule so you post at least two things a day," she advises.

When also asks, "When were you last covered by the media outlet?" If you were just on *The View* last week, they probably will not be asking you back for a while. The same is true with your arts editor at the local newspaper. The media has a lot of ground to cover and must keep content fresh.

WHERE?

Where is your target market? Does your target market prefer newspapers over online news? Do they prefer to pin rather than tweet? Are they sitting in the salon next to you? This will help you better select the public you are pitching and the messages that go out through social media. You will very likely have multiple target markets so make sure you identify all of them and know where they live.

WHY?

Why did you write your book? Why do you write? Every writer has a backstory and many times it is just as compelling as the writer's work. This backstory may lend itself to your PR. Say you wrote a book on autism because your child is autistic. Include your "why" when pitching. It gives the gatekeepers a more rounded picture of who you are and also lends gravitas to the book. You aren't just selling your book's story. You are selling the story of you.

Now that we know the who, what, where, why and how of public relations, you will need to invest some time into getting your public relations campaign rolling. It will take work but it won't be too taxing since you have already jumpstarted the campaign with your writing platforms.

Writing platforms are more than gateways to your words. They also act as your personal publicist. "Early on in my blog [bikesnobnyc.blogspot.com], I was lucky that journalists and publications would contact me," says Eben Weiss (pen name BikeSnobNYC) who authored two cycling books and is a columnist for *Bicycle* magazine. Prior to his blog, Weiss had never written professionally and credits his blog for getting him noticed. "It is an extension of my PR in that people are reading it and the nature of the internet is to promote things that are interesting."

Now it is the time tell everyone why you and your work are interesting and go beyond the internet to do it. Sure, you are going to have to write more. But if you do your job well as a publicist, you will be writing more than just press releases.

LORENA BENIQUEZ has employed her skills as a celebrity publicist, reporter, filmmaker, and freelance writer. As a publicist, Beniquez has worked with Ray Romano, CBS Newworks, Showtime, and Sundance Channel to name a few. She is currently scripting a documentary film commissioned by the Lucille Ball Desi Arnaz Center for Comedy, which Beniquez also directed.

SPEAK MORE, SELL MORE

by Dianna Graveman

Book signings are a great way to network, but most indie authors average fewer than two sales per signing, not counting purchases from family members and friends. Speaking events are a much more effective sales tool. Special interest groups and target audiences are more likely to buy your book than are random shoppers.

Let's face it: Indie authors who have not been traditionally published face harsh competition. It can be tough to convince the buying public you have something worthy to offer when you don't have a publishing house behind you.

The trick is to think like a businessperson. Successful authors know that book promotion is not just a hobby. Don't treat it like one. Find your target audience and invite them to learn from you. Offer them value, and make them want your product.

GET THE GIG

Start local. Offer a workshop to area writing groups. Pitch to clubs who may have a special interest in your book's topic or theme. Both historical fiction and nonfiction can land you a gig at your county or state historical society. Contact the event coordinator at your library district or a nearby community college and offer to speak. Investigate the adult and continuing education programs at area school districts; many hire published authors to teach, with no college degree required.

If your book is of interest to seniors, contact the recreation director at a retirement center or try OASIS, a national organization with community chapters that host programs for adults over 50. Not all of these groups will allow you to sell books at the event, but all will provide word-of-mouth publicity and, in some cases, media exposure.

"If you are just starting out, your best bet is to network within the area you have expertise," said fiction writer J. A. Konrath, an outspoken champion of self-publishing who has also published traditionally. "Give free books to schools, businesses, and conferences—anywhere they hire speakers—and be able to pitch your speech in a compelling, succinct way."

Konrath also suggests e-book authors use CreateSpace or Lightning Source to make print copies for speaking events. Make sure your business card has a link to the site where your e-book is sold.

....

Check the events section of your local paper for area business groups who may want to hear about indie publishing or book marketing topics.

....

Book clubs are an obvious audience for published authors. Readerscircle.org lists the location and description of book clubs around the world, searchable by country and zip code. An added bonus is that authors can request that their books be featured at the site and offer to do a half-hour phone chat with interested book clubs.

Check the events section of your local paper for area business groups who may want to hear about indie publishing or book marketing topics. Look for relevant support groups, if you've written a nonfiction book involving a health or social issue.

Award-winning sportswriter and journalist Mike Eisenbath self-published a memoir in 2009 and quickly realized his most effective speaking engagements would be opportunities to talk to people directly interested in his book's topic: clinical depression.

"My memoir had a somewhat focused subject, since it was about clinical depression and how to combat that with spiritual faith," Eisenbath said. "So people who have suffered from the disease or who have had a loved one with the disease were the logical audience. It meant most of the engagements I had were small. And I had to accept that as okay, especially given the intimate and sensitive nature of the topic."

FIND YOUR AUDIENCE ON THE WEB

Special interest groups are searchable by location and topic at Meetup.com. You likely won't be paid to speak to the group, but you will gain word-of-mouth publicity, and you'll walk away with a pocketful of business cards to add to your e-mail list.

Speakerfile is also a great place for authors and topic experts to promote. Set up a profile complete with book covers, slides, links to media interviews, lists of affiliations and accomplishments—even video or photos from previous speaking engagements. Set your rates and availability as a speaker. When you pitch your talk to an organization or group, include a link to your Speakerfile and showcase your talent.

Togather.com is a site exclusively for authors who want to speak, but with a twist: speakers can require a minimum number of attendees for an event, which is canceled if enough registrations aren't received. After the event, fans can leave feedback.

Don't forget to add "Speaker" to your bio on all of your existing online profiles, including Linkedin, Facebook, Twitter, and Goodreads. Make sure your author website announces you are a speaker, too.

PROMOTE YOUR EVENT

Congratulations, you've booked an event! Now it's time to promote.

- Create a Facebook event and invite your contacts.
- Send a press release to your local paper or news site. If Patch.com publishes in your area, pitch yourself as the subject of an article. Create a login so you can post the event on the site yourself.
- Prepare a simple poster or flyer to announce your event and post it on community bulletin boards around town.
- Add an events page to your website or blog. Post upcoming events as well as past events (to show a following) and a list of potential speaking topics for future engagements.
- Radio and television shows can be a tough sell, but blog talk radio hosts are *always* looking for interviewees. Google "blog talk radio" plus "writers," or search for a program with a theme related to your book. Get scheduled as a guest, then promote your upcoming event on the show. Don't forget to promote the interview, too, and post a link to the recorded show on your website.

Add an events page to your website or blog. Post upcoming events as well as past events (to show a following) and a list of potential speaking topics for future engagements.

- Set up a page at Eventbrite.com, then use the site to send custom e-mail invitations and list the event on search engines and in the Eventbrite directory. If you choose to host your own event, you can sell tickets and track your attendance.
- List your event at Zvents.com, and it will be distributed across the site's media network.

- Blog and tweet about your event. Announce it on Linkedin. Set up a Goodreads giveaway in advance of the event to drum up interest.

PREPARE FOR YOUR EVENT

Arlynn Greenbaum, President of Authors Unlimited, is a lecture agent and former Director of Marketing for Little, Brown and Company. Her clients include literary heavyweights Jodi Picoult, Jeffrey Eugenides, and Taylor Branch.

Greenbaum cautions new authors who hope to promote their books through speaking events to get coaching if they're not experienced speakers. "Writing is introverted, and speaking is extroverted," she said. "Not all writers are good speakers. People don't want to just hear you read; they want to listen to you talk about the creative process. If you're going to do it, be good at it."

One way to get coaching and build confidence is through Toastmasters International. You can search for a chapter near you at www.toastmasters.org. The site also hosts several free articles on topics related to public speaking.

Offer a few copies of your book as door prizes. Invite audience members to throw their business cards into a hat for the drawing, with the understanding you have permission to add those contacts to your e-mail list.

Several weeks before your event, send your host a .jpeg file of your book cover, a synopsis of your book, a brief bio, and a headshot of you for posting on the organization's website.

Ask your event organizer if you can sell books at the event, and request an estimate of the expected number of guests. If you can't sell your books, you may still choose to accept the invitation in exchange for publicity. If you do plan to sell, bring a friend to handle your sales so that you can spend all of your time interacting with your audience.

Consider offering a small percentage of your sales from the event to the host organization or a related charity, and ask the event planner to announce that agreement to your audience. You'll make up the lost percentage in sales and good will.

Prepare a thank you note, along with an offer to send a summary of your talk afterward for inclusion in the organization's newsletter.

Remember to pack plenty of bookmarks or business cards. Offer a few copies of your book as door prizes. Invite audience members to throw their business cards into a hat for the drawing, with the understanding you have permission to add those contacts to your e-mail list.

DON'T HARD SELL—ENTERTAIN!

Of course you want to sell books—but don't make sales the obvious point of your talk.

"Give content, not a sales pitch," said travel and history writer Sean McLachlan. "Give them an interesting lecture on Jesse James, and then happen to mention he's a supporting character in your novel."

McLachlan, a former archeologist who has traveled to more than 30 countries in his quest for adventure and the perfect story, enjoys using personal anecdotes to entertain his audience.

"Everyone is interested in hearing about rock climbing in Ethiopia or visiting Babylon in Iraq," he said. "If people think you're an interesting person, they're more likely to give your books a try."

DIANNA GRAVEMAN is a former corporate training designer, teacher, staff editor, and MFA faculty member whose portfolio includes over 160 publishing credits, 22 awards, and coauthorship of four regional histories. Graveman owns 2 Rivers Communications & Design, which provides writing, editing, and marketing services for businesses, and co-owns Treehouse Publishing Group, which provides author services. Learn more at www.2riverscommunications.com and www.treehousepublishinggroup.com..

HOW TO BREAK INTO THE GIFT MARKET

....

by Claire Bateman

Know how to get your self-published book placed right next to the register? How about being the only book in a retail store? The secret is simple; market your title as a gift and sell it to gift and specialty stores, hospital gift shops, stationers, or children's boutiques across the country.

Most gift shop and boutique owners do their own buying and travel several times a year to gift shows in search of new and unique gifts. They love meeting an author and unlike the big box book outlets they don't need to work through a distributor to buy books for their stores.

CHOOSING THE RIGHT GIFT MARKET

Location, Location, Location

The four largest US gift markets are in Atlanta (www.americasmart.com), Dallas (www.dallasmarketcenter.com), Las Vegas (www.giftandhomely.com), and New York (www.nynow.com). Each venue offers at least two large shows a year attracting thousands of exhibitors and buyers and lasts five to six days. Some also host several smaller two to three day shows per year with fewer participants.

Temporary Booth Space

Also known at the Temps, this booth space is leased to individual manufacturers (like you) for the length of the show. Temps is divided into product categories; home decor, culinary, children, stationery, bridal, spa, holiday, etc. To select the category that best suits your book, imagine the type of store that would carry a book like yours and what types of products would compliment your title? If you've written a children's book, lease booth space in children. Cookbooks sell in culinary, a memoir about your wedding is well suited for bridal or stationery, etc.

Business consultants, product developers, and national sales reps come to the Temps section of markets looking for the next great unknown product. Temps is a hotbed of creative entrepreneurs and a great place to network and share ideas. You may find someone with a complimentary product willing to share booth space and expenses for the next show (a children's artist pairs well with a children's book, collegiate decor is a nice match for a sports memoir etc).

Each venue's website has an application process and information for first time exhibitors. If the bigger shows are intimidating to you, consider doing a smaller market. The booth fees are less expensive and because they only last a few days, lodging costs will be more economical as well. These smaller markets are also a great way for new exhibitors to get the lay of the land before committing to a week-long show.

PREPARING FOR THE SHOW

Marketing before market

Once you've chosen the show that's right for you, look through the market's website and take advantage of free mailing lists, complimentary product listings, and other pre-market advertising opportunities. Sending postcards or email blasts ahead of the show gives buyers a preview of your book. The venue will have a sales person assigned to you. Ask them for help.

Booth selection and display

Most temp booths are rented by the square foot and the standard booth size is 10' by 10'. Displaying one title does not require this much space. Ask your sales person if there are any booths that are 5' deep and 10' wide. This will cut booth cost and simplify booth set-up and break-down.

Booth Display

You will need a banner, an adequate display for your book, and a table for your paperwork and invoices with a spot for pamphlets and business cards. If you are driving to the show, be sure you can fit your booth setup in your vehicle. If you are flying, you will have to ship your setup to the show ahead of time. Simple is better, have your booth decor and banner match your ad, email blast, and promotional material. The more consistent your artwork, the easier it is for buyers to find you. For booth ideas, look at photos from the market website.

Pricing your book for the gift market

Traditionally, gift stores use keystone markup. This is the practice of marking merchandise for resale at double the wholesale price. If the retail price you have chosen for your title is $10.00 the wholesale price you will charge at market is $5.00. Choose your price carefully and keep it consistent for your entire customer base.

Quantity per order

Gift buyers are used to buying in multiples. When choosing your order size remember to sell what you think the store can sell. You want the books to 'move well' for your customers. Repeat customers in this industry are your bread and butter. If the order size is too big and the books sit on the shelf, your customer is less likely to re-order.

Pre-printed promotional materials and signage

- Pamphlets or fliers. Great for the buyer who wants to 'think about it." In addition to listing your contact information these should include a brief description of your book, cover art, and a pricing chart.
- Business cards.
- Carbonless Invoice tablets. An absolute must for taking orders. These should have all of the pertinent information for billing the customer and for shipping your product: customer's billing and shipping address, telephone number, email address, credit card information, order date, ship date, quantity ordered, pricing information, and shipping costs. You will fill out the invoice at the show. One copy for you, the carbonless copy goes to your customer. It is industry standard to get credit card information at these shows. Some businesses may request different terms (this is especially common for hospital gift shops). In these cases it is ok to ask for a credit reference list or to express your willingness to work with terms after the first order.
- A "Meet the Author" sign.
- Show special signage. See below.

SHOW TIME

Show specials

The show special is designed to help you close the sale at the show. Some common ideas are to offer free shipping, an additional book for free, or to sign all books in orders placed at the show. Offer something of value to the customer that doesn't cut into your profit (like autographing books).

Professionalism

Dress professionally and comfortably. Be courteous and available, limit computer and smart phone time. Buyers come to shows to buy. Remember that when they say, "I'm just looking."

FULFILLING ORDERS

Invoicing

It is important to have a reliable bookkeeping program to manage your new customer base. After the credit card transaction has been processed, create a paid invoice in your bookkeeping program to be included with the order.

Shipping

Having the right materials is key. Find a box that fits your quantity per order. When your books fit snugly in their package there is less risk of damage during shipping. Shipping and handling costs are commonly paid by the customer. Include these costs in your invoice.

In closing, remember that most buyers are small business owners who, like you, are trying to make it in the world of big business. Selling your book means selling yourself and chances are if they identify with you a sale is inevitable. People love meeting a real-life author. Your job title gives you immediate credibility. Use it and above all, have fun.

Claire Bateman's second title, *This Little Light of Mine*, won Honorable Mention in the Writers Digest International Self-Published Book Contest. Her work has appeared in *Country Roads Magazine*, *The Catholic Commentator* and *Jubilee Literary Magazine*.

AUTHOR'S GUIDE TO CREATING AN E-MAIL NEWSLETTER

....

by Dana Sitar

If you've ever Googled "building a platform," you've likely been told it's time to start a newsletter. "It's all about the list," everyone says, and you're starting to believe it. But you don't want to be another among the slew of salesmen who invade your readers' inboxes every day, and you're not sure where to even begin or how you might benefit.

You may have already read dozens of articles telling you an e-mail list is your best possible marketing tool, and you're eager to add another weapon to your bookselling arsenal. The fantastic power of "The List," however, is not in its potential to garner book sales, but in its ability to help you build genuine relationships with your readers—which leads to not only sales, but to a dedicated, loyal fanbase who will stick with you and your books for years to come.

THE BENEFITS TO THE AUTHOR

A reader signing up for your list gives you something simple but of great value: permission. Through your newsletter, you earn permission to contact readers directly through e-mail, and they may even come to expect and look forward to your correspondence. Creating and meeting that expectation helps you foster goodwill, and the opportunity to touch base with a reader one-on-one will help each of them connect with and remember you.

THE BENEFITS TO THE READER

Many of the tips for writing e-mail newsletters warn you that your readers are overwhelmed with e-mail, that you have to fight to get their attention, that you have to take care not to annoy them with your correspondence—but what if your readers enjoy what you have to say?

While keeping up with an overflowing inbox can be overwhelming, if your newsletter is helpful and entertaining, people will make time to read it. If you focus on fostering relationships, rather than on selling your books or pushing your blog, they'll look forward to the opportunity to connect with you—you're that interesting, and they respect your work!

HOW TO GET STARTED

Follow these simple steps to get started on an e-mail newsletter that will engage your readers and help you build a loyal fanbase for your books.

Step 1: Start with stating your goals.

Before you set anything up, state your goals and determine how your newsletter can support them. Are you trying to sell your book? Build your blog readership? Draw more people to your events? Connect with your loyal community?

Knowing your end goals will help you determine the best format and content for your newsletter, the best way to encourage readers to sign up, and the optimal schedule. Consider a clear action step or two for subscribers: Should they go to your blog after reading each e-mail, share a tweet with a particular message, or hop over to Amazon to pick up your latest book? Once you know where you want to guide readers, your correspondence can be driven by that end goal.

....

Knowing your end goals will help you determine the best format and content for your newsletter, the best way to encourage readers to sign up, and the optimal schedule.

....

Step 2: Pick a direction.

Once you know your goals, you can determine the best type of newsletter to help you achieve them. Here are some common directions your author newsletter could take:

- Occasional news—This type of newsletter is best-suited for authors with an already-established fan base. If your goal is to keep readers abreast of your latest releases and upcoming events, you can focus on sharing these updates through your e-mail list.
- How-to or Informational articles—While time-intensive, this type of newsletter is a great way to offer additional value that attracts new readers. You can write unique articles for each edition of your newsletter, exploring topics of interest to readers in your genre.

- Resources—This round-up style newsletter is another way to offer additional value, but with less of a writing commitment than full articles. You can write a less extensive update that includes categorized links to articles and resources for readers in your genre.
- Blog digest or full posts—If you also write an author blog, your newsletter is a natural traffic-driver. You can send an e-mail when you publish a new blog post that teases the post, or e-mail the full post for readers who prefer to read it in their inbox.

Along with determining the overall direction, decide early on what topics you'll cover. Similar to creating an author blog, knowing the theme of your newsletter from the beginning will ensure consistency in your messages to readers.

Will you stick to personal messages, or include helpful information? If helpful information or resources, will they be on broad topics loosely related to your other work, or will they have a narrower focus for specific readers?

Step 3: Set your schedule.

Once you know the direction you'll take, promise readers a schedule and content. Telling them what to expect and when to expect it will encourage readers to look forward to your correspondence.

....

Before you send your first newsletter, determine your frequency and your theme. Prep your messages ahead just as you would for your blog or a magazine column.

....

Of course, if you make that promise, follow through to foster goodwill and confidence. Forecasting a schedule and straying from it could confuse readers and potentially cause them to unsubscribe. If you don't expect to stick to a particular schedule—especially if you're sharing only occasional news—don't try to promise one.

Before you send your first newsletter, determine your frequency and your theme. Prep your messages ahead just as you would for your blog or a magazine column. Commit to planning a topic, headline, and outline for several editions of the newsletter. This will help you ensure these messages match the tone and quality of your other writing, rather than taking on the hurried, careless tone of e-mail correspondence.

Step 4: Choose a service.

Dozens of services exist to help you manage your e-mail list and send professional-looking newsletters to your readers with little technical know-how on your part. Look around the web before settling for your provider or paying for services you don't need.

Subscribe to the newsletters of your favorite authors and bloggers to get a reader's perspective on the services they use. How do the newsletters look in your inbox? Is subscribing—and unsubscribing—easy or too complicated? Then look at these services from an editorial perspective. Do they offer sufficient support for the size of your audience? Will managing your e-mails and your list be simple enough for your level of technical expertise? Do they offer strong customer service and tutorials to help when it's not?

Step 5: Create an incentive to join.

Unless you have a strong fan base, you may not convince readers to subscribe for the updates alone. Offer an additional incentive to encourage and reward them for sharing their e-mail address. This incentive often takes the form of a free gift to subscribers: a short ebook, a manifesto, a report for your niche, a short story.

You can also create an educational series (a simple e-course) exclusive to subscribers, a series of blog posts only they can access, or offer exclusive discounts on your products and services.

Step 6: Promote the sign-up to your readers.

A flashing pop-up at your website will certainly get readers' attention, but don't miss opportunities for subtler and less-offensive ways to encourage readers to subscribe. A link or embedded sign-up form in your website's sidebar gets attention without disturbing the readers' experience so much.

Also, don't forget to include a link to sign up in your byline for articles at blogs and newsletters, share it with your Twitter followers and Facebook fans, and bring an old-fashioned piece of paper to book signings and events for attendees to add their e-mail address before they leave.

Step 7: Send your e-mails and engage with readers.

Once you start sending e-mails to your list, remember to maintain a focus on reader engagement. This list is an opportunity for readers to touch base and get to know you better, and a great way for you to connect personally. Write personal messages that prompt readers to follow up with you. Pose direct questions, and encourage them to "hit reply" to answer them. This is a great chance to learn from your most dedicated fans exactly what they want from you!

Adding a P.S. to the end of your e-mail is one of the best ways to encourage readers to take action—put your link there, or ask a question you'd like them to answer. After the headline, the P.S. is the second most-read part of an e-mail; you'll be astounded by how much engagement and clicks will increase from this simple addition!

THE MOST IMPORTANT PART

Overall, the most important thing to remember about your e-mail list is that this correspondence is all about the reader. Readers offer you incredible value and faith by signing up, so be sure to return the favor by consistently offering the engagement and value they're expecting.

DANA SITAR is a freelance journalist and indie author. She's been a freelancing (editor and writer) since 2004 with two self-published short story collections out and an information e-book for writers. She's written for *The Daily Cardinal, The Onion, Baystages, SF Weekly, Laughspin,* and *Maximum Ink*; as well as dozens of writing and career blogs, including The Creative Penn, Musings from the Slushpile, and Brazen Life. Learn more at http://danasitar.com.

BLOGGING BASICS

Get the Most Out of Your Blog

....

by Robert Lee Brewer

In these days of publishing and media change, writers have to build platforms and learn how to connect to audiences if they want to improve their chances of publication and overall success. There are many methods of audience connection available to writers, but one of the most important is through blogging.

Since I've spent several years successfully blogging—both personally and professionally—I figure I've got a few nuggets of wisdom to pass on to writers who are curious about blogging or who already are.

Here's my quick list of tips:

1. **START BLOGGING TODAY.** If you don't have a blog, use Blogger, WordPress, or some other blogging software to start your blog today. It's free, and you can start off with your very personal "Here I am, world" post.

2. **START SMALL.** Blogs are essentially very simple, but they can get very complicated (for people who like complications). However, I advise bloggers start small and evolve over time.

3. **USE YOUR NAME IN YOUR URL.** This will make it easier for search engines to find you when your audience eventually starts seeking you out by name. For instance, my url is http://robertleebrewer.blogspot.com. If you try Googling "Robert Lee Brewer," you'll notice that My Name Is Not Bob is one of the top 5 search results (behind my other blog: Poetic Asides).

4. **UNLESS YOU HAVE A REASON, USE YOUR NAME AS THE TITLE OF YOUR BLOG.** Again, this helps with search engine results. My Poetic Asides blog includes my name in the title, and it ranks higher than My Name Is Not Bob. However, I felt the play on my name was worth the trade off.

5. **FIGURE OUT YOUR BLOGGING GOALS.** You should return to this step every couple months, because it's natural for your blogging goals to evolve over time. Initially, your blogging goals may be to make a post a week about what you have written, submitted, etc. Over time, you may incorporate guests posts, contests, tips, etc.

6. **BE YOURSELF.** I'm a big supporter of the idea that your image should match your identity. It gets too confusing trying to maintain a million personas. Know who you are and be that on your blog, whether that means you're sincere, funny, sarcastic, etc.

7. **POST AT LEAST ONCE A WEEK.** This is for starters. Eventually, you may find it better to post once a day or multiple times per day. But remember: Start small and evolve over time.

8. **POST RELEVANT CONTENT.** This means that you post things that your readers might actually care to know.

9. **USEFUL AND HELPFUL POSTS WILL ATTRACT MORE VISITORS.** Talking about yourself is all fine and great. I do it myself. But if you share truly helpful advice, your readers will share it with others, and visitors will find you on search engines.

10. **TITLE YOUR POSTS IN A WAY THAT GETS YOU FOUND IN SEARCH ENGINES.** The more specific you can get the better. For instance, the title "Blogging Tips" will most likely get lost in search results. However, the title "Blogging Tips for Writers" specifies which audience I'm targeting and increases the chances of being found on the first page of search results.

11. **LINK TO POSTS IN OTHER MEDIA.** If you have an e-mail newsletter, link to your blog posts in your newsletter. If you have social media accounts, link to your blog posts there. If you have a helpful post, link to it in relevant forums and on message boards.

12. **WRITE WELL, BUT BE CONCISE.** At the end of the day, you're writing blog posts, not literary manifestos. Don't spend a week writing each post. Try to keep it to an hour or two tops and then post. Make sure your spelling and grammar are good, but don't stress yourself out too much.

13. **FIND LIKE-MINDED BLOGGERS.** Comment on their blogs regularly and link to them from yours. Eventually, they may do the same. Keep in mind that blogging is a form of social media, so the more you communicate with your peers the more you'll get out of the process.

14. **RESPOND TO COMMENTS ON YOUR BLOG.** Even if it's just a simple "Thanks," respond to your readers if they comment on your blog. After all, you want your readers to be engaged with your blog, and you want them to know that you care they took time to comment.

15. **EXPERIMENT.** Start small, but don't get complacent. Every so often, try something new. For instance, the biggest draw to my Poetic Asides blog are the poetry prompts

and challenges I issue to poets. Initially, that was an experiment—one that worked very well. I've tried other experiments that haven't panned out, and that's fine. It's all part of a process.

SEO TIPS FOR WRITERS

Most writers may already know what SEO is. If not, SEO stands for *search engine optimization*. Basically, a site or blog that practices good SEO habits should improve its rankings in search engines, such as Google and Bing. Most huge corporations have realized the importance of SEO and spend enormous sums of time, energy and money on perfecting their SEO practices. However, writers can improve their SEO without going to those same extremes.

In this section, I will use the terms of *site pages* and *blog posts* interchangeably. In both cases, you should be practicing the same SEO strategies (when it makes sense).

Here are my top tips on ways to improve your SEO starting today:

1. **USE APPROPRIATE KEYWORDS.** Make sure that your page displays your main keyword(s) in the page title, content, URL, title tags, page header, image names and tags (if you're including images). All of this is easy to do, but if you feel overwhelmed, just remember to use your keyword(s) in your page title and content (especially in the first and last 50 words of your page).

2. **USE KEYWORDS NATURALLY.** Don't kill your content and make yourself look like a spammer to search engines by overloading your page with your keyword(s). You don't get SEO points for quantity but for quality. Plus, one of the main ways to improve your page rankings is when you...

3. **DELIVER QUALITY CONTENT.** The best way to improve your SEO is by providing content that readers want to share with others by linking to your pages. Some of the top results in search engines can be years old, because the content is so good that people keep coming back. So, incorporate your keywords in a smart way, but make sure it works organically with your content.

4. **UPDATE CONTENT REGULARLY.** If your site looks dead to visitors, then it'll appear that way to search engines too. So update your content regularly. This should be very easy for writers who have blogs. For writers who have sites, incorporate your blog into your site. This will make it easier for visitors to your blog to discover more about you on your site (through your site navigation tools).

5. **LINK BACK TO YOUR OWN CONTENT.** If I have a post on Blogging Tips for Writers, for instance, I'll link back to it if I have a Platform Building post, because the two complement each other. This also helps clicks on my blog, which helps SEO. The one caveat is that you don't go crazy with your linking and that you make sure your links are relevant. Otherwise, you'll kill your traffic, which is not good for your page rankings.

6. **LINK TO OTHERS YOU CONSIDER HELPFUL.** Back in 2000, I remember being ordered by my boss at the time (who didn't last too much longer afterward) to ignore any competitive or complementary websites—no matter how helpful their content—because they were our competitors. You can try basing your online strategy on these principles, but I'm nearly 100 percent confident you'll fail. It's helpful for other sites and your own to link to other great resources. I shine a light on others to help them out (if I find their content truly helpful) in the hopes that they'll do the same if ever they find my content truly helpful for their audience.

7. **GET SPECIFIC WITH YOUR HEADLINES.** If you interview someone on your blog, don't title your post with an interesting quotation. While that strategy may help get readers in the print world, it doesn't help with SEO at all. Instead, title your post as "Interview With (insert name here)." If you have a way to identify the person further, include that in the title too. For instance, when I interview poets on my Poetic Asides blog, I'll title those posts like this: Interview With Poet Erika Meitner. Erika's name is a keyword, but so are the terms *poet* and *interview*.

8. **USE IMAGES.** Many expert sources state that the use of images can improve SEO, because it shows search engines that the person creating the page is spending a little extra time and effort on the page than a common spammer. However, I'd caution anyone using images to make sure those images are somehow complementary to the content. Don't just throw up a lot of images that have no relevance to anything. At the same time...

9. **OPTIMIZE IMAGES THROUGH STRATEGIC LABELING.** Writers can do this by making sure the image file is labeled using your keyword(s) for the post. Using the Erika Meitner example above (which does include images), I would label the file "Erika Meitner headshot.jpg"—or whatever the image file type happens to be. Writers can also improve image SEO through the use of captions and ALT tagging. Of course, at the same time, writers should always ask themselves if it's worth going through all that trouble for each image or not. Each writer has to answer that question for him (or her) self.

10. **USE YOUR SOCIAL MEDIA PLATFORM TO SPREAD THE WORD.** Whenever you do something new on your site or blog, you should share that information on your other social media sites, such as Twitter, Facebook, LinkedIn, online forums, etc. This lets your social media connections know that something new is on your site/blog. If it's relevant and/or valuable, they'll let others know. And that's a great way to build your SEO.

Programmers and marketers could get even more involved in the dynamics of SEO optimization, but I think these tips will help most writers out immediately and effectively while still allowing plenty of time and energy for the actual work of writing.

BLOG DESIGN TIPS FOR WRITERS

Design is an important element to any blog's success. But how can you improve your blog's design if you're not a designer? I'm just an editor with an English Lit degree and no formal training in design. However, I've worked in media for more than a decade now and can share some very fundamental and easy tricks to improve the design of your blog.

Here are my seven blog design tips for writers:

1. **USE LISTS.** Whether they're numbered or bullet points, use lists when possible. Lists break up the text and make it easy for readers to follow what you're blogging.
2. **BOLD MAIN POINTS IN LISTS.** Again, this helps break up the text while also highlighting the important points of your post.
3. **USE HEADINGS.** If your posts are longer than 300 words and you don't use lists, then please break up the text by using basic headings.
4. **USE A READABLE FONT.** Avoid using fonts that are too large or too small. Avoid using cursive or weird fonts. Times New Roman or Arial works, but if you want to get "creative," use something similar to those.
5. **LEFT ALIGN.** English-speaking readers are trained to read left to right. If you want to make your blog easier to read, avoid centering or right aligning your text (unless you're purposefully calling out the text).
6. **USE SMALL PARAGRAPHS.** A good rule of thumb is to try and avoid paragraphs that drone on longer than five sentences. I usually try to keep paragraphs to around three sentences myself.
7. **ADD RELEVANT IMAGES.** Personally, I shy away from using too many images. My reason is that I only like to use them if they're relevant. However, images are very powerful on blogs, so please use them—just make sure they're relevant to your blog post.

If you're already doing everything on my list, keep it up! If you're not, then you might want to re-think your design strategy on your blog. Simply adding a header here and a list there can easily improve the design of a blog post.

GUEST POSTING TIPS FOR WRITERS

Recently, I've broken into guest posting as both a guest poster and as a host of guest posts (over at my Poetic Asides blog). So far, I'm pretty pleased with both sides of the guest posting process. As a writer, it gives me access to an engaged audience I may not usually reach. As a blogger, it provides me with fresh and valuable content I don't have to create. Guest blogging is a rare win-win scenario.

That said, writers could benefit from a few tips on the process of guest posting:

1. **PITCH GUEST POSTS LIKE ONE WOULD PITCH ARTICLES TO A MAGAZINE.** Include what your hook is for the post, what you plan to cover, and a little about who you are.

Remember: Your post should somehow benefit the audience of the blog you'd like to guest post.

2. **OFFER PROMOTIONAL COPY OF BOOK (OR OTHER GIVEAWAYS) AS PART OF YOUR GUEST POST.** Having a random giveaway for people who comment on a blog post can help spur conversation and interest in your guest post, which is a great way to get the most mileage out of your guest appearance.

3. **CATER POSTS TO AUDIENCE.** As the editor of *Writer's Market* and *Poet's Market*, I have great range in the topics I can cover. However, if I'm writing a guest post for a fiction blog, I'll write about things of interest to a novelist—not a poet.

4. **MAKE PERSONAL, BUT PROVIDE NUGGET.** Guest posts are a great opportunity for you to really show your stuff to a new audience. You could write a very helpful and impersonal post, but that won't connect with readers the same way as if you write a very helpful and personal post that makes them want to learn more about you (and your blog, your book, your Twitter account, etc.). Speaking of which...

5. **SHARE LINKS TO YOUR WEBSITE, BLOG, SOCIAL NETWORKS, ETC.** After all, you need to make it easy for readers who enjoyed your guest post to learn more about you and your projects. Start the conversation in your guest post and keep it going on your own sites, profiles, etc. And related to that...

6. **PROMOTE YOUR GUEST POST THROUGH YOUR NORMAL CHANNELS ONCE THE POST GOES LIVE.** Your normal audience will want to know where you've been and what you've been doing. Plus, guest posts lend a little extra "street cred" to your projects. But don't stop there...

7. **CHECK FOR COMMENTS ON YOUR GUEST POST AND RESPOND IN A TIMELY MANNER.** Sometimes the comments are the most interesting part of a guest post (no offense). This is where readers can ask more in-depth or related questions, and it's also where you can show your expertise on the subject by being as helpful as possible. And guiding all seven of these tips is this one:

8. **PUT SOME EFFORT INTO YOUR GUEST POST.** Part of the benefit to guest posting is the opportunity to connect with a new audience. Make sure you bring your A-game, because you need to make a good impression if you want this exposure to actually help grow your audience. Don't stress yourself out, but put a little thought into what you submit.

ONE ADDITIONAL TIP: Have fun with it. Passion is what really drives the popularity of blogs. Share your passion and enthusiasm, and readers are sure to be impressed.

SOCIAL MEDIA PRIMER FOR WRITERS

How to Use Social Media the Right Way

by Robert Lee Brewer

Beyond the actual writing, the most important thing writers can do for their writing careers is to build a writer platform. This writer platform can consist of any number of quantifiable information about your reach to your target audience, and one hot spot is social media.

Here's the thing: I think it's more important to chase quality connections than quantity connections on social media. More on that below.

So social media is one way to quantify your reach to your target audience. If you write poetry, your target audience is people who read poetry (often other folks who write poetry). If you write cookbooks, your target audience is people who like to cook.

And in both cases, you can drill down into more specifics. Maybe the target audience for the poetry book is actually people who read sonnets. For the cookbook, maybe it's directed at people who like to cook desserts.

4 SOCIAL MEDIA TIPS FOR WRITERS

Anyway, social media is one way to connect with your target audience and influencers (like agents, editors, book reviewers, other writers) who connect to your target audience. Sites like Facebook, Twitter, LinkedIn, YouTube, Pinterest, Goodreads, Red Room, and so many more–they're all sites dedicated to helping people (and in some cases specifically writers) make connections.

Here are my 4 social media tips for writers:

1. **Start small.** The worst thing writers can do with social media is jump on every social media site ever created immediately, post a bunch of stuff, and then quit because they're overwhelmed on the time commitment and underwhelmed by the lack of

response. Instead, pick one site, complete all the information about yourself, and start browsing around in that one neighborhood for a while.

2. **Look for connections.** Notice that I did not advise looking for leads or followers or whatever. Don't approach strangers online like a used car salesman. Be a potential friend and/or source of information. One meaningful connection is worth more than 5,000 disengaged "followers." Seriously.

3. **Communicate.** There are two ways to make a mistake here. One, never post or share anything on your social media account. Potential new connections will skip over your ghost town profile assuming your account is no longer active. Plus, you're missing an opportunity to really connect with others. The other mistake is to post a million (hopefully an exaggeration) things a day and never communicate with your connections. It's social media, after all; be social.

....

One meaningful connection is worth more than 5,000 disengaged 'followers.'

....

4. **Give more than you take.** So don't post a million things a day, but be sure to share calls for submissions, helpful information (for your target audience), fun quotes, great updates from your connections (which will endear you to them further). Share updates from your end of the world, but don't treat your social media accounts as a place to sell things nonstop. Remember: Don't be a used car salesman.

One final tip: Focus. Part of effective platform building is knowing your target audience and reaching them. So with every post, every status update, every Tweet, every connection, etc., keep focused on how you are bringing value to your target audience.

POPULAR SOCIAL NETWORKING SITES

The social media landscape is constantly shifting, but here are some that are currently popular:

- Bebo (http://bebo.com)
- Digg (http://digg.com)
- Facebook (http://facebook.com)
- Flickr (http://flickr.com)
- Google+ (http://plus.google.com)
- Habbo (http://habbo.com)
- Hi5 (http://hi5.com)
- Instagram (http://instagram.com)

- LinkedIn (http://linkedin.com)
- MeetUp (http://meetup.com)
- Ning (http://ning.com)
- Orkut (http://orkut.com)
- Pinterest (http://pinterest.com)
- Reddit (http://reddit.com)
- StumbleUpon (http://stumbleupon.com)
- Twitter (http://twitter.com)
- Yelp (http://yelp.com)
- YouTube (http://youtube.com)
- Zorpia (htttp://zorpia.com)

9 THINGS TO DO ON ANY SOCIAL MEDIA SITE

Not all social media sites are created the same. However, there are some things writers can do on any site to improve the quantity and quality of the connections they make online.

1. Use your real name. If the point of social media is to increase your visibility, then don't make the mistake of cloaking your identity behind some weird handle or nickname. Use your real name—or that is, use your real byline as it appears (or would appear) when published.

2. Use your headshot for an avatar. Again, avoid concealing your identity as a cartoon image or picture of a celebrity or pet. The rules of online networking are the same as face-to-face networking. Imagine how silly it would be to see someone holding up a picture of a pet cat while talking to you in person.

3. Complete your profile. Each site has different ways to complete this information. You don't have to include religious or political views, but you do want to make your site personal while still communicating your interest and experience in poetry. One tip: Give people a way to contact you that doesn't involve using the social networking site. For instance, an e-mail address.

4. Link to websites. If you have a blog and/or author website, link to these in your profile on all social media sites. After all, you want to make it as easy as possible for people to learn more about you. If applicable, link to your previously published books at points of purchase too.

5. Make everything public. As a poet, you are a public figure. Embrace that state of mind and make everything you do public on social media. This means you may have to sacrifice some privacy, but there are pre-Facebook ways of communicating private matters with friends and family.

6. Update regularly. Whether it's a status update or a tweet, regular updates accomplish two things: One, they keep you in the conversation; and two, they let people

you know (and people you don't know) see that you're actively using your account. Activity promotes more connections and conversations, which is what writers want on social media sites.

Give people a way to contact you that doesn't involve using the social networking site. For instance, an e-mail address.

---

7. Join and participate in relevant groups. One key to this tip is relevancy. There are lots of random groups out there, but the ones that will benefit you the most are ones relevant to your interests and goals. Another key is participation. Participate in your group when possible.

8. Be selective. Piggybacking on the previous tip, be selective about who you friend, who you follow, which groups you join, etc. Don't let people bully you into following them either. Only connect with and follow people or groups you think might bring you value—if not immediately, then eventually.

9. Evolve. When I started social media, MySpace was the top hangout. Eventually, I moved on to Facebook and Twitter (at the urging of other connections). Who knows which sites I'll prefer in 5 months, let alone 5 years, from now. Evolve as the landscape evolves. In fact, even my usage of specific sites has had to evolve as user behavior changes and the sites themselves change.

FINAL THOUGHT

If you have a blog, be sure to use it to feed your social media site profiles. Each new post should be a status update or tweet. This will serve the dual purpose of bringing traffic to your blog and providing value to your social media connections.

AUTHOR PLATFORM 2.0

....

by Jane Friedman

You've been through the drill already. You know about establishing your own website, being active on social media, plus networking up and down the food chain. You've heard all the advice about building your online and offline presence—and perhaps you've landed a book deal because of your strong platform.

But platform building is a career-long activity. It doesn't stop once your website goes live, or after you land a book deal. In fact, your continued career growth depends on extending your reach and uncovering new opportunities. So what's next?

I'll break it down into three categories:

- Optimize your online presence.
- Make your relationships matter.
- Diversify your content.

OPTIMIZE YOUR ONLINE PRESENCE

First things first. You need your own domain (e.g., JaneFriedman.com is the domain I own), and you should be self-hosted. If you're still working off Blogger or Wordpress.com, then you won't be able to implement all of my advice due to the limitations of having your site owned or hosted by someone else.

Once you truly own your site, hire a professional website designer to customize the look and feel to best convey your personality or brand. If you don't yet have a grasp on what your "personality" is, then hold off on a site revamp until you do. Or you might start simple, by getting a professionally designed header that's unique to your site.

Website and blog must-haves

Here's a checklist of things you should implement aside from a customized design.

- Readers should be able to subscribe to your blog posts via e-mail or RSS. You should be able to track the number of people who are signing up, and see when they are signing up.
- Customize the e-mails sent to anyone who subscribes to your blog posts. This can be done if you use Feedburner (free service) or MailChimp (free up to 2,000 names). Each e-mail that your readers receive should have the same look and feel as your website or whatever branding you typically use. You should also be able to see how many people open these e-mails and what they click on.
- If you do not actively blog, start an e-mail newsletter and post the sign-up form on your site. This way you can stay in touch with people who express interest in your news and updates. Again, MailChimp is a free e-mail newsletter delivery service for up to 2,000 names. You should also have e-newsletter sign-up forms with you at speaking engagements.
- Install Google Analytics, which offers valuable data on who visits your site, when they visit, what content they look at, how long they stay, etc.
- Add social sharing buttons to your site and each post, so people can easily share your content on Facebook, Google, etc. This functionality might have to be manually added if you have a self-hosted site.

Review your metrics

As I hope you noticed, many of the above items relate to metrics and measurement. Advance platform building requires that you study your numbers. Especially think about the following:

- How do people find your site? For example, if you're dumping a lot of energy into Twitter to drive traffic to your blog posts, but very few people visit your site from Twitter, that means your strategy is not working, and you might need to course correct.
- What content is the most popular on your site? This is like a neon sign, telling you what your readers want. Whatever it is, consider how you can build on it, repurpose it, or expand it.
- What causes a spike in traffic, followers, or subscribers? When you achieve spikes, you've done something right. How can you repeat the success?
- What's extending your reach? Most days, you're probably talking to the same crowd you were yesterday. But every so often, you'll be opened up to a new audience—and from that you can find new and loyal readers. Identify activities that have a broad ripple effect, and make you heard beyond your existing circles. (In Google Analytics, this would mean tracking how new visitors find you.)

Advanced social media monitoring and involvement

Just about everyone by now has a Facebook profile or page, a LinkedIn profile, a Twitter account, etc. But static profiles can only do so much for you. Social media becomes more valuable when you decide how to interact and how to facilitate valuable discussion among your followers. Here are a few areas to consider.

- Implement an advanced commenting system. Sometimes the most valuable part of a blog is having a comments section where people can contribute and interact with each other. But this usually means actively filtering the good comments from the bad. Using a robust system like Disqus or Livefyre (and paying for access to their filtering tools) can help you develop a quality discussion area that rewards the most thoughtful contributors.
- Add a forum or discussion board. Very popular bloggers, who may have hundreds of comments on a post, will often add a forum or discussion board so their community can interact in an extended way. If your site is Wordpress-based, plug-ins can help you add a forum to your site in one step. Or you can consider using a private Facebook group or Ning (ning.com) as the base for your community.
- Use HootSuite to be strategic with your social media updates. HootSuite is a free, Web-based software that helps you schedule updates primarily for Twitter, but also for other sites. It also helps you analyze the effectiveness of your tweets (e.g, how many people clicked on a link you tweeted?).
- Use Paper.li (free service) to automatically curate the best daily tweets, updates, and posts on whatever subject you're an expert on—based on the people or organizations you follow and trust. Sometimes curating is one of the best services you can provide for your community—not only do you provide valuable content, you help people understand *who else* provides valuable content!

A final word about social media: Everyone knows about the usual suspects (Facebook, Twitter, Google Plus). Make sure you're not missing a more niche, devoted community on your topic. For example, All About Romance (www.likesbooks.com) is a very popular site for readers and authors of romance.

MAKE YOUR RELATIONSHIPS MATTER

A key component to platform is the relationships you have and grow. Often when you see a successful author, it's only the *visible* aspects of their online presence or content that are apparent. What you can't see is all of the relationship-building and behind-the-scenes conversations that contribute to a more impactful and amplified reach.

Am I saying you have to know big-name people to have a successful platform? No! Do you need to build relationships with successful or authoritative people (or organizations/ businesses) in your community? Yes. Here's how to amplify your efforts.

Make a list of who's interacting with you the most

Regardless of where it's happening (on your site or on social media), take note of who is reading, commenting on, or sharing your content. These are people who are already paying attention, like what you're doing, and are receptive to further interaction.

If you're ignoring these people, then you're missing an opportunity to develop a more valuable relationship (which will likely lead to new ones), as well as reward and empower those you're already engaged with.

What does "rewarding" and "empowering" look like? You might drop a personal note, offer an e-book or product for free, or involve them somehow in your online content. You might have a special newsletter for them. Do what makes sense—there are many ways to employ this principle. Christina Katz, who teaches classes to writers, creates "Dream Teams" of writers who are selected from previous students. It's a great idea that rewards both Christina and the students she coaches.

Make a list of your mentors and how you can help them

You should have a list (or wish list!) of mentors. If not, develop one. We all have people who are doing something we dream of, or operate a few steps beyond where we're currently at.

> Do not approach this as something you're going to "get something" out of, or it will backfire.

If you're not already closely following your mentors on their most active channels of communication (blog, Twitter, Facebook, etc), then start. Begin commenting, sharing, and being a visible fan of what they do. Consider other ways you can develop the relationship, e.g., interview them on your blog or review their book. But most of all, brainstorm how you can serve them.

If you engage mentors in an intelligent way (not in a needy "look at me" sort of way), then you may develop a more meaningful relationship when they reach out to acknowledge your efforts. But be careful: Do not approach this as something you're going to "get something" out of, or it will backfire.

Do watch for opportunities that mentors will inevitably offer (e.g., "I'm looking for someone to help moderate my community. Who wants to help?") I once helped an author arrange a book event when he stopped in Cincinnati, and that helped solidify a relationship that had only been virtual up until that point.

Finally, don't forget a time-honored way to cozy up to mentors: offer a guest post for their blog. Just make sure that what you contribute is of the highest quality possible—more high quality than what you'd demand for your own site. If you bring a mentor considerable traffic, you'll earn their attention and esteem.

Look for partnerships with peers

Who is attempting to reach the same audience as you? Don't see them as competitors. Instead, align with them to do bigger and better things. You can see examples of partnership everywhere in the writing community, such as:

- Writer Unboxed website (where I participate)
- Jungle Red Writers blog
- The Kill Zone blog

We all have different strengths. Banding together is an excellent way to extend your platform in ways you can't manage on your own. When presented with opportunities to collaborate, say yes whenever you'll be exposed to a new audience or diversify your online presence.

Stay alert to your influencers and who you influence

There are many ways to identify important people in your community, but if you're not sure where to start, try the following.

- Blog rolls. Find just one blog that you know is influential. See who they're linking to and recommending. Identify sites that seem to be on everyone's "best of" list— or try searching for "best blogs" + your niche.
- Klout. This social media tool attempts to measure people's authority online by assigning a score. It will summarize who you influence, and who you are influenced by.
- If you use the Disqus commenting system, it will identify the most active commenters on your site.

DIVERSIFY YOUR CONTENT

Writers can easily fall into the trap of thinking only about new *written* content. It's a shame, because by repurposing existing content into new mediums, you can open yourself up to entirely new audiences.

For example, I have a friend who has a long solo commute by car, plus he walks his dogs while listening to his iPod. Nearly all of his media consumption is podcast driven. He rarely reads because his lifestyle doesn't support it. That means that if he can't get his content in audio form, he won't buy it.

Envision a day in the life of your readers. Are they likely to be using mobile devices? Tablets? (Guess what: Google Analytics tells you the percentage of mobile and tablet visits to your site!) Do your readers like to watch videos on YouTube? Do they buy e-books? Are they on Twitter?

If you adapt your content to different mediums, you will uncover a new audience who didn't know you existed. While not all content is fit for adaptation, brainstorm a list of all the content you currently own rights to, and think of ways it could be repurposed or redistributed.

If you adapt your content to different mediums, you will uncover a new audience who didn't know you existed.

A popular repurposing project for longtime bloggers is to compile and edit a compilation of best blog posts, and make it available as an e-book (free or paid). Some bloggers will even do that with a handful of blog posts that can serve as a beginner or introductory guide to a specific topic. Fiction writers: How about a sampler of your work in e-book or PDF form? Poets: How about a podcast of you reading some of your favorite poems?

Some forms or mediums you might want to explore:

- Creating podcasts and distributing through your own site (or via iTunes)
- Creating videocasts and distributing through YouTube or Vimeo (did you know that YouTube is now the No. 2 search engine?)
- Creating tips or lessons in e-mail newsletter form
- Creating PDFs (free or paid), and using Scribd to help distribute
- Creating online tutorials or offering critiques through tools such as Google Hangouts, Google Docs, and/or Screencast.com
- Creating slide presentations and distributing through SlideShare

The only limit is your imagination!

HOUSEKEEPING

On a final note, I'd like to share a few housekeeping tips that can help boost your image and authority online. While they may seem trivial, they go a long way in making a good impression and spreading the word about what you do.

- Get professional headshots that accurately convey your brand or personality—what people know you and love you for.
- For your social media profiles, completely fill out *all* fields and maximize the functionality. This is important for search and discoverability. For instance, on LinkedIn, add keywords that cover all of your skill sets, pipe in your Twitter account and blog posts, and give complete descriptions of all positions you've held. On Google Plus, list all the sites that you're a contributor for. On Facebook, allow people to subscribe to your public updates even if they aren't your friends.

- Gather updated testimonials and blurbs, and use them on your site and/or your social media profiles if appropriate.

However you decide to tackle the next stage of your platform development, ensure consistency. Whether it's your website, e-newsletter, Facebook profile, business cards, or letterhead, be consistent in the look and feel of your materials and in the message you send. Unless you are appealing to different audiences with different needs, broadcast a unified message no matter where and how people find you. Believe me—it doesn't get boring. Instead, it helps people remember who you are and what you stand for.

JANE FRIEDMAN is a former publishing and media exec who now teaches full-time at the University of Cincinnati. She has spoken on writing, publishing, and the future of media at more than 200 events since 2001, including South by Southwest, BookExpo America, and the Association of Writers and Writing Programs. Find out more at http://janefriedman.com.

BOB MAYER

The Hybrid Author and Changing Times

....

by Olivia Markham

In the fall of 2010, *New York Times* best-selling author Bob Mayer had already traditionally published over 40 books, but was frustrated with traditional publishing's slow schedule and unresponsiveness to change. So, he and now-business-partner Jen Talty formed what has become Cool Gus Publishing to publish his backlist as e-books. In January 2011, they sold 347 e-books. By July 2011, after a lot of hard work and long hours, they were selling 65,000 e-books a month, and by the end of 2011, they had sold over 400,000 e-books. In March of 2012, they were averaging 50,000 e-books a month, and had built a 7-figure indie publishing house in just two years.

This author has written a number of series—the Atlantis series, the Area-51 series, the Green Beret series, the Shadow Warrior series, the Presidential series, and, most recently, the Nightstalkers series. Some of his more recent titles have been *Chasing the Lost, The Jefferson Allegiance,* and *The Kennedy Endeavor.* From 2007 to 2011, he co-wrote three books with *New York Times* best-selling author Jennifer Crusie: *Don't Look Down; Agnes and the Hitman;* and *Wild Ride.* He's also written a number of nonfiction titles, including *The Novel Writer's Toolkit; Write It Forward: From Writer to Successful Author;* and (as a former Green Beret) *Who Dares Wins: Special Operations Strategies for Success,* and *The Green Beret Survival Guide.*

Now, after four years of self-publishing and about a dozen more books written and released as e-books—more than half of those self-published—we're asking Bob about his success in self-publishing as a Hybrid author (a term he coined), one who contracts with traditional publishers while also self-publishing.

What projects are you currently working on?

I'm writing my fourth Nightstalkers book. Which is interesting because although this interview is about self-publishing, my first three Nightstalker books were published by 47North, which is Amazon's science fiction imprint. This book is not part of that three-book contract, so the plus of self-publishing is, if Amazon doesn't pick it up, I can simply publish it myself. Even though I mainly "self" publish, I also believe in having multiple income streams. More importantly, publishing with Amazon increases my marketing footprint, as 47North has its own marketing arm.

What lead you to write Sci-Fi—the Atlantis series and the Area 51 series?

I just did a "True Lies" blog post (January 2014) about my four pillars of story: reading, my military background, history, and last, but not least, myths and legends. Atlantis is one of the most ancient myths, and Area 51 is a modern one. I'm interested in those stories. What's true? What's fiction? Is the line blurred? Actually, I put a lot more fact in my novels than most people suspect.

What would you liken your writing process to?

It's a creative flow. I trust my subconscious more and go with the flow. But I also focus more on pushing into the depth of my characters more. After almost 60 books written, I know a lot more about this than I did when I started. So if I'm starting to go in the wrong direction, I pick up on that immediately.

Any new projects on the horizon?

Series are the key to success. So I'm doing something momentous after 56 books. I'm wrapping several of my series into each other. I've already brought the main character from *The Green Berets: Chasing the Ghost* into my very successful Dave Riley Green Beret series, and they'll be together in future books. I've also brought my main two characters from my Cellar books into my Nightstalker books.

In my current *Nightstalkers*, I'm also integrating some aspects of *Psychic Warrior* and eventually wrapping it back to my No.1 bestselling Atlantis series. My head hurts to think of it, because we're talking pulling together a lot of people and story-lines, but so far it's working.

How did you get started writing?

I was living in the Orient studying martial arts and had some time on my hands. So I simply began writing to keep sane. I didn't think about getting published. I was more focused on simply telling a story.

Why did you decide to self-publish?

In late 2009 I looked at the publishing landscape and saw a lot of change on the horizon. I'd always described publishing as slow and techno-phobic, and that didn't bode well.

I also had the rights back to a lot of my backlist, and those books were sitting around doing nothing. Note that I didn't "self" publish. Jen Talty and I formed Cool Gus Publishing, because with the number of titles I have, it was impossible for me to do it myself. Also, I simply didn't want to do all that work because my primary work is being a writer. We now have published other authors. Jennifer Probst and Colin Falconer are doing quite well for us, and we have others whose sales are increasing.

In your opinion, what is the biggest benefit to self-publishing vs. traditional publishing?

Besides higher royalties [in self-publishing]? Creative and business control. We view ourselves as a publishing partnership where the author comes first. The author gets final say over content, cover, copy, marketing, price, etc. etc. We advise the authors, but ultimately they are the ones who create story, which is the content that is sold to readers. We facilitate that.

It's also much, much faster. I still see announcements in Publishers Marketplace about deals for publication two years out. Who knows what the landscape will be two years out? We just launched a bunch of backlist for Janice Maynard, a rising star in romance, and got 7 titles out in two months from the time we agreed to do it. We're in the digital age, and the business has to reflect that.

How has self-publishing made a difference in your writing career?

It's totally transformed it. I earn more than I ever did in traditional publishing, even when I was a *New York Times* bestseller. I get paid every month. I know exactly how much is coming in and from where.

I also believe it's changed the actual writing. I was worried when *Nightstalkers: The Book of Truths* came out (2013), because it didn't fit the traditional novel style, but readers have really liked it. I've found that readers want more information, shorter books, and are more open to free-flowing narrative, rather than the traditional five-part structure.

What is the secret to your success?

Lots of books and hard work. Every successful indie author I know works very, very hard. The best promotion is a good book; better promotion is more good books.

In your opinion, what is the hardest part of self-publishing a book?

Writing a good book. I think because it's relatively easy to self-publish, people take short cuts. When you had to fight to get an agent, an editor, and a publisher, you had to work hard on craft. I don't see people doing that as much. They just slap stuff up there and are shocked when it doesn't sell.

Readers are tougher than agents, editors, and publishers, so we have to work that much harder.

Where did you find your team of editors and cover artists?

We do our covers in-house. That was a steep learning curve, but one we've mastered. It involved a lot of back and forth with the author. We definitely want authors to be happy with their covers. And it has to pop in thumbnail.

We hire freelance editors as needed. It's the only thing we don't do inside of Cool Gus.

How do you market your books to reach readers and get real results?

That's the first question writers ask us when they consider Cool Gus. And we're honest—while there are things we can do, and we know how to work the system, it's extremely difficult to market fiction. While everything is happening faster, the truth is that marketing requires a long term plan. Consistency is key. Series are key. Finding your core group of readers and cultivating them is critical. My objective in 2014 is to focus much more on readers.

Any suggestions about how to find that core group of readers?

That's a big goal in 2014. To build up that core group, I'm doing my "True Lies" blog every Tuesday which is more personal than I have done in the past. We're building up our mailing list. I give out free Advance Reading Copies [ARCs] of upcoming books to fans, in the hope that they will write reviews.

Reviews are really important. What a lot of readers don't know is you can probably get a free e-book from an author if you promise to write a review. At least from authors who are "self" published.

Bottom line is that readers are the most important part of publishing, so we keep our focus on building our relationship with them.

How do you balance your writing time with everything else that goes with self-publishing?

The writing has to come first. I write in the mornings and spend the afternoon running my business. But I've learned you have to write whenever you can: on planes, in hotel rooms. Wherever. The easiest thing to slack off on is the writing. Everything about being an author is great; the writing is the hardest part.

What do you know now about the business that you wished you'd known when you started writing?

Take charge of your own career. No one else can do it for you. Network a lot. This is a people business. To think you can just sit back and write is naïve. I just got back from visiting my Amazon editor in New York City and Audible ACX in New Jersey (audiobooks). I learn from those meetings, and I also put a face on my books for them.

Practically speaking, I'd focus more on series. Very few authors can make a living doing stand alone books. Series, with intriguing characters, is key.

If you could pass on one piece of advice to other writers who are interested in self-publishing, what would it be?

Be willing to learn and change. Even in traditional publishing, I found few writers were willing to change what they were doing. I have my three rules of rule breaking for success: 1. Know the rule; 2.Have a good reason for breaking the rule; 3. Accept the consequences of breaking the rule.

We wrote a book on what we learned in digital publishing: *How We Made Our First Million on Kindle: The Shelfless Book.*

What advice would you give midlist authors who are looking to self-publish?

If you have more than a couple of titles, you really can't "self" publish. You can hire out a lot of it, but then you're dealing with multiple points of contacts. There are a lot of people trying to make money off writers. At Cool Gus we don't make money if our authors don't make money. They don't pay us anything. We have to believe in them, and we give them a single point of contact plus a lot of experience. We also provide the contacts we've cultivated over the years. We put our authors first, because they are the creators of content.

I'd recommend checking out many of the blogs about the business, and going to Kindleboards where there's a thread about pretty much every aspect of self-publishing with a lot of good information.

Understand you have to be an entrepreneur now, even if you're traditionally published. You're self-employed in the world of publishing. Focus on the business. Have a long-term goal and a business plan.

Distribution is no longer an issue; it's discoverability. I believe it's the best time ever to be a writer because the only person who can stop us is ourselves.

Olivia Markham is a freelance writer, with 4 years of experience. She's also a freelance editor with 10 years of experience and a Master's degree in Writing. She edits short stories and novels, and offers classes and workshops at conferences and elsewhere, to writers at all levels. She's a member of NW Independent Editors Guild, the National Writers Union, RWA, and the Oregon Writers Colony, and networks on Twitter, Facebook, LinkedIn, and Google+.

BEN GALLEY

Self-Publishing Was Not a Last Resort

....

by S.K. Valenzuela

Self-publishing has finally come into its own. New data on industry trends reveals the sizable niche that self-publishing has carved for itself and just how competitive Indie authors are in the marketplace.

This is fantastic news for Ben Galley, whose e-bookstore Libiro Books is one of the hottest developments in the self-publishing industry. Launched in September 2013, Libiro exclusively carries Indie books, offering self-published authors unique exposure and industry-leading royalties. I sat down with Ben to discuss the state of self-publishing and his work as an author, consultant, and book distributor.

Let's talk a bit about Ben Galley the author. What books do you have out currently, and what factors influenced your decision to pursue self-publishing?

Self-publishing wasn't a last resort to me—it was my first choice. When I put the final touches to my debut book in 2010, I wanted desperately to see it on the shelves, both digital and physical. But what I didn't want was to spend the next year or more going from publisher to publisher, and possibly failing in my quest. I was working a number of dead-end jobs at the time, and wanted out of the monotony. Self-publishing, for me, was a way of taking my future into my own hands, keeping more of my rights and royalties in the process. And so, in late 2010, I self-published my first book—The Written, a dark fantasy novel that was the first in what would turn out to be an epic series. In 2012 came the sequel Pale Kings, and in 2013, the final two books, Dead Stars and Dead Stars—Part Two. But I'm not stopping there. In the next few months I'm publishing a graphic novel version of The Written, and Shelf Help—a guide to self-publishing.

Shelf Help—your online self-publishing site—was launched after you had already released your first two books. What did you learn from your own experience that you wanted to share with other Indie authors?

> Purely and simply, I knew that self-publishing was difficult. When I first started out there was very little information on the subject. I had to do a lot of research and make quite a few mistakes to learn the path. But thanks to my trial and error, I managed to create a solid method of publishing, my Shelf Help method. I knew that there were other authors out there just like me, desperate to publish. I knew I could help them, and so I built and launched Shelf Help to do it!

As an Indie author, you proudly and passionately embrace the do-it-yourself aspects of publishing and marketing. Was there a time when you didn't feel confident in your ability to manage all of this, and how did you overcome it?

> There are always going to be times when you don't feel confident, or that you doubt yourself. The way I overcome them is by treating doubt positively. If I ever get doubts, I make myself sit down and address them, analyzing if they're at all rational. If they are, I end up refining something, or raising my game. Doubt can be useful, as long as you can rationalize!

If an author finds some aspect of this business intimidating—whether it's editing, or marketing, or managing an online presence, or all of the above—how can he or she build confidence?

> Feeling intimidated is perfectly understandable when it comes to self-publishing. It's a DIY process, and therefore there's a lot to do and a lot of pressure to do it right. Truth is, not every author can do everything, and not every author should. That's why I always recommend using professionals such as cover designers and editors to help take some of the work off my plate, and to reach a professional standard at the same time. It's worth the cost. Another way to build confidence is to just get stuck in and keep trying, especially with marketing and an online presence. Watch how the best do it, and then emulate! You'll soon build up the skills.

What's the most common question you've fielded on Shelf Help regarding Indie publishing, and how have you answered it?

> Besides: "How do I publish a book?", the most common question is: "What's the secret to success?" The answers to this question are quite straight forward. Firstly, you need to write the very best book you can. This is paramount, as this is what all your sales and reviews will ultimately be based on. Don't rush into publishing with something half-baked. Your book needs to move people, to ignite discussion, like all great books do. Secondly, you need to be professional. This means a great cover and highly-edited prose. You might have written the best book the world has ever seen, but it will fail if

its supporting elements are poorly executed. By sticking close to these two rules, you'll have a good shot at success.

Do you have any mentors that have inspired you in your career as an author, a self-publishing consultant, and now as the co-founder of an e-bookstore?

I have many indeed! My leap back into writing, way back in 2008, was thanks to the astounding prose of Mr Neil Gaiman. He's an incredible author, and has achieved so much in his time. My other inspirations are the greats, people like Henry Ford and Howard Hughes who saw the world at a different angle and spent their lives dedicated to invention and progress. That's what drives me—to be remembered alongside men like them.

Speaking of that e-bookstore, let's talk about Libiro Books. Can you tell the story of how you and co-founder Teague Fullick came up with the idea for an Indie-only e-bookstore?

Myself and Teague have worked together for a number of years now, and the result of Libiro was, believe it or not, the result of a long walk around a car-park and a heated discussion about the book industry. At that time, company after company was wading into the market, but there still seemed to be something lacking for me as an author—an eBook store that could offer better royalties and be more indie-centric, something to tick every box on the author's wish-list. I believe Teague's exact words were: "We should just build one." Teague wasn't joking, and we were suddenly very inspired. Thanks to Teague's background in web design and technology and my knowledge of the book industry, we spent the next few weeks furiously planning and building sites to see if it could be done. The weeks stretched into months, and after a year of hard work and investment, we finally cracked it. From that moment on, Libiro grew from an eager experiment into a fully fledged business and bookstore, launching in September 2013 to an eager audience.

As an Indie author yourself, what is the most exciting aspect of Libiro Books for authors?

I think the most exciting thing about Libiro is its royalty rate. Where most stores and publishing platforms offer 60-70%, we offer that bit extra—75%. What this means for the author is that they make more for every book sold, supporting them and spurring them on.

How is Libiro uniquely designed to help Indie authors reach and engage their readers?

Essentially, we provide a dedicated and exciting space. It can be hard for indie authors to stand out from the crowd at the immense stores like Amazon. At Libiro, we're indie-exclusive, which means that we only sell indie books by indie authors. This means authors have a better chance of standing out, as well as showcasing to the world what they're capable of. But that's not all—we've put a lot of effort into making a store that's not only beautiful to look at but easy to use. We also like to put a bit of fun into the store, and inject our personalities. This means that readers are also getting a great experience, and return time and time again.

Amazon continues to be such a dominant force in the e-publishing world. As authors weigh their publishing strategies, what are some of the advantages to offering their books in multiple marketplaces and for multiple e-reader platforms?

The simple fact of the matter is that availability is more important than exclusivity. Amazon is a brilliant and dominant force, but its market share isn't 100%, and isn't ever likely to be. By being exclusive to just one store, an author runs the risk of alienating readers who use other stores and read on other devices. Plus, availability also means a higher chance of discovery and alternate revenue streams.

Self-publishing opens doors for so many authors, and while this is one of its most profound advantages, it's also a double-edged sword. How can Indie authors gain visibility in a crowded marketplace?

That's a good question. Not only can it be hard to stand out without the big marketing punch of the publishing houses, but there are many readers out there that are of the opinion that all self-published books are poor quality. I know for a fact this isn't true, and it's a stigma I'm constantly campaigning against. The key to shrugging off such stigma, and to standing out, is again down to a damn good book and professionalism. Good reviews and word-of-mouth are hugely important to indies and can really help us to climb the ranks towards the bestseller spots. That's why we need to nail top notch quality. Visibility is also down to perseverance in your marketing. There are days when progress seems non-existent, but all it means is that you have to keep reassessing and keep working. As they say—hard work pays off!

How do you think traditional categories and boundaries between genres will shift as authors refine their niche markets? Is this something you're already seeing?

Absolutely. Publishers are naturally cautious about taking on new books, as it means a financial risk. But indie authors, on the other hand, can publish cheaply and quickly, and we can also publish whatever we want. Occasionally, yes, this can be a bad thing, but what it means is that even the smallest niches and strangest sub-genres are experiencing the time of their lives. With so much literature being poured onto the market, the variety and experimentation has become endless. It's an exciting time for readers as well as authors, as the lines are now well and truly, and gloriously, blurred.

What's the most exciting trend you see in self-publishing right now?

The most exciting trend in my mind would be the trend towards hybrid publishing deals. It signifies a change of mind for traditional publishers, as well as an evolution of the traditional way of doing business. Indies are increasingly more prevalent in the bestsellers these days, and publishers are taking notice. They've seen that there is value in successful indie authors that go out and build fan bases by themselves. Authors like Hugh Howey and Amanda Hocking are now landing deals with publishers that are very unusual indeed—involving higher royalties and varying ebook and print rights. In other words, joining forces in a near-equal and profitable way.

Where can authors find out more about you, Shelf Help, and Libiro Books?

You can find out more about me and my books at www.bengalley.com, or on Twitter @BenGalley. Shelf Help can be found at www.shelfhelp.info, and Libiro is ready and waiting at www.libiro.com!

S.K. Valenzuela is an author, freelance writer, and marketing consultant. She is the author of the Silesia Trilogy, a New Adult sci-fi adventure series, and the co-founder of the SisterMuses imprint. She has served as a judge for the Writer's Digest Self-Published Book Awards for several years. You can find her blogging about writing and the creative life at www.sistermuses.com, keep current with her works in progress at www.skvalenzuela.com, and follow her on Twitter at @skvalenzuela.

HUGH HOWEY

This Brave New World

of Indie Publishing

by Maureen Dillman

Hugh Howey, best known for his popular sci-fi series *Wool*, made history when he refused to bow to traditional publishing pressures by the major houses, and instead issued his own terms. He's a shining example of what can happen when an indie creator sticks by their principles and doesn't lose sight of what writing is all about—telling a story. But how did Howey get there, and why did he feel that a partnership between publishers and authors was so important? After hearing so much about him across the interwebs, I was eager for a chance to ask him about his journey through self-doubt and obscurity, to land a major publishing contract with Simon & Schuster on his own terms.

Did you ever have doubts that you would achieve success by publishing independently?

Every single day. I still do. But I would have these doubts however I published. I had these doubts as I queried my first book and signed with a small publisher. I never expected to make a living doing this. It's a passion. I feel the same way about photography, except that hobby costs me money. How's this: If writing was something that required monthly dues, I'd still pay to do it. I'm not in this to get rich, and I can't imagine anyone with that goal surviving the heartbreak of the years of obscurity. You have to write because you love it. That's my opinion, anyway.

How do you tackle self-doubt?

I don't. It tackles me. It's crippling. And the more success I have, the more I have to ignore the size of my audience and tell myself that I'm just writing for my wife and my mom. No one is ever going to see this. I'm safe here.

I'm like that kid who hides under the table and thinks if he can't see anyone, no one can see him back. That attitude gets me through the writing process. And then I tackle the publishing process as if millions of people will see this."

What would you say to someone else currently battling with self doubt or the harsh critics and naysayers in their lives?

I've coined a new phrase to help myself deal with this: Huggers gonna hug. Fill yourself with love, even if you don't feel it at first, especially if you don't feel it at first. Understand that what people think of you *has nothing to do with you*. It has everything to do with them. It's not your business. Only you know who you are and what you're capable of. Concentrate on that. And feel love and pity for the people who bring negativity into the world. Be thankful that this isn't you.

Would you suggest that writers test their abilities in different styles, genres, or age categories?

Absolutely! Until you've tried it, you don't know if you like it or have an affinity for it. Don't keep punching the same ticket hoping for a different result. One of the biggest mistakes I see from new writers is sequelitis. Now that they have that first book and those characters they love, they keep writing in that world. Which leaves them selling their first book over and over, and that won't be their strongest book. Diversify. Explore. Try different POVs and tenses. Try different length works.

Do you agree that most writers generally can't make a living with their writing?

Yes, but only because most writers won't put the hours in. They won't dedicate themselves to this. This is like any other art. If you expect to pick up a paintbrush or a guitar and knock out a masterpiece, you aren't going to make it. You're going to get frustrated. How many people can write ten novels before they care about their first sale? Not many. And the reason people have this misconception about their chances is simple: We all spend a good amount of our lives writing. We think we have this nailed. But we haven't even started yet. Not until you get through that first draft.

The writers who approach this with passion and conviction can make a living at it. Those are precisely the ones I see doing well. How bad do you want this? Ask yourself that every day.

There's been a lot of speculation to this as of late, but do you feel the current abundance of self-published works is hurting the industry?

Not at all. Nor do I think my ability to surf the web and find interesting content is affected by the millions of new websites and blogs that go up every week. Stifling voices is a far greater concern. And as publishers move toward the Hollywood model of gambling on blockbusters instead of nurturing new writers, self-publishing becomes even more important. It's a fantastic way to start a career, build an audience, and improve one's craft. Musicians play small gigs and even street corners before they make it. Now authors have a similar path to success. It's no guarantee, but it has opened the door for thousands of writers to make a living doing what they love. And it has rewarded readers with affordable and exciting content.

Were you ever concerned that your independently published work would be judged as mediocre as compared to traditionally published work?

I don't know of anyone who assumes that every book in a bookstore is a great book. You have to read to know if it appeals to you. The opinions I care about are from those who pick up my book and give it a chance.

This is going to sound heretical and a bit nuts, and I totally get that, but one of the reasons I turned down offers from major publishers is that I worried about the stigma of being with a Random House or a HarperCollins. I explained this to editors at those houses during negotiations. My book was already a *New York Times* bestseller with a major film deal from Ridley Scott. These things mean more to me knowing that it was readers who made it happen, not a major publisher with a huge marketing budget. It happened organically. It was word of mouth. It may even have had something to do with the story I wrote. Signing all of that away would be to obscure the communal nature of the work's success. Even 7-figure offers weren't enough for me to turn my back on that.

....

We all spend a good amount of our lives writing. We think we have this nailed. But we haven't even started yet. Not until you get through that first draft.

....

As a small business owner and the employee of a large corporation, both of whom make the same amount and work the same hours, and see which of them takes more pride in their work.

Who do you feel truly determines success in the publishing industry? The publishers? The distributors? The public? Other writers?

The public, without a doubt. It isn't even close. I've watched publishers market the heck out of books only to see them flounder. The readers are in charge.

Now moving on to the thing a lot of our readers are probably curious about, your groundbreaking contract with Simon & Schuster. Can you tell us a little more about the contracts negotiations?

We told publishers what we wanted. They offered piles of money instead. We kept saying no.

Really? What were your reasons for holding out? What was missing from those first rounds of contracts?

All three rounds of offers wanted the digital rights to WOOL. I don't think any author should sign those rights over until the 25% of net ceiling is broken. Publishers are making record profits right now because of the rise of eBooks. They are raking in those profits by taking advantage of writers. Hollywood went through this a few years ago, and a strong union helped fight for fairer deals for streaming content. Unfortunately, writers are represented by a union that doesn't care about them. Our union spends all of its time fighting for bookstores and publishers. Because the people at the top are getting fat advances that effectively pay them higher royalties. New authors, meanwhile, are stuck. The rich get richer and the poor get poorer.

Even when my advance would've put me in the 'richer' category, I still believed this. We should stand together and demand change, demand that those record profits go toward helping nurture the careers of aspiring writers.

After you turned down the first round of offers from traditional publishers did you feel that you had made a terrible mistake?

I went back and forth. It wasn't easy. And we went through three rounds of offers over the course of a year, with 5-figure deals turning into 6-figure deals turning into 7-figure deals. It was never easy, but my agent and I held to our convictions. And our spouses were awesome and supportive (even if they gave us funny looks now and then).

What made you finally choose to sign with Simon & Schuster?

Simon & Schuster, which hadn't been a part of this exchange to that point, came to us with a brave and amazing deal. It was exactly what we had asked for. I think they deserve a lot of credit for treating us like partners rather than something to acquire. We got a print-only deal that left all other rights with me (digital, audio, foreign, everything). It also has a finite term, and so I get those print rights back six years from now. This is what authors deserve. It just requires walking away, which is scary. I can attest to that.

What excited you most about teaming up with a traditional publisher? What concerned you the most?

I was excited about trying something new. I love to diversify and experiment. I enjoy seeing so many sides of the publishing business. And even though my print on demand book was stocked in Barnes & Nobles and indie bookstores like Powell's and elsewhere, I knew that this would help new readers discover my story. That was exciting.

What concerned me the most was all the extra work being with a traditional publisher entails! Book tours and promo videos and a surge of interviews. It was intense. I missed the self-publishing days when I could spend most of my time just writing.

And lastly before we let you go, what would you say to other writers who are embarking on their own self-pub journey?

I'd really ask yourself why you are doing this. There are no guarantees. There is a lot of luck involved. Talent can go unnoticed. Hacks like me can have phenomenal success. Can you handle writing every day without promise of a single reader? If you can, and you stick with it, you can't lose.

Maureen Dillman is the author of *Crafting aProfessional Independent Novel* as an eBook, and a contributing author and layout and design editor of *The Writing Life*. Maureen currently lives in the San Francisco Bay Area with her husband, and rescue dog. When not writing, she enjoys exploring science and technology, cycling, and snapping pictures of the world around her.

DELILAH MARVELLE

Making the Choice to Switch

....

by Olivia Markham

Delilah Marvelle knows how to find and use unique historical facts. She combines those details to create historical romance with a twist. Her unusual characters and plotting keep readers glued to the pages. Her first books were traditionally published, beginning in 2008. She's authored eight novels and two novellas in her three series—the Scandal series, the Rumor series, and the School of Gallantry series. In March 2013, she switched to self-publishing, coming out with *Lady of Pleasure*, the third book in the School of Gallantry series. To many of her writing friends, this seemed very brave. Later that year, she published *Romancing Lady Stone*, a School of Gallantry novella. She's the winner of *Romantic Times* Reviewer's Choice for Best Sensual Historical Romance of 2011 for *Prelude to a Scandal* (the Scandal series) and had Booklist name her historical romance *Forever and a Day* (the Rumor series) as one of the Top 10 Romances of 2012.

The author isn't afraid to tackle sensitive and complex subjects, but does so tastefully, with strong unique heroines, tantalizing heroes, and witty dialogue. People of the 1830s weren't much different from the people of today, and Delilah paints them with a deftness that shows them having all the passions that struggle and strain beneath the surface, especially in such a tightly laced, and unforgiving era in society.

When Delilah isn't writing, of course, she's digging through inappropriate research books that include anything in history having to do with courtesans, sexual contraptions that were never properly used, and other fascinating uncensored history that never made it into college textbooks.

What inspired you to write Prelude to a Scandal, the first book in the Scandal series, released in 2011?

My reasoning for writing Prelude to a Scandal extends to my genuine fascination toward human behavior and history itself. People have a tendency to think that people in the past were somehow different from the people of today. The more you dig into history, however, the more you begin to realize that the only difference between the people of the past and the people of today is our environment. In the end, we emotionally respond to the world around us in the same way.

After reading Casanova's memoires as well as My Secret Life (by Anonymous), I realized that these two men had serious sexual issues—what we today would identify as sexual addiction. The only difference is that in history, the only name they might have had for sexual addiction is what we know as the "rake." And with that thought and my genuine need to explore a topic most historical romances would shy away from, my hero, Bradford, was born.

What projects are you currently working on?

I am currently finishing up Book 4 in my School of Gallantry series, Night of Pleasure. The entire series centers on a school that educates men in the art of love and seduction. It explores the sexy and outrageous aspects of romance based on real history.

Any new projects on the horizon?

I'll be releasing a sizable novel by early 2015 that will introduce my upcoming Whipping Society series which will be my longest running series, to date. We're talking as many as 10 books (or more, depending on how readers respond to it). It's based on real history and will center on a brothel dedicated to the art of pain (historical BDSM). It's fascinating history and gives me so much to play with.

What would you liken your writing process to?

I first do all my historical research prior to writing a new book. Once that's done, I sit down and write. I'm a pantster. Which means that when I have an idea, I build my characters around it and write by the seat of my pants. I usually don't know anything about my characters and learn more about them as I write. Obviously, I scrap a lot of what I write as a result of that, but it's an exciting process I enjoy every single time. Because to me, my characters turn into real people. Like real people, you have to spend time with them to get to know them. And that's what I do.

Without knowing who they are, I spend time with them and find out who they are. I find if I know too much of what is going to happen in the story, I lose interest. I want to be surprised. Because I know if I'm surprised, then my readers will be. And that's what I strive for. To surprise my readers every single time.

Why did you decide to self-publish?

Hoo-boy. This is going to be rather long winded. Why did I self-publish? Because too much of the business has changed, but not much of New York has. I'm crushed knowing it. After all, no one understands how to edit and create the product better than they do. Part of the problem with New York is that they've created outrageous costs for themselves, like having expensive leases in the most expensive area in the United States: New York City. Historically, it made a lot of sense. It was the hub of how business was run.

Now? Everything has gone digital. So with publishing not being grounded to snail mail or one area, the idea of paying multi-million dollar leases to maintain their "business" and then rationalizing it by taking from an author's check 92 percent for print and 75 percent for digital is just astounding. And that's just one way they're not financially handling the digital revolution.

In addition, publishers have created a serious quandary for themselves by allowing distributors and bookstores to control everything. In what line of business does it make sense to send out a product to a store and when the product doesn't sell, the store destroys that product (the stripping of print books) and then gets money back because it didn't do its job of selling the book? Not only is it environmentally disturbing, but the bookstores get away with not being responsible for their sales. If a bookstore can't sell a book, guess what? They make the publisher (and ultimately the author) pay for it. Financially and environmentally, it's not a rational way of running a business anymore. And yet, no one seems to want to make any changes.

In self-publishing, the only control I don't have is who buys the book.

The bottom line is this: my hourly wage with a traditional publishing company turned out to be less than minimum wage with almost every book I've published, given the amount of time I've put in. Why would any rational person continue to put in any hours knowing that those hours are never rewarded?

It was pretty obvious what I needed to do. In exchange for the money I didn't make via traditional publishing, New York did teach me how to be a better writer. They taught me the business. But this is a business, and my love for traditional publishing has no place when it comes down to what I need to do to succeed. It's me or them. And guess what? I chose me. I basically gave myself a raise.

In your opinion, what is the biggest benefit to self-publishing vs. traditional publishing?

The biggest benefit is getting control of the product from beginning to end. That wasn't the case with traditional publishing. Not only was the writing sometimes out of my control, but I had no say on covers, prices, distribution, marketing or when the book was going to be released. It's a lot not to be in control of. In self-publishing, the only control I don't have is who buys the book.

How has self-publishing made a difference in your writing career?

I feel like I've finally returned to enjoying writing the way I used to. It's a combination of a sense of pride and joy that when I finish a book, I know exactly what is going to happen to it. It's incredible to feel rejuvenated and excited about the writing process all over again.

What is the secret to your success?

There is no one answer to what makes me a success. But I will say the one thing that has helped me get to where I am is plain old hard work. From beginning to end. I challenge myself to write the best book I can every single time. I also believe in making time for my readers.

Whether it's fan mail, or on Twitter or Facebook, I try to interact with the people who make it possible to be successful. Without them, there is no me. So I always look to give them time and genuinely show my love.

In your opinion, what is the hardest part of self-publishing a book?

Believe it or not, I'd say writing the dang book and making sure it's what you want to give to the readers. Because I now hire my editors, I get the final say. Not the editor. So it's all on me, and I think that's the hardest part of self-publishing. There's no one else to take the blame but you.

How do you market your books to reach readers and get real results?

Although I do BookBub, blog tours, and advertise with *Romantic Times* magazine, I've actually slowed down on my marketing. I've grown my audience to a point that I can announce a book is out via my newsletter, Twitter, and Facebook, and it drives sales. That said, I haven't hit the New York Times (NYT) or USA Today lists, but honestly, I don't feel like I need to. I'm thrilled with the money I'm making. My readers treat me well.

How do you balance your writing time with everything else that goes with self-publishing?

I always dedicate one day a week to online stuff and self-publishing stuff that needs attention and leave the rest to writing. Sometimes that fluctuates. I may have to spend an entire week dedicated to self-publishing items on my agenda, but I find by setting boundaries for myself and ensuring that I am always focusing on my writing, everything falls into place. Every time.

I can always use more hours in the day, but I never feel like I'm abusing my hours. Which makes a big difference when an author is self-publishing.

Are you still repped by literary agent Don Maass and what has that been like?

Yes, Donald Maass is still my agent. He's been incredibly supportive of the route I've taken. Working with him from the beginning was a dream. He knows so much about the industry and writing itself, I feel I'm constantly growing as professional. Although I'm not publishing traditionally anymore, that isn't to say I've turned my back on it and Don knows that.

If you could pass on one piece of advice to other writers who are interested in self-publishing, what would it be?

Have patience with your career. A lot of authors go into self-publishing thinking that if they don't make money off of the first one or two or three or four books they put out, they're a failure. And that's just not true. It takes time. You simply have to deliver quality every time. It took Nora Roberts 16 years to get to number one using the traditional publishing route. That seems like a lifetime to people in the self-publishing world. And it is. But writing is a life-long career. It's usually not a quick roaring success story.

I like the fact that my career has been slowly evolving into its own success, year after year, as opposed to getting slapped with the *New York Times* and *USA Today* listing right away. Because I'm learning so much by my disappointments, failures, and successes. I'm learning about my writing, my brand, and what makes my readers happy. Over time, if a self-published author has 30 books and never hits a list, but is consistently selling 5 books a day for all 30 books, that's dang good money. Better money than an author would see from New York.

Olivia Markham is a freelance writer, with 4 years of experience. She's also a freelance editor with 10 years of experience and a Master's degree in Writing. She edits short stories and novels, and offers classes and workshops at conferences and elsewhere, to writers at all levels. She's a member of NW Independent Editors Guild, the National Writers Union, RWA, and the Oregon Writers Colony, and networks on Twitter, Facebook, LinkedIn, and Google+.

SELF-PUBLISHING COMPANIES

Finding a self-publishing company willing to work with you on your book project is relatively easy. However, some self-publishing companies are better fits for your specific project than others. For instance, some companies may specialize in e-publishing but not do much in print. Others may have a long history in print but not cover every platform you want in digital publishing.

On top of that, some self-publishing companies offer an array of extra services, including assistance with editing, proofing, design, promotion, and more. Depending on the goals for your self-published book, you may or may not want to spend a lot of money on these extras. Since pricing can add quick if you do go with these extras, shop around before settling on the first company you find.

You may find that extra expenses for book design are more affordable by using a freelance designer. Also, editing-related expenses may be better serviced by a freelance editor. Check pricing and experience before spending a lot of money you may never recoup.

If you're unsure of what reasonable freelance rates are for a service, check out the "How Much Should I Charge?" pay rate chart. It lists various services with their most common pay scales, including highs, lows, and averages.

KEEP IN MIND

Self-publishing requires a lot of research and iniative. After all, self-publishers wear more hats than anyone else in publishing: author, publisher, marketer, publicist, accountant, designer, editor, and more. While writers can see that success is possible by reading the interviews in this book, it should also be noted that it's a competitive business. As such, avoid letting any service provider "sweep you off your feet" and/or put "stars in your eyes" when it comes to self-publishing. Rather, stay grounded and price conscious.

Writers can have a very successful self-publishing experience, but the whole point behind self-publishing is that they're now in control of the business side of publishing, in addition to the writing. As a business owner, do your due diligence and research which options are best for your book project.

1 CREATIVE ADVANTAGE

311 W. Main St., Sun Prairie WI 53590-2909. (608)834-8291. **Website:** dwightclough.com. **Contact:** Dwigth Clough, ghostwriter/publisher. Estab. 1982. Experience in writing, rewriting, editing, and ghostwriting services specializing in life story, Christian inspirational, educational, devotional, and leadership books. Services include any or all of the following: book planning, concept development, writing, rewriting, editing, self-publishing on Create Space and Kindle (including book cover design, ISBN, bar code, print on demand). Limited web development services available as well. National award-winning writer; experienced, published author.

48 HOUR BOOKS

2249 14th St. SW, Akron OH 44314. (800)231-0521. **E-mail:** info@48hrbooks.com. **Website:** www.48hrbooks.com. Offers services including PDF proof, b&w interior pages, b&w interior photos, full-color covers, and more.

ADDITIONAL INFORMATION "By simply uploading a ms and selecting various options available, authors will be supplied with a professionally printed, designed, and perfect-bound book at whatever quantity they desire, shipped in 48 hours."

ABBOTT PRESS

1663 Liberty Dr., Bloomington IN 47403. (866)697-5310. **Website:** www.abbottpress.com.

ADDITIONAL INFORMATION "Abbott Press offers publishing services that will help your book stand out in the marketplace. Throughout the entire publishing process you have the freedom to determine when and how your book is published. No matter if your goal is to publish for family and friends or advance an already successful writing career, we can help you achieve your goals."

SHAILA ABDULLAH

8408 Dulac Dr., Austin TX 78729. (512)924-7674. **E-mail:** info@myhouseofdesign.com. **Website:** www.myhouseofdesign.com. **Contact:** Shaila Abdullah, owner. Estab. 1995. Offers web, multimedia, and print services.

ADDITIONAL INFORMATION Services for web & multimedia include websites, content management systems, Wordpress sites, landing pages, book launch campaigns, e-mail campaigns, e-newsletters, social media pages, web banners and ads, multimedia demos, presentations, and online courses. Services for print include book covers, book interiors, book design, e-book design, flyers and sell sheets, postcards, posters, business cards, stationery, ads, brand, and identity.

ABSOLUTE LOVE PUBLISHING

6044 Mesa Verde Circle, Austin TX 78749. **E-mail:** editor@absolutelovepublishing.com. **Website:** www.absolutelovepublishing.com. **Contact:** Sarah Hackley, editor. Estab. 2009.

ADDITIONAL INFORMATION "Our mission is to create and publish projects promoting goodness in the world. Absolute Love and its imprint, Spirited Press, offer popular categories of books to change your life. We can also offer reviewing and editing services."

ACCURATE WRITING & MORE

16 Barstow Lane, Hadley MA 01035. (413)586-2388. **E-mail:** shel@principledprofit.com. **Website:** www.frugalmarketing.com. **Contact:** Shel Horowitz, owner. Estab. 1982. Offers book marketing and book shepherding services.

ADDITIONAL INFORMATION For book marketing, develops marketing strategy and individualized marketing plans for authors, books, and book series. For book shepherding, helps make the decision to publish traditionally, self-publish, e-publish, or publish through a subsidy publisher and to implement the chosen strategy.

A FONTLIFE PUBLICATION, LLC

5809 Lunenberg Dr., Raleigh NC 27603. (919)604-5828. **E-mail:** info@fontlifepublications.com. **Website:** fontlifepublications.com. **Contact:** Victor M. Font, Jr., owner. Estab. 2012. "A FontLife Publication, LLC is a Christian-based, family-owned publishing organization with a passion for discovering unknown authors. We provide self-publishing, editorial, marketing, education, and Web development/eCommerce services for authors primarily writing for the Christian, Inspirational, Technology, Business, Children, and Leadership genres. We'll consider any book, however, in any genre, that we find interesting and meets our family-friendly standards. We do not publish graphic material and language. We pay authors the highest royalties you'll find anywhere! We are known for personal service, editorial excellence, and dedication to detail, handling all aspects of publishing including editing, design, distribution, and printing: both Print-on-Demand (1 book at a time) and offset (larger print runs); copyright registration and e-Book conversion. We provide professional writers, out-of-print writers, and aspiring writers with high-quality books and e-Books. With our help, even non-writers can turn their ideas into marketable, high-quality publications ready for distribution on the Internet, in bookstores, and specialty shops around the world."

AMADOR PUBLISHERS, LLC

611 Delamar NW, Albuquerque NM 87107. **E-mail:** zelda@amadorbooks.com. **Website:** www.amadorbooks.com. **Contact:** Zelda Gatuskin, editor-in-chief. Estab. 1986.

ADDITIONAL INFORMATION Offers ms review service, developmental editing, book design, cover design, custom website design, and complete self-publishing packages under Worldwind Books imprint.

ARBOR BOOKS

244 Madison Ave., #254, New York NY 10016. (877)822-2500. **E-mail:** info@arborbooks.com. **Website:** www.arborbooks.com. **Contact:** Marketing Director: Olga Vladimirov.

ADDITIONAL INFORMATION "Arbor Books is a full-service ghostwriting and book-packaging company with a full-time staff of 15 writers, designers, and publicists, as well as 85 subcontractors, including the world's top printers, distributors, and other publishing experts and services. Arbor Books ghostwrites and publishes fiction and nonfiction including business books, novels, children's books, memoirs, and every other literary form and genre. Arbor Books services include ghostwriting, editing, rewriting, proofreading, research, typesetting, cover design, registrations (copyright, Library of Congress, ISBN, Books In Print), getting reviews and endorsements, printing, e-books, audio books, POD (print on demand) books, book marketing, kits, press releases, booking TV and radio programs, book and author publicity, speaking tours and book signings, negotiating with producers and agents, and more. Cost: Submit quote request online or contact by phone. See website for additional information

ARCTICHOUSE PUBLISHING

P.O. Box 2949, Kingston NY 12402. **E-mail:** arctichousepublishing@gmail.com. **Website:** arctichousepublishing.com. **Contact:** Dorothy Wills-Raftery, publisher. Estab. 2011.

ADDITIONAL INFORMATION Offers a complete one-stop shop of professional services including editing, proofing, illustration, layout and design, ISBN and Copyright registration, and printing services to bring a book concept to a printed reality the author can then market.

ART BOOKBINDERY LTD.

Suite 5-1377 Border St., Winnipeg Manitoba R3H 0N1 Canada. (866)944-2999. **E-mail:** info@artbookbindery.com. **Website:** www.artbookbindery.com.

ADDITIONAL INFORMATION "Our self-publishing company is Empowering Writers to Self Publish™ by simplifying the self-publishing process while providing the highest level of customer service, detailed information on the self-publishing process, expert advice, technical support, creative cover design, and the highest quality book printing and binding; all at an affordable price."

ARTISAN BOOKWORKS

Sequim WA 98382. (425)954-5277. **E-mail:** contact@artisanbookworks.com. **Website:** www.artisanbookworks.com. **Contact:** Kelly Lenihan, publisher. Estab. 2008.

ADDITIONAL INFORMATION "If you're considering self-publishing your book but don't want to jump through all the hoops yourself and would prefer to partner with a small, artisan publisher, Artisan Bookworks can help. We offer all-inclusive packages as well as an array of editorial and book-formatting services, enabling you to customize your experience at each stage of your publishing journey. Whether you simply need your book formatted for print or digital production, or everything in between—from copyediting to final cover design—you're in good hands with Artisan Bookworks."

ASTA PUBLICATIONS

P.O. Box 1735, Stockbridge GA 30281. (678)814-1320. **Fax:** (678)814-1370. **E-mail:** info@astapublications.com. **Website:** www.astapublications.com.

ADDITIONAL INFORMATION "Our mission is to continue building Asta Publications into company that is respected by our authors, our clients, and our peers, while maintaining our firm resolve to effectively deliver a superior product."

AUTHOR HOUSE

1663 Liberty Dr., Bloomington IN 47403. (888)519-5121. **E-mail:** authorsupport@authorhouse.com. **Website:** www.authorhouse.com. Offers one-on-one author support, custom full-color cover, custom interior design, ISBN assignment, electronic proof, online distribution, bookstore availability, and more. Packages start at $749 for paperback/hardcover, $899 for children's/color book, and $349 for e-book publishing.

ADDITIONAL INFORMATION Also offers public relations, direct marketing, custom domain name, and more. Standard packages include author copy.

AVENTINE PRESS

55 E. Emerson St., Chula Vista CA 91911. (866)246-6142. **E-mail:** info@aventinepress.com. **Website:** www.aventinepress.com. **Contact:** Keith Pearson. POD press offering electronic proofs, custom cover design, bar code, websites, LOC number, press releases, and more.

ADDITIONAL INFORMATION "Aventine Press is a service organization. We provide the author who has decided to invest in his or her own work the tools to bring it to fruition quickly, expertly, and economically. Our services encompass everything you'll need, start to finish, in the book publishing process while making it an easy, step-by-step experience."

BELLE ETOILE STUDIOS

112 Reton Ct., Cary NC 27513. **E-mail:** michael@belleetoilestudios.com. **Website:** www.belleetoilestudios.com. **Contact:** Michael Trudeau, editorial manager/co-owner. Estab. 2009. Belle Etoile is a 2-person publishing services studio from principals Michael Trudeau and Jamie Kerry.

ADDITIONAL INFORMATION "We offer design, production, and editorial to book-publishing houses and self-publishing authors." Editorial services include developmental editing, substantive editing, copyediting, proofreading, fact-checking, editorial project management, copywriting, and ms review and consultation. Design and production services include typesetting/page layout, book cover design, book interior design, book production management, logo design, branding, general graphic design, and e-book creation. "We work primarily with literary fiction, genre fiction, general nonfiction, and poetry. Our genre fiction experience includes titles in crime, fantasy and science fiction, horror, mystery and suspense, romance, young adult, and more. Our trade nonfiction experience includes titles in autobiography and biography, cultural studies and social sciences, ecology, health, history, humor, memoir, politics, sports, the occult, and more."

BOOKBABY

(877)961-6878. **E-mail:** books@bookbaby.com. **Website:** www.bookbaby.com.

ADDITIONAL INFORMATION Offers print and e-book services with e-book publishing packages that start as low as free. In addition to self-publishing, BookBaby offers editorial, design, and promotion services.

THE BOOK DOCTOR IS IN

San Pedro CA 90732. (310)346-8852. **E-mail:** stacey@thebookdoctorisin.com. **Website:** thebookdoctorisin.com. **Contact:** Stacey Aaronson, fulfiller of publishing dreams and founder. Estab. 2011. Offers market analysis program, professional editing, artistic book cover design, standout book layout and design, writing services, superb e-book design, custom graphics creation, publishing facilitation, engaging promo materials, creative website design, attentive communication, and handholding from start to finish.

ADDITIONAL INFORMATION "I take you by the hand as a self-publishing author and transform your ms into the book you've dreamed of—from impeccable editing and proofreading to engaging, audience-targeted cover and professional interior design—rivaling or exceeding a traditional house publication."

BOOKLOCKER.COM, INC.

5726 Cortez Road W., #349, Brandenton FL 34210. **Website:** www.booklocker.com.

ADDITIONAL INFORMATION Booklocker is a print-on-demand and e-book publishing services and distribution company. "According to attorney Mark Levine, author of The Fine Print, BookLocker is: 'As close to perfection as you're going to find in the world of e-book and POD publishing. The e-book royalties are the highest I've ever seen, and the print royalties are better than average.' BookLocker helps authors get their books on the market quickly (usually within a month) and for far less than most POD publishers charge."

BOOKMASTERS, INC.

30 Amberwood Pkwy., Ashland OH 44805. (877)312-3520. **Fax:** (419)281-0200. **Website:** www.bookmasters.com. Printing options include web and sheet-fed offset and digital (e-book). Offers perfect binding, case binding, saddle stitch, double wire-o, GBC comb, plastic coil, Lay-Flat, and trim-four/drill three for loose leaf.

ADDITIONAL INFORMATION "When it comes to book printing and production, BookMasters takes pride in managing every detail so you can focus on the business of publishing. Because of our state-of-the-art capabilities and great passion for providing exceptional service, publishers get exactly what they want: more choices and fewer hassles."

BOOKSTAND PUBLISHING

FastPress Publishing, Inc., 305 Vineyard Town Center, Suite 302, Morgan Hill CA 95037. (866)793-9365. **Fax:** (408)413-5443. **E-mail:** support@bookstandpublishing.com. **Website:** www.ebookstand.com. Estab. 1996. Offers POD and e-books. Services include full-color cover, electronic proof, ISBN number and bar code, e-commerce page, and more.

ADDITIONAL INFORMATION "We take your ms and transform it into a professionally published book. We handle all the back office tasks of printing, order processing, royalty collection, distribution, and much more."

BRAVADO PUBLISHING

1196 Echo Dr., Roseburg OR 97470. (541)673-0636. **E-mail:** kristen@bravadopublishing.com. **Website:** www.bravadopublishing.com. **Contact:** Kristen James, Editor.

ADDITIONAL INFORMATION "Editing, critiquing, book and e-book formatting for a variety of platforms." See website for additional information.

BROWN BOOKS PUBLISHING GROUP

16250 Knoll Trail, Suite 205, Dallas TX 75248. **E-mail:** publishing@brownbooks.com. **Website:** www.brownbooks.com. Ian Birnbaum, editor. **Contact:** Kathryn Grant, acquisitions editor. "Brown Books Publishing Group provides a wide variety of professional book publishing services that will put your book on the road to book publishing success. Our publishing services offer various combinations of publishing, marketing and editorial features. Perhaps most importantly, you retain all the rights to your book and you are in control of its production."

ADDITIONAL INFORMATION Brown Books Publishing Group is a full-service independent publisher committed to producing high quality, award-winning books of all genres for authors who choose to retain the rights to their intellectual property. Milli Brown formed Brown Books Publishing Group based on one central concept, "building successful relationships with authors in order to develop Manhattan quality books for those who wish to retain the rights to their intellectual property and keep the profits from their books' sales. Brown Books Publishing Group ushered in a New Era in Publishing, helping authors navigate the often complicated world of publishing and offering expert guidance in ms development, creative design, fulfillment, distribution, marketing and public relations. At Brown Books, authors gain the best of both worlds by taking advantage of over fifteen years of publishing expertise while retaining complete control over their projects."

CAMP POPE PUBLISHING

P.O. Box 2232, Iowa City IA 52244. (319)351-2407. **Fax:** (319)339-5964. **E-mail:** mail@camppope.com. **Website:** www.camppope.com. **Contact:** Clark Kenyon. Estab. 1991.

ADDITIONAL INFORMATION "I am not a commercial publisher and do not accept unsolicited mss. But I am here to help you get your book into print by providing the services you need, from editing, design, and layout to complete printing and binding." Services include text editing, design and layout, proofreading, formatting, annotating, and scanning of art; binding (perfect bound or Smyth sewn) and printing (offset and digital); and marketing assistance and book distribution. Cost: Contact or use online quote form for prices. See website for additional information.

CCB PUBLISHING

E-mail: info@ccbpublishing.com. **Website:** www.ccbpublishing.com.

ADDITIONAL INFORMATION Print-on-demand book and e-book publisher. Distribution channels include Ingram Books, Baker & Taylor, and the Espresso Book Machine® (EBM), an ATM-style on-site book printer. Distribution channels in Europe include Gardners Books and Bertram Books, and distribution into Australia, New Zealand and the Asia-Pacific region is provided by Dennis Jones & Associates. Contact or see website for additional information.

CHANGEMAKERS PUBLISHING AND WRITING

750 La Playa, #952, San Francisco CA 94121. (415)571-8282. **E-mail:** info@changemakerspublishingandwriting.com. **Website:** www.changemakerspublishingandwriting.com. **Contact:** Gini Graham Scott, Ph.D., J.D. Estab. 1968.

ADDITIONAL INFORMATION "I consult with and write books, articles, and scripts for clients, working from rough drafts, notes, interviews, tapes of workshops/seminars, and other materials. I also help clients publish and promote their books or find mainstream publishers, agents, and film producers. I have published more than 50 books of my own, have written 15 original scripts, several under option, and have written, produced, and sometimes directed more than 40 short films, including book and script trailers, which can be seen at www.youtube.com/changemakersprod. I also conduct workshops, seminars, teleseminars, and Webinars on writing, publishing, and promoting one's books and articles."

COLORPAGE

formerly Tri-State Litho, 71 Ten Broeck Ave., Kingston NY 12401. (800)836-7581. **Fax:** (845)331.1571. **Website:** www.colorpageonline.com.

ADDITIONAL INFORMATION Print-on-demand publisher. "We can create unique publications in short-runs, at affordable prices. Use our instant, online book price wizard for your next project." Cost, additional information, and free publishing guide available.

CREATESPACE

Amazon, 100 Enterprise Way, Suite A200, Scotts Valley CA 95066. **E-mail:** info@createspace.com. **Website:** www.createspace.com. Estab. 2007. POD publisher offering full-color covers, b&w books, ISBNs, and more.

ADDITIONAL INFORMATION "Choose the do-it-yourself publishing option with no setup fees if you have print-ready PDF files or take advantage of professional book design, editing, and marketing services if you're looking for more assistance. Network with thousands of other authors and industry professionals in the free online CreateSpace Community. Gather feedback on your work using the free Preview tool."

CREATIVELINK

P.O. Box 318, Hammondsport NY 14840. **E-mail:** info@creativelinkgraphics.com. **Website:** creativelinkgraphics.com. **Contact:** Anne Kiley, sole proprietor. Estab. 1995. Creativelink is a complete design service; check website for portfolio.

ADDITIONAL INFORMATION Offers innovative, production-oriented book design services for authors wanting to self-publish, but who want their books to look as individual as they are themselves. Also complete writing and editorial service.

DADIVAN BOOKS

3104 E. Camelback Road #160, Phoenix AZ 85016. (347)291-1779. **Fax:** (928)268-9181. **E-mail:** dadivanbooks@gmail.com. **Website:** www.dadivanbooks.com. **Contact:** Bootsie Martinez, editor. Estab. 1989. "We are professional writers, editors, and publishers with more than a century of combined experience in the publishing world."

ADDITIONAL INFORMATION Dadivan Books also offers complete self-publishing from soup-to-nuts, including economical subsidy publishing services. "We specialize in helping authors achieve their individual dreams, whether that dream is improving a ms through proofreading or editing, preparing a ms in e-publishing formats, preparing a ms in paperback layout, designing the perfect cover, or fulfilling another editorial need, including ghostwriting and book doctoring. All services are available a la carte or as part of an economical package."

DOG EAR PUBLISHING

4010 West 86th St., Suite H, Indianapolis IN 46268. (866)823-9613. **Fax:** (317)489-3506. **E-mail:** helpme@dogearpublishing.net. **Website:** www.dogearpublishing.net. **Contact:** Alan Harris, Miles Nelson, Ray Robinson.

ADDITIONAL INFORMATION "At Dog Ear Publishing, you can publish a book in about 12 weeks. You own the copyright and you are in control of how we publish your book. Our site is full of resources for self publishing, and we'll help you all along your journey answering all your questions of how to publish a book, from book publishing basics to book marketing and selling. Need only self publishing printing? We can provide those services too."

DORRANCE PUBLISHING CO.

701 Smithfield St., 3rd Floor, Pittsburgh PA 15222. (800)695-9599. **Website:** www.dorrancepublishing.com. **Contact:** Author Relations Representative. Estab. 1920. POD publisher that offers full-color cover, perfect binding, copyright, ISBN, and more.

ADDITIONAL INFORMATION Books are not edited or proofread. Books are generally printed and shipped to buyer within 48 hours.

E-BOOK TIME, LLC

6598 Pumpkin Road, Montgomery AL 36108. (877) 613-2665. **E-mail:** publishing@e-booktime.com. **Website:** www.e-booktime.com. Estab. 2004.

ADDITIONAL INFORMATION "Whether it's Christian publishing, poetry publishing, or some other genre, we can make your dream of getting your book published a reality. Don't worry about formatting your ms. We will take care of everything needed to format your ms into a published book you can be proud of. Important points to consider: Paperback $395. Hardcover and paperback $695. Sold by BarnesandNoble.com, Amazon.com and others. Five free copies. You keep all rights. Discounted book price for authors. Printed mss accepted. Ready in 4-6 weeks. Excellent royalty rates. ISBN assigned to print books. Copyright registration service. Copyedit service available."

EQUILIBRIUM BOOKS

P.O. Box 1456, Mandurah WA 6210 Australia. +61 418 954 470. **E-mail:** info@equilibriumbooks.com. **Website:** www.equilibriumbooks.com. Estab. 2002.

ADDITIONAL INFORMATION Print-on-demand publisher. "Equilibrium Books is a small, family-owned Australian business, started, owned and operated by a part-time writer who understands fully the frustrations of turning a ms into a printed book." Cost: Prices range from $184.33USD to $415.91USD depending on package and exchange rate at time of purchase. Offers online comparison of each publishing package's elements. See website for additional information.

ERIAKO ASSOCIATES

(310)392-6537. **E-mail:** eriakoassociates@gmail.com. **Contact:** Erika Fabian, CEO. Estab. 1982. Offers design, editing, and overseeing entire publishing process. Erika Fabian of Eriako Associates is an international book designer as well as writer and editor. She has personally written 22 books, some published by the likes of Putnam, Ballantine, and Harlequin. Her books have also been translated and published in several languages.

ADDITIONAL INFORMATION "We cover essentially all phases of publishing for books, brochures, and advertising materials. We also do professional photography of authors, and for the material if it needs photo illustration."

FIRST CHOICE BOOKS

Unit 2, 460 Tennyson Place, Victoria BC V8Z 6S8 Canada. (250)383-6353. **Fax:** (250)383-2247. **E-mail:** info@firstchoicebooks.ca. **Website:** www.firstchoicebooks.ca. **Contact:** Patrick O'Connor, co-owner, operations manager.

ADDITIONAL INFORMATION "Book publishers, small publishing presses and independent authors who wish to self publish will find our self publishing company affordable, trustworthy and dependable. Quotations are provided within 2 to 3 business days and a hardcopy proof within 2 weeks. Our high-tech book printing equipment and experienced, friendly team of professionals will make your publishing experience enjoyable and informative. For a quick estimate, use our Quick Price Calculator. For more accurate pricing, use our Self-Publishing Quote form. For additional information about the publishing process, download our Free Self Publishing Guide. Find out more about our lay-flat, durable, smyth-sewn, soft and hard cover coffee-table style books—great for photography, children's, and edition books. First Choice Books is dedicated to helping publishers and self-published authors make and save money."

G AND J PUBLISHING

15826 Cherry Cove, Palm Springs CA 92262. (760)202-4878. **E-mail:** info@gandjpublishing.com. **Website:** www.gandjpublishing.com. Gayle Farmer, editor. **Contact:** Gayle Farmer, editor; Jeff Farmer, publisher.

ADDITIONAL INFORMATION "Set-up fees: $900 e-books only; $1,050 Basic Paperback Package; $1,350 Paperback plus E-book Package. Standard products/services: POD publishing, editing, page layout, cover design. Additional services: e-book setup, hardcover and paperback editions, Kindle Editions, full distribution, author market material, author websites, press kits, copywriting. Details: When it comes to producing books, speed is not the only consideration and POD printers are as different as night and day. Attention to detail is job one at G and J Publishing. From editing your ms to designing your book cover we work to make your book the best it can be. Our printer pays close attention to craftsmanship when producing your book. Ten quality control checks on each book, sharp cover graphics and crisp text. You will find the quality of your book is superior to many of the books on bookstands today."

GLOBAL AUTHORS PUBLICATIONS

E-mail: gapbook@yahoo.com. **Website:** www.globalauthorspublications.com. **Contact:** Kathleen Walls. **ADDITIONAL INFORMATION** "GAP offers the best of both worlds. Now you can have the convenience and low cost of print-on-demand and the returnability and pricing of your own self-publishing company." Books must be at least 48 pages and not more than 700 pages. Cost: $2,000 (payable in 2 installments) with an annual $150 fee to cover recordkeeping. Cost includes one copy of book, copyediting, formatting, photographic cover design, ISBN, registration in *Books in Print*, a Library of Congress number, and book link on the GAP website. Contact or see website for additional information.

GLOBE PUBLISHING

2856 Utah Road, Rantoul KS 66079-9027. **E-mail:** carla@globepublishingandgraphics.com. **Website:** globepublishingandgraphics.com. **Contact:** Carla Russell, co-owner. Estab. 2013. "Whether a writer's ms needs are tweaking (copy editing and/or proofreading) or the complete interior (typesetting) and exterior (cover) design, we can walk with you though every step to the printing process."

GOOSE RIVER PRESS

3400 Friendship Road, Waldoboro ME 04572. (207)832-6665. **E-mail:** gooseriverpress@roadrunner.com. **Website:** www.gooseriverpress.com.

ADDITIONAL INFORMATION Traditional royalty publisher who also offers a self-publishing option. "Self-publishing services are offered to those books that do not meet our high standards for publication or those who simply choose to publish themselves. We offer copy editing and typesetting services for those who need help preparing camera-ready copy, complete book production (we can print as few as 50 copies), and promotion. We work with Ingram, Baker & Taylor, Barnes & Noble, Amazon.com, and more. For those who wish to self-publish under another press name, Goose River Press can provide fee-based editing and printing services at competitive rates." Send SASE for complete information or send us e-mail.

GREY SWAN PRESS

Boston MA (978)979-2000. **E-mail:** jim@greyswanpress.com. **Website:** www.greyswanpress.com. Estab. 2004. Grey Swan Press is a full-service independent publishing company.

ADDITIONAL INFORMATION "We offer editorial services, cover and interior design, book layout, copyright and registration services. We create e-book, Kindle, hardcover and paperback editions. We also offer book distribution through major channels. We are affiliated and work closely with Kelley & Hall Book Publicity."

IBJ BOOK PUBLISHING

IBJ Media, 41 East Washington St., Ste. 200, Indianapolis IN 46204. (317)634-6200. **Fax:** (317)263-5402. **E-mail:** info@ibjbp.com. **Website:** www.ibjbookpublishing.com.

ADDITIONAL INFORMATION "We are a full-service resource for authors who want to self-publish the highest quality book in a professional, cost effective and timely manner, including corporate anniversaries, artist portfolios, children's and cookbooks." Optional services available include book coaching, copyediting, proofreading, ebook conversion, print on demand services, an online bookstore, placement and marketing collateral. Cost: Contact for a quick estimate.

INFINITY PUBLISHING

1094 New Dehaven St., Suite 100, W. Conshohocken PA 19428. (610)941-9999. **Fax:** (610)941-9959. **Website:** www.infinitypublishing.com. **Contact:** Author Advocates. Estab. 1997. Offers ISBN assignment, custom-made barcode, custom-designed cover, and more.

ADDITIONAL INFORMATION "Authors pay a one-time setup fee to have their book file added into Infinity's unique print on demand book publishing system. Self publishing authors retain all rights to their book, they own the copyright, and they may remove their book from the book publishing system at any time. Authors have total creative control over the content and all aspects of their book during publishing within production limitations. Suggested retail prices are based on page count, however, with Infinity's value-added feature, authors may increase the price of their nonfiction book. Self-publishing success is a two-fold process where quality writing and effective marketing equal sales. We offer professionally designed and quality printed promotional materials for our authors as well as highly respected marketing books that will help you find your audiences. Our newsletters, author advocates, conferences and wealth of online articles featuring expert advice and successful campaign strategies focus on teaching authors how to be effective in their efforts to promote and market their published books. Enhance your book with a CD inside through our CD in a Book Program."

INGRAMSPARK

Website: www1.ingramspark.com.

ADDITIONAL INFORMATION "IngramSpark is the only publishing platform that delivers fully integrated print and digital distribution services to the book industry through a single source. What does that mean? Once you finish and format your book we make it possible to share it with the world."

INNOVO PUBLISHING

3541 Waterford Cv N., Collierville TN 38017. (888)546-2111. **Website:** www.innovopublishing.com.

ADDITIONAL INFORMATION "Innovo Publishing provides full-service publishing and marketing of multiple editions of your Christian ms." Publishing options include hardbacks, paperbacks, e-books (Kindle, iPhone, iPad, Adobe), and CD and MP3 audio books. Services include editing, proofreading, interior design and layout, cover design and layout, e-book and audio book creation, ISBN, and on-demand ordering and printing. Cost: Hardback and paperback publishing packages start at $679; audio book packages (with professional narration) start at $150; e-book packages start at $599. See website for pricing for individual services. Offers free self-publishing guide. Contact online for consultation and additional information.

INSIDEOUT PRESS

P.O. Box 2666, Country Club Hills Illinois 60478. (708)957-6047. **E-mail:** kim@insideoutpress.com. **Website:** www.insideoutpress.com. **Contact:** Kim Olver, president. Estab. 2009.

ADDITIONAL INFORMATION "We are a full-service self-publishing company, providing cover design, personalized back cover, interior page layout, image insertion, ISBN assignment, eBook formatting, Amazon and Barnes & Noble set-up, Amazon search inside program, personalized InsideOutPress Bookstore page, promotional materials, social media set-up, book signing kit, index service, Library of Congress control number, US copyright registration, author website set-up, media kit set-up, and printer estimates."

INSTANTPUBLISHER

410 Hwy 72 West, P.O. Box 340, Collierville TN 38027. (800)259-2592. **Fax:** (901)853-6196. **E-mail:** questions@instantpublisher.com. **Website:** www.instantpublisher.com. Short-run press (minimum order of 25 books). Mss accepted through company's unique software that gives authors the ability to proof online before the book is sent to press.

ADDITIONAL INFORMATION "Instantpublisher.com is the short run book publisher division of Fundcraft Publishing Company, the world's largest personalized cookbook publisher. Fundcraft started as a small publishing house in eastern Kansas in the early 30's specializing in short-run custom cookbooks for groups and organizations across the country. Our book printing success is directly related to our ability to accept mss straight from customer's desktop publishing programs. Customer's can proof the book online, select book printing options and publish the book quickly and affordably directly from our large book printing facility—all from the ease of a home or office computer. We do not buy any mss outright, do not pay any royalties, and do not market or distribute your books, except for free listings on our website. Authors pay the entire cost to publish a book. Authors have complete design control over the text, cover and binding style. Instantpublisher.com does not set any type or compose any pages. The finished copies, the copyright and all subsidiary rights belong exclusively to the author. Instantpublisher.com [a book printing company] can provide an ISBN number for your book for an additional charge."

IUNIVERSE

1663 Liberty Dr., Bloomington IN 47403. (800)288-4677. **Fax:** (812)355-4085. **Website:** www.iuniverse.com. Estab. 1999. Self-publishing company that offers a range of services for authors trying to get their work published.

ADDITIONAL INFORMATION "iUniverse is a self-publishing company that makes it possible for writers to achieve the dream of becoming a published author. With leadership that brings expertise in publishing, sales and marketing and technology, iUniverse offers a unique mix of self-publishing products and services and the skills of a professional team dedicated to enabling authors to see their books in print. By offering a variety of affordable publishing, editorial and marketing services, iUniverse helps authors get their mss off their desks and into the marketplace faster than traditional publishing companies. "

JADA PRESS

P.O. Box 672825, Marietta GA 30006. (904)226-8876. **E-mail:** jadapress@aol.com. **Website:** www.jadapress. com. **Contact:** Glenda Ivey, publisher.

ADDITIONAL INFORMATION "Set-up fees: Executive Program: $1,250• Standard products/services: author royalties at 80% net; bookstore return policy; custom book covers; choice of sizes; copyediting; ISBN; Library of Congress Number; listed in Books In Print; listing in JADA Press Bookstore; 6 free copies; JPG file; distribution with Baker & Taylor and Ingram• Additional services: $200 per year archive fee; press releases; advertising; professional press kits; website• Details: Books are completed in three to four months. Books carry the JADA Press logo."

JANET SPENCER KING, BOOK DEVELOPMENT GROUP

595 Main St., #1602, New York NY 10044. (212)371-1479. **E-mail:** janet@bookdevelopmentgroup.com. **Website:** www.bookdevelopmentgroup.com. **Contact:** Janet Spencer King. Estab. 2007. Book Development Group is a group of three independent editors.

ADDITIONAL INFORMATION King offers services in concept development, ms evaluations, ms content editing, and line editing. Works with fiction writers of most genres, consulting on plotting, pacing, point of view, and the many other aspects of a novel. Also works with nonfiction writers in a wide variety of topics from health, fitness, and nutrition to self-help and personal growth, among others. For authors who wish to self-publish, King provides customized personal production management. Works with copy editors as well as cover and interior designers to turn mss into widely distributed, beautifully crafted books. Provides e-book conversion and distribution as well.

KELLEY & HALL BOOK PUBLICITY

5 Briar Lane, Marblehead MA 01945. (617)680-1976. **E-mail:** jocelyn@kelleyandhall.com. **Website:** www. kelleyandhall.com. **Contact:** Jocelyn Kelley, partner. Estab. 2004. Kelley & Hall is a literary publicity company that is dedicated to helping authors and publishers with their promotion, marketing, and media relations.

ADDITIONAL INFORMATION "We create effective book buzz as well as author recognition that will increase book sales. We help writers build their author brand. Book marketing and book promotion are the cornerstones of Kelley & Hall. We have recently partnered with an independent publishing company, Grey Swan Press (www.greyswanpress.com)."

LAREDO PUBLISHING

465 Westview Ave., Englewood NJ 07631. (201)408-4048. **Fax:** (201)408-5011. **Website:** www.laredopublishing.com. Estab. 1991.

ADDITIONAL INFORMATION Co-edition publisher. "We are a seasoned publishing company, providing editorial, production, translation, and creative services to help our clients develop content-driven products." Cost: General Publications: Economy ($299), Executive ($1.499), and Ambassador ($2,199). Star ($499), Gold ($899), and Platinum ($2,899) children's book packages. See website for additional information.

LB PRESS

750 Putnam Dr., Reno NV 89530. **Website:** lbpresspublishing.com. **Contact:** Cindie Geddes, co-owner. Estab. 2009. LB Press, a subsidiary of Lucky Bat Books, is a full-service fee-based publishing company, offering one-on-one project management and personalized care for writers wanting full control of their work.

ADDITIONAL INFORMATION "We work with writers to find just the right combination of services to help make each project a success. We do not upsell; our fees are all listed on our site; we take no percentages and we encumber no rights. You wrote it; you own it."

LENTINI DESIGN

1626 Virginia Road, Los Angeles CA 90019. (323)766-8090. **E-mail:** info@lentinidesign.com. **Website:** www.lentinidesign.com. **Contact:** Hilary Lentini, owner. Estab. 1990.

ADDITIONAL INFORMATION Services include branding development, marketing pieces/deliverables, web development/deliverables, social media.

LIGHTNING SOURCE, INC.

1246 Heil Quaker Blvd., La Vergne TN 37086. (615)213-5815. **Fax:** (615)213-4725. **E-mail:** inquiry@ lightningsource.com. **Website:** lightningsource.com.

ADDITIONAL INFORMATION "For independent publishers, as well as medium and large publishers. Our print on demand distribution service is the fastest and most economical way to get your books to consumers around the world."

LLUMINA PRESS

7580 NW 5th St., #16535, Fort Lauderdale FL 33318. (954)726-0902. **Fax:** (954)726-0903. **Website:** www.llumina.com. **Contact:** Deborah Greenspan.

ADDITIONAL INFORMATION *"Llumina Press* was created by writers for writers. We know how to help you because we've been there. We know how it feels to get a rejection letter, and how it feels to finally get that book published. We've been through writer's block, torn our collective hair out trying to find exactly the right words, and suffered over whether to leave our finest phrases in or take them out. We are experienced writers and editors, and after eleven years of publishing, we've got a handle on that too."

LULU

860 Aviation Pkwy., Suite 300, Morrisville NC 27560. (919)459-5858. **Website:** www.lulu.com. Founder/CEO: Bob Young.. POD publisher that makes works available in print and electronic formats.

ADDITIONAL INFORMATION "Lulu enables authors to sell their work directly to their particular audience. Using Lulu's simple publishing tools, they format and upload their digital content. Then they can take advantage of Lulu's global marketplace, social networking and author services, free customized storefronts and retail listings on Amazon, Barnes & Noble and much more."

DICK MARGULIS CREATIVE SERVICES

284 W. Elm St., New Haven CT 06515. (203)389-4413. **E-mail:** dick@dmargulis.com. **Website:** www.dmargulis.com. **Contact:** Dick Margulis, owner. Estab. 2004. Offers high-quality printed and electronic books for discerning clients. Thoughtful editing, appropriate design, expert production, comprehensive project management, for publishers of all sizes and for all kinds of books.

ADDITIONAL INFORMATION "If you are an author, agent, publisher, or other organization considering a book project, I'd like the opportunity to quote on the services you need. I have been involved in both editing and typography in one way or another for over half a century; my experience is broad and deep."

MILL CITY PRESS

322 First Ave. N., Suite 500, Minneapolis MN 55401. (612) 455-2294, ext. 206. **E-mail:** info@millcitypress.net. **E-mail:** michelle@millcitypress.net. **Website:** www.millcitypress.net. Emily Weiss, Dir. of Publicity. **Contact:** Michelle Brown, Dir. of Sales.

ADDITIONAL INFORMATION "Mill City Press offers a new way of looking at self-publishing. We use our industry experience and e-commerce insight to give you the most cost-effective tools for self-publishing, marketing, and selling your book. What Makes Mill City Press Different? We pass along wholesale printing costs to our authors. Most self-publishing companies use the same printer for their book publishing projects. We charge you what the printer charges us and we show you the bill. Our competitors mark up those costs between 50%-100%. Compare self-publishing mark-ups on printing costs. You make 100% of the Royalties. You're paying us to help launch your book, you don't need to pay us a percentage of each sale too. See how much you'll make on each book you sell as a Mill City Press author. Then compare 100% royalties from us to the royalties paid by other self-publishing companies."

MORRIS PUBLISHING

3212 E. Highway 30, Kearney NE 68848. (800)650-7888. **Fax:** (308)237-0263. **Website:** www.morrispublishing.com. Estab. 1993. The company has a separate division specializing in cookbooks.

ADDITIONAL INFORMATION "We specialize in short-run book printing for self-published authors and have printed millions of books for individuals, businesses, and small book publishers. From cover design to book printing, Morris Publishing provides for all your self-publishing needs."

MYSTIC PUBLISHERS

614 Mosswood Dr., Henderson NV 89015. (866)869-7842. **E-mail:** joawilkins@mysticpublishers.com. **Website:** www.mysticpublishers.com. Estab. 2001.

ADDITIONAL INFORMATION "Mystic Publishers strives to bring a cost-effective alternative to all who want to see their work in print." A la carte services offered at individual costs include typing, formatting, proofreading, editing, graphic design, ISBN and copyright, and book promotion; see website for fees. Cost: Basic publishing package, $650; basic publicity package (personalized postcards, bookmarks, press releases, and more), $255. Contact or see website for additional information.

ODELL COETZEE

566 Dakota St., Elardus Park, Pretoria Gauteng 0181 South Africa. **Website:** http://k-shandra.elance.com. **Contact:** Odell Coetzee. Estab. 2010.

ADDITIONAL INFORMATION Services offered include e-book interior layout, design and proof for Kindle and Smashwords, including linked and functioning TOC; Createspace book layout, design, and proof with picture resolution formatting. Virtual flipbook is provided to access layout before finalizing.

OSMOND MARKETING

29 via Regalo, San Clemente CA 92673. (949)813-0182. **E-mail:** amy@osmondmarketing.com. **Website:** www.osmondmarketing.com. **Contact:** Amy Cook, publisher. Estab. 2009. Osmond Marketing creates and manages premium-quality content for businesses, brands, and authors. "Prices are affordable to help individuals and small businesses build their platforms, engage their audiences, and identify with their consumers right along with Fortune 500 companies."

ADDITIONAL INFORMATION Services include book publishing, website design and hosting, press releases, publicity tours, blog tours, marketing materials, social media management, ghostwriting, list building, newsletters, contests and giveaways, audiobooks, videography, photography, illustration, business and legal services, affiliate marketing, and market research.

OUTSKIRTS PRESS

10940 S. Parker Road - 515, Parker CO 80134. (888) OP-BOOKS. **E-mail:** info@outskirtspress.com. **Website:** www.outskirtspress.com. Offers POD, e-books, and off-set print runs. Packages run from $199 for an Emerald package to $1,099 for the Pearl package.

ADDITIONAL INFORMATION "Outskirts Press offers you the best of both worlds by combining the advantages of independent self-publishing with the advantages of traditional book publishing. Before, during, and after publication you will receive the assistance of a dedicated group of publishing professionals, all the while maintaining all your publishing rights and setting your own retail price, royalty, and author discount."

PROFESSIONAL PRESS

P.O. Box 3581, Chapel Hill NC 27515. (800)277-8960. **Fax:** (919)942-3094. **Website:** www.profpress.com.

ADDITIONAL INFORMATION "Professional Press helps you create a salable, readable, and attractive book, designed and edited professionally. Our service is dependable, fast, and always accessible." Offers offset printing and print-on-demand. Cost: Price lists available online broken out according to soft cover, hard cover, and print-on-demand. See website for additional information.

RICHMOND PICKERING LTD

Denmark Cottage, Lower Hengoed, Oswestry Shropshire SY10 7EF England. 01691-679711. **Fax:** 01691-679711. **E-mail:** richmondpickeringltd@gmail.com. **Website:** www.writershouse.co.uk. **Contact:** Claire Pickering, director/editor; Rebecca Richmond, director/coach. Estab. 2013. Provides self-publishing, book coaching, editing, and book marketing services. Publishes 6-10 titles/year, generally mass market paperback originals and electronic originals. Receives 30 queries/year. Pays authors 10% royalty (minimum) and 15% for e-books. Responds in 1-3 months on any query, proposal, or ms. Interested in nonfiction (how-to, self-help, wellness). All mss must be fully edited to a professional standard before submission. Any submission must complement the existing titles within the "My Guide" series of self-help, wellness, and how-to books. See website for details. Query with SASE and mss for consideration to be self-published. Contact for any other services.

SAME OLD STORY PRODUCTIONS

P.O. Box 606, Halfway OR 97834. (541)742-4121. **E-mail:** submissions@sameoldstory.net. **Website:** www.sameoldstory.net. **Contact:** Doug McKim, editor and founder; Cindy Womack-Steele, editor. Estab. 2012. A self-publishing, subsidy publisher. Offers competitive rates that are both fair and affordable. For price details or further information, see website or e-mail. Publishes hardcover, trade paperback, mass market paperback, and electronic originals or reprints. Publishes 12-24 titles/year. 50-100% of books from first-time authors. 100% from unagented writers. Publishes ms 6 months after acceptance. Accepts simultaneous submissions. Responds to queries, proposals, and mss in 1 month. Catalog available online. Guidelines available by e-mail. Query with SASE. Submit proposal package including an outline and 3 sample chapters.

SELF PUBLISHING, INC.

93 Lake Ave., Tuckahoe NY 10707. (800)621-2556. **Fax:** (914)222-9228. **Website:** www.selfpublishing.com. **Contact:** Ron Pramschufer.

ADDITIONAL INFORMATION Services include book printing (web, offset, digital) in single- and full-color text; mechanical, substantive, and comprehensive editing; indexing; book layout and cover design; and author website design. Cost: Provides online quote request form for printing services. Also offers editorial services (packages range from $250 to $1,950 for children's books; rates are 14 cents to 35 cents/word for editing, $3.75-5.25/page for indexing). Offers free publishing guide and monthly e-newsletter. See website for additional information.

SMASHWORDS, INC.

15951 Los Gatos Blvd., Suite 16, Los Gatos CA 95032. **Website:** www.smashwords.com. Services include free downloads of marketing and style guides.

ADDITIONAL INFORMATION "Smashwords is an e-book publishing and distribution platform for e-book authors, publishers, and readers."

SOURCED MEDIA BOOKS

29 via Regalo, San Clemente CA 92673. (949)813-0182. **E-mail:** amy@sourcedmediabooks.com. **Website:** www.sourcedmediabooks.com. **Contact:** Amy Cook, publisher. Estab. 2009. Sourced Media Books is a traditional and self-publishing company based in Southern California.

ADDITIONAL INFORMATION Offering a full spectrum of services, from developmental editing to final press production, Sourced Media Books offers high-end publishing quality at self-publishing prices. Some of these services include coaching, copy editing, typesetting, proofreading, cover design, ISBN registration, Library of Congress registration, working with digital and/or offset presses, and distribution (national, online, or both). Website design and marketing services are also available upon request.

SPEEDY PUBLISHING

40 E. Main St., Newark DE 19711. (855)262-3719. **E-mail:** info@speedypublishing.com. **Website:** www.speedypublishing.com. **Contact:** Colin Scott. Estab. 2013. Speedy Publishing is a hybrid publisher offering multi-platform publishing training online. "We offer authors the ability to format their content for print, e-book, and audio just to name a few. We also offer access to one of the best distribution services in the industry."

ADDITIONAL INFORMATION Speedy books are available through most online bookstores, including Amazon, B&N, Apple, Lulu, Kobo, Ingram, Baker & Taylor, and more. "Our books are also accessible to hundreds of physical bookstores and libraries throughout the USA and overseas."

SPIRE PUBLISHING LTD.

P.O. Box 678, Salt Spring Island BC V8K 2W3 Canada. **E-mail:** info@spirepublishing.com. **Website:** www.spirepublishing.com. Estab. 2002.

ADDITIONAL INFORMATION "Whether it's a work of fiction with worldwide online distribution, a family memoir with a short run, or a cookbook just for your kitchen club, Spire Publishing can start you on your self-publishing journey." Book options include softcover (trade paperback), hardcover (laminate or cloth), and color softcover (saddle stitched or perfect bound). Cost: Professional Package, $999 (£799); Essentials Package, $799 (£599); Print Ready Package, $599 (£399), Print Ready Plus Package, $699 (£499). See website for package details and comparison of features. Proofreading available at additional cost. Contact or see website for additional information, including book pricing.

SPRINGBOARD CONTENT & PUBLISHING, LLC

10720 E. Sahuaro Dr., Scottsdale AZ 85259. (602)432-3094. **E-mail:** info@springboardpublishing.com. **Website:** www.springboardpublishing.com. **Contact:** Ellen J. Nusbaum, Program Manager. Estab. 2005.

ADDITIONAL INFORMATION Print-on-demand; ebooks• Set-up fees: A-List Package: $829 Economy Package: $279 Co-Writing Package: $500 plus 25% of profits• Standard products/services: Basic package (Economy) includes proofing; Desktop publishing; PDF; Express jacket design; press release; basic distribution through Cyberread and Lulu as PDF and bound (no ISBN)• Additional services: editing; copyright procurement and submission; ISBN; ghost writing; feedback review; conversion of handwriting ms; Website creation and hosting; print fulfillment• Details: The Co-Writing Package includes the A-List package plus writing; co-writing or rewriting a book based on author's subject matter expertise. Springboard shares copyright and byline. Flat $500 fee for Co-Writing Package.

STORY ARTS MEDIA

777 Pearl St., Suite 211, Boulder CO 80302. **Website:** www.storyartsmedia.com. **Contact:** Joseph Daniel, publisher. Estab. 1979.

ADDITIONAL INFORMATION "Boutique publishing and creative services company. Publishes 10-12 titles a year under own imprint as well as provides comprehensive publishing services to a small, selective group of independent authors."

SYNTAX AND STYLE

North Andover MA 01845. **E-mail:** mary@syntaxandstyle.com. **Website:** www.syntaxandstyle.com. **Contact:** Mary McAvoy, owner/founder. Estab. 2006. Syntax and Style will customize a web platform for an author. Web platform consists of website, blog, Facebook fan page, LinkedIn profile, Twitter account.

ADDITIONAL INFORMATION Syntax and Style will also guide an author through the process of self-publishing.

TO PRESS & BEYOND

825 E. Pedregosa St., Suite 2, Santa Barbara CA 93103. (805)898-2263. **E-mail:** info@topressandbeyond.com. **Website:** www.topressandbeyond.com. **Contact:** Gail M. Kearns, president. Estab. 1995.

ADDITIONAL INFORMATION "Gail M. Kearns and her team at To Press & Beyond are specialists in book publishing consulting and support services. With over 16 years of experience, they skillfully and successfully guide your print and/or e-book project from ms to finished book, educating and coaching every step of the way. Their comprehensive range of services include writing, developmental editing and copyediting, proofreading, design and layout, printing, distribution, sales and promotion, both in trade and niche markets and on the web. Our books consistently win editorial and design awards."

TRAFFORD PUBLISHING

1663 Liberty Dr., Bloomington IN 47403. **E-mail:** customersupport@trafford.com. **Website:** www.trafford.com. Offers one-on-one author support, custom full-color cover, custom interior design, ISBN assignment, electronic proof, online distribution, bookstore availability, and more. Packages range from $549 for the E-novo package to $10,999 for Tapestry (and many packages in between).

ADDITIONAL INFORMATION Also offers advanced distribution, international book fair displays, personalized business cards, and more. Standard packages include author copies.

TREEHOUSE PUBLISHING GROUP LLC

8734 Norcross Dr., St. Louis MO 63126. (314)363-4546. **E-mail:** authorservices@treehousepublishinggroup.com. **Website:** treehousepublishinggroup.com. **Contact:** Kristina Makansi, managing partner. Estab.

2013. Treehouse Publishing Group offers a full menu of a la carte author services as well as assisted self-publishing under our Treehouse imprint.

ADDITIONAL INFORMATION "At TPG, we believe that every project is as unique as the author who created it. That's why we individually tailor each package—from developmental edits to book layouts to website design—to suit your specific goals."

TRINITY PRESS

3190 Reps Miller Rd, Suite 360, Norcross GA 30071. (770)248-1964. **Fax:** (770)248-1013. **E-mail:** joe@trinitypress.com. **Website:** trinitypress.com. **Contact:** Joe Dye, president. Estab. 1984.

ADDITIONAL INFORMATION Offers the print and distribution of paperback books as well as printing of business supplies and materials and full binding services.

UBUILDABOOK, LLC

20 N. Aviador St., Ste. C, Camarillo CA 93010. (866)909-3003. **E-mail:** info@ubuildabook.com. **Website:** www.ubuildabook.com.

ADDITIONAL INFORMATION Print-on-demand publisher. "UBuildABook is a creative book publishing platform. Supply us with your book content. You design the custom book cover and the page layout and leave the rest to us." Offers download of book-building software or photo book software from website. Cost: Provides pricing information online for 1-24 books; use online quote request for 25+ books. For orders of less than 25, standard books include 80# glossy paper (or equivalent matte paper), full-color laminated cover, up to 500 color pages interspersed with b&w pages, perfect binding, and text on spine (if spine is large enough); additional options available for orders of over 25 books. See website for additional information.

VIRTUALBOOKWORM.COM PUBLISHING INC.

P.O. Box 9949, College Station TX 77842. (877)376-4955. **Website:** virtualbookworm.com.

ADDITIONAL INFORMATION "Virtualbookworm.com was established as a 'clearinghouse' for authors, since it offers virtually everything under one roof. Although we now charge setup and design fees, those costs are kept to a minimum so as to cover all expenses. And, as with 'traditional' publishers, we carefully review each ms and only offer contracts to authors who truly have exceptional mss. We don't print garbage, and we want our authors to proudly say they were published by Virtualbookworm. You'll receive some of the best royalties in the business!"

VOLUMES

M & T Printing Group, 907 Frederick St., Kitchener ON N2B 2B9 Canada. (888)571-2665. **Fax:** (519)578-4743. **Website:** www.volumesdirect.com.

ADDITIONAL INFORMATION Print-on-demand publisher. Services include front and back cover design, interior formatting, author's proof, archiving for future orders, ISBN, Library of Congress, EAN barcode, copyright, and availability in publisher's online bookstore. Cost: Launch Package, $799; Folio Package, $1,699; see website for breakdown and comparison of services in each package. Contact or see website for additional information.

WALDORF PRESS

2140 Hall Johnson Road, #102-113, Grapevine TX 76051. (303)550-8186. **E-mail:** barbara@barbaraterry.com. **E-mail:** driversseatmedia@aol.com. **Website:** www.waldorfpress.com. **Contact:** Karen Davis, partner. Estab. 2013. Small self-publishing company (50% author-subsidy). Determines if an author should be subsidy published by quality of work and public interest. Publishes about 7 books/year. Receives 40 queries and mss/year. Authors are paid between 20-50% royalties on wholesale and retail price. Responds to writers within 1 month. Publishes book 6 months after acceptance. Interested in any mss, fiction and nonfiction. Query with SASE and complete ms via e-mail.

WESTBOW PRESS

Thomas Nelson, Inc., 1663 Liberty Dr., Bloomington IN 47403. (866)928-1240. **E-mail:** lmurphy@westbowpress.com. **Website:** www.westbowpress.com. **Contact:** Lisa Murphy, Imprint Manager. Estab. 2009.

ADDITIONAL INFORMATION "At WestBow Press we help authors self-publish books of all genres, specializing in books with Christian morals, inspirational themes and family values. Whether you have goals of commercial success or simply desire to publish a book for friends and family, WestBow Press can help you create your book in your vision."

WHEATMARK, INC.

1760 E. River Road, Suite 145, Tucson AZ 85718. (888)934-0888. **Fax:** (520)798-3394. **E-mail:** info@wheatmark.com. **Website:** www.wheatmark.com. Estab. 1999.

ADDITIONAL INFORMATION "Wheatmark is a publishing company that offers a complete set of editing, book publishing, and book marketing services." Services include ms evaluation, copyediting, page layout, cover design, book marketing, printing and production, author website, and a Great Expectations credit program. Cost: Contact for rates. Provides free book marketing guide and e-newsletter. Contact or see website for additional information.

WHITEHALL PRINTING COMPANY

4244 Corporate Square, Naples FL 34104. (800)321-9290. **Fax:** (239)643-6439. **E-mail:** info@whitehall-printing.com. **Website:** www.whitehallprinting.com. Estab. 1959.

ADDITIONAL INFORMATION Book printer. Softcover book manufacturing from 100 to 25,000 copies. Design, editing and fulfillment. Contact or see website for additional information.

WINGSPAN PRESS

WingSpan Press, Inc., P.O. Box 2085, Livermore CA 94551. (866) 735-3782. **E-mail:** info@wingspanpress.com. **Website:** www.wingspanpress.com.

ADDITIONAL INFORMATION "WingSpan Press is a a group of writers helping writers achieve their dreams at a fair price while allowing them to earn a good return on their investment. Our focus is on quality and customer service. Our business rules are simple: Answer the phone, tell people the truth, and do what we say we'll do. We're willing to answer all your questions and help you understand the ins and outs of self-publishing before you sign an agreement or lay out any money. We're constantly striving to provide services to assist you in positioning your book for success, including excellent design, distribution, marketing tools, website sales and customer support."

WISDOM HOUSE BOOKS

(919)883-4669. **E-mail:** clara@wisdomhousebooks.com. **Website:** www.wisdomhousebooks.com. **Contact:** Clara Jackson.

ADDITIONAL INFORMATION "Full service VIP publishing for independent authors. Wisdom House Books, we represent the best of you. We provide all the services of a major publisher, but you retain 100% of the royalties and 100% of the selling profits. There are no 'Publishing Packages' or 'Levels' here; we simply offer a list of services that you may select from based on what you feel works best for you, your goals, and your budget."

WORD ASSOCIATION PUBLISHERS

205 5th Ave., Tarentum PA 15084. (800)827-7903. **E-mail:** tom@wordassociation.com. **Website:** www.wordassociation.com. **Contact:** Dr. Tom Costello.
ADDITIONAL INFORMATION "At Word Association, we offer writers a way to publish their books with all of the advantages of self-publishing and none of the negatives of a vanity press. We are a one-stop shop, offering all of the services and expertise you may want or need." Services include editing and proofreading, ms consultation, co-writing, ghostwriting, ms preparation (typesetting or page formatting), cover and interior design, credentials (ISBN, Library of Congress, copyright), printing and binding, promotion and marketing, and distribution and fulfillment. Cost: Offers two publishing packages; see website for breakdown of services for each and related costs. Also offers editing and marketing and promotions services. See website for additional information.

XLIBRIS

1663 Liberty Dr., Suite 200, Bloomington IN 47403. **E-mail:** info@xlibris.com. **Website:** www.xlibris.com. Offers one-on-one author support, image adjustments and placement, ISBN assignment, and more. Variety of packages available.
ADDITIONAL INFORMATION Also offers specialty publishing packages for poetry, science fiction, children's, and Christian books. Standard packages include author copies.

XULON PRESS

2301 Lucien Way, Suite 415, Maitland FL 32751. (866)381-2665. **Website:** www.xulonpress.com. **Contact:** Jim Kochenburger.

ADDITIONAL INFORMATION "We are the original print-on-demand self-publisher for Christian authors. We can turn your ms into a quality Christian book and get it into the hands of readers through 25,000 bookstores and on the Internet. You may purchase copies in any quantity from 1 to 10,000 or more. There is no minimum order to get self-published, no obligation on your part to buy copies of your book. Just submit your ms and let us take care of the rest." Services include book cover design, professionally formatted interior text, ISBN, marketing and advertising programs, and Christian staff. Quarterly royalty payments. No minimum book order. See website for additional information.

Y24K PUBLISHING SERVICES

55 Beacon St., Arlington MA 02474. **E-mail:** writeray@y42k.com. **Website:** www.y42k.com/bookproduction.html. **Contact:** Ray Charbonneau, proprietor. Estab. 2010.
ADDITIONAL INFORMATION "I can help you design and publish your book quickly, professionally, and at a low cost. Unlike other services that automate the process, I'll work directly with you every step of the way to ensure you get the book you want. You end up with a paperback book listed on Amazon.com and an e-book listed on Amazon, Barnes & Noble, Apple's iBookstore, Kobo, and many other outlets. You also get the ability to order paper books at a steep discount, which you can use for review copies, for gifts, to stock local bookstores, or to sell yourself. I also send you all the final copies of the various files that I've used to publish your book. And I publish links to your book on Facebook, Google+, Twitter, and my website."

EDITORIAL
SERVICES

///

Finding the right editor for your project can make the difference between success and failure. One knock against self-publishing that still persists is that self-published books are of lesser quality. By using freelance editors, you can work to overcome that specific hurdle in the self-publishing process.

However, there are a variety of editing services available with different pricing structures. It's important to remember that sometimes you get what you pay for, and it's possible to pay (or overpay) for services you don't really need. The "How Much Should I Charge?" pay rate chart should help with determining an appropriate fee with your freelance editor.

Beyond determining a fair rate, self-publishers need to know what type of editorial assistance they need. For instance, do you just need someone to read through the ms for bad spelling and grammar? Do you need fact checking assistance? Could you use help with the structure and pacing?

Each service may have a different fee and a different amount of time required to complete the work. In determining freelance rates, you'll need to know the hourly rate and time requirement to assign a fair fee that will result in quality work. Setting unfair expectations is bad for the freelancer, but it also puts your project at risk, because you're counting on the freelancers to give their best.

KEEP IN MIND

Starting locally will allow you to research each company carefully and learn about their past performance and make it easier to have face-to-face discussions about the ms. Realize that any face-to-face time and time on the phone may be considered "billable hours" by your freelancer. Be sure to agree on all such fees and get it in writing before starting work. It will help ensure a more professional working relationship and provide both sides with more security.

Going local is not a requirement. In fact, you may find that going with another editor outside of your area is more affordable or provides you with a freelancer who has better qualifications. Always ask for previous experience and consider checking references, especially if you're investing a lot of money in the editorial process. After all, you want to make sure your money will be money well spent.

ABSOLUTE EDITING & PROOFREADING

25620-G Cross Creek Dr., Yorba Linda CA 92887. **Fax:** (714)660-9060. **E-mail:** romwriterskb@yahoo.com. **Website:** www.sandrakayauthor.com. **Contact:** Sandra Kay, owner. Estab. 2012.

ADDITIONAL INFORMATION "If you are considering self-publishing, a good edit is a must. I offer editing and proofreading services for all types of mss (sorry, I do not edit erotic). I work through e-mail using Word Tracker."

ACCENTUATED BRANDNAME CREATIVITY, INC.

P.O. Box 426067, Cambridge MA 02142. (617)492-5650. **E-mail:** acreatyv1@earthlink.net. **Contact:** Chuck Brandstater, founding owner. Estab. 1996.

ADDITIONAL INFORMATION Offers copyediting, proofreading, translating a broad variety of nonfiction materials, electronic or on paper, book-length or shorter.

ACCURATE WRITING & MORE

16 Barstow Lane, Hadley MA 01035. (413)586-2388. **E-mail:** shel@principledprofit.com. **Website:** www.frugalmarketing.com. **Contact:** Shel Horowitz, owner. Estab. 1982. Offers book marketing and book shepherding services.

ADDITIONAL INFORMATION For book marketing, develops marketing strategy and individualized marketing plans for authors, books, and book series. For book shepherding, helps make the decision to publish traditionally, self-publish, e-publish, or publish through a subsidy publisher and to implement the chosen strategy.

A+EDITHER

Las Vegas NV **E-mail:** susangarcia@aplusedither.com. **Website:** aplusedither.com. **Contact:** Susan Garcia, editor.

ADDITIONAL INFORMATION Years in field: 5. Years as a freelancer: 1. "Primary Services I Provide: Editing (nonfiction preferred): I bring a unique editing perspective to material on leadership and management, human resources, or self-help topics. As a former senior leader and instructor at a military academy, I not only "walked the talk" but also taught curriculum on conflict management, organizational behavior, team-building, communication skills, personality assessments (e.g., Myers-Briggs Type Indicator, DiSC), motivational theory, etc. Editing (technical): As a full-time technical editor, I ensured subject matter experts clearly conveyed their ideas and research to a wider audience. My focus is always to improve the clarity of the language without "dumbing down" the content. I not only improve the narratives of technical documents but also enhance accompanying tables, graphs, figures, and maps. Always seeking to improve my skills, I am currently enrolled in the Technical Communication certification at the University of California, San Diego. Copyediting/Proofreading: Naturally meticulous and detail oriented, I have an affinity for editing each line of your writing. I will find and resolve the grammar, syntax, punctuation, and formatting issues, being careful not to change your stylistic voice or intended meaning. I am certified in the Professional Sequence in Editing program, University of California, Berkeley." See resume at www.the-efa.org/members/data/resumes/garcias.pdf.

ANGELA AIDOO

E-mail: angela@aidoo-edit.com. **Website:** www.aidoo-edit.com. **Contact:** Angela Aidoo.

ADDITIONAL INFORMATION Over 10 years experience offering personalized editorial services to new and experienced writers of fiction and nonfiction. Comfortable editing books and materials produced by non-native speakers of English. Services include developmental editing, copyediting, proofreading, research, and fact-checking. Accustomed to meeting tight deadlines.

TIINA ALEMAN

P. O. Box 6635, Jersey City NJ 07306. (551)580-0428. **E-mail:** tiinaaleman@gmail.com. **Contact:** Tiina Aleman.

ADDITIONAL INFORMATION Editor specializing in translation editing. Translates from the Estonian into English. Received her editorial certification from NYU. Skills: Ms editing, copyediting, line editing, translation editing, copywriting, proofreading, typography, desktop publishing, prepress, production management, project management. Off-site freelance editorial and production projects preferred.

ALL MY BEST

5852 Oak Meadow Dr., Yorba Linda CA 92886. (714)777-1238. **E-mail:** lynette@allmybest.com. **Website:** www.allmybest.com. **Contact:** Lynette M. Smith.

ADDITIONAL INFORMATION "Contact Lynette Smith, owner of All My Best Business and Nonfiction Copyediting, to benefit from her 30 years' experience in copyediting and proofreading, up to and including the level of minor rewrites. Lynette can help you, whether you're a nonfiction author, publisher, printing firm, small business, corporation, consultant, speaker, marketer, teacher, or graduate student. She is most familiar with APA (American Psychological Association) and AP (Associated Press) style formats and can adapt to your house style or personal writing style as needed. Visit website for more information, including testimonials and free writing tips. When you're ready for assistance (or you would like a free, no-obligation sample edit and quote on a ms of at least 35,000 words), send an e-mail."

ALWAYS WRITE PROOFREADING & EDITING

Ingram TX (936)825-1900. **E-mail:** writingspecialist@alwayswrite.us. **Website:** www.alwayswrite.us. **Contact:** Dawn S. Herring, Owner/Writing Specialist.
ADDITIONAL INFORMATION Dawn Herring has been in the field for over 20 years, with 6 years as a freelancer. She provides affordable and professional proofreading, editing, and revising services. Dawn has both a BA and an MA in English, with a specialization in linguistics/grammar. She has over 20 years combined professional experience in the following: proofreading and editing scholarly articles, theses and dissertations, website content, creative works, newsletters, resumes, technical reports, and numerous types of business documents; teaching college writing and grammar courses; tutoring writing and grammar; and developing and presenting seminars on her skills.

JOHN C. ANDERSON

1117 Sherwood Ave., San Jose CA 95126. (415)574-1051. **E-mail:** jcax01@gmail.com. **Website:** jca01. wordpress.com. **Contact:** John Anderson, owner. Estab. 2000.
ADDITIONAL INFORMATION Offers writing and editing services, including copywriting, copyediting, proofing for publication, marketing communications, ghostwriting, news writing, feature writing, marketing and promotional copy.

A+ EDITING AND PROOFREADING

20407 39th Place NE, Lake Forest Park WA 98155. (206)786-0560. **E-mail:** julie@jklein-editor.com. **Website:** www.jklein-editor.com. **Contact:** Julie Klein, owner/operator. Estab. 2012.
ADDITIONAL INFORMATION Line editor, copy editor, and proofreader with experience in fiction genres,

especially women's, LGBT, literary, and historical. Your dictated, handwritten, typed, or word-processed ms converted and developed for e-publication.

CARL ARNOLD

156 Prospect Park, West Brooklyn NY 11215. (718)788-5944 (phone & fax); (347)254-0527 (cell). **E-mail:** carlarnold@mac.com. **Website:** http://www. edit1to1.com/. **Contact:** Carl Arnold.
ADDITIONAL INFORMATION For 25 years Carl Arnold has worked in areas of publishing (mostly book mss and large education projects for Scholastic and McGraw-Hill), advertising, finance and law, and has also worked one-to-one with people writing dissertations as well as essays for college and graduate school applications, helping them with English. He has varying ability with Greek, French, German, Turkish, Hebrew and Arabic. See more at http://www. the-efa.org/members/data/resumes/arnoldc.pdf.

NICOLE ARONIS

809 E. 23rd St., Newton NC 28658. **Website:** writerlywonderings.tumblr.com. **Contact:** Nicole Aronis. Estab. 2014.
ADDITIONAL INFORMATION "I have experience with editing fiction and new mss." Wants to work with new authors or new books, "whether this is help with developmental editing or a final copyedit/proofreading before sending to agents/publsihers."

ARTIS LINGUA CONTENT CREATION & TRANSLATION

P.O. Box 3646, Wichita Falls TX 76301. (940)257-2118. **E-mail:** artislingua@gmail.com. **Website:** www.artslingua.com. **Contact:** Ysabel de la Rosa.
ADDITIONAL INFORMATION 25+ years in business communications, including publishing, advertising, and public relations. "I provide editorial and design services in English and Spanish. My experience includes working with books, magazines, feature articles, profile articles, and poetry. I work in translation and translation management in Latin American and Castilian Spanish." Skilled in translation management of complex communications in multiple languages. Winner of 170+ awards for editorial, advertising, and public relations work.

GILLIAN BAGWELL

549 Vistamont Ave., Berkeley CA 94708. **E-mail:** gillianbagwell@hotmail.com. **Website:** gillianbagwell. com. **Contact:** Gillian Bagwell. Estab. 2012.

ADDITIONAL INFORMATION Offers all levels of editing, including writing critique and coaching. Specializes in historical fiction. Also, coaches for author readings and other public speaking.

BALAGOT COMMUNICATIONS, INC.

Chicago IL **E-mail:** ChicagoWriter@outlook.com. **Contact:** Maija Rothenberg. "Years in field: 27. Years as freelancer: 27. Award-winning business and healthcare writer, editor, and collaborator with 27 years' experience developing books, articles, newsletters, and marketing communications. My goal is to make ideas fly off the page into the reader's mind through graceful, insightful writing, laser-sharp editing, and compulsive fact checking. Former president of Independent Writers of Chicago. Former instructor in the University of Chicago Publishing Program."

NICOLE BALANT EDITING

Newcastle ME (207)319-9522. **E-mail:** NicoleBalant@roadrunner.com. **Contact:** Nicole Balant, copyeditor/proofreader.
ADDITIONAL INFORMATION Years in field: 33. Years as a freelancer: 26. "Versatile and experienced copy editor and proofreader of humanities, social and hard sciences, business, and fiction; trained in-house at Greenwood Publishing Group and as a graphic designer; MS technical writing (Rensselaer Polytechnic); BA psychology and English (Bryn Mawr College). Nonfiction projects for academic presses, college textbook publishers, and business references; fiction projects include a suspense novel that debuted at #1 on the New York Times bestseller list."

KATHLEEN A. BARRY

San Diego CA (858)433-6885. **E-mail:** katieabarry@gmail.com. **Website:** www.linkedin.com/in/katie-barry. **Contact:** Katie Barry, writer/editor. Estab. 2012.
ADDITIONAL INFORMATION Writing and editing for businesses, with a focus on marketing communications.

ROBIN GANT BASKETTE

3361 Grasmere Dr., Lexington KY 40503. **E-mail:** robgabas@gmail.com. **Contact:** Robin Baskette, founder/CEO. Estab. 2013.
ADDITIONAL INFORMATION "Robin offers proofreading and copyediting services in all types of writ-

ing. Her other specialty is in math, science, and technical writing."

VICTORIA BELL EDITORIAL SERVICES

ON Canada. **E-mail:** vbell@editors.ca. **Website:** www.vmbell.com. **Contact:** Victoria Bell, editor. Estab. 2000.
ADDITIONAL INFORMATION "I'm a certified professional editor, and I hold a Master of Fine Arts in Creative Writing from the University of British Columbia. I edit and proofread fiction, whether for self-publishing or for submission to an agent or publisher."

BELLE ETOILE STUDIOS

112 Reton Ct., Cary NC 27513. **E-mail:** michael@belleetoilestudios.com. **Website:** www.belleetoilestudios.com. **Contact:** Michael Trudeau, editorial manager/co-owner. Estab. 2009. Belle Etoile is a 2-person publishing services studio from principals Michael Trudeau and Jamie Kerry.
ADDITIONAL INFORMATION "We offer design, production, and editorial to book-publishing houses and self-publishing authors." Editorial services include developmental editing, substantive editing, copyediting, proofreading, fact-checking, editorial project management, copywriting, and ms review and consultation. Design and production services include typesetting/page layout, book cover design, book interior design, book production management, logo design, branding, general graphic design, and e-book creation. "We work primarily with literary fiction, genre fiction, general nonfiction, and poetry. Our genre fiction experience includes titles in crime, fantasy and science fiction, horror, mystery and suspense, romance, young adult, and more. Our trade nonfiction experience includes titles in autobiography and biography, cultural studies and social sciences, ecology, health, history, humor, memoir, politics, sports, the occult, and more."

FRAN BERMAN

12 Locust Ave., Exeter NH 03833. (603)772-3995. **E-mail:** f.berman@comcast.net. **Contact:** Fran Berman.
ADDITIONAL INFORMATION Fran Berman has been a freelance editor for 18 years. She copyedits and proofreads copy for feature articles, academic journal articles, reference publications, websites, newsletters, press releases, and annual reports; fact checks citations and journal content. Ensures consistency of style, spelling, punctuation. Has an undergraduate degree in English and an MBA with a concentration

in finance and marketing. Has worked on a *pro bono* basis for nonprofits, producing annual reports, newsletters, and press releases. Clients have included Sloan Management Review, Cambridge University Press, Reader's Guide to Periodical Literature, the New York Philharmonic, Jewish Federation of New Hampshire, nonfiction authors, and *Consumer Guide*." See resume at http://www.the-efa.org/members/data/resumes/bermanf.pdf.

JOE BIEL DESIGN

2752 N. Williams Ave., Portland OR 97227. (503)232-3666. **Fax:** (888)503-0599. **E-mail:** joe@microcosmpublishing.com. **Website:** microcosmpublishing.com. **Contact:** Joe Biel, designer. Estab. 1995. Specializes in one and two color design interiors and two and four color book covers.

ADDITIONAL INFORMATION "We've designed hundreds of books over the life of a teenager, and we'd be happy to consider designing your book. Rates are based on how much affinity we have for your job, your budget, and how much time is presently available but can be tailored to fit any reasonable budget."

JENNIFER BILLOCK CREATIVE SERVICES

12004 255th Ave., Trevor WI 53179. **E-mail:** jenniferjoanbillock@gmail.com. **Website:** www.jenniferbillock.com. **Contact:** Jennifer Billock, owner. Estab. 2012.

ADDITIONAL INFORMATION Jennifer Billock Creative Services offers editing, writing, and layout design services. Specialties include developmental and copy editing for self-publishing mss, travel material, recipe and cookbook writing and editing, book proposals, and magazine work of all types.

BIOMEDISYS, INC.

230 E. Ohio St., Suite 702, Chicago IL 60611. (312)470-6330. **E-mail:** info@biomedisysinc.com. **Contact:** Julie Phelan, MD, MBA, president. Estab. 2012. "At Biomedisys, we write and edit biomedical communications materials for many different audiences, ranging from patients to physicians and researchers, in a variety of formats, including abstracts, mss for peer-reviewed journals, news stories and articles, scripts for presentations and multimedia, books, slide decks, training modules, web content, white papers, and business reports. Additionally, we have extensive experience in writing reports and other materials for business audiences."

ADDITIONAL INFORMATION "Along with these services, we also edit mss and reports. We have worked with clients worldwide and have experience working with non-native English-speaking writers."

CHRIS BIRGE PROOFREADING SERVICES

710 Valley View Circle, Bloomington IL 61705. (309)830-1379. **E-mail:** cubn3914@yahoo.com. **Contact:** Chris Birge, owner-operator. Estab. 2014.

ADDITIONAL INFORMATION "I am a freelance writer with the ability to offer proofreading services. The return of your materials will be prompt. Proofreading services will normally be priced at 1¢ for every 5 words. However, rates may increase if expedited service is required."

BIRTH THAT BOOK

P.O. Box 2324, Loves Park IL 61131. (888)637-3563. **E-mail:** info@kellyepperson.com. **Website:** kellyepperson.com. **Contact:** Kelly Epperson, founder. Estab. 2012.

ADDITIONAL INFORMATION Offers book coaching, editing, self-publishing. "Kelly Epperson has written 25+ books, some for New York Times bestselling authors, one that sold 3 million copies. She's been writing her weekly newspaper column since 2001 and is a judge for the International Erma Bombeck essay contest."

JENNIFER BISHOP

Bethesda MD (240)340-1149. **E-mail:** jbishop@gmail.com. **Contact:** Jennifer Bishop, editor/writer.

ADDITIONAL INFORMATION Years in field: 10. Years as a freelancer: 3. "Jennifer Bishop is a skilled editor, writer, designer, and publications manager with more than 11 years' experience serving federal agencies and science advisory groups. She has written conference proceedings and meeting minutes; developed annual reports, brochures, fact sheets, posters, and websites; and has edited technical reports, regulatory documents, and journal articles. She has worked on publications for the National Institutes of Health, Centers for Disease Control and Prevention, Department of Education, Interagency Committee on Disability Research, Nuclear Regulatory Commission, National Institute of Standards and Technology, American Library Association, and the National Academy of Sciences, among others. She has a B.F.A from Cornell University and is pursuing an M.S. in technical communication at Northeastern University."

BJORNER & ASSOCIATES

1110 Springfield Pike #8, Cincinnati OH 45215. **E-mail:** bjorner@earthlink.net. **Website:** www.bjorner.info.

ADDITIONAL INFORMATION Bjørner & Associates provides contracted services to publishers, authors, researchers and librarians to assist them in distributing high quality work in print and online. Susanne Bjørner will write, edit, and proofread for publication of: Web sites, journals, magazines, newsletters, books. She has experience with academic (college and university; K-12), library, business, and technical markets. Her prior career as a librarian and information professional assures excellent fact-checking skills in a wide range of subjects. Languages: American English native; knowledge of Danish and Spanish.

CYNTHIA BLAIR

Stony Brook NY (631)689-6119; (631)880-0432 (cell). **E-mail:** cynthiawriter@gmail.com. **Contact:** Cynthia Blair.

ADDITIONAL INFORMATION Cynthia Blair has 20 years in field and is an experienced, versatile writer and editor who is thorough, works quickly, and never misses a deadline. She is the author of more than 50 published books and is widely-published in newspapers, magazines, and trade publications "in a wide range of nonfiction topics, especially business (MBA from the M.I.T. Sloan School of Management)." Specialties: business; health, diet, and nutrition; travel; fiction. "My specialty [in nonfiction] is taking other people's thoughts and ideas, either written or oral, and turning them into a coherent, well-written piece. I am particularly adept at "translating" complicated or obscure information about every possible topic into prose that can be easily understood."

BLOOM INK

Bloomfield Hills MI 48301. (248)642-1816. **E-mail:** info@bloomwriting.com. **Website:** bloomwriting.com. **Contact:** Barbara Bloom, founder and principal. Estab. 2008. Barbara Bloom of Bloom Ink is a detail-oriented, committed writer and editor. Barbara brings more than 20 years of successful publishing and communication experience to her work. She has worked for Simon & Schuster Trade and Wayne State University Press and managed the publishing program at the Norton Simon Museum. As a freelance editor, writer, and writing coach, she promotes clear writing across a range of genres and styles. Barbara works with clients to put their best narrative forward, whatever the form: fiction or nonfiction mss (trade, academic, children's, self-publishing) or B2B and B2C communications (white papers, marketing materials, and more). **ADDITIONAL INFORMATION** Offers copyediting, developmental editing, proofreading, e-books, self-publishing, abridging, book proposals, query letters, ghostwriting, and coaching services.

BLOSSOM EDITING

E-mail: carol@blossomediting.com. **Website:** www.blossomediting.com. **Contact:** Carol Hansson.

ADDITIONAL INFORMATION "With over 14 years of experience in both copyediting and proofreading, you will receive a clean copy in a short amount of time." Example projects include: novels, resumes, cover letters, essays, and articles. Resume and references available upon request. Simple editing (including spelling and grammar): For all documents under and including 40 pages*: $5 a page. Substantitive editing (including spelling, grammar, point-of-view and continuity errors): For all documents under and including 40 pages: $7 a page. Also specializes in web editing and writing. See more pricing and information on website.

BLUE HORIZON COMMUNICATIONS

Rehoboth Beach DE (302)227-1749. **E-mail:** books@bluehorizoncommunications.com. **Website:** www.bluehorizoncommunications.com. **Contact:** Laurel Marshfield.

ADDITIONAL INFORMATION Laurel has 25 years' experience working with physicians, lawyers, educators, holistic practitioners (healers, intuitives), healthcare professionals, and business people shaping their prose. See website for more information.

BMF ENTERPRISES

6749 Shady Hollow Dr., Pace FL 32571. **E-mail:** bmf99@att.net. **Contact:** Constance Marse, editor-in-chief. Estab. 2010.

ADDITIONAL INFORMATION Offers editorial services by a professional editor and writer with more than 30 years experience. "Constance Marse specializes in editing and proofreading books, blogs, website material and brochures for individuals, businesses, and publishers. This editing/proofreading service includes a review for readability, consistent style, punctuation, typographical errors, and grammar usage while retaining the tone, style, and voice of the author."

BOOK COMPLETION

2407 California St. SE, Huntsville AL 35801. **E-mail:** cara@bookcompletion.com. **Website:** bookcompletion.com. **Contact:** Cara Stein, owner. Estab. 2012. Services include weaving and melding content into a ms; editing and polishing mss; designing cover to match branding, attract readers, and convey the feel and message of book's content; designing an interior layout to go with the cover and help communicate the message; producing the book as a PDF e-book for sale or distribution on your website; producing the book as an e-book in Kindle and e-pub formats for sale on Amazon, Barnes & Noble, etc.; and producing the book for print.

ADDITIONAL INFORMATION "We do the whole process, from writing and editing to layout and design. The result will be an attractive, professional book that showcases your work. Let us be your one-stop shop to get your book finished and fabulous!"

THE BOOK DOCTOR IS IN

San Pedro CA 90732. (310)346-8852. **E-mail:** stacey@thebookdoctorisin.com. **Website:** thebookdoctorisin.com. **Contact:** Stacey Aaronson, fulfiller of publishing dreams and founder. Estab. 2011. Offers market analysis program, professional editing, artistic book cover design, standout book layout and design, writing services, superb e-book design, custom graphics creation, publishing facilitation, engaging promo materials, creative website design, attentive communication, and handholding from start to finish.

ADDITIONAL INFORMATION "I take you by the hand as a self-publishing author and transform your ms into the book you've dreamed of—from impeccable editing and proofreading to engaging, audience-targeted cover and professional interior design—rivaling or exceeding a traditional house publication."

BOOK EDITING ASSOCIATES

(469)789-3030. **E-mail:** editor@ms-editing.com; bookeditors@msediting.com. **E-mail:** editingnetwork@gmail.com. **Website:** book-editing.com; editing-writing.com; childrensbookeditors.com. **Contact:** Lynda Lotman.

ADDITIONAL INFORMATION "Book-Editing.com is a service for writers that screens, tests, and monitors book editors, proofreaders, indexers, and publishing consultants."

THE BOOK EDITOR: LAURIE ROSIN

P.O. Box 7688, Sarasota FL 34278. (941) 921-0906. **E-mail:** laurie@thebookeditor.com. **E-mail:** thebookeditor@aol.com. **Website:** www.thebookeditor.com. Estab. 1979.

ADDITIONAL INFORMATION Laurie Rosin has more than 35 years editing and consulting experience in all genres for clients worldwide. Has edited 38 national best sellers. Over 50 million copies in print. Writing Fellow, National Endowment for the Humanities. Offers comprehensive chapter-by-chapter critiques and line editing; also offers one-on-one Master Class. Fee determined by word count.

BOOKING AUTHORS INK

E-mail: lynda@bookingauthorsink.com. **Website:** bookingauthorsink.com. **Contact:** Lynda Bouchard, chief inspiration officer. Estab. 1999.

ADDITIONAL INFORMATION Offers a boutique public relations firm dedicated to authors. "I do publicity and marketing, editing, speech writing, guest blog posts, event planning, and concierge services for authors."

BOOKMARK EDITING

Austin TX (512)318-8259. **E-mail:** kelly@bookmarkediting.com. **Contact:** Kelly Besecke.

ADDITIONAL INFORMATION Years as freelancer: 5. "I am a developmental editor and copyeditor for scholars, students, nonfiction authors, and organizations. I draw on 15 years of experience with academic writing and publishing to ensure focused arguments, clear explanations, and an organized and reader-friendly presentation of ideas. My greatest strengths as an editor are organizing ideas, explaining complex ideas clearly, and helping writers develop their thinking about works in progress. My copyediting services emphasize clarity, flow, and grammatical correctness. My developmental editing services can involve coaching and consulting with authors from the beginning to the end of their writing projects or simply helping them take a draft to the next level. I listen hard and read carefully to fully understand authors' intentions so I can help them think through and develop their ideas and communicate them well." See resume at www.the-efa.org/members/data/resumes/beseckek.pdf.

BOOKMARKER EDITORIAL SERVICES

20 Lower Via Casitas, Unit #3, Greenbrae CA 94904. (415)785-4985; (732)513-1276 (cell). **Fax:** (415)785-

4836. **E-mail:** cnixon@bookmarker-es.com. **E-mail:** bookmarker_es@yahoo.com. **Website:** www.bookmarker-es.com. **Contact:** Cindy B. Nixon. Estab. 1996.
ADDITIONAL INFORMATION Years in field: 22 Years as freelancer: 18. "Bookmarker Editorial Services can meet any and all of your editorial needs, whether basic or detailed proofreading; light or heavy copyediting; minor or major copy revisions; full-service writing projects from scratch; and everything in between—like fact-checking, ghostwriting, line editing, project management, and desktop publishing. Bookmarker serves large and small clients as well as simple and complex projects. "Clients can feel completely confident knowing that publications will be thoroughly consistent, accurate, and error-free, so that they'll look and read their best. Owner and operator Cindy B. Nixon has been specializing in promotional copywriting, fiction/nonfiction copyediting, and general proofreading since earning her master's in English from Rutgers University in 1991."

BOOKMARK SERVICES

P.O. Box 793, Housatonic MA 02136-0793. **E-mail:** victoria@bookmarkservices.net. **Website:** bookmarkservices.net. **Contact:** Victoria Wright, owner. Estab. 1995. Special rates for seniors and students. MasterCard, VISA, and PayPal accepted.
ADDITIONAL INFORMATION Victoria and her merry band of experts offer assistance for your written words: ms evaluation, developmental editing, copyediting, proofreading, ghostwriting, fact-checking, research, APA formatting, audio transcription, layout, cover design, query letters, book proposals, self-publishing. "We are happy to work with writers of every level of skill and experience, in virtually every area of focus: fiction, nonfiction, young adult, memoirs, business, technical, and academic."

MARK BOSS

1005 Huntingdon Road, Panama City FL 32405. **E-mail:** mark@chimpwithpencil.com. **Website:** www.chimpwithpencil.com. **Contact:** Mark Boss, editor. Estab. 2011.
ADDITIONAL INFORMATION "I freelance for tech companies, novelists and nonfiction writers, and edit web content, blog posts, novels, short stories, academic papers, query letters, and business books. My rates are competitive. If you have something you need edited, I may be able to help."

BOUTIQUE LITERARY CONSULTANCY

2932 B. Langhorne Road, Lynchburg VA 24501-1734. (615)681-9977. **E-mail:** lspain@laboutiqueave.com. **Website:** www.laboutiqueave.com. **Contact:** John Gosslee, executive editor. Estab. 2012. Boutique is a literary consultant agency and editing house. "Our group of award-winning and widely-published authors provide personalized, nurturing support for your work. We pass work on to a number of literary agents and publishers. Boutique has placed mss with Big Six publishers like Random House, Simon & Schuster, and HarperCollins, as well as with Atlantic Grove, Farrar, Straus & Giroux, and Knopf, in addition to numerous mid-sized and small publishers nationwide. We've additionally placed short fiction, poems, essays, and other work with a long list of top literary magazines through our referrals. We also develop a sound approach to a range of career objectives, including university teaching placement, book touring, fellowship applications, author visibility, creating an extended readership around an author's work, and other specific career-building objectives."

BETHANY BRENGAN, EDITING SERVICES

(360)390-5618. **E-mail:** bfbrengan@gmail.com. **Website:** www.brenganedits.com. **Contact:** Bethany F. Brengan. Estab. 2007.
ADDITIONAL INFORMATION "Bethany Brengan, Editing Services, offers high-quality, professional content and copyediting to those looking to self-publish or who are trying to prepare a ms to send to publishers and agents. Fiction and nonfiction mss of all genres are accepted, excluding erotica. The editor has years of experience from her freelance career and her work at an independent publisher, and she is familiar with several style guides, including Chicago, MLA, and APA."

MARLENE BROEMER, PH. D.

6827 SW Montauk Circle, Lake Oswego OR 97035. (503)372-6325; (503)902-2380. **E-mail:** marlenemp@yahoo.com. **Contact:** Marlene Broemer, Ph.D.
ADDITIONAL INFORMATION Marlene Broemer has 25 years in the field. "My personal experience as a writer includes both fiction and poetry, but I have worked most of my life with practical texts—grant applications, business proposals, essays, journal articles for academic and business publications, documentation for government agencies, including groups such as the United Nations and the European Union.

One specialty I have is working with writers for whom English is a 2nd or 3rd language. Depending on my familiarity with the native language I may be able to help the writer to better conceptualize materials in English. My languages are: French, Russian, Swedish, and Finnish." Education and degrees: Univ. of Helsinki, Ph.D. Comparative Literature; San Francisco State University., M.A., Comparative Literature; Michigan State Univ., B.A. English &Education. See resume at www.the-efa.org/members/data/resumes/broemerm.pdf.

KIM BROOKS

(773)654-1968 (home); (312)953-0076 (cell). **E-mail:** kabrooks@mac.com. **Contact:** Kim Brooks.
ADDITIONAL INFORMATION Years in field: 6. Years as freelancer: 6. "A published author and experienced editor with a Masters degree in creative writing from the Iowa Writers' Workshop at the University of Iowa, Kim approaches all projects with enthusiasm, creativity, and a well-honed editorial eye. Her own work has appeared in such publications as Salon.com, Babble.com, Glimmer Train, One Story, and Epoch. From years of practicing her craft, Kim understands both the hard work and imagination that goes into good writing. She has eight years experience teaching creative writing and composition on the college level, and is comfortable working with clients on everything from concept and narrative to line editing."

VALERIE BROOKS

The Write Edit, Santa Fe New Mexico 87507. **Fax:** (505)988-1473. **E-mail:** valerie@thewriteedit.com. **Website:** thewriteedit.com. **Contact:** Valerie Brooks, M.A.
ADDITIONAL INFORMATION Valerie Brooks has worked in the field for 15 years as a substantive editor, copy editor, and proofreader, specializing in fiction and nonfiction mss. She follows Chicago and AP style. Her "areas of expertise include health and wellness, mainstream literature, women's literature, performing arts, animals, spiritual, memoir, spas, and travel. She earned a M.A. in Writing and Publishing from Rosemont College, PA and a B.A. in Journalism from Hofstra University, NY. For more information, see www.the-efa.org/members/data/resumes/brooksv.txt.

WYNNE BROWN LLC

2733 W. Hilltop Road, Portal AZ 85632. (520)558-1131. **E-mail:** wynnebrown@mac.com. **Website:** www.wynnebrown.com. **Contact:** Wynne Brown,

owner. Estab. 2012. Wynne Brown has spent 35 years as a freelance graphic designer, writer, and editor. Design services include book design, presentations, brochures, newsletters, technical illustrations, logo development.
ADDITIONAL INFORMATION She also spent 6 years as a copy editor at a mid-sized daily newspaper and has edited books, magazine articles, and academic publications. She is comfortable with Associated Press, Chicago Manual of Style, and American Psychological Association stylebooks.

SHEILA BUFF

500 Milan Hill Road, Milan NY 12571. (845)758-3035. **E-mail:** sheilabuff@frontiernet.net. **Website:** www.sheilabuff.com. **Contact:** Sheila Buff.
ADDITIONAL INFORMATION Sheila Buff brings 20 years of successful experience in publishing to her clients. She specializes in health, nutrition, and consumer medicine and is the ghostwriter or co-author of 7 national bestsellers. Her editorial skills can help you with book proposals, ms reviews, editorial input, book coaching, and self-publishing. Her recent book projects have been with HarperWave, Kaplan, Globe Pequot, Hyperion, and other trade publishers. "In addition to my medical book work, I am the author of numerous titles on birdwatching, natural history, gardening and the outdoors." See publication list at http://www.the-efa.org/members/data/resumes/buffs.pdf.

BUILD AN ONLINE PLATFORM THAT WORKS

22 Chestnut Way, Manalapan NJ 07726. **E-mail:** karencioffi@ymail.com. **Website:** karencioffi.com. **Contact:** Karen Cioffi, owner. Estab. 2012.
ADDITIONAL INFORMATION Offers an online course focuses on "how to create and build online platforms, starting with the website. A version of the course is offered as an e-class through WOW! Women on Writing."

STACY BURNS

Denver CO **E-mail:** stacylburns@gmail.com. **Contact:** Stacy Burns.
ADDITIONAL INFORMATION "I hold an MFA in Creative Writing and have five years of editing experience and three years of experience teaching college-level composition and creative writing courses. I have worked in all stages of the written communication process—from brainstorming, research, and

outlining to writing, proofreading, fact checking, and line editing, to designing layout, typesetting, and publishing. The publications I have worked on range from literary journals to church newsletters to international computer specification standards." See resume at http://www.the-efa.org/members/data/resumes/burnss.pdf.

CINDY BUSHONG

4083 Sheridan Ave., Loveland CO 80538. **E-mail:** cindybushong.1@gmail.com. **Website:** linkedin.com/pub/cindy-bushong/9/330/163. **Contact:** Cindy Bushong, owner/editor. Estab. 2009.

ADDITIONAL INFORMATION Offers editing, copyediting, and proofreading print and online content related to technology and science.

JEFF BUTLER

600 Arbor Dr., #629, Dry Ridge KY 41035. **E-mail:** c.jeffbutler@gmail.com. **Contact:** Jeff Butler, owner. Estab. 2014.

ADDITIONAL INFORMATION "My work on a ms can be as detailed as the client needs. I work closely with the writer/publisher to make sure that a ms is not only readable, but also accurate in the instance of nonfiction. If a detailed copy edit is not desired or needed, I am also available for proofreading."

THE BUTTERFLY TYPEFACE

1303 Calla Circle, Fayetteville NC 28303. (501)251-8118. **E-mail:** butterflytypeface.imw@gmail.com. **Website:** www.thebutterflytypeface.com. **Contact:** Iris Williams McGee, owner. Estab. 2014.

ADDITIONAL INFORMATION Offers editing, writing, ms typeset and design.

CAROL'S CORRECTIONS

P.O. Box 381, Cedar Bluffs NE 68015-0381. **E-mail:** carolweber@windstream.net. **Website:** www.carolscorrections.weebly.com. **Contact:** Carol Weber. Estab. 2012.

ADDITIONAL INFORMATION "Please note that I will not do erotica, the occult or horror. Period. All services require a 50% deposit before I begin, with the second half due upon receipt of the edited work. What I offer: A Sample Edit. You'll want to ensure you're going to like my editing style; I will want to ensure your ms is ready for editing, and that I'll be a good fit for your ms. I'll be happy to edit, for free, five to ten pages of your ms. My work is content editing, or line editing, depending on whose definition you use. This is intended to be the final look-through a book before you call it done, and declare it ready for the public."

LEE E. CART

15 Taylor Cemetery Road, Wellington ME 04942. **E-mail:** lee.e.cart@gmail.com. **Website:** www.leeecart.com. **Contact:** Lee E. Cart, owner/author. Estab. 2010.

ADDITIONAL INFORMATION Offers developmental editing, line editing, writing coach, proofreading, Spanish translation, and advice on becoming a book reviewer.

KATHY CARTER

Peoria IL (309)685-6389. **E-mail:** kathy@carteredit.com. **Website:** www.carteredit.com. **Contact:** Kathy Carter.

ADDITIONAL INFORMATION Kathy Carter has edited books since 1982 andstarted her own editing business in 2006. She is a "reliable freelanceeditor specializing in nonfiction books. Meticulous editing with special emphasis on structure and organization." Services include developmental, structural, substantive, and copy editing. Clients include Beacon Press, Unitarian Universalist Association, and numerous individual authors. Kathy can be contacted through her website.

KAREN CARTER COMMUNICATIONS

10604 Lieter Place, Lone Tree CO 80124. **E-mail:** karen.carter7@gmail.com. **Website:** kccommunications.blogspot.com. **Contact:** Karen Carter, copy editor. Estab. 2003.

ADDITIONAL INFORMATION "I am a copy editor with more than 25 years of experience. When you hire me to edit your ms, you can be confident not only in my abilities as an editor, but in the professional caliber of every interaction you will have with me. I enjoy working with authors and have edited dozens of books that range from business and self-help titles to memoirs and poetry collections to novels in just about every genre."

CASTLE COMMUNICATIONS

3900 Balcones Woods Dr., Austin TX 78759-5006. (512)413-5059. **Fax:** (512)231-0966. **E-mail:** lc@castlecommunications.com. **Website:** www.castlecommunications.com. **Contact:** Lana Castle, owner. Estab. 1996. Castle Communications provides expert editing, production services, and publishing advice. The owner, Lana Castle, provides the inside scoop on publishing, helps clients choose the best pathways, and steers them clear of common pitfalls. Her company helps writers publish outstanding printed books, ebooks, audiobooks, and media materials that meet their timeline, budget, business experience, quality expectations, and needs for prestige and creative control. Lana's diverse experience includes writing, editing, design, graphics, layout, and audio and video production. She is also an internationally published author of four trade books, the editor of an anthology, and she launched and runs two publishing companies.

CENTER FOR WRITING EXCELLENCE

1164 W. 21st Ave., Apache Junction AZ 85120. (928)458-5861. **E-mail:** janiewrites1@gmail.com. **Website:** janiewrites.com. **Contact:** Janie Sullivan, director. Estab. 2009.

ADDITIONAL INFORMATION The Center for Writing Excellence offers professional, customized writing services. "We pride ourselves in professional work, quick turnaround, and reasonable prices. If you have a writing project coming up, consider the C4WE. Our writing staff is standing by ready to help get your writing projects done on time and on budget!"

C.F. EDITORIAL SERVICES

624 E. 18th St. N., Newton IA 50208. (641)417-9378. **E-mail:** cfedits@hotmail.com. **Contact:** Cynthia Freeman, copyeditor.

ADDITIONAL INFORMATION "Copyeditor/developmental editor with 19 years experience, specializing in peer reviewed scientific publishing, ESL or native English, in subjects ranging from physics and materials engineering to tire science and technology. Editing for organization, subordination, and redundancy, as well as grammar and syntax, punctuation, form and use of symbols, nomenclature, and clarity of expression. CMS and ACS style, and meticulous use of house styles." For more information, see www.the-efa.org/members/data/resumes/freemanc.pdf.

CHANGE IT UP EDITING AND WRITING SERVICES

5580 G. Coach House Cricle, Boca Raton FL 33486. (954)348-1963. **E-mail:** cyjohnson5580@gmail.com. **Website:** http://changeitupediting.com. **Contact:** Candace Johnson, editor/owner. Estab. 2012.

ADDITIONAL INFORMATION Editorial services offered include copyediting/line editing, content editing, proofreading, article/blog editing, and mss evaluations.

CHANGEMAKERS PUBLISHING AND WRITING

750 La Playa, #952, San Francisco CA 94121. (415)571-8282. **E-mail:** info@changemakerspublishingandwriting.com. **Website:** www.changemakerspublishingandwriting.com. **Contact:** Gini Graham Scott, Ph.D., J.D. Estab. 1968.

ADDITIONAL INFORMATION "I consult with and write books, articles, and scripts for clients, working from rough drafts, notes, interviews, tapes of workshops/seminars, and other materials. I also help clients publish and promote their books or find mainstream publishers, agents, and film producers. I have published over 50 books of my own, have written 15 original scripts, several under option, and have written, produced, and sometimes directed over 40 short films, including book and script trailers, which can be seen at www.youtube.com/changemakersprod. I also conduct workshops, seminars, teleseminars, and Webinars on writing, publishing, and promoting one's books and articles."

DANIELLE JANE CHOUHAN

9 Highland Park, Malden MA 02148. (617)818-7123. **E-mail:** dchouhan@pagetoportal.com. **Contact:** Danielle Jane Chouhan, editor.

ADDITIONAL INFORMATION Years in field: 8; years as freelancer: 5. "I offer editorial services and production project management for a variety of projects—big and small. I am a full-time, freelance editorial specialist with experience in K-12 as well as the college and higher-education markets." Danielle offers project management, copyediting, and proofreading, and prefers—but am not limited to—online mark-up and softproofing. Experience includes: school curriculum textbooks, scholarly journals, software instructional textbooks, corporate materials, and online database/encyclopedia content. Education: Napier University: Edinburgh, Scotland, UKMaster's Diploma in Publishing with Business; Brandeis University: Waltham, MABA in Sociology; Humanities Interdisciplinary Minor; La Sorbonne: (Université de Paris VII): Paris, France. Completed Spring Semester Abroad through the New York University program in France. See resume: www.the-efa.org/members/data/resumes/chouhand.pdf.

CHRYSALIS EDITORIAL

6439 Barnaby St., NW, Washington DC 20015. (301)704-1455. **Website:** www.chrysaliseditorial.com.

Contact: Herta B. Feely, owner; Emily Williamson, senior editor.

ADDITIONAL INFORMATION Offers editing and writing services by award-winning, published writers. "Chrysalis Editorial serves writers in a variety of capacities. Our ms critiques have helped countless writers hone and revise their work into publishable shape. We also offer ghostwriting, copy editing, provide agent and publishing advice (e-books too), and act as writing coaches for numerous clients, many of whom have gone on to obtain agents and publish their work."

CLEAR COPY EDITORIAL SERVICES

Boise ID (208)426-0772. **E-mail:** editors@clearcopy.com. **Website:** www.clearcopy.com. **Contact:** Harvey McCloud.

ADDITIONAL INFORMATION "Our business is writing, editing, and proofreading text documents, both technical and nontechnical, nonfiction and fiction." Services include writing, structural editing, rewriting, copyediting, proofreading, research, academic consultation and guidance, research design, statistical analysis. Contact for a quote or additional information.

CLOSE READER EDITING

(832)428-7651. **E-mail:** closereaderedit@aol.com. **Contact:** Stephen Delaney.

ADDITIONAL INFORMATION Stephen Delaney is an editor and proofreader of fiction and nonfiction with 10 years in the field, 8 as a freelancer. Specialties: short stories, novels, poetry, science fiction, fantasy, memoir, and creative nonfiction. See more info at www.the-efa.org/members/data/resumes/delaneys.pdf.

CMF EDITORIAL SERVICES

6465 Sagebrush Ct., Westerville OH 43081-3720. **E-mail:** christinefil@yahoo.com. **Contact:** Christine Filippetti, editor/proofreader. Estab. 2009.

ADDITIONAL INFORMATION Editorial services include editing, proofreading, fact checking and research, page layout, assessment test correlations, and item writing.

COACH BONNIE

P.O. Box 6075, Evanston IL 60204. (847)962-4770. **E-mail:** bonfire770@gmail.com. **Website:** www.coachbonnie.com. **Contact:** Bonnie Kustner. Estab. 1999. Offers one-on-one coaching services for the writer,

the writer-to-be, the writer who thinks he can, the writer who is stuck, and the writer who is soaring. "Coaching brings consistency, accountability, and sometimes (but only when needed) a major kick in the butt."

ADDITIONAL INFORMATION "Terrific for the writer who isn't sure how to get started, fabulous for the writer who got started but then got stuck, and pure genius for the writer who needs to finish, edit, proof, polish, and publish their extraordinary oeuvre."

COFFEE HOUSE FICTION EDITING SERVICES

Forest Hills MD 21050. **E-mail:** info@coffeehousefiction.com. **Website:** www.coffeehousefiction.com. Estab. 2007.

ADDITIONAL INFORMATION "To advance our objective of elevating excellent fiction, we've been supplying editing services to promising authors for over two years. We can focus on grammar, punctuation, and basic elements of style, readability, and sentence structure. We can also provide you with content editing, a more involved holistic reading of the fiction, and work with you on overall style, theme, complexity, and structure of a story. While fiction is a passion, we've worked with a number of authors of nonfiction; and we happily and meticulously edit documents of all types." Cost: generally runs 2¢ per word. Other editorial services and assistance are available upon request. Accepts submissions and inquiries by e-mail only.

BRUCE COLE

726 Tyner Way, Incline Village NV 89451. (775)831-7747. **E-mail:** rbacole@hotmail.com. **Contact:** Bruce Cole.

ADDITIONAL INFORMATION Bruce Cole has spent 34 years in thie field as freelancer. He was first published in 1980. His articles and reviews have appeared in *Worldview Magazine, The Willamette Valley Observer, The Catholic Sentinel, The Portland Oregonian, The Downtowner, The North Lake Tahoe Bonanza, and Tahoe World.* His extensive proof-reading experience was acquired at The Liturgical Press, Yale University Press, and various magazines and newspapers. He has expertise in history and biography, theology and philosophy, current events, literature, health and insurance issues. Available for articles, book reviews, and editorials; proofing and editing of mss of all sizes. He is affiliated with Editorial Freelancers Association. See resume: www.the-efa.org/members/data/resumes/coleb.pdf.

JULIE COLLINS WRITES

725 Decatur St., Lincoln IL 62656. **E-mail:** juliecbates@yahoo.com. **Website:** juliecollinswrites.com. **Contact:** Julie Collins Bates, owner. Estab. 2004.
ADDITIONAL INFORMATION Offers writing, editorial project management, copy editing, proofreading.

COMMA SENSE EDITING

252 Bayview Ave., East Patchogue NY 11772. **E-mail:** lvediting@gmail.com. **Website:** www.commasense.net. **Contact:** Lourdes Venard, president. Estab. 2010. CommaSense Editing was founded by Lourdes Venard, an editor with more than 20 years experience.
ADDITIONAL INFORMATION "We offer developmental editing, copyediting, proofreading, and translations (from Spanish to English). We work mostly with individual authors, whether they plan to self-publish or are seeking an agent/publishing house. CommaSense specializes in crime fiction, science fiction, YA, Hispanic-themed books, and memoirs."

COPY A LA CARTE

484 W. 43rd St., Apt. 24F, New York NY 10036-6341. (212)564-6343. **E-mail:** macle8@aol.com. **Contact:** Chris MacLeod. Estab. 1992.
ADDITIONAL INFORMATION Offers editing, writing, and customized copywriting services.

THE COPYMANCER

Brooklyn NY **E-mail:** rose@copymancer.com. **Website:** www.copymancer.com. **Contact:** Rose Jasper Fox, editor.
ADDITIONAL INFORMATION Years in field: 17. Years as a freelancer: 11. "I edit short and long fiction, primarily focusing on genre fiction. I specialize in helping new authors get their first novels ready for querying agents or self-publishing." Types of work: Copy editing, proofreading, line editing, project editing, substantive editing, critique, research. Types of material: Books, mss, short stories, novels. Subjects covered: Fiction (science fiction, fantasy, horror, romance, erotica, pornography) related to mythology, folklore, history, geography and travel, language and linguistics, spelling and grammar, writing and journalism, mathematics, science, medicine, sexuality, sex and gender, politics and activism, technology, crafts, food and cooking, dance, and music.

JUDY CORCORAN

325 West 52nd St., 2G, New York NY 10019. (212)315-2449. **E-mail:** judycorc@aol.com. **Website:** www.JudyCorcoran.com. **Contact:** Judy Corcoran.
ADDITIONAL INFORMATION "Judy Corcoran is a highly respected writer, copywriter, copyeditor and proofreader. She has worked at magazines such as *Real Simple, Good Housekeeping, Better Homes and Gardens, Time, Fortune, Money,* and *Golf Digest*, writing advertorials, marketing materials and merchandising proposals. She authored *The Concise Guide to Magazine Marketing: Tips, Tools and Best Practices* and the co-author of *Joint Custody with a Jerk: Raising a Child with an Uncooperative Ex* and *Volleyball: Playing with Your Head at Any Height.* Judy offers professional service, a quick turn-around time, and crisp, accurate copy at an affordable price." She has been in the field for 25 years, 15 as a freelancer. See more information at www.the-efa.org/members/data/resumes/corcoranj.pdf.

CREATIVELINK

P.O. Box 318, Hammondsport NY 14840. **E-mail:** info@creativelinkgraphics.com. **Website:** creativelinkgraphics.com. **Contact:** Anne Kiley, sole proprietor. Estab. 1995. Creativelink is a complete design service; check website for portfolio.
ADDITIONAL INFORMATION Offers innovative, production-oriented book design services for authors wanting to self-publish, but who want their books to look as individual as they are themselves. Also complete writing and editorial service.

CRITIQUE MY NOVEL

2408 W. 8th Ave., Amarillo TX 79106. **E-mail:** questions@critiquemynovel.com. **Website:** critiquemynovel.com. **Contact:** Catherine York, owner/chief editor. Estab. 2011.
ADDITIONAL INFORMATION "We offer free sample critiques, several editing services for all levels of ms, and easy payment plans. Combine our services to cover all stages of your revisions, and we'll include e-book formatting once your book is ready."

CROSS-BORDER EDITORIAL SERVICES

San Diego CA (858)243-0781. **E-mail:** gaddis@cbes.biz. **Contact:** David Gaddis Smith.
ADDITIONAL INFORMATION Year in field: 30. Years as a freelancer: 4. "David Gaddis Smith is a writer, editor, researcher and Spanish-to-English translator with extensive knowledge about Mexico, border,

Middle East, and other international issues. Long the foreign editor of the San Diego Union-Tribune, he now edits for the Al-Monitor website and writes and edits for MexicoPerspective.com and other organizations involved with Mexico and border issues."

KIM CROZIER

(616)235-8300. **Fax:** (616)235-8340. **E-mail:** kbcandmk@gmail.com. **Contact:** Kim Crozier, owner. Estab. 1999.

ADDITIONAL INFORMATION Offers developmental and copy editing, technical/copy and creative writer, large contracts, negotiations, and business/corporation formation.

CSINCLAIRE WRITE-DESIGN

3405 Old Chapel Hill Road, Unit B, Durham NC 27707. (919)260-0031. **E-mail:** info@cswritedesign.com. **Contact:** Charlotte Sinclaire, owner. Estab. 1992.

ADDITIONAL INFORMATION Offers services in both graphic design and editorial evaluation. Editorial is to the extent requested, anything from a simple read-through with comments to red-lining, rewriting, or even ghostwriting. Fiction or nonfiction welcome.

MEGHAN CUNNINGHAM

2611 Formosa Ave., Orlando FL 32804. (321)480-2558 (cell); (407)893-5296. **E-mail:** mcunigan@bellsouth.net. **Contact:** Meghan Cunningham.

ADDITIONAL INFORMATION Meghan Cunningham has 18 years in the field. "I have textbooks published with both Cengage and McGraw-Hill; in addition, I have worked on website content for developmental readers for McGraw-Hill. My writing and editing skills are extremely adaptable; I have worked on legal documents, magazines, textbooks and educational materials, dissertations, health materials, and classified goverment material. For 10 years, I taught college-level developmental reading and writing. In addition to teaching developmental English, I have taught research-based composition courses and ESL courses. My teaching experience has given me an edge in meeting the demands of today's students and being able to adapt my teaching style to many different types of students. I have extremely high standards, am a strict grammarian, and am interested in producing only quality work." Provides writing samples and references. See CV at www.the-efa.org/members/data/resumes/cunninghamma.pdf

KAREN CURE

Hastings on Hudson NY (917)975-1727 (cell). **E-mail:** karencure@gmail.com. **Contact:** Karen Cure.

ADDITIONAL INFORMATION "Years in field: 35. Years as freelancer: 17. Books and magazine articles mix with grant applications, business proposals, and advertising on my lifetime writing and editing project list. I have a nuanced ear for language, and I'm adept at copyediting in Chicago and AMA styles as well as resourceful and experienced at research, proficient at leading and managing complex projects, and enthusiastic as a collaborator. I give 110 percent to channel clients' ideas and thoughts into smart, polished editorial packages. Highlights: Held editorial director-level positions at Fodor's/Random House and Globe Pequot Press. Wrote the best-selling travel guidebook of all time. For an international AIDS program, helped compile and edit dozens of grant proposals ranging in length from 300 to 4,000 pages. Designed, edited, and did layout for the national guidelines for adult and pediatric HIV care and treatment. Have written and edited documents about how to get new business for accountants and how to establish a residential program for at-risk youth. Designed and edited a master plan for a landscape architecture firm and researched printing-and-binding options."

D&R WORDSMITHS

12500 Trinity Hills, Kemp TX 75143. **E-mail:** drwordsmiths@mail.com. **Website:** drwordsmiths.weebly.com. **Contact:** Debra Smith, co-founder. Estab. 2014.

ADDITIONAL INFORMATION Offers editing, proofreading, book/ms reviews, and copywriting.

DADIVAN BOOKS

3104 E. Camelback Road #160, Phoenix AZ 85016. (347)291-1779. **Fax:** (928)268-9181. **E-mail:** dadivanbooks@gmail.com. **Website:** www.dadivanbooks.com. **Contact:** Bootsie Martinez, editor. Estab. 1989. "We are professional writers, editors, and publishers with over a century of combined experience in the publishing world."

ADDITIONAL INFORMATION Dadivan Books also offers complete self-publishing from soup-to-nuts, including economical subsidy publishing services. "We specialize in helping authors achieve their individual dreams, whether that dream is improving a ms through proofreading or editing, preparing a ms in e-publishing formats, preparing a ms in paperback layout, designing the perfect cover, or fulfilling another editorial need, including ghostwriting and book doctoring. All services are available a la carte or as part of an economical package."

CHARLES DELAFUENTE

New York City NY (845)638-2160. **E-mail:** charles-delafuente@gmail.com. **Contact:** Charles DeLa-Fuente. "Years in field: 35 Years as freelancer: 10. Experienced *New York Times* copy editor with law degree available for freelance editing, writing and research assignments. I've got decades of experience as a copy editor and line editor at *The Times* and several other newspapers. I've been a freelance editor for magazine articles and books for more than 10 years. I've also done fact-checking and proofreading for authors and publishers. I'm also an experienced newspaper and magazine reporter, available to write magazine articles. I've written appellate briefs, and I'm available to write or edit them, or do substantive legal research. In fact, because I'm licensed in New York and in the federal courts, I can even sign a brief in some circumstances."

DESIGNWRITE

12 Bourne Rise, Collingbourne Ducis, Marlborough Wiltshire SN8 3HG United Kingdom. **E-mail:** simon@designwrite.co.uk. **Website:** www.designwrite.co.uk. **Contact:** Simon Carreck. Estab. 1998. **ADDITIONAL INFORMATION** Offers content/copy/line editing, ghostwriting, and audio/video scripting. Also, book/magazine/catalogue layout and page design.

ALYSSA DI RUBBO

86 Bay State Road, Boston MA 02215. **E-mail:** adirubbo@bu.edu. **Website:** alyssadirubbo.tumblr.com. **Contact:** Alyssa Di Rubbo, writer/blogger/editor. **ADDITIONAL INFORMATION** Offers various editorial and blogging services.

DOCUMENT DRIVEN

16420 SE McGillivray #103-103, Vancouver WA 98683. (360)991-2121. **E-mail:** janice@documentdriven.com. **Website:** www.documentdriven.com. **Contact:** Janice Hussein, MS in writing/publishing. Estab. 2003. **ADDITIONAL INFORMATION** The editorial services include developmental editing, substantive editing, light and heavy copyediting, proofreading, ms critiques, submission critiques and development (query letters and synopses), and book proposal development. 12 years experience as freelance editor. In addition, she worked for a literary agent for 3 years. She works with both fiction and nonfiction writers, as well as publishers.

DOVE MEDIA GROUP INC.

6505 E. Central #301, Wichita KS 67206. **E-mail:** dovemedia@cox.net. **Website:** meetdmg.com. **Contact:** Laurie Dove, president. Estab. 1999. **ADDITIONAL INFORMATION** Offers custom print and web design, full-service editorial.

DR. TOD EDITING SERVICES

8 American Court, Catonsville MD 21228. (410)744-9349; (410)782-5646. **E-mail:** marytod@me.com; mary@drtodediting.com. **Website:** www.drtodediting.com. **Contact:** Mary Tod. "Whether you are a medical publisher or an academic researcher looking for an experienced copyeditor, I can provide you with just the right dose of medical editing. My background as a medical scientist ensures that I know and understand the scientific lingo, and my excellent language skills and training as a copyeditor allow me to polish scientific writing in a way that conforms to my publishing clients' style guides and formats." **ADDITIONAL INFORMATION** Freelance editor since 1996. Medical journal and book editing. Trade book proofreading, both fiction and nonfiction. Board-certified Editor in Life Sciences. PhD in Physiology. 10 years' experience as medical researcher on faculty of medical school. Experienced editor for ESL authors in medical fields. Author or coauthor of more than 30 scientific articles published in peer-reviewed journals.

DRYDENBKS LLC

336 Central Park W., 3F, New York NY 10025. (718)213-2127. **E-mail:** emmaddryden@gmail.com. **Website:** www.drydenbks.com. **Contact:** Emma D. Dryden, principal/founder. Estab. 2010. **ADDITIONAL INFORMATION** Offers a variety of editorial and creative services; workshops and presentations; and consultancy services. Specializes in children's books.

HEATHER DUBNICK EDITORIAL SERVICES

39 Dodge St. #356, Beverly MA 01915. (508)932-6955. **E-mail:** hdubnick@gmail.com. **Website:** www.heatherdubnick.com. **Contact:** Heather Dubnick. Estab. 2004. Heather Dubnick Editorial Services offers copyediting, developmental editing, ms evaluation,

coaching, researching, fact-checking, proofreading, formatting, and indexing.

ADDITIONAL INFORMATION "I work in Spanish as well as English."

PAIGE DUKE

North Richland Hills TX 76180. **Website:** www.thepaigeduke.com. **Contact:** Paige Duke, copy editor/proofreader. Estab. 2007.

ADDITIONAL INFORMATION "Whether you need a basic proofread or a high-level copyedit, Paige Duke would love to help you polish your ms for publication. Trust your work to an editor with an eagle eye for detail, extensive knowledge of Chicago style, and dedication to timely delivery."

THE ECLECTIC EDITOR

Lansing MI 48910. (224)999-0779. **E-mail:** brenda@eclecticeditor.com. **Website:** www.eclecticeditor.com. **Contact:** Brenda Errichiello. Estab. 2011.

ADDITIONAL INFORMATION "My editorial services are designed primarily for the first-time, self-publishing author looking for an editorial partner to make their book or novel as effective and immaculate as possible. My packages are focused on content (primarily developmental and substantive editing), and it is my goal to help bridge the gap between your first draft and the book that you always dreamed you could write. I also offer coaching services for authors who may need an accountability partner or who would like some more support during the writing process, whether that's just an encouraging word or assistance brainstorming characters out of a sticky situation."

ECO-WRITE, LLC

Environmental and Life Science Writing and Editing, Warriors Park PA (814)692-7440. **E-mail:** jdrohan@nasw.org. **Website:** www.eco-write.com. **Contact:** Joy R. Drohan.

ADDITIONAL INFORMATION Joy Drohan is a freelance science editor and award-winning writer whose clients include the U.S. Forest Service, National Park Service, Delaware Department of Natural Resources and Environmental Control, Island Press, Carnegie Institution, Grand Canyon Association, The Conservation Fund, Penn State University, University of Delaware, University of Maryland, and University of Nevada, Las Vegas, and Engineering Service (NRAES), Cornell University, NATO.

EDITING BY DEBORAH

254 Reuter Lane, Forest Grove OR 97116. (503)327-9629. **E-mail:** info@editingbydeborah.com. **Website:** editingbydeborah.com. **Contact:** Deborah Bishop, owner. Estab. 2012.

ADDITIONAL INFORMATION Refer to website for more on editing services available.

THE EDITING COMPANY

27 Carlton St., #404, Toronto ON M5B 1L2 Canada. (416)924-3856. **Fax:** (416)924-6227. **E-mail:** editor@theeditingco.com. **Website:** theeditingco.com. **Contact:** Beth McAuley, senior editor. Estab. 2009. Offers a range of services for writers, including substantive, stylistic, and copy editing; proofreading; indexing; e-book conversion; photo research; permissions editing; and photo research. "We specialize in nonfiction works, including memoirs, scholarly books and essays, self-help books, and literary nonfiction in all genres."

ADDITIONAL INFORMATION "Our publishing consulting services help guide an author through the process of traditional or independent publishing, providing advice on finding appropriate publishers and agents, querying, synopsis writing, networking and promotion, selling, and more."

EDITING EXCELLENCE

P.O. Box 2071, Spokane WA 99210. **E-mail:** barbara@barbarahollace.com. **Website:** barbarahollace.com. **Contact:** Barbara Hollace, editor/owner. Estab. 2004.

ADDITIONAL INFORMATION "My business has one standard—the standard of excellence. Whether you are a first-time author or a veteran, you deserve the best. I am a freelance editor and published author. Areas of focus include proofreading, substantive (developmental) editing, website content and ghostwriting."

EDITLAW

Sharon C. Rutberg, Seattle WA (206)409-2604. **E-mail:** legaleditor@comcast.net. **Contact:** Sharon C. Rutberg.

ADDITIONAL INFORMATION Sharon Rutberg has 28 years in the field; 8 as a freelancer. "As an attorney, I specialize in editing legal publications, including treatises for practicing lawyers, articles for professional journals, and books by attorney-authors. My goal is to help you create a clear, accurate, elegant presentation of your complex information. I bring to every project a love of order and logic, an eye for detail and visual harmony, and a passion for perfection. Whether you need help developing and organizing your ideas (developmental editing), revising your rough draft (copyediting), polishing your final draft (line editing), or proofreading the end product, I will bring out the best in your publication. I work on-line in Word using TrackChanges or in hard copy, and am familiar with Chicago and AP styles and the Bluebook. I am also comfortable working with your house style, or I can help you develop one."

EDITMORE EDITORIAL SERVICES

501-I South Reino Road #194, Newbury Park CA 91320. **E-mail:** tammy@editmore.com. **Website:** www.editmore.com. **Contact:** Tammy Ditmore, owner/editor. Estab. 2011. Offers copyediting, proofreading, and developmental editing for nonfiction authors. **ADDITIONAL INFORMATION** "I have been working with words for more than 3 decades—editing and writing for a wide range of authors and publications. I can help you get the most out of your words whether you are creating a book, article, website, annual report, or grad school assignment. Let me focus on the details so you can concentrate on the ideas."

EDITOR EXTRAORDINAIRE

Calgary AB Canada. **Fax:** (206)352-8418. **E-mail:** editor.extraordinaire@gmail.com. **Website:** editorextraordinaire.com. **Contact:** Audra Gorgiev.
ADDITIONAL INFORMATION Years in field: 15; Years as freelancer: 12. "I am a professional freelance editor (copyediting, line editing, technical editing, and substantive editing) and proofreader offering a wealth of experience editing a wide variety of written material (including textbooks, scientific, medical, and technical journal articles, academic documents, marketing materials, ESL documents, as well as other nonfiction work)."

EDITORIAL ALCHEMY

Carol Gaskin, (941)377-7640. **E-mail:** carol@editorialalchemy.com. **Website:** www.editorialalchemy.com. **Contact:** Carol Gaskin, Editor.
ADDITIONAL INFORMATION Services include ms critiques, marketing materials, line editing, development for fiction and nonfiction, writing tutorials, and occasional ghostwriting.

EDITORIAL INSPIRATIONS

15086 Brown Pleasants Road, Montepelier VA 23192. (804)883-7480. **E-mail:** editor@editorialinspirations.com. **Website:** www.editorialinspirations.com. **Contact:** April Michelle Davis, owner.
ADDITIONAL INFORMATION Editorial Inspirations provides editing, indexing, and proofreading services to both publishers and authors. April Michaelle Davis has been a freelance editor, indexer, and proofreader since 2001. She has a B.A. in English from Messiah College, a M.P.S. in publishing from The George Washington University, and several field-related certificates, including ones in book publishing and editing from the University of Virginia, along with one in professional editing from EEI Communications. April has worked with authors and publishers in a variety of genres, including training, engineering, carpentry, real estate, law, memoir, self-help, historical, biographical, scholarly, children's literature, and religion.

THE EDITORIAL NOTE

Wilmette IL **E-mail:** calcohen75@gmail.com. **Website:** www.editorialnote.net. **Contact:** David H. Cohen.
ADDITIONAL INFORMATION "David Cohen has been a professional writer and editor for over two decades. His work has appeared in the Financial Times of London, Crain's Chicago Business, Time magazine, Chicago Wilderness and other publications. His corporate editorial clients have been in the areas of healthcare and financial services. A long-term conservationist, Cohen was formerly a writer and editor for the Chicago Audubon Society, and has worked in Europe, Asia and Latin America. As a professional educator, Cohen has taught at Chicago-area universities and has developed workplace literacy programs."

EDITORIAL SERVICES OF LOS ANGELES (ESOLA)

Los Angeles CA **E-mail:** EditorialServicesofLA@gmail.com. **Website:** http://editorialservicesofla.com. **Contact:** Lisa Rojany Buccieri, proprietor.
ADDITIONAL INFORMATION ""Editorial Services of Los Angeles (ESOLA) has been in business for over 20 years and has helped hundreds of writers of both children's and adult books of fiction and nonfiction get published by traditional means and self-publishing. ESOLA offers everything from detailed content/line editing with critique letter, writing and ghostwriting, to eBook editing and pdf typesetting." Other services include book doctoring, copyediting, proofreading, ms evaluation, and more. Cost: E-mail for

quote; professional membership discounts available. Offers free query letter edit with service. See website for additional information.

EDITWRITEDESIGN

E-mail: editwritedesign@yahoo.com. **Website:** www.editwritedesign.com.

ADDITIONAL INFORMATION Editorial services include comprehensive editing. Other services include cover design and interior design and layout. Cost: Contact for quote. See website for additional information.

JOHANNA EHRMANN

Auburndale MA 02466. (617)558-9373. **E-mail:** johanna@herworkplace.com. **Contact:** Johanna Ehrmann.

ADDITIONAL INFORMATION "More than 20 years spent editing and copyediting textbooks have given me a good understanding of what works and what doesn't in a book or series. I bring a laser-sharp focus to each project, and I think about the text on many levels—content, flow, style, and grammar. I also enjoy writing for young people and have written leveled readers and graphic novels—both fiction and nonfiction—and SE and TE copy for literature, math, and social science books. Though much of my experience has been with textbooks, I welcome projects that push me into new areas. Americanizing a cookbook, copyediting mythology reference works, and even proofreading a company history were great fun." Johanna earned a B.A. in psychology from Brandeis Univ. See more information at http://www.the-efa.org/members/data/resumes/ehrmannj.pdf.

ELEPHANT ROCK

88 Clarence Ave. SE, Minneapolis MN 55414. (612)244-0865. **E-mail:** elephantrockretreats@gmail.com. **Website:** elephantrockretreats.com. **Contact:** Jeannine Ouellette, director. Estab. 1995.

ADDITIONAL INFORMATION Offers writing and editing services and creative writing retreats by Jeannine Ouellette. Jeannine has written several books and collaborated on and/or edited many others.

EMBREE LITERARY SERVICES

138 W. Alta Green, Port Hueneme CA 93041. (805)985-1113. **E-mail:** maryembree@gmail.com. **Website:** www.maryembree.com. **Contact:** Mary Embree, owner/manager. Estab. 1990. Mary Embree is an author, freelance editor, literary consultant, seminar and workshop presenter, and public speaker. Since 1990, she has helped writers with their book mss from first to final draft, guiding and editing their book projects according to professional book publishing standards. Her services include writing and editing book proposals, query letters to literary agents and book publishers, and preparing mss for presentation.

ADDITIONAL INFORMATION If authors choose to self-publish, she guides them through the entire process, such as registering their copyright and getting ISBNs, barcodes, and Library of Congress Control numbers. Embree and her associates design and typeset interior pages of the book as well as eye-catching book covers, providing print-ready PDF files.

EPIC VISION MARKETING

4427 Fessenden St. NW, Washington DC 20016. (301)639-8204. **E-mail:** amknoop@epicvisionmarketing.com. **Website:** www.epicvisionmarketing.com. **Contact:** Aphrodite Knoop, chief editor and marketing consultant. Estab. 2014.

ADDITIONAL INFORMATION "Aphrodite Knoop (DBA Epic Vision Marketing) leverages 15 years experience working with publishers, writers, and marketers to help writers refine and promote their work: developmental editing, copyediting, proofreading, and social media/marketing support."

THE EQUALIZER

Bob MacKenzie, B.A., M.A., B.Ed., (613)329-9942. **E-mail:** bob@communication.ca. **Website:** www.communication.ca/editor. **Contact:** Bob MacKenzie.

ADDITIONAL INFORMATION "WRITE, REVISE, EDIT, PROOFREAD. 40+ years experience. Published author, poet, critic. Marketing professional. Bob MacKenzie, B.A., M.A., B.Ed."

ERIAKO ASSOCIATES

(310)392-6537. **E-mail:** eriakoassociates@gmail.com. **Contact:** Erika Fabian, CEO. Estab. 1982. Offers design, editing, and overseeing entire publishing process. Erika Fabian of Eriako Associates is an international book designer as well as writer and editor. She has personally written 22 books, some published by the likes of Putnam, Ballantine, and Harlequin. Her books have also been translated and published in several languages.

ADDITIONAL INFORMATION "We cover essentially all phases of publishing for books, brochures, and advertising materials. We also do professional photography of authors, and for the material if it needs photo illustration."

ERLICK EDITORIAL AND RESEARCH SERVICES

Silver Spring MD 20902. **E-mail:** lerlick@hotmail. com. **Contact:** Louise Erlick, sole proprietor. Estab. 2002.

ADDITIONAL INFORMATION Offers editing, proofreading, and research for hourly rate.

DAVID J. ESTRIN

0305 SW Montgomery St., #408, Portland OR 97201. (503)820-9647. **E-mail:** theeditor@mindspring.com. **Contact:** David J. Estrin. Estab. 1998.

ADDITIONAL INFORMATION Full-time freelance editor and consultant. Ms development, project management, copyediting, seminars on writing and publishing, consulting. Disciplines: anthropology, art history, business, criminal justice, critical theory, gay studies, history, comparative literature, education, economics, geography, law, philosophy, political Sscience, public administration, policy studies, psychology, religion, sociology, social work/social welfare, urban affairs, and women's studies. Recommended editor, Columbia Univ. School of Social Work. Earned a B.A. in Government, Oberlin College. "I have worked in academic publishing for more than 33 years. I was an acquisition editor at Longman and Garland, during which time I signed and developed dozens of textbooks in the social sciences... and more than 100 scholarly works and textbooks in a variety of disciplines." David Estrin is currently the copy editor of the International Journal of Africana Studies. See resume at www.the-efa.org/members/data/resumes/estrindj.pdf.

GAIL FAY

270 Malabar Rd SW, Box 108, Palm Bay FL 32907. (321)243-8599. **E-mail:** gail@faywordworks.com. **Website:** www.faywordworks.com. **Contact:** Gail Fay, writer/copyeditor.

ADDITIONAL INFORMATION Years in field: 8. Gail Fay is a professional copyeditor, proofreader, writer specializing in the nonfiction educational market. Gail is a former English teacher. She works with the Chicago Manual of Style and Publication Manual of the APA. She copyedits educational, scholarly, reference, and trade titles; works in MS Word using track changes, querying the author and incorporating the author's responses into the final version; creates a detailed style sheet including decisions on punctuation, capitalization, spelling, and style; proofs electronically using Adobe Acrobat Professional. Gail has been the only proofreader of the Scarecrow Press journal *Teacher Librarian* for over 2 years.

ASHLEY FESTA WRITING

San Antonio TX (210)373-8681. **E-mail:** ashley@ashleyfesta.com. **Website:** www.ashleyfesta.com. **Contact:** Ashley Festa, owner/editor. Estab. 2010.

ADDITIONAL INFORMATION Offers developmental editing, copy editing, and proofreading.

FINAL DRAFT INC.

517 MacDonald Road, Oakville ON L6J 2B7 Canada. (289)242-4873. **E-mail:** nancyforn@yahoo.com. **Website:** nancyforn.wix.com/finaldraft. **Contact:** Nancy Fornasiero, editor/writer. Estab. 2000.

ADDITIONAL INFORMATION "Drawing on over 20 years in the book publishing industry, I provide a wide range of editorial services: substantive editing, copy editing, project management, ghost writing, proposal writing, and more. My specialties areas include nonfiction, illustrated, and educational titles. No fiction. French-to-English translation services also available."

FIRSTLIGHT VENTURES, INC.

Santa Fe NM 87507. (505)428-0905. **E-mail:** cynthiawrites@msn.com. **Contact:** Cynthia Lane, MA.

ADDITIONAL INFORMATION Cynthia Lane is a writer, ghostwriter and substantive and developmental editor with more than 28 years experience. Her fields of experience include personal and spiritual development, the environment, complementary healthcare/stress management international development. Ghostwriting projects have included books and journal articles on the environment, complementary healthcare and personal growth.

MARTIN FISCHER

Oak Park IL **E-mail:** martinfischer@hotmail.com. **Website:** http://martinfischer.webs.com. **Contact:** Martin Fischer.

ADDITIONAL INFORMATION "Experienced amateur genealogist Martin Fischer is available to conduct freelance family history projects including searching online databases, building family trees, editing memoirs and creating genealogical websites."

HEIDI FITZGERALD

14420 43rd Ave. N., Plymouth MN 55446. **Website:** heidifitzgerald.com. **Contact:** Heidi FitzGerald, editor. Estab. 2013.

ADDITIONAL INFORMATION Offers editing, proofing, researching, and ghostwriting. 20+ years of experience with editing of books, academic papers, newsletters, directories, copywriting/editing.

FLORIDAWENDY PRODUCTIONS

2306 NW 46th Terrace, Gainesville FL 32606. (352)373-9619. **E-mail:** floridawendy@cox.net. **Website:** www.floridawendy.typepad.com. **Contact:** Wendy Thornton. Estab. 2012.

ADDITIONAL INFORMATION Services include comprehensive editing, including novels, memoirs, ESL, and formal academic prose, including papers, theses, and dissertations. Areas of expertise include medicine, engineering, computer science, journalism, environmental, education, etc.

KATHLEEN FLORIO

16645 S.E. 18th St., Bellevue WA 98008. (425)746-8525. **E-mail:** klflorio@msn.com. **Contact:** Kathleen Florio.

ADDITIONAL INFORMATION Years in field: 30. Years as freelancer: 25. "I provide editing and writing services to deliver print and online materials that are accurate, clear, and tailored to the target audience. Areas of interest include education (including education technology), arts and culture, nature, environmental issues, business and finance, history, politics, travel, food, music, and gardening. I work with individual authors, publishers, corporations, nonprofits, and universities. Sample clients include the Panasonic Foundation, ASCD (the Association for Supervision and Curriculum Development), Princeton University, Microsoft, the Merck Institute for Science Education, and Susquehanna University." See resume at http://www.the-efa.org/members/data/resumes/floriok.pdf.

A FONTLIFE PUBLICATION, LLC

5809 Lunenberg Dr., Raleigh NC 27603. (919)604-5828. **E-mail:** info@fontlifepublications.com. **Website:** fontlifepublications.com. **Contact:** Victor M. Font, Jr., owner. Estab. 2012. "A FontLife Publication, LLC is a Christian-based, family-owned publishing organization with a passion for discovering unknown authors. We provide self-publishing, editorial, marketing, education, and Web development/eCommerce services for authors primarily writing for the Christian, Inspirational, Technology, Business, Children, and Leadership genres. We'll consider any book, however, in any genre, that we find interesting and meets our family-friendly standards. We do not publish graphic material and language. We pay authors the highest royalties you'll find anywhere! We are known for personal service, editorial excellence, and dedication to detail, handling all aspects of publishing including editing, design, distribution, and printing: both Print-on-Demand (1 book at a time) and offset (larger print runs); copyright registration and e-Book conversion. We provide professional writers, out-of-print writers, and aspiring writers with high-quality books and e-Books. With our help, even non-writers can turn their ideas into marketable, high-quality publications ready for distribution on the Internet, in bookstores, and specialty shops around the world."

ERIN FOSTER BOOKS

3741 Cason Cove Dr., Apt. #1308, Orlando FL 32811. **E-mail:** erinfosterbooks@gmail.com. **Website:** erinfosterbooks.com. **Contact:** Erin Foster, editor. Estab. 2008.

ADDITIONAL INFORMATION "I do substantive edits, copyediting, and proofreading, depending on what the author is interested in and how in depth they would like my comments to be. The prices are dependent on word count and type of editing, but are all listed on my website and indvidualized quotes can be made via e-mail."

FOUR EYES EDIT

(646)234-2628 (Margarita); (917)561-5616 (Adela). **E-mail:** foureyesedit@gmail.com. **Website:** www.foureyesedit.com. **Contact:** Margarita R. Kurtz; Adela Brito. Estab. 2008.

ADDITIONAL INFORMATION "Four Eyes Edit is a partnership of 2 professional editors who have worked together since 2006. Adela Brito and Margarita Kurtz have served as developmental editors and copy editors to bestselling authors and first-time writers."

SYLVIA FRANCES

407 Hart Place, Jonesboro LA 71251. **Website:** www.sylviafrances.weebly.com. **Contact:** Jamie Stephens, editor/author. Estab. 2013.

ADDITIONAL INFORMATION Offers editing and proofreading of articles and books.

PENELOPE FRANKLIN

E-mail: info@creativeliteraryalliance.com; penelope@creativeliteraryalliance.com. **Website:** www.creativeliteraryalliance.com. **Contact:** Penelope Franklin.

ADDITIONAL INFORMATION Penelope Franklin is a versatile editor and writer who has been in the field for over 25 years. She is associated with such major publishers as Reader's Digest Books, Columbia University, the United Nations, Oxford University Press, American Heritage magazine and Current Biography magazine. As a consultant to UNICEF, she assisted writers around the world who used English as a second language. She works with first-time authors and established ones, with an emphasis on developing each client's unique voice. She studied at the Publishing Institute of New York University and is a graduate of Columbia University. Her services include ms evaluation; developmental, line and substantive editing; rewriting; ghostwriting and co-authorship; and production of personal histories. She is also a skilled writing coach and does copywriting for advertisements, brochures and other promotional materials.

REBEKAH L. FRASER

P.O. Box 81, Petersham MA 01366. (203)606-2929. **E-mail:** rebekahlfraser@gmail.com. **Website:** www.rebekahlfraser.com. **Contact:** Rebekah Fraser. Estab. 2007.

ADDITIONAL INFORMATION "I offer more than words; I offer ideas translated through editing, writing, ghost writing, copywriting, messaging strategy, logo design, journalism, scriptwriting, and new media production (social, video, etc.)."

FREESTYLE EDITORIAL SERVICES

Ellicott City MD (410)999-5426. **E-mail:** jlatta@freestyleservices.com. **Website:** www.freestyleservices.com. **Contact:** Joseph Latta, editor.

ADDITIONAL INFORMATION Years in field: 15. Years as a freelancer: 4. "I specialize in developing clear, concise business and marketing content for professional services companies and nonprofits. With nearly 15 years of writing, editing, and management experience in the corporate environment, I have worked closely with organizations to create persuasive sales/grant proposals, white papers, marketing brochures, website content, business books, corporate communications, and other business development

materials. I am passionate about helping my clients stand apart from the competition."

CASSANDRA FREY

1421 Yale Dr., Holiday FL 34691. **E-mail:** cassf316@gmail.com. **Contact:** Cassandra Frey.

ADDITIONAL INFORMATION Offers proofreading, editing (books, advertisements, etc.), design assistance, ghost writing, assistance with speaking engagements, and more.

FRIDAY & FRIENDS

P.O. Box 370, Hot Springs MT 59845. (406)210-8701. **E-mail:** fridayandfriends@z9mail.com. **Contact:** Susan Campbell, principal. Estab. 2004.

ADDITIONAL INFORMATION Offers ms evaluation; comprehensive edit; rewrite and/or ghostwrite; instruction in Chicago Manual of Style; book design, format, and conversion to pdf. Competitive rates.

EMMA FULENWIDER

220 Touchstone Place, West Sacramento CA 95691. (530)613-2647. **E-mail:** emmafulenwider@gmail.com. **Website:** www.ideagirl.com. **Contact:** Emma Fulenwider. Estab. 2013.

ADDITIONAL INFORMATION "Emma Fulenwider is a freelance editor and ghost blogger. She comes from an education in journalism and public relations and has 7 years of writing, editing, and blogging experience. Emma is also a marketing consultant."

FULL STOP EDITORIAL

Fort Collins CO (970)266-9157. **Website:** www.fullstopeditorial.com. **Contact:** Lisa Péré.

ADDITIONAL INFORMATION Editing, Writing, Project Management; 20 years' experience. "Full Stop Editorial excels in clarifying your message, on time and on budget. The result: Winning proposals, educated end users, increased readerships, satisfied clients, and greater profitability." Lisa Péré lets you choose the depth of edit you want—surface (copy) edit or deep (developmental) edit. She provides fast, efficient review of existing material. Proficient in French. Affiliated with Editorial Freelancers Association, Northern Colorado Writers, SCBWI, and Society for Technical Communication. See www.linkedin.com/in/llpere.

GAL-FRIDAY PUBLICITY

308-1114 Howie Ave., Coquitlam BC V3J 1V1 Canada. (604)366-7846. **E-mail:** rachel@gal-fridaypublicity.com. **Website:** www.gal-fridaypublicity.com. **Con-**

tact: Rachel Sentes, founder/publicist. Estab. 2009. Offers business and book publicity, e-book publicity/publishing, media kit creation and design, editing, ms consultations, ghostwriting, Wordpress websites, copy editing, proposal writing, and literary agent and publishing consultations.

ADDITIONAL INFORMATION "We have worked in all aspects of the book industry behind and in front of the scenes."

DONNA J. GARZINSKY

Wharton NJ (973)361-5224. **E-mail:** garwarnj@yahoo.com. **Contact:** Donna J. Garzinsky, editorial.

ADDITIONAL INFORMATION Donna Garzinsky has been in the field for 18 years, and as freelancer 8. She has worked with publishers and curriculum developers, with focus on reading comprehension, leveling, and/or assessment; phonics; grammar/usage/mechanics; writing process; spelling; and for ESL/ELD students. Donna is experienced in using InCopy and Acrobat.

GD PROOFS

Marco Island FL 34145. (201)988-2658. **E-mail:** gdproofs@yahoo.com. **Website:** www.gdproofs.vp-web.com. **Contact:** Gabriella Deponte.

ADDITIONAL INFORMATION Gaby Deponte is a versatile copy editor, proofreader, and translator who's been in the field for more than 20 years. She has experience editing and writing in the financial, fiction, and nonfiction areas. Gaby edits book mss as well as brochures, articles, marketing letters, and presentations. Her expertise includes refining the work of non-native speakers. With excellent written and verbal communications skills, she works collegially and respects deadlines. For more information, please visit her website or see her resume at http://www.the-efa.org/members/data/resumes/deponteg.pdf.

GEEKY GIRL, LLC

128 Wentworth Dr., Lansdale PA 19446. (215)393-8740. **E-mail:** rex@karinrex.com. **Website:** www.geekygirlonline.com. **Contact:** Karin Rex, president. Estab. 1989.

ADDITIONAL INFORMATION "Geeky Girl offers technical and professional writing services and instructional design."

KRISTEN GEORGI, MAT/MAT, DMH(C)

37 Bellvale Lakes Road, Warwick NY 10990. (845)986-8175; (845)597-4148. **E-mail:** kgeorgi@optonline.net.

Website: www.kristengeorgi.com. **Contact:** Kristen Georgi.

ADDITIONAL INFORMATION Kristen Georgi has "18 years as a freelance and staff editor and writer; Writer/editor of healthcare industry B-to-B reports; Editor of Current Clinical Practice for primary care physicians; Editor of APCToday.com for nurse practitioners and physician assistants; Editor-in-chief of national newspaper of Chinese medicine; Healthcare journalist for daily newspaper and national consumer magazines; High level decision-making and problem-solving capabilities with exceptional multitasking capacity. Member, American Medical Writers Association." See resume at http://www.the-efa.org/members/data/resumes/georgik.pdf.

GHOSTWRITER CENTRAL

Hatteras St., Tarzana CA 91356. (888)743-9939; (818)433-4050; (747)333-8660 (text only). **E-mail:** mikemckla@aol.com. **Website:** www.ghostwords.com. **Contact:** Michael McKown, editor. Estab. 2002.

ADDITIONAL INFORMATION "Every project undertaken by Ghostwriters Central, from a one-page document to a 300-page ms, is handled with the utmost care. We always deliver clients' projects with excitement, secure in the knowledge that we have devoted great effort to the cause." Services offered: book mss, scripts, speeches, wedding vows, resume, copywriting, script doctoring, letter writing, editing, and rewriting. See website for fee schedule.

LYNNE GLASNER

27 West 96th St., New York NY 10025. (917)744-3481. **E-mail:** lyngla@rcn.com. **Contact:** Lynne Glasner.

ADDITIONAL INFORMATION Lynne Glasner has 20 years of experience in the field and 10 years as a freelancer in coaching, developmental and line editing, copy editing, fact checking, and proofreading, including trade books (nonfiction and fiction) and textbooks. "Textbook focus: teacher and pupil editions for all populations, including ESL and special needs, in basal reading, math, science, and social studies series, and supplementary printed matter; high school texts; teacher training materials. Trade book focus: politics, contemporary social issues, media issues." She also offers contract writing services and ghostwriting.

GOLDEN GRAPHICS

314 W. Franklin St., Kenton OH 43326. (419)673-6260. **Fax:** (419)675-3133. **E-mail:** robin@golden-graphics.

com. **Website:** http://booksbyrobincarrig.com. **Contact:** Robin Carrig, partner. Estab. 1983.

ADDITIONAL INFORMATION As a partner in Golden Graphics, Robin offers proofreading and editorial services. She has a BS in journalism with a minor in English, years in the communications and printing businesses, and experience in self-publishing her own works of fiction. "Golden Graphics has the capabilities to help you with self-publishing your own books."

GOLDENWEST EDITING

9735 Castaic Court, Santee CA 92071. (619)324-3348. **E-mail:** leslie@goldenwestediting.com. **Website:** www.goldenwestediting.com. **Contact:** Leslie O'Brien, editorial director. Estab. 1996.

ADDITIONAL INFORMATION "No matter how comprehensively researched and how well written, all documents benefit from editing and proofreading to ensure that ideas are communicated in the best possible way."

ELLEN GOLDSBERRY

76 Quaker St., Weare NH 03281. (603)660-8080. **E-mail:** goldsberry@gsinet.net. **Website:** www.ellengoldsberry.com. **Contact:** Ellen Goldsberry, editor. Estab. 2010.

ADDITIONAL INFORMATION "I offer ms critiques (first 20 pages for a nominal fee), content editing, line editing, and coaching throughout the writing process. My specialties are memoirs, literary fiction, historical fiction, business writing. Sorry, I do not edit mysteries, westerns, fantasy, or science fiction. If you are considering self-publication or submission to an agent I can help you refine and elevate your work."

GRAPHICS AND EDITING IN A FLASH

P.O. Box 466, Sharon MA 02067. **E-mail:** njpmail@mindspring.com. **Website:** www.facebook.com/graphicsandeditinginaflash. **Contact:** Yael Resnick, owner. Estab. 1996.

ADDITIONAL INFORMATION Offers book design, cover design, all phases of editing. "Reasonable rates, fast turnaround times, and work is always done with great crae and attention to detail. Warm, personal, one-on-one service."

SARAH HACKLEY

Driftwood TX 78619. (512)773-1723. **E-mail:** sarah@sarahhackley.com. **Website:** www.sarahhackley.com. **Contact:** Sarah Hackley, author/editor. Estab. 2009.

ADDITIONAL INFORMATION "As a bestselling nonfiction editor and professional ghostwriter, Sarah's talent lies in helping writers find their individual voices and tell their stories in the most compelling way possible. She has helped professional athletes, award-winning businessmen and women, CEOs, doctors, attorneys, financial professionals, professional speakers, and many others share their messages with the world." Services offered: developmental editing, substantive editing, line editing, proofreading, ms review, and self-publishing advice.

MAUREEN HAGGERTY

320 Patrick Pl., Chalfont PA 18914. (215)822-2229. **E-mail:** maureenhaggerty@verizon.net. **Contact:** Maureen Haggerty.

ADDITIONAL INFORMATION Maureen is an established freelance writer/editor/proofreader who has been in this field for 30 years. "I thrive on the challenges a diversified assignment docket affords. Corporations, associations, research and patient-care facilities, publishers, marcom agencies, and individuals benefit from my creativity, resourcefulness, and ability to see the big picture without losing sight of critical details. Specializing in memoir/personal and local history and health- and/or aging-related topics, I preserve the author's voice while enhancing clarity and providing context and empower consumers to make informed healthcare/lifestyle decisions. I've edited a national association's award-winning magazine, created patient information materials and print and PowerPoint CME programs, and "translated" scripts written by non-native speakers of English into English as it's spoken in America. I've also edited or proofed novels, memoirs; travel, relationship, and investment guides; and a ms introducing a novel management theory. Recent projects have included adding historical context to transform a client's genealogical research into a prized family heirloom and chronicling the first 100 years of a township's history. References and estimates for long- or short-term projects and rush jobs are available on request."

JJ HALL

Sewickley PA (724)759-8183 or (888)433-1187. **E-mail:** jthepersonalassistant@yahoo.com. **Contact:** JJ Hall.

ADDITIONAL INFORMATION JJ Hall lives near Pittsburgh and has been in the field for 12 years, 4 as a freelancer. "I help writers stay on task by compiling a list of due dates, assignments, tasks, projects, and timelines. I check grammar, syntax, punctuation, spelling, clarity, and consistency. Upon request, I can transform a series of jumbled words into a sentence, a paragraph, or a written conversation. I have formatted fiction, how-to books, administrative manuals, speeches, reports, newsletters, proposals, and presentations. I enjoy working with authors who would like assistance formatting or coordinating interior layout for their publications. My personality—calming, low-key and mellow; my skills—personable, tenacious and detail-oriented. Contact me for further information."

HAMILTON DRAMATURGY

P.O. Box 906, Quakertown PA 18951. **E-mail:** hamiltonlit@hotmail.com. **Website:** www.hamiltonlit.com. **Contact:** Anne Hamilton, founder. Estab. 1991.
ADDITIONAL INFORMATION "Hamilton Dramaturgy is an international consultancy offering script development, dramaturgy, new musical development, editing, self-publishing, and career advisement services."

JENNIFER READ HAWTHORNE

Vero Beach FL (772)774-8260 (land); (612)865-4550 (cell). **E-mail:** jennifer@jenniferhawthorne.com. **Contact:** Jennifer Read Hawthorne.
ADDITIONAL INFORMATION "Jennifer Read Hawthorne is an award-winning author/editor specializing in editing books, book proposals, articles, and blog posts. Genres include business, self-help, spirituality, health, memoir, and how-to. Her extensive writing/editing experience includes books; newspaper, magazine and broadcast journalism; poetry; and technical writing. She has also taught business and technical writing at the Master's level and in the corporate world. Jennifer is the author/editor of 7 books (four bestsellers), including the #1 bestsellers *Chicken Soup for the Woman's Soul* and *Chicken Soup for the Mother's Soul*. Her books have sold more than 14 million copies."

HEATHER DUBNICK EDITORIAL SERVICES

39 Dodge St. #356, Beverly MA 01915. (508)932-6955. **E-mail:** hdubnick@gmail.com. **Website:** www.heatherdubnick.com. **Contact:** Heather Dubnick, principal. Estab. 2004. Offers "copyediting, developmental editing, ms evaluation, coaching, researching, fact-checking, proofreading, formatting, and indexing. I work in Spanish as well as English."

THE HELP

648 Rivenhurst St., Bremerton WA 98310. (360)440-5795. **E-mail:** admin@thehelpbyastrids.com. **Website:** www.thehelpbyastrids.com. **Contact:** Marie Astrid Stanek, owner/manager. Estab. 2008. The Help is a fast growing virtual assistance agency.
ADDITIONAL INFORMATION Services provided include administrative support, writing and translation, and multimedia and graphic design.

HERR'S INDEXING SERVICE

P.O. Box 5378, Kailua Kona HI 96745. (802)585-6844. **E-mail:** lindahallinger@gmail.com. **Website:** www.herrsindexing.com. **Contact:** Linda Herr Hallinger, owner. Estab. 1944.
ADDITIONAL INFORMATION "Herr's Indexing Service provides quality and affordable indexes for books and journals on a variety of topics, including medicine, health, nursing, social sciences, business, education, and agriculture."

M.J. HINKO

23 Tejano Canyon Road, Sandia Park NM 87047. (505)281-4655. **E-mail:** mjhinko@aol.com. **Contact:** M.J. Hinko.
ADDITIONAL INFORMATION 12 years in the field. Proofreader and copy editor with experience working in a wide variety of fields. Specialties include educational, psychological, and scientific publishing (including educational/psychological assessments and supporting materials), marketing materials (print ads, catalogs, PowerPoint presentations) and proposals. Clients include Riverside Publishing. "I am a proofreader and copy editor with experience working in a wide variety of fields, including educational and psychological publishing, marketing materials, adult nonfiction, and YA fiction." See www.the-efa.org/members/data/resumes/hinkom.pdf.

HISTORICAL EDITORIAL

6420 Toney Lane, Spotsylvania VA 22553. **E-mail:** jennyq@historicaleditorial.com. **Website:** historicaleditorial.com. **Contact:** Jennifer Quinlan, owner. Estab. 2010.
ADDITIONAL INFORMATION Offers developmental editing, copyediting, and cover design.

NINA HNATOV

51 Roslyn Dr., Glen Head NY 11545. (516)532-3535. **E-mail:** nina.hnatov@gmail.com. **Contact:** Nina Hnatov.

ADDITIONAL INFORMATION Freelance editor/copyeditor/proofreader; well-versed in a variety of disciplines. "I have many years of varied editorial experience, ranging from educational textbooks and testing materials (Kindergarten-University Press) to books, periodicals, newsletters, magazines, catalogs, art publications, research studies, annual reports and financial materials. Areas of expertise include art history, bioinformation/genetics, business/marketing, calculus, child development, computer architecture, economics, English language arts, fine arts, health care/nursing, history, mathematics, parenting, physics, psychology, science, self-help, social studies and sociology. I live on Long Island, New York, and am available on a per project/ongoing basis. My fees are reasonable and I am certain you will find my work to be meticulous, thorough and conscientious, and always completed on your time schedule." See resume at www.the-efa.org/members/data/resumes/hnatovn.pdf.

CAROL HOLMES

New York NY (917)941-9476. **E-mail:** inastrongcity@aol.com. **Contact:** Carol Holmes.

ADDITIONAL INFORMATION Carol Holmes specializes in academic and nonfiction proofreading, knows a footnote from an endnote, and has worked on large bibliographies. Her work is in many Scribner and Oxford University Press sets. She also works for Rutgers University, Kent State University Press, and Unicef. "I'm the one called in when the job has gone wrong, when it's been worked on by too many hands, or when it hasn't been worked on at all. I look for the fix that entails the fewest changes, and I won't copyedit in proof—unless you ask me to." Consistency of style is an obsession. For more information, see www.the-efa.org/members/data/resumes/holmesc.pdf.

MARY HORNER

St. Peters MO **E-mail:** mehorner@charter.net. **Website:** www.writrteachr.blogspot.com. **Contact:** Mary Horner. Estab. 2011. Award-winning journalist with more than 15 years experience in the publishing industry and author of *Strengthen Your Nonfiction Writing* provides editing services that include content, grammar, and style.

ADDITIONAL INFORMATION References available.

JANA HUNTER WRITING SERVICES

2900 Saint Paul Rivera, Round Rock TX 78665. (206)913-3334. **E-mail:** jana@janahunterwriter.com. **Website:** janahunterwriter.com. **Contact:** Jana Hunter, owner/writer/editor. Estab. 2000.

ADDITIONAL INFORMATION Offers writing, editing, conceptualizing, developing, researching, publishing, formatting, and consulting. "We can be as involved in or peripheral to your project as you need or want."

INDEX WEST

P.O. Box 615, Olympia WA 98507. (360)870-4384. **E-mail:** indexer@karikells.com. **Website:** www.karikells.com. **Contact:** Kari Kells, owner/indexer. Estab. 1994.

ADDITIONAL INFORMATION "I'm dedicated to creating quality indexes at competitive rates since 1994. My indexes bridge the gap between ideas in an author's text and terms that readers will look for when they're hunting for specific information. I provide print and back-of-the-book indexes, editing services for authors and editors writing their own indexes, and training for people who want to learn how to write effective indexes."

INDIGO EDITING & PUBLICATIONS

917 SW Oak St., #302, Portland OR 97205. (503)629-9216. **E-mail:** info@indigoediting.com. **Website:** www.indigoediting.com. **Contact:** Ali McCart, senior editor. Estab. 2006.

ADDITIONAL INFORMATION "Indigo started as a firm of freelance editors. It's now grown to offer design, e-book conversion, and publishing project management services in addition to editing. With multiple publishing professionals on hand, authors can rest assured that their book will be professionally edited by an expert in their genre, designed with a keen eye toward readability, and produced with all the latest publishing trends in mind."

INFINITE PATHWAYS

Caledon Village ON Canada. **E-mail:** administration@infinite-pathways.org. **Website:** infinite-pathways.org. **Contact:** M.J. Moores, editor. Estab. 2013.

ADDITIONAL INFORMATION "Infinite Pathways and M.J. Moores will provide a free assessment of any 1 page of poetry or flash fiction, 1 scene of play, or the first 10 pages of your story to allow you to evaluate my work and our ability to communicate prior to purchasing services." Offers ms critiques, content edit, line edit, copyedit, proofreading, and more.

INFORMATION PLUS PROFESSIONAL SERVICES

2438 Athens Road, Olympia Fields IL 60461. (866)391-2234. **Fax:** (866)576-4491. **E-mail:** wp@information-pluspro.com. **Website:** www.informationpluspro.com. **Contact:** Walter M. Perkins, principal and editorial director. Estab. 2009. Information Plus Professional Services is an independent publisher. Current tile, *Write Right - Right Now*, covers key steps in the writing and publishing process. Perkins has been a journalist for 30+ years and has also ghost-written speeches.

ADDITIONAL INFORMATION Services offered include: book publication, writing coaching, editing and proofreading, and legal review (has a J.D., not a licensed attorney).

INNATE PRODUCTIONS

371 Barrie Road, P.O. Box 244, Pakenham ON K0A 2X0 Canada. (613)623-1029. **E-mail:** innateproductionsmail@gmail.com. **Website:** innateproductions.ca. **Contact:** Ellen Gable Hrkach, James Hrkach. Estab. 2005.

ADDITIONAL INFORMATION Offers self-publishing book coaching (assisting new authors to self-publish their own books, guiding them through the various steps), formatting for print, formatting for Kindle, cover design, and editorial (developmental editing for novels).

JANET SPENCER KING, BOOK DEVELOPMENT GROUP

595 Main St., #1602, New York NY 10044. (212)371-1479. **E-mail:** janet@bookdevelopmentgroup.com. **Website:** www.bookdevelopmentgroup.com. **Contact:** Janet Spencer King. Estab. 2007. Book Development Group is a group of three independent editors.

ADDITIONAL INFORMATION King offers services in concept development, ms evaluations, ms content editing, and line editing. Works with fiction writers of most genres, consulting on plotting, pacing, point of view, and the many other aspects of a novel. Also works with nonfiction writers in a wide variety of topics from health, fitness, and nutrition to self-help and personal growth, among others. For authors who wish to self-publish, King provides customized personal production management. Works with copy editors

as well as cover and interior designers to turn mss into widely distributed, beautifully crafted books. Provides e-book conversion and distribution as well.

MARY JASKIEWICZ

San Francisco CA **E-mail:** jaskiem@yahoo.com. **Contact:** Mary Catherine Jaskiewicz.

ADDITIONAL INFORMATION Experienced Writer, Copyeditor, Developmental Editor, Proofreader, Writing Tutor/Instructor with over 17 years of writing, editing and research experience. Clients include a Kuwaiti client whose investment company introduces new technologies to the Gulf region (12 years); the Middle East/Africa Regional Head at a major European multi-national firm (Enterprise Solutions Division) (10 years). Mary Jaskiewicz's skills: "Demonstrated ability to develop a general concept into a focused, quality document and/or improve on a communication. Can comprehend the gist of an assignment quickly and complete it with minimal direction from the client. Am also an experienced English as a Second Language (ESL) instructor. To this effect, have taught writing for academic and professional purposes."

LINDA JAY EDITORIAL SERVICES

323 Post St., Petaluma CA 94952. (415)320-0083. **E-mail:** lindajay@aol.com. **Contact:** Linda Jay, copywriter/copyeditor. Estab. 2001. Offers promotional writing for self-published authors, including: Back jacket copy, flap copy, press releases, website text, brochures, newsletters, magazine profiles, feature stories, case studies, titles, and captions. Also copy edits book mss for self-published and traditionally published authors. Has edited more than 75 mss in past 3 years, including the following genres: business, memoir, fantasy, novels, spirituality, and women's issues.

JD WORDSMITH LLC

Millstone Township NJ (732)598-7724. **Fax:** (732)308-9498. **E-mail:** jane@jdwordsmith.com. **Website:** www.jdwordsmith.com. **Contact:** Jane DeTullio, editor.

ADDITIONAL INFORMATION Years in field: 12. Years as a freelancer: 3. "I currently write articles for a local medical center and press releases and web pages for businesses. I edit mss, business correspondence, websites, dissertations, theses, resumes, and curricula vitae. My 12 years in academia, both as a professor of English and director of a university writing center have provided me with incisive writing and editing skills."

JEWELL COMMUNICATIONS

Dona Hightower Perkins, 9205 Seven Oaks Ln., Denton TX 76210. (940)891-4240. **E-mail:** donaperkins@verizon.net. **Contact:** Dona Perkins.

ADDITIONAL INFORMATION Dona Perkins has 20 years of experience in editing, copyediting, and proofreading for publishers, small and large businesses, and individual clients. This includes content editing, developmental editing, copyediting, proofreading, and electronic editing; developmental editing and copyediting of college textbooks; editing of course curriculum, guidelines, articles, journals, and dissertations for major universities. "Expert proficiency in standard copyediting and proofreading guidelines. More than 15 years of experience with the Chicago Manual of Style, Publication Manual of the American Psychological Association, and American Medical Association Manual of Style." See resume at www.the-efa.org/members/data/resumes/perkinsd.txt.

JIM BARRETT, AUTHOR

13923 Dusty Oaks Trail, Bella Vista CA 96008. (530)605-9322. **Fax:** (530)472-3648. **E-mail:** jimbarrett18592@aol.com. **Website:** http://maduncanbook.com. **Contact:** Jim Barrett, author, police procedure consultant. Estab. 2009. Jim Barrett is the author of five published books and several screenplays, one of which is currently under option.

ADDITIONAL INFORMATION Offers a unique service as a police procedure consultant. "My mission is to create true to life police procedures for your book or screenplay. Don't let a gaff or misstatement cause your readers to close your book in disgust. Ensure that your novel or screenplay contains authentic police procedures, not your best guess at how the police operate. With thirty years in law enforcement coupled with writing experience, I can answer your questions and solve your problems so your work will always ring true."

JLMORENO EDITING, PRODUCTION & DESIGN

When Clarity Counts, (480)540-7637. **E-mail:** jlmoreno@whenclaritycounts.com. **Website:** www.whenclaritycounts.com. **Contact:** Jerryll L. Moreno, MA, Certified Scholoary Editor.

ADDITIONAL INFORMATION JLMoreno is a freelance and academic editor providing production management, editing, proofing, and design that transform information into knowledge and connects content with scholars worldwide. Currently, Jerryll works closely with authors, typesetters, indexers, publishers, and acquisition managers to provide a wide variety of publishing expertise. As a publishing professional, she believes that negotiating best practices and competing interests is critical to successfully transform information into knowledge, create quality content, and build lasting relationships with authors and presses.

BRYAN JOHNSON

P.O. Box 382, Houghton MI 49931. **E-mail:** bryanjohnson333@att.net. **Contact:** Bryan Johnson.

ADDITIONAL INFORMATION Offers editing, indexing, research for nonfiction, particularly history, science/engineering, techology, religion.

KATHERINE JOHNSON

707 Alvin Ave., Salisbury MD 21804. **E-mail:** kjohnson.editing@gmail.com. **Website:** kjohnsonediting.wordpress.com. **Contact:** Katherine Johnson, editor. Estab. 2013.

ADDITIONAL INFORMATION Offers freelance editing and proofreading for works of all lengths. Pricing: $2 per every 1,000 words. References available.

KARICK & ASSOCIATES

4520 E. Hillshire Dr., Richmond IL 60071. **Fax:** (847)841-3787. **E-mail:** kari@karick.com. **Website:** www.karick.com. **Contact:** Kari Turco, owner/proofreader. Estab. 1996.

ADDITIONAL INFORMATION Offers proofreading, copy editing, formatted typing for publishing, re-formatting for e-publishing, inside jacket copy.

KARR EDITORIAL, LLC

1148 Lakepointe St., Grosse Pointe Park MI 48230. (313)821-0778. **E-mail:** leslie@karreditorial.com. **Website:** www.karreditorial.com. **Contact:** Leslie Karr, president. Estab. 2004.

ADDITIONAL INFORMATION Offers professional copyediting, proofreading, project management, and "comprehensive editing solutions tailored to meet the specifications of your project."

KAT EDITS

3010 14th St. E., Saskatoon SK S7N 2W4 Canada. **E-mail:** k-duncombe@hotmail.com. **Website:** katedits.wordpress.com. **Contact:** Katherine Duncombe, editor. Estab. 2013.

ADDITIONAL INFORMATION Offers substantive or structural editing, stylistic editing, proofreading, copy editing.

THERESA L. KAY

398 Nordstrasse, Fairbanks AK 99709. **E-mail:** theresa.ae@gmail.com; treekay@cowboys.uwyo.edu. **Contact:** Theresa Kay Communications. Estab. 2002.

ADDITIONAL INFORMATION As a freelance proofreader and copy editor, Theresa Kay's subject specialties include education (theory, practice, all levels kindergarten through college, administration, textbooks), social sciences, anthropology, psychology, sociology, criminology, American studies, cultural studies, history, reference materials and encyclopedias, and fiction. She worked full-time as the senior editorial associate for a nonprofit education journal for five years. She is skilled at copyediting using Word and proofreads on paper or electronically. See more information at www.the-efa.org/members/data/resumes/kaytl.pdf.

ESTHER KEANE COMMUNICATIONS

834 Point Way, Virginia Beach VA 23462. (757)652-4874. **E-mail:** esther@estherkeane.com. **Website:** estherkeane.com. **Contact:** Esther Keane, editor. Estab. 2012.

ADDITIONAL INFORMATION Offers ms evaluation/line editing, copyediting/proofreading, fact check, book cover design, and writing (ghostwriting, back flap synopsis for book cover, press release, reviews, and more).

KELLEY & HALL BOOK PUBLICITY

5 Briar Lane, Marblehead MA 01945. (617)680-1976. **E-mail:** jocelyn@kelleyandhall.com. **Website:** www.kelleyandhall.com. **Contact:** Jocelyn Kelley, partner. Estab. 2004. Kelley & Hall is a literary publicity company that is dedicated to helping authors and publishers with their promotion, marketing, and media relations.

ADDITIONAL INFORMATION "We create effective book buzz as well as author recognition that will increase book sales. We help writers build their author brand. Book marketing and book promotion are the cornerstones of Kelley & Hall. We have recently partnered with an independent publishing company, Grey Swan Press (www.greyswanpress.com)."

KIMBERLY K. KELLY

9801 E. Homestead Road, Poplar WI 54864. **Contact:** Kimberly K. Kelly, editor.

ADDITIONAL INFORMATION "Have been a technical/freelance writer since August 1986 in areas of university research, computer manuals, crude oil engineering, European travel, disability services, college-level English tutoring, Public Arts and Sister Cities commissions, and nonprofits."

ANNE KEMPER

127 W 79th St., #3, New York NY 10024. (917)603-3995. **E-mail:** akemper@gmail.com. **Website:** www.linkedin.com/in/annekemper. **Contact:** Anne Kemper.

ADDITIONAL INFORMATION With 13 years in the field, Anne Kemper is an "editor of print and digital instructional materials with a successful track record of bringing profitable multi-authored projects from conception to publication. Specialties: Print and digital instructional materials for college, test-prep, trade, and educational markets. Subjects include English, psychology, history, political science, neuroscience, languages, biology." Education: New York Univ. Summer Publishing Institute, New York, NY. June–July 1999. Yale Univ., New Haven, CT. B.A. in English, *magna cum laude*, May 1999.

SUSAN E. KENNEDY

Londonderry NH **E-mail:** skennedy09@yahoo.com. **Contact:** Susan E. Kennedy.

ADDITIONAL INFORMATION Years in field: 6. Years as freelancer: 4. "Thorough line editor, proofreader, and copyeditor who enjoys all types and lengths of fiction and nonfiction mss. I correct grammar and punctuation, improve sentence structure, word flow, and clarity. Experience includes literary and genre novels (adult and YA), memoirs, scholarly texts, short story anthologies, technology how-to, nonprofit publications (such as membership newsletters), and general interest nonfiction." Susan has worked with a wide range of clients, including college professors, new writers, established authors, and publishers. She has been in the field for 6 years and holds a Master of Fine Arts in Fiction and Nonfiction from Southern New Hampshire University. As a freelancer, she is particularly interested in fiction and mss on historical topics.

ANNE KETCHEN

446 Brook St., Carlisle MA 01741. (978)369-1661. **E-mail:** anneketchen@comcast.net. **Website:** anneketcheneditor.yolasite.com. **Contact:** Anne Ketchen.

ADDITIONAL INFORMATION For 18 years, Anne Ketchen has been a freelance editor specializing in corporate training and education. She provides a variety of instructional editing and copyediting services, primarily to the training industry and to educational publishers. Anne holds a B.A. in English from Univ. of Maine and MS in Occupational Therapy from Columbia University. Her related experience includes 10 years as a Registered Occupational Therapist (working with spinal cord injury patients, muscular dystrophy patients, and children with learning disabilities). She has a Certificate in Native Plant Studies from New England Wild Flower Society and a strong interest in natural history, especially native plants." See resume at www.the-efa.org/members/data/resumes/ketchena.pdf.

KICK BUTT MARKETING

P.O. Box 236, Tiverton RI 02878. **E-mail:** leslie@kickbuttmktg.com. **Website:** www.kickbuttmktg.com. **Contact:** Leslie Lindeman, commander in chief. Estab. 1990.

ADDITIONAL INFORMATION Offers strategic planning, direction, and writing services for comprehensive marketing plans, public relations campaigns, printed materials, advertising programs, websites, and social media pages.

KM EDITORIAL

P.O. Box 4451, Glendale CA 91222. **E-mail:** info@katiemccoach.com. **Website:** www.katiemccoach.com. **Contact:** Katie McCoach, owner. Estab. 2012.

ADDITIONAL INFORMATION "Freelance developmental book editor Katie McCoach runs KM Editorial. She works with writers and authors of all kinds and in all genres. Get a consult today!"

TERESE LOEB KREUZER

377 Rector Place, Apt. 10H, New York NY 10280. (212)807-7509. **E-mail:** tereseloeb@mac.com. **Contact:** Terese Loeb Kreuzer.

ADDITIONAL INFORMATION Terese Loeb Kreuzer is a journalist, writer, editor, photographer, multimedia producer/director and project manager. She has been freelancing for 32 years. She is the founder and editor of the Travel Arts Syndicate and co-author with Carol Bennett of *How to Move to Canada: A Primer for Americans.* She is also the publisher and editor of Downtown Post NYC, a newsletter about news and events in Lower Manhattan. See more information at: www.the-efa.org/members/data/resumes/kreuzertl.pdf.

KRISTEN CORRECTS

1063 Casa Loma Dr., Meridian ID 83642. (208)447-0860. **E-mail:** kristen@kristencorrects.com. **Website:** www.kristencorrects.com. **Contact:** Kristen House, owner. Estab. 2012. Kristen Corrects provides professional ms editing and business writing services at a competitive price. "Kristen House, a certified editor with an impressive portfolio, offers high-quality editing and writing work at a competitive price."

ADDITIONAL INFORMATION "With astounding qualifications and flawless master of the complexities of the English language, Kristen has the editing skills to bring refinement to any ms." Kristen specializes in editing fiction (SFF) mss, website content, and blogs.

MARCELA LANDRES

Brooklyn NY (718)208-5810. **E-mail:** marcelalandres@yahoo.com. **Website:** www.marcelalandres.com. **Contact:** Marcela Landres.

ADDITIONAL INFORMATION "A former Simon & Schuster editor, Marcela Landres helps writers get published by editing their work and educating them on the business side of publishing. She edits a wide variety of fiction and nonfiction including but not limited to: novels (literary, mainstream, commercial, adult, young adult, chick lit, street lit, women's, romance, historical, mystery, thriller, suspense), short story collections, memoirs, self-help, inspiration, pop culture, and New Age. She does not, however, edit cookbooks, poetry, children's books (specifically, anything for middle grade or younger readers), works in Spanish, science fiction and fantasy. Her clients range from best-selling and/or award-winning authors to self-published authors. While she works with writers of all backgrounds, as one of the few Latina editors in the book business she has extensive experience in Latino/Hispanic and multicultural publishing." For more, go to website, click on Services. Memberships: Women's Media Group, Editorial Freelancers Association, and Las Comadres. A graduate of Barnard College, she is a co-founder of the Comrades and Compadres Writers Conference, has served on the Brooklyn Literary Council which helps organize the Brooklyn

Book Festival, and was a judge for the Beyond Margins Award for PEN.

MARY LANG

Torrance CA (877)620-2626. **E-mail:** langm@comadrona.com. **Contact:** Mary Lang.

ADDITIONAL INFORMATION "Editorial and marketing talent for nonfiction authors who want to develop concepts, understand the market, structure proposals, and then write and polish their best ms. Mary knows what sells and why." Mary Lang has been in the field for 15 years, 10 as a freelancer. She provides developmental, substantive, and stylistic editing. She holds a B.A. from UC San Diego (literature/writing), M.A. University of Southern California. She has been an editor for Fortune 500 organizations, NASA and others. She has been a writing instructor and lecturer at Stanford University, UCSD, CSULA. Marketing Experience: Random House.

LAST SYLLABLE COMMUNICATIONS

953 N. Carlson Dr., Stanton MI 48888. **E-mail:** editing@lastsyllable.net. **Website:** www.lastsyllable.net. **Contact:** Rachel Lee Cherry, editor. Estab. 2010.

ADDITIONAL INFORMATION Offers basic copyediting, line editing, and proofreading for fiction and nonfiction texts. "I'll make sure sentences are clearly understandable and flow into one another, grammar and spelling are correct, facts are right, the ms adheres to applicable style guidelines, page designs are followed correctly, and the whole of the text makes sense. Self-publishing and traditionally publishing authors equally welcome. Formatting services also available."

LAWRENCE JUNIOR EDITORIALS

P.O. Box 9007, Queenstown RSA 5320 Australia. **Contact:** Lazola Pambo. Estab. 2006.

ADDITIONAL INFORMATION Offers editing articles, essays and proofreading the grammatical content. Checking for misspelling or irrelevant word usage. The cost for the services depends on the scope of the content as larger texts need critical attention as well as smaller texts.

LEGAL PRO EDITORS

5619 Knobby Knoll, Houston TX 77092. (832)444-6623. **E-mail:** editors@legalproeditors.com. **Website:** legalproeditors.com. **Contact:** Brooke E. Smith.

ADDITIONAL INFORMATION "I am a Harvard Law graduate with over 20 years litigation experience who became a full-time freelance editor over 5 years ago. I have either done content edit, developmentally edited, or done both on over 150 books. Fiction ranges from mainstream through most genres, including legal suspense, mystery/suspense, historical, science fiction/fantasy, romance/erotica, and young adult. Nonfiction works include motivational, memoir, religious/New Age, how-to, and promotional. While I still do a lot of legal editing (journal articles and treatises) for attorneys, my current focus is books, particularly novels involving attorney characters or legal issues/procedure for which I do developmental as well as content/line editing." See more information at http://www.the-efa.org/members/data/resumes/smithb.txt.

LIGHTWORDS EDITORIAL SERVICES

167 West 71st St., New York NY 10023. (212)799-4365. **E-mail:** True. **E-mail:** phyllisstern2002@yahoo.com. **Website:** lightwords-editorial.com. **Contact:** Phyllis Stern.

ADDITIONAL INFORMATION Phyllis Stern is an "Experienced editor, specializing in books on health, psychology, spirituality, the arts and education, as well as fiction and memoir. Skilled at editing for grammar, usage and clarity of style with attention to the writer's voice. Strong interest in creative work and books on personal growth and conscious living." Phyllis holds an M.A. in English literature, and has published articles in major magazines. "I have taught creative writing with grants from the New York State Council on the Arts, and am also a practitioner of holistic healing. As a writer myself, I am sensitive to preserving the tone and nuance of the author's style, while helping to polish the work for publication. I help present your work with clarity and vision."

MAUREEN LILLA

77 State Road, Plymouth MA 02360. **E-mail:** mlilla777@aol.com. **Contact:** Maureen Lilla, principle. Estab. 1986. Offers developmental editing for authors, professionals, and business writers; development of query letters and book proposals; writing and ghostwriting; book doctoring; book and book cover design.

ADDITIONAL INFORMATION Client list available upon request.

THE LINGUISTIC EDGE

1024 Bayside Dr., #301, Newport Beach CA 92660. (714)637-6264. **Website:** www.linguisticedge.com. **Contact:** Dorothy M. Taguchi.

ADDITIONAL INFORMATION Dorothy Taguchi specializes in developing and editing award-winning educational programs. With over 20 years in the industry, her roles for educational publishers include educational advisor, producer, editorial director, curriculum developer, editor, and proofreader. Her experience ranges from K-2 reading and math instruction to a wide range of graduate courses. She also edits children's books, nonfiction books, and reports, as well as exhibit text panels and supporting materials.

MAGGIE LYONS

P. O. 291, Callao VA 22435. **E-mail:** maggielyons66@gmail.com. **Website:** lyonseditorialservices.yolasite.com. **Contact:** Maggie Lyons.

ADDITIONAL INFORMATION Maggie Lyons' editorial services include academic documents (theses, textbooks, articles, papers), fiction and nonfiction mss, query/cover letters, children's literature, marketing, PR, and fundraising communications, corporate reports, manuals, ESL documents, U.K. English documents, resumes. She has international experience (30+ years) in academic publishing, educational, business, and corporate communications in the U.S.A., Europe, and the U.K. through trade, federal sales, public affairs, legal, manufacturing, and nonprofit organizations, Oxford University, and academic publishing. Recent editing projects include a thesis, academic and legal documents in English by nonnative writers (ESL), marketing materials for a renewable energy company, marketing materials and Web content for a marketing company, and a language. "As an academic editor I have worked with university professors to review and develop mss in a broad variety of disciplines through to textbook and electronic publication. Humanities and sciences include, but are not restricted to, history, literature, religion, music, art, geology, and astronomy." Maggie has a B.A. in French (German and music minors) and M.A. in Public Communications and has spent 30 years in the editing field, 10 as a freelancer.

KIM MACQUEEN

47 Maple St., Suite #206, Burlington VT 05401. **E-mail:** kim@barnesmacqueen.com. **Website:** kimmacqueen.com; barnesmacqueen.com. **Contact:** Kim MacQueen.

ADDITIONAL INFORMATION Kim brings 25 years of progressively responsible editorial experience to her new company, Barnes MacQueen Publishing Re-sources, with partner Cindy Barnes. BMPR provides editorial, layout production, distribution and marketing services to indie authors nationwide.

MALLORY EDITING

Saint Petersburg FL **E-mail:** malloryediting@gmail.com. **Contact:** Jeannine Mallory.

ADDITIONAL INFORMATION 15 years in the field. 15 years as a freelancer. Specialties include fiction, health, and self-help.

ROBIN MALTZ

9 Orchard St., Northampton MA 01060. (347)276-3211. **E-mail:** robin.maltz@gmail.com. **Contact:** Robin Maltz.

ADDITIONAL INFORMATION Robin Maltz is a nonfiction editor, writer, and indexer, with more than 20 years experience in book, magazine, academic, and business publishing. She has a client-centered approach with proven ability to meet deadlines, produce excellent results, and exceed expectations. Her skills include substantive editing, copy editing, article writing, brochures, reports, and web copy, back-of-book indexing, proofreading, research, fact checking, copyright permissions. Her interests are in self-published books, small presses, journal articles, academic books in all fields, marketing materials, business and legal reports. See more information at www.the-efa.org/members/data/resumes/maltzr.pdf.

MANSBRIDGE EDITING & TRANSCRIPTION

149 Cedar Ridge Circle, St. Augustine FL 32080. (904)461-9564. **Contact:** Beth Mansbridge. Estab. 1998.

ADDITIONAL INFORMATION Years in field and as freelancer: 16. Beth edits fiction and nonfiction "of many genres, query and proposal letters, promotional materials, and websites. Business has thrived through word of mouth and repeat clients. Beth strives for excellence and is pleased to say that her clients often win literary awards and contests."

MS CRITIQUE

Michael Garrett, Creative Inspirations, Inc., P.O. Box 362, Clay AL 35048. **E-mail:** mike@mscritique.com; mgteach352@gmail.com. **Website:** www.mscritique.com. **Contact:** Michael Garrett.

ADDITIONAL INFORMATION Editor of over 2,000 books. "As credited in Mr. King's nonfiction book *On Writing: A Memoir of the Craft*, I served as Stephen

King's first editor. 25 years of professional book editing experience with New York publishers. Your best choice among all book editors for mystery, suspense, romance, thriller, horror, mainstream, and nonfiction." Services offered include ms critique and editing, and comprehensive structural advice.

STEVEN J. MARCUS

Newton MA (617)964-1580. **E-mail:** smarcus@nasw.org. **Contact:** Steven J. Marcus.

ADDITIONAL INFORMATION Harvard educated, Steven J. Marcus has been in this field 30 years; 12 as a freelancer. As an experienced editor, Steven is "especially adept at transforming the writing of 'expert authors' into engaging and useful communications for general audiences. I'm also a very capable editor of professional writers." His assignments involve science, technology, or medicine, but he also edits copy from other fields, such as economics and cultural affairs. See resume at www.the-efa.org/members/data/resumes/marcussj.txt.

DICK MARGULIS CREATIVE SERVICES

284 W. Elm St., New Haven CT 06515. (203)389-4413. **E-mail:** dick@dmargulis.com. **Website:** www.dmargulis.com. **Contact:** Dick Margulis, owner. Estab. 2004. Offers high-quality printed and electronic books for discerning clients. Thoughtful editing, appropriate design, expert production, comprehensive project management, for publishers of all sizes and for all kinds of books.

ADDITIONAL INFORMATION "If you are an author, agent, publisher, or other organization considering a book project, I'd like the opportunity to quote on the services you need. I have been involved in both editing and typography in one way or another for over half a century; my experience is broad and deep."

MARKETING MEYVN CONSULTING

312 Ronalds St., Iowa City IA 52245. (319)354-5692; (319)621-4671. **E-mail:** wasson.julia@gmail.com. **Contact:** Julia Wasson.

ADDITIONAL INFORMATION "Energetic and creative writer with special expertise in marketing communications that give businesses personality and interest. Also skilled at ghostwriting for executives, writing press releases and other public relations pieces, creating scripts for marketing or instructional videos,writing advertising copy. Careful and thorough copy editor with an eye for detail. Experienced educator with extensive background in writing for educational publishing, including the test preparation and testing industry."

MARVELOUS EDITIONS

E-mail: marlene@fixyourbook.com. **Website:** www.marvelouseditions.com. **Contact:** Marlene Adelstein or Alice Peck. Estab. 2014.

ADDITIONAL INFORMATION "Marvelous Editions is the partnership of respected independent editorial consultants Marlene Adelstein and Alice Peck. We both have over 2 decades of experience." See website for bios and further information.

JILL MASON

Winooski VT (802)655-8915. **E-mail:** jill@masonedit.com. **Website:** www.masonedit.com.

ADDITIONAL INFORMATION Jill Mason edits books—nonfiction and fiction, scholarly and trade—as well as journals, magazines, business materials, theses and dissertations. "I do all levels of editing—copyediting, substantive editing, and developmental editing—as well as proofreading and indexing. I am familiar with the Chicago Manual of Style and the APA Publication Manual. I typically work in Word using its Track Changes feature but am also used to working with hard copy. I'm accustomed to working with authors whose first language is not English, and I have at least some familiarity with French, Spanish, German, and Italian. I try always to retain the author's voice, no matter what I'm editing and what shape it's in." Education: B.A. in psychology, University of Vermont; Workshop for Experienced Ms Editors, University of Chicago; Grantwriting for Nonprofit Organizations Workshop

PEARL MATIBE

15480 Annapolis Road, Suite 202, Bowie MD 20715. **E-mail:** pearlmatibe@gmail.com. **Website:** www.pearlmatibe.com. **Contact:** Pearl Matibe. Estab. 2013.

ADDITIONAL INFORMATION Offers book reviews (nonfiction, biographies, memoirs), copy editing and proofing, and ms assessment in .pdf format.

DANIEL MCCOURT

65 Cottage St., Apt. 2B, Port Chester NY 10573. (914)393-1136. **E-mail:** danmccourt@optonline.net; dan@takehimdowntown.com. **Contact:** Daniel McCourt.

ADDITIONAL INFORMATION Daniel McCourt is experienced in Freelance Copy Editing, Proofreading, Inputting Corrections and Electronic Production. "I have primarily checked copy and proofread around book closings, but I have also helped working in InDesign, and in Quark." See resume at www.the-efa. org/members/data/resumes/mccourtd.pdf.

WILLIAM MCGEVERAN

147-36C Charter Rd. #C, Jamaica NY 11435. (718)969-4101. **E-mail:** gmcgeveran@gmail.com. **Contact:** William McGeveran.

ADDITIONAL INFORMATION William McGeveran is a longtime staff and freelance editor with 37 years in the field, 3 as a freelancer. He has "varied experience in content editing, review-editing, rewriting/writing, copyediting, and project management, espec. in adult reference and in nonfiction bks/textbks for children/ young adults. Former editorial director, World Almanac Books (2000-06), responsible for The World Almanac, World Alm. for Kids, Funk & Wagnalls Encyclopedia, World Alm. Book of Records, etc. Seeking editing/writing assignments or consultancy. Glad to discuss how I might possibly meet your needs. Available on-site locally."

MCLAMB COMMUNICATIONS

630-203 St. Joseph St., Carolina Beach NC 28428. (910)520-9035. **E-mail:** mclambcommunications@ gmail.com. **Contact:** Teresa McLamb, owner.

ADDITIONAL INFORMATION Years in field: 40 Years as freelance author and journalist. Professional History: Owner, McLamb Communications - public relations, special events, freelance writing and editing, business communications. Communication Specialist and Event Coordinator for GE. Reporter/Photographer. Education: MA - English, UNC Wilmington; BA - Journalism, UNC Chapel Hill NC. Licensed Real Estate Broker. Selected Professional Honors/Affiliations: Editorial Freelancers Association, Greater Wilmington Communicators Roundtable, Brunswick County TDA, Brunswick County Chamber Board, Chair 2001. CASE Grand Award - Radio Programs CASE Award of Excellence - Radio Programs Outstanding Leadership Award, Wilmington Leadership Institute Communication Excellence Award, GE Corporate Communications. See resume PDF at: http://www.the-efa. org/members/data/resumes/mclambt.pdf.

MEDIANEIGHBOURS.COM

20 Via del Vaquero, Santa Fe NM 87508. **Website:** www.medianeighbours.com. **Contact:** Mary Neighbour, owner/editor. Estab. 2009.

ADDITIONAL INFORMATION "At MediaNeighbours.com, we translate real-world challenges to e-world results. We help authors, artists, small businesses, and nonprofits who are looking for ways to represent themselves across the internet and promote their products and services."

MELISWENK: THE MS PERFECTIONIST

1512 Jefferson Ave., Joplin MO 64801. **E-mail:** meliswenk@gmail.com. **Website:** meliswenkediting. wordpress.com. **Contact:** Melissa A. Swenka, owner/ editor. Estab. 2011.

ADDITIONAL INFORMATION Offers professional, publishable prose from a passionate and dedicated reader of creative, academic, and promotional mss; an eagle eye with a friendly hand; familiarity with MLA, APA, and Chicago style guides; experience with memoir, genre fiction, literary, satire and dark comedy, self-help, how-to, academic research; proofreading, copy editing; negotiable rates and personalized service.

JUDYTH MERMELSTEIN

3838 Evelyn, Verdun, Montreal QC H4G 1P6 Canada. **E-mail:** lapomme@postaccess.com. **Website:** about. me/mermelsteinjudyth. **Contact:** Judyth Mermelstein, writer/editor/translator. Estab. 1970.

ADDITIONAL INFORMATION Customized editorial and support services for individual authors, small presses, and organizations outside mainstream publishing, based on client needs and preferences. "One size fits all solutions fit no one very well. Once the scope of the project has been well defined, I will gladly issue a firm quote to your specifications. Please e-mail with a description of your project and any deadlines involved before sending attachments. I normally respond within 48 hours."

MIDDLEOFTHENIGHT EDITORIAL SERVICES

31 Lorraine St., Roslindale MA 02131. (617)553-2999; (617)413-7204 (cell). **E-mail:** middleofthenight@comcast.net. **Website:** www.middleofthenight.org. **Contact:** Ellen Kaplan-Maxfield.

ADDITIONAL INFORMATION Complete editorial services, including back-of-the-book scholarly indexing (specializing in psychology and philosophy works); developmental editing, substantive editing, and copyediting; and InDesign book design, typesetting and layout, creating print and ebooks ready for publication. Years in field: 10; Years as freelancer: 30.

Specializing in back-of-the-book indexing of scholarly mss with expertise in psychology and philosophy. Familiarity with SKY indexing software and embedded indexing in MS Word. "Working on deadline, skillful and sensitive editing as well as perfectionist proofreading of book mss (list of published titles available upon request; see work references. Familiarity with Track Changes in Word and with typemarking." See resume at http://www.the-efa.org/members/data/resumes/kaplanmaxfielde.pdf.

GEORGE A. MILITE

P.O. Box 7352, Lancaster PA 17604. (717)299-2932. **Fax:** (866)709-4847. **E-mail:** militeg@gmedit.com. **Contact:** George A. Milite.

ADDITIONAL INFORMATION With more than 30 years' experience as a writer, editor, and teacher, George Milite specializes in business management, education, and reference publishing. Instructor, Temple University. Former Adjunct Professor, Dept. of English Language Studies, The New School.

JESSICA MORELAND

22 Audry Lane, Westford VT 05494. (802)355-3408. **E-mail:** info@jessicamoreland.com. **Website:** www.jessicamoreland.com. **Contact:** Jessica Moreland.

ADDITIONAL INFORMATION Years in field: 10. Years as freelancer: 10. "Jessica Moreland is an award-winning freelance writer, editor, and book designer from Vermont. She finds it extremely rewarding to work one-on-one with authors, and her best recommendations are from happy clients. Jessica graduated Magna Cum Laude from Brigham Young University in English with an emphasis in editing, and she received an MFA in Creative Writing from the University of Massachusetts-Boston.

MUCHMORE, INC.

Quality editorial services since 1998, P.O. Box 373, Perry Kansas 66073. (785)550-1715. **E-mail:** nicole_muchmore@yahoo.com. **Website:** www.muchmore-inc.com. **Contact:** Nicole Muchmore.

ADDITIONAL INFORMATION Nicole Muchmore has been a full-time freelance copy editor for 15 years, with a focus on scientific and academic publishing. "I have had long and productive relationships with publishing houses such as Nature Publishing and Oxford University Press, among others." Nicole's specialty subjects include biological and genetic sciences, and medical specialties such as urology. She is skilled at editing the science research reports of English-as-second-language authors. For more information see www.nicolemuchmore.com.

MYERS PRODUCTIONS

P.O. Box 4201, Scottsdale AZ 85261. **E-mail:** psmyers1@cox.net. **Contact:** Patricia Myers, president. Estab. 1985. Offers writing, editing, press releases, publicity, public relations.

ADDITIONAL INFORMATION Specializes in business and personality profiles, food, dining, nightlife, music, travel, books, and local history.

LISA NEFF EDITORIAL SERVICES

150 Hart Ln., Springfield PA 19064. (610)328-0768. **E-mail:** neffeditorial@gmail.com. **Contact:** Lisa Neff.

ADDITIONAL INFORMATION Lisa Neff has edited medical mss for 26 years, 14 of them freelancing. She states her goals include: editing pre-pubilcation ESL journal mss for foreign authors; editing medical books; and editing and writing patient education materials. Her experience includes the fields of ESL medical editing as well as regular editing of nursing, psychology, and environmental mss. She received thorough training in-house at W. B. Saunders, Philadelphia, in all aspects of medical journal production, including ms, first and second pages, bluelines, and advanced-copy review. She has some book-production experience as well. See resume at www.the-efa.org/members/data/resumes/neffl.pdf.

MICAH NEWMAN

945 Kight St., Stephenville TX 76401. (860)455-3503. **E-mail:** micah.newman@gmail.com. **Contact:** Micah Newman.

ADDITIONAL INFORMATION "I have more than 7 years' experience in developmental editing with science textbooks, workbooks, and web-based materials with Holt McDougal, Rinehart & Winston, and have done extensive freelance work in that and on a wide variety of other subjects since then. My bachelor's is in Biology and my master's is in philosophy. I'm an excellent writer, and have published works in academic journals. I can deliver quality results for most any writing or editorial task you may have."

THE NEW YORK BOOK EDITOR

Erin Niumata, **E-mail:** nybookeditor@hotmail.com. **Website:** www.nybookeditor.blogspot.com. **Contact:** Erin Niumata. Estab. 2004.

ADDITIONAL INFORMATION "We have provided valuable proofreading, copy editing, critiques and much more. We have worked with many best-selling authors as well as first-time writers. Additional editors: Foster Niumata, Mira Park, Tracy Cartwright and more."

NOLA EDITING

Gail Naron Chalew, 6310 Fontainebleau Dr., New Orleans LA 70125. (504)864-0266. **E-mail:** nolaeditor@gmail.com. **Contact:** Gail Naron Chalew.

ADDITIONAL INFORMATION Gail Chalew has spent 25 years in the field; 23 years freelancing. "Substantive editing of academic works and dissertations, with a focus on the social sciences, humanities, and Judaica; particularly skilled in working with material written by non-native English speakers. Edited books for Cambridge University Press, Stanford University Press, Elsevier, Greenwood, Lawrence Erlbaum, and Temple University Press, as well as dissertations in the social sciences and library science." "A graduate of the Baltimore Institute for Jewish Communal Service in which she earned a Masters of Social Work and a Masters of Jewish History, Gail has worked both in the editing field and in Jewish journalism. Since, 1989, she has been editor of the Journal of Jewish Communal Service, a professional journal distributed internationally to people working for Jewish agencies. From 2000 to early 2005, Gail was the editor of The New Orleans Jewish News, the Jewish newspaper for the New Orleans community." Education: 1973: B.A. in anthropology, Vassar College, Poughkeepsie, New York; 1975: M.S.W., University of Maryland School of Social Work, Baltimore, Maryland; 1975: M.A. in Jewish History, Baltimore Hebrew University, Baltimore; Professional memberships: American Jewish Press Association, Editorial Freelancers Association. See resume: www.the-efa.org/members/data/resumes/chalewgn.pdf.

NP SOLUTIONS

P.O. Box 585, Buffalo NY 14207. (716)783-9926. **E-mail:** normallen958@aol.com. **Website:** www.npsolutions.co. **Contact:** Norm R. Allen, Jr. Estab. 2011. Offers proofreading, editing, ghostwriting, writing advice, and assistance. Provides help with mss, articles, essays, theses, family histories, biographies, autobiographies, fiction, nonfiction, letters, etc. Provides advice for getting published. Provides speaking tours on ethics, progressive politics, current events, the need for critical thinking, etc.

ROLF OLSEN

San Bartolome 26, Xchitepec Morelos 62790 Mexico. (918)636-1636. **E-mail:** rolf37@gmail.com. **Website:** sites.google.com/site/2tulsatranslations. **Contact:** Rolf Olsen. Estab. 2011.

ADDITIONAL INFORMATION Offers writing, editing, and proofreading written material in Spanish or English, and translation of Spanish to English and English to Spanish.

1 CREATIVE ADVANTAGE

311 W. Main St., Sun Prairie WI 53590-2909. (608)834-8291. **Website:** dwightclough.com. **Contact:** Dwigth Clough, ghostwriter/publisher. Estab. 1982.

ADDITIONAL INFORMATION Experience in writing, rewriting, editing, and ghostwriting services specializing in life story, Christian inspirational, educational, devotional, and leadership books. Services include any or all of the following: book planning, concept development, writing, rewriting, editing, self-publishing on Create Space and Kindle (including book cover design, ISBN, bar code, print on demand). Limited web development services available as well. National award winning writer; experienced, published author.

PAGE TURNER EDITING

Oakland CA (510)655-7301. **E-mail:** deniseleto@att.net. **Contact:** Denise Michelle Leto.

ADDITIONAL INFORMATION "Currently, I am a freelance substantive and developmental editor. For 7 years I was a Senior Editor at the University of California, Berkeley. During the last 15 years, I have edited work by faculty and post-doctoral scholars for university presses, nonfiction professional and trade authors, and work by creative writers, such as personal essays, novels, and poetry for literary journals and publishers. I earned a Masters in Fine Arts at Saint Mary's College of California. Prior to that, I graduated Valedictorian and Phi Beta Kappa in Legal Studies and Social Policy from UC Berkeley. I have edited writing from a range of disciplines and genres: environmental science, psychology, sociology, literary scholarship as well as the creative arts. I am a published poet and author."

PAPER STAR EDITORIAL & DESIGN

33846 Fourteenth St., Union City CA 94587. (831)402-2074. **E-mail:** tomiko@paperstareditorial.com. **Website:** www.paperstareditorial.com. **Contact:** Tomiko Breland, owner. Estab. 2013.

ADDITIONAL INFORMATION "Paper Star Editorial & Design offers editing, graphic design, and ms review services. Based in the Bay Area in California, we believe that everyone deserves the opportunity to present the best version of themselves, and that sometimes it takes a little help (and professional expertise) to achieve that version."

BARBARA J. PARKER

13 Burnham Pl., Fair Lawn NJ 07410. (201)475-1525. **E-mail:** bjparker100@gmail.com. **Contact:** Barbara J. Parker.

ADDITIONAL INFORMATION "I have enjoyed a varied career as a writer and editor, including work for newspapers, non-profit organizations, trade organizations, pharmaceutical firms, educational publishers, magazines, newsletters and Web sites. I'm looking for assignments that will best use my skills and professional background and that will match one of my many interests. I have written about everything from the arts and literature to finance and business and have served as a feature writer, magazine editor, newspaper and reporter. I have a particular interest in putting my abilities to work for an environmental organization, but I am open to all suitable freelance opportunities. For details, see resume at www.the-efa. org/members/data/resumes/parkerbj.pdf.

LINDA AU PARKER

P.O. Box 133, New Brighton PA 15066. **E-mail:** linda@ lindamaubooks.com. **Website:** www.lindamaubooks. com. **Contact:** Linda Au Parker, independent contractor. Estab. 2006.

ADDITIONAL INFORMATION "I have been proofreading professionally for more than 27 years. I have worked for various publishers, including F+W Publications, Crown & Covenant, Carroll & Graf, and more. Most of my work now is with independent authors who need help cleaning up their mss before submitting to agents or publishers or who need help polishing those final mss before self-publishing."

PASTIME PUBLICATIONS

1370 Trancas St., #372, Napa CA 94558. (707)252-4062. **Fax:** (707)252-4062. **E-mail:** dona@napavalleypastime.com. **Website:** www.napavalleypastime. com. **Contact:** Dona Bakker, owner. Estab. 2003.

ADDITIONAL INFORMATION Editorial services offered include proofreading, editing, and coaching in memoir writing.

PAX STUDIO LLC

20515 Bunker Hill Dr., Fairview Park OH 44126. **E-mail:** lori@loripax.com. **Website:** loripax.com. **Contact:** Lori Paximadis, principal. Estab. 1991.

ADDITIONAL INFORMATION Offers copyediting, line editing, developmental editing, proofreading, and project management.

PENULTIMATE EDITORIAL SERVICES

#27-4520 Gallagher's Lookout, Kelowna BC V1W 3Z8 Canada. (778)478-0877. **E-mail:** info@penultimateword.com. **Website:** www.penultimateword.com. **Contact:** Arlene Prunkl, editor.

ADDITIONAL INFORMATION "I specialize in working with first-time, self-publishing authors." Services include ms consultation, developmental editing, structural and stylistic editing, copyediting, proofreading, writing and rewriting, indexing, research, and fact checking/reference checking. Cost: $45US/hour for proofreading and copyediting; $50US/hour for substantive editing, structural editing, consultation, critique, or indexing. Receive free estimate through online submission form. See the website for additional information.

CAROL ANNE PESCHKE

Greenbank WA (360)678-0761. **Fax:** (360)222-3732. **E-mail:** CAPeschk@aol.com. **Contact:** Carol Anne Peschke.

ADDITIONAL INFORMATION Carol Anne Peschke has 20 years in the field, 16 as a freelancer. Copyediting, rewriting, and proofreading of STM academic and professional publications, specializing in environmental science and healthcare. Electronic ms coding, cold reads, design surveys, permission tracking, author contact, and other production and editorial services. Copyeditor of *The American Journal of Psychology* since 1997. Carol Anne Peschke is skilled at editing translated and second-language mss. "As former editing manager of a full-service house, I have in-depth knowledge of prepress production. I work independently and have earned a reputation in the industry for fast, efficient, thorough editing." See more information at www.the-efa.org/members/data/resumes/peschkec.pdf.

PICKWICK WRITING SERVICES

140 Lazy Willow Lane, Unit 102, Myrtle Beach SC 29588. (843)582-2197. **E-mail:** mdevlin30@gmail. com. **Website:** pickwickwritingservices.wordpress.

com. **Contact:** Matthew Devlin, lead editor. Estab. 2008.

ADDITIONAL INFORMATION "The Pickwick Writing Team consists of 2 published, well-educated, professional writers. We are dedicated to providing our clients with quick and high quality services at reasonable rates. The services we offer include, but are not limited to, ms and website editing; creating dynamic written content for websites, brochures, marketing e-mails, etc.; ghost writing and co-writing."

DIANE PINIARIS

2621 Palisade Ave., Apt. 14E, Bronx NY 10463. (718)548-7859. **E-mail:** dianepiniaris@gmail.com. **Contact:** Diane Piniaris.

ADDITIONAL INFORMATION Diane has been in the field for over 30 years. "My specialty is ELT (EFL/ESL) writing/editing - I have written a series of highly successful ELT test preparation textbooks for the Greek market for University of Michigan Proficiency (ECPE) and Competency (ECCE) exams. Previously, I worked for 5 years at Oxford University Press as an ELT developmental editor and I have over 20 years of ELT classroom experience. Before getting into ELT, I was in trade publishing (4 years with Scribners in the late 1960s-early 1970s and 5 years with Paddington press, a now-defunct Anglo-America publisher based in London)."

HILARY POWERS

385 Palm Ave., #5A, Oakland CA 94610. (510)834-1066. **E-mail:** hilary@powersedit.com. **Website:** www.powersedit.com. **Contact:** Hilary Powers.

ADDITIONAL INFORMATION Hilary Powers has a journalism degree from Stanford. She has spent more than 20 years as a freelance editor. Hilary can help with editing from the lightest of copyediting to polishing and developmental work, as well as radical revision for tone and focus.

PRO NOVEL EDITING SERVICES

3805 Burke, Cheyenne WY 82009. (307)772-1741. **Fax:** (501)325-0305. **E-mail:** proediting@earthlink.net. **Website:** www.pronovelediting.com. **Contact:** Michael McIrvin, founding writer and editor. Estab. 2003. Pro Novel Editing Services can provide the following for fiction writers of all skill levels: line editing, developmental (content) editing, novel ms critiques, and query letters.

ADDITIONAL INFORMATION Pro Novel Editing Services can also facillitate the following for self-pub-

lishers: book layout in the appropriate program files required by your POD company, book cover design, conversion to all digital formats, e-book layout and design, and website design.

PROOFED TO PERFECTION EDITING SERVICES

PO Box 71851, Durham NC 27722. (919)732-8565. **E-mail:** inquiries@proofedtoperfection.com. **Website:** www.proofedtoperfection.com. **Contact:** Pamela Guerrieri.

ADDITIONAL INFORMATION Pamela works with most genres of fiction, both secular and inspirational, in the capacity of a proofreader, content editor, developmental editor, and ghostwriter. Her genres include general fiction, romance, thrillers, sci-fi, fantasy, and literary fiction, as well as memoirs, narrative nonfiction, educational, and inspirational books. Pamela currently does contract editing work for several major publishing houses and editorial firms as a ms evaluator and content editor. Information on rates and services available on website.

PROOFMYSPEC.COM

4733 Ternstone Ave., Orlando FL 32812. **E-mail:** editor@proofmynovel.com. **Website:** proofmyspec.com. **Contact:** Tammy Gross, owner. Estab. 2009.

ADDITIONAL INFORMATION Services offered include edit, proofread, analyze, transcribe.

PROOF POSITIVE

10 Amherst Road, Marlboro NJ 07746. **E-mail:** proofpositivepro@gmail.com. **Website:** proofpositivepro.com. **Contact:** Christie Stratos, owner. Estab. 2013.

ADDITIONAL INFORMATION "Proof Positive is an editing, beta reading, and proofreading business dedicated to making your work the best possible version of itself. It's not just about finding grammatical errors and plot inconsistencies; it's also about preserving your author's voice, tone, and style while enhancing writing that's already great. Pre- and post-release publicity for your book are part of the package, no matter how big or small your ms is. Let's work together to make your work shine above the rest."

JAYA RAMCHANDANI

29 C Sagar Sangeet, Colaba, Mumbai 400005 India. (91)9967967693. **E-mail:** jayar@siriusinteractive.co.in. **Website:** siriusinteractive.co.in. **Contact:** Jaya Ramchandani.

ADDITIONAL INFORMATION Jaya offers all levels of editing from a simple proofread to developmental editing. She is widely read in the areas of astronomy, physics, psychology, neurology, nanotechnology, and linguistics, and has edited over 3,000 papers to date. More recently, she's been spending half her time in astronomy and physics outreach projects.

RASILLIANT ENTERPRISES

1160 E. Lexington Ave. #21, El Cajon CA 92019. **E-mail:** info@rasilliantenterprises.com. **Website:** rasilliantenterprises.com. **Contact:** Jason Scott, founder. Estab. 2012.

ADDITIONAL INFORMATION Offers copy editing, proofreading, content writing, curriculum writing, ghost writing, and business writing.

READWRITE PUBLISHING SERVICES, INC.

7672 Montgomery Road, #234, Cincinnati OH 45236. (513)502-0264. **E-mail:** readwritepub@gmail.com. **Contact:** Audrey Pettengill, president. Estab. 2014.

ADDITIONAL INFORMATION Offers freelance copy, developmental, and technical editing (higher education, software industries; project management (agile); and process improvement (lean six sigma).

REAL WRITERS APPRAISAL SERVICE AND EDITORIAL CONSULTANCY

E-mail: info@real-writers.com. **Website:** www.real-writers.com. **Contact:** Lynne Patrick, Coordinator.

ADDITIONAL INFORMATION "Our appraisal and editorial service is available to anyone. Send us your ms and we will provide comprehensive feedback on anything from a haiku to a family saga. We also edit mss for conventional or self-publication." Accepts online submissions only. Cost: basic fee of £30 per hour covers a full professional evaluation of prose, poetry, or script of any length, or £20 per hour for detailed copy editing. Introductory packages also available

RECOMMENDED READER

Tucson AZ (520)327-3312. **E-mail:** sc@recommended-reader.net; mossdreams@live.com. **Contact:** Susan Elizabeth Campbell, proofreader/copyeditor.

ADDITIONAL INFORMATION Years in field: 14. "Susan Campbell is a freelance proofreader and copyeditor specializing in scholarly, literary, and scientific work (including the social sciences) for university presses and other institutions and individuals. She has worked on titles and materials for Harvard University Press, Cornell University Press, University Press of New England, Rutgers University Press, Oregon State University Press, Penn State Press, Cedars-Sinai Medical Center LA, the Arizona Department of Game and Fish, the Arizona-Sonora Desert Museum, astronomers of the UA Vatican Observatory, and the University of Arizona Press (where she completed her editorial internship), among others. Susan is a meticulous and focused editor and proofreader, always on time, with particular reading experience and education in horticulture, agriculture, natural history, botany, and ornithology, as well as the social sciences, biology, ethnobotany, ethnoarchaeology, and astronomy. For UA Press she has also worked on dozens of titles in fiction, history, memoir, and poetry. She is conversant in CMS, APA, and AP style. Clients note she is thoughtful, flexible, intelligent, and easy to work with." See resume at www.the-efa.org/members/data/resumes/campbellse.pdf.

REFINER'S FIRE EDITING

P.O. Box 986, Loveland CO 80538. (970)219-9897. **E-mail:** etrup219@aol.com. **Website:** www.refinersfireediting.com. **Contact:** Eleanore D. Trupkiewicz, owner. Estab. 2011.

ADDITIONAL INFORMATION Offers proofreads, line-by-line copyedits, and content edits for fiction mss and academic (humanities-themed) papers. Proofreads and overall content edits for poets. Edits include informational flyers about common editing errors (grammar, punctuation, etc.).

WENDY REIS EDITING AND PROOFREADING

Stratford ON N5A 5L9 Canada. **E-mail:** wendyreisediting@gmail.com. **Website:** www.wendyreiseditingandproofreading.com; www.wendyreisediting.wordpress.com. **Contact:** Wendy Reis.

ADDITIONAL INFORMATION "I do a mandatory 2,000-word sample edit before accepting a project. (This applies to first time clients only.) I need to know if your work is ready for a professional edit. This will also give you valuable feedback." Editing: All projects are 1¢/word of original word count.

RHOADES EDITING SERVICES

2318 Appletree Lane, Arlington TX 76014. (817)247-4374. **E-mail:** rhoadesediting@att.net. **Contact:** Elaine Rhoades. Estab. 2012. Provides following services: 1. Editing to include comprehensive conceptual, line, and copy for the ms; 2. Editor will provide a written critique and analysis of the ms; 3. Client is allowed one round of follow-up questions about the ms and critique via e-mail and phone, and is limited to a half-hour or less of the editor's time.

ADDITIONAL INFORMATION "For a negotiable lower fee at client's discretion, the Editor will provide a more basic ms reading and written analysis without line and copy edit if agreed on by both parties in writing."

RICHMOND PICKERING LTD

Denmark Cottage, Lower Hengoed, Oswestry Shropshire SY10 7EF England. 01691-679711. **Fax:** 01691-679711. **E-mail:** richmondpickeringltd@gmail.com. **Website:** www.writershouse.co.uk. **Contact:** Claire Pickering, director/editor; Rebecca Richmond, director/coach. Estab. 2013. Provides self-publishing, book coaching, editing, and book marketing services. Publishes 6-10 titles/year, generally mass market paperback originals and electronic originals. Receives 30 queries/year. Pays authors 10% royalty (minimum) and 15% for e-books. Responds in 1-3 months on any query, proposal, or ms. Interested in nonfiction (how-to, self-help, wellness). All mss must be fully edited to a professional standard before submission. Any submission must complement the existing titles within the "My Guide" series of self-help, wellness, and how-to books. See website for details. Query with SASE and mss for consideration to be self-published. Contact for any other services.

RIGHT TOUCH EDITING

4 Country Spring Loop, Haverhill MA 01832-1272. (978)996-0389. **Fax:** (978)374-1557. **E-mail:** erin@righttouchediting.com. **Website:** www.right-touchediting.com. **Contact:** Erin Brenner. Estab. 2005. Erin Brenner has been editing for 2 decades. She founded Right Touch Editing to offer writers just what they need for editorial services: highly skilled editing, decades of expertise in publishing, and top-notch professionalism. Erin holds a master's degree in literature and works with other editors who are equally knowledgeable about literature and book publishing. Works with writers to determine: what kind of editing their book needs, how to publish the book, and how to market the book.

DEBORAH A. RING

Professional Writing & Editing Services, 198 Chapmans Ave., Warwick RI 02886. **E-mail:** ring@wordbirdonline.com. **Contact:** Deborah A. Ring, writer/editor.

ADDITIONAL INFORMATION Deborah Ring has 21 years in the field, 9 years as a freelancer. Deborah is a full-time freelancer providing professional copyediting, proofreading, and writing services to publishers of academic, reference, and professional books and journals. Her areas of specialty include literature, history, arts, humanities, business and economics, and social sciences.

RING OF TRUTH WRITING AND EDITING

693 Spruce St. #1, Oakland CA 94610. (510)465-3935. **E-mail:** ralphdranow@yahoo.com. **Website:** essentialwriting.com/ringoftruthwritingandediting.htm. **Contact:** Ralph Dranow, editor and ghostwriter. Estab. 2007.

ADDITIONAL INFORMATION "I do substantive editing and copy editing on a wide variety of types of writing—memoir writing, novels, poetry, nonfiction articles, essays, personal statements, and application essays for college and graduate school. I also do ghostwriting, primarily helping clients write their memoirs. I have also ghostwritten letters and bios. And I can coach clients, providing guidance and support for their writing projects."

KIMBERLY RINKER

12A Kingery Quarter, Willowbrook IL 60527. (708)557-2790. **E-mail:** trotrink@aol.com. **Website:** www.kimberlyrinker.com. **Contact:** Kimberly Rinker, award-winning freelance journalist. Estab. 1984.

ADDITIONAL INFORMATION "Multiple-award winning journalist with 30+ years experience. Provides feature writing, copy editing, nonfiction journalism, ghostwriting, press releases, web design and content input. See my website for a list of clients and to view my recent projects."

JUDITH ROBEY

1721 Scott St., Conway AR 72034. (501)205-1681. **E-mail:** judith-robey@sbcglobal.net. **Contact:** Judith Robey.

ADDITIONAL INFORMATION "I am a copyeditor with 7 years of experience and an academic background (Ph.D. Russian literature, Indiana University; B.A. Russian and German, the University of Virginia). I currently work as a freelance editor for Cambridge-eEds and Oxford Editing, where I specialize in academic proposals and dissertations, particularly for nonnative English speakers. I also work for university presses and academic clients as an independent copyeditor, specializing in humanities and social sciences." See resume at www.the-efa.org/members/data/resumes/robeyj.pdf.

ARLENE W. ROBINSON

E-mail: bettyboopwrites@aol.com. **Contact:** Arlene W. Robinson.

ADDITIONAL INFORMATION "Arlene W. Robinson has developed and edited 500+ full-length mss in a variety of genres since 1996. Her clients include Angie Daniels, Catherine G. McCall, Sue Dent, Daleen Berry, and Hannah R. Goodman. Arlene welcomes new or published authors as clients, and enjoys helping journalistic, business and academic writers transform their writings into marketable, polished products for mainstream readers." Specializes in substantive and structural editing adn critique, developmental editing and critique, stylistic editing and style conversions, and copyediting and proofreading.

BEV KATZ ROSENBAUM

Canada. **E-mail:** bevrosenbaum@yahoo.ca. **Website:** www.bevkatzrosenbaum.com. **Contact:** Bev Katz Rosenbaum.

ADDITIONAL INFORMATION Offers ms critiques. Former editor at Harlequin and McGraw-Hill Ryerson.

ROTH EDITORIAL SERVICES

Lebanon PA **E-mail:** kristin@rotheditorial.com. **Website:** www.rotheditorial.com. **Contact:** Kristin Roth.

ADDITIONAL INFORMATION "As a professional editor with over 9 years experience in the publishing industry, I am detail oriented and effective at meticulously evaluating and enhancing the quality of written communication. I will provide you with quality editorial services to meet your needs, whether you require an edit of your business plan, fiction ms, brochure, media kit, or scholarly work. I edit for several major publishers, including Penguin, Simon & Schuster, Grand Central Publishing, HarperCollins, W.W. Norton, St. Martin's Press, Brill, and Palgrave Macmillan. I also edit for businesses and first-time authors."

RUTHLESS EDITOR

27070 W. Escuda Dr., Buckeye AZ 85396-7416. (928)252-6410. **E-mail:** contact@ruthlesseditor.com. **Website:** ruthlesseditor.com. **Contact:** Kathleen Watson, founder/owner. Estab. 1989. Editing services: websites, books blogs, articles for trade publica-

tion, and employer manuals. Writing services: websites, blogs, newsletters, articles for trade publication, company histories, and commemorative poetry. Experience in manufacturing, construction, employee relations, senior care, and academic writing.

SANDYEW PRE-PUBLISHING SERVICES

Providence RI (401)338-9092. **E-mail:** alcyew@gmail.com. **Contact:** Alice Yew. Estab. 2008.

ADDITIONAL INFORMATION Alice Yew has worked 5 years in the field as a freelancer. Edits or proofreads books, journal articles and websites of any subject matter. Education: BA Mathematics, MSc Applied Mathematics, PhD Applied Mathematics. Skills: copyediting, proofreading. Subjects: mathematics, physics, environmental studies, engineering, education, Chinese. Clients include Pearson, Hodder, Wiley, Harcourt, Oxford University Press, Cambridge University Press. "Given my former 10-year career as an academic mathematician, I especially welcome opportunities to work on texts with mathematical, scientific, or educational content and typescripts in LaTeX."

SAVVY COMMUNICATION LLC

P.O. Box 6746, Louisville KY 40206. (502)632-2241. **E-mail:** susanlindsey@savvy-comm.com. **Website:** www.savvy-comm.com. **Contact:** Susan E. Lindsey, owner. Estab. 2010.

ADDITIONAL INFORMATION Offers editing in a range of genres, style expertise (Chicago, MLA, AP), copyediting, content editing, proofreading, freelance writing services, and public speaking on a range of topics.

SCHOON CREATIVE

3009 Hoosier Creek Road NE, Cedar Rapids IA 52404. **E-mail:** christianschoon@christianschoon.com. **Website:** christianschoon.com. **Contact:** Christian Schoon, owner/head wrangler. Estab. 1999.

ADDITIONAL INFORMATION Offers editorial consultations for self-publishing/traditional publishing (specializing in young adult novels), plus scriptwriting and copywriting consultations and services with experience including Walt Disney Studios copywriter and freelance scriptwriter for Warner Bros. TV, Saban/Fox Kids, Hanna-Barbera, Hallmark, and others.

KIRSTEN SCHUDER

1319 Hardys Creek Road, Jonesville VA 24263. (276)346-3625. **E-mail:** kirsten.schuder@gmail.

com. **Website:** www.linkedin.com/pub/kirsten-schuder/72/a06/161/. **Contact:** Kirsten Schuder, M.S. Estab. 2013.

ADDITIONAL INFORMATION "Kirsten comes from a strong academic background. She has worked on several book projects as both a ghost writer and editor."

BRETTE SEMBER

Clarence NY **E-mail:** Brette@BretteSember.com. **Website:** www.brettesember.com. **Contact:** Brette Sember.

ADDITIONAL INFORMATION Years as a freelancer: 16. "Brette Sember B.A., J.D., is an experienced author, freelancer, ghostwriter, book doctor, blogger, indexer, and copyeditor. She writes often about food, travel, travel shopping, parenting, divorce, business, law, books, lifestyle, pregnancy, health, how-to, education, learning skills, women's and family issues, adoption, reproductive technology, finance, writing, children's books, senior issues, and more. She is the author of more than 40 books and many ebooks. As a ghostwriter and book doctor, Brette has worked on a variety of projects and topics including project management, college textbooks, test-taking skills, self-tutoring, adoption, business, virtual assistants, conversation starters, and many more. As an indexer and copyeditor, she has worked on over 300 titles." She also does online content production and social media management for brands and authors.

SERENDIPITY BLU WRITING SERVICES

Tehucacana TX 76686-0134. **E-mail:** katiebluephotography@yahoo.com. **Website:** http://katiebluephotography.smugmug.com. **Contact:** Virginia Riddle, photojournalist, editor. Estab. 2009.

ADDITIONAL INFORMATION Services include editing, facting checking, and research of mss from magazine to book length; ghost, blog, bussiness letter, and resume writing; compilation of information into cookbooks and handbooks; conducting seminars and workshops on writing and getting published and educational issues; photographing of special events, specializing in sports, nature, and event cameo photography. All services are offered by an experienced, master-degreed, college English professor with teaching certificates in English and English-as-a-Second Language (ESL) who is also a published magazine and book writer and editor.

FRAN SEVERN

6397 Oliver Road, Salisbury MD 21801. (443)782-2462 (bus); (443)260-2390 (c). **Fax:** (443)782-2464. **E-mail:** fran@fransevern.com. **Website:** www.fransevern.com. **Contact:** Fran Severn.

ADDITIONAL INFORMATION "Years in field: 20. Years as freelancer: 27. Writer, editor, publisher, producer, blogger, technical writer, university instructor (mass communications), special events coordinator, voice-over artist, on-air anchor/reporter/DJ, still and video photographer. My skills are varied and—after nearly three decades in the field of communications—they are well-honed. I do more than edit copy. With my background, I see the complete picture and how well your material connects with your audience. When more than one approach is used, I know how to integrate them for the more effective, most efficient program and results. And if 'all' you want is line or copy editing, I love red ink. The first call and consultation are free. This gives you a chance to define your needs and gives me information so I can develop a plan that's cost-effective and successful for you. Within a week, you'll have a detailed proposal, including price, timeline, and specific documents and services I'll deliver. The price includes the draft document(s) and two re-writes, if needed. Simple projects, like copy editing or proofreading existing documents, are priced at a flat rate, based on the number of pages. Complex or on-going projects are billed on an hourly rate. Legitimate non-profits and charities receive a 25% discount."

THE SHARP PENCIL

East Meadow NY **Website:** www.thesharppencil.com. **Contact:** Elaine Will Sparber.

ADDITIONAL INFORMATION Elaine Will Sparber offers substantive editing, line editing, copyediting, cleanup editing, and proofreading for book publishers, packagers, and authors. Her nonfiction specialties include health, nutrition, dieting, cooking, fitness, pregnancy and childbirth, parenting, relationships, psychology, self-help, lifestyle, politics, mind/body/spirit, and pet care. Her fiction specialties are general fiction, mystery, suspense, thriller, romance, fantasy, LGBT, and YA. Please visit her website for further information.

MISSY SHEEHAN

P.O. Box 362, Hedgesville WV 25427. (304)584-7534. **E-mail:** missy@missysheehan.com. **Website:** www.

missysheehan.com. **Contact:** Missy Sheehan, owner. Estab. 2010.

ADDITIONAL INFORMATION "With 5 years of experience editing and writing for magazines and newspapers, I help other writers make their work clear and compelling. I offer proofreading, copy editing, and substantive editing of short stories, articles, essays, novels, and more."

SILVERMIST INSPIRATIONS

3730 Greenbook Ln., Mt. Pleasant WI 53406. **E-mail:** kruth626@yahoo.com. **Website:** www.silvermistinspirations.com. **Contact:** Kimberly Yoghourtjian. Estab. 2012.

ADDITIONAL INFORMATION Services are primarily for those in the Christian marketplace. Includes editing and proofreading books, articles, sales and news letters, pamphlets, etc.

SISTER MUSES

P.O. Box 14201, Irving TX 75014. **E-mail:** inquiries@sistermuses.com. **Website:** www.sistermuses.com. **Contact:** S.K. Valenzuela, lead editor. Estab. 2014.

ADDITIONAL INFORMATION SAs an independent publishing imprint, we offer authors a wide array of professional services, including ms proofreading, editing, and design, cover design, and story doctoring and analysis. "We offer a complimentary review of the first 10 pages of a ms in order to assist our clients in choosing the package that will provide the best results for the best value."

ELIZABETH SMITH

Brooklyn NY (917)974-1879. **E-mail:** esmithwrite@gmail.com. **Contact:** Elizabeth Smith.

ADDITIONAL INFORMATION "Available for writing, editing, copyediting, and proofreading of print or online projects. Experienced in fiction and nonfiction. Also experienced in editing translations for American markets, both nonfiction and fiction. Organized, creative, dependable, and interested in developing projects for children, teens, or adults. Familiar with InDesign and writing for Web-based publications. Over 5 years experience as editor, copyeditor, and proofreader. Also available as writing coach and mentor. Clients: Rizzoli International Publications, Penguin Books, Harry N. Abrams, Inc., Harlequin, Random House, Inc., Museum of Modern Art." See resume at www.the-efa.org/members/data/resumes/smithe.pdf.

KIMBERLY M. SMITH

Jacksonville FL (904)742-7359. **E-mail:** kmsmithwrites@yahoo.com. **Contact:** Kimberly Smith.

ADDITIONAL INFORMATION "I have a master's degree in English and have taught English and creative writing to writers of all ages. With 20 years of experience writing, editing, and proofreading, I have created business documents, organizational reports, press releases, fiction, and poetry for small businesses, educational and nonprofit organizations, literary magazines, and college and university students. I live and work in Jacksonville, Florida, and enjoy an open and flexible schedule, which enables me to work around any project's schedule and produce a quick turnaround time. You will find my assistance helpful, courteous, and fresh with ideas."

SOMATIC ARTS EDITING

9611 Rainier Ave. S., Seattle WA 98118. **E-mail:** leslie.eliel@gmail.com. **Website:** http://somatic-arts.weebly.com. **Contact:** Leslie Eliel, owner. Estab. 1988.

ADDITIONAL INFORMATION Offers book design and book production from idea to product for writers in the Somatic Arts and related fields—popular neuroscience; somatic psychology; mindfulness training; and body-based moralities for treating PTSD, trauma, nervous-system disregulation, anxiety, and chronic pain. Will work with trade books, booklets, and coffee table books.

SOUTHERN ROAD PRESS

12A Windcreek St., Friendswood TX 77546. **E-mail:** diane@thedianekrause.com. **Website:** www.thedianekrause.com. **Contact:** Diane Krause, owner. Estab. 2011.

ADDITIONAL INFORMATION Offers content editing, copy editing/line editing, proofreading, website content editing/coaching, and ghostwriting.

SPLICKETY PUBLISHING GROUP

P.O. Box 513, Bettendorf IA 52722. **E-mail:** 1benwolf@gmail.com. **Website:** www.splicketypubgroup.com. **Contact:** Ben Wolf, executive editor. Estab. 2011.

ADDITIONAL INFORMATION "Ben Wolf has experience editing everything from graduate papers to novels in excess of 150,000 words. One of his clients was offered contracts from 2 competing publishing houses after he edited her ms. Ben offers various types of edits ranging from basic proofreading for grammar, spelling, and syntax to full line and copy edits."

SPLITSEED

5007-C Victory Blvd., #164, Yorktown VA 23693. (757)240-4241. **E-mail:** amanda@split-seed.com. **Website:** www.split-seed.com. **Contact:** Amanda Rooker. Estab. 2007.

ADDITIONAL INFORMATION Offers full-service custom editing and publishing packages for nonfiction authors and professionals, including critique and consultation, project management, developmental editing, copyediting, proofreading, electronic publishing, and press-ready book design (Adobe InDesign). "We specialize in helping professionals translate their expertise into a polished, publishable, true-to-self ms to meet their professional goals, and are passionate advocates for writers and independent publishing." Member, Editorial Freelancers Association. Cost: free phone consultation for project fee estimates (please provide sample).

SPRINGLEY EDITORIAL SERVICES

Gina Springer Shirley, 4715 Alta Loma Dr., Austin TX 78749. (512)947-5586. **E-mail:** gina@springley. net. **Website:** www.springley.net. **Contact:** Gina E. Springer Shirley, writer/editor/translator.

ADDITIONAL INFORMATION Years in the field: 15. Years as a freelancer: 6. Gina E. Springer Shirley, MA, is a writer and editor of educational materials and an English/Spanish translator. During a 15-year career in educational publishing, Ms. Springer Shirley has written and edited supplemental and intervention programs in the subjects of English, Reading, Language Arts, and ELL/ESL. Some of the programs she has developed include Oxford Picture Dictionary for the Content Areas, Elements of Reading: Fluency, Elements of Reading: Phonics & Phonemic Awareness, and Critical Reading: Differentiated Instruction Across Genres. She remains connected to students and their needs by tutoring and mentoring K-12 students.

FRED STANTON

94 Geiser Road, Wynantskill NY 12198. (518)283-1864. **E-mail:** fredstanton1@gmail.com. **Contact:** Fred Stanton.

ADDITIONAL INFORMATION Fred Stanton is a copy editor, proofreader, indexer, and technical writer with over 33 years of experience in the field, 13 as a freelancer. With a strong background in the sciences (B.S. in physics, M.S. in molecular biology), he has copy edited the United Nations International Labour Organization's *Encyclopaedia of Occupational Safety & Health*, monographs in molecular biology, and the *Journal of Biomolecular Techniques*. He has also copy edited books on history, labor, and African-American studies, as well as business newsletters. His desktop publishing skills include formatting and page design in Adobe InDesign. Fred is also a poet and songwriter.

STARUSNAK'S EDITORIAL SERVICES

629 County Route 57, Phoenix NY 13135. **E-mail:** starusnakseditorialservices@gmail.com. **Website:** www. willowtree.b-town.us. **Contact:** Wendi Starusnak, senior copy editor. Estab. 2013.

ADDITIONAL INFORMATION "Starusnak's Editorial Services offers light, medium, and heavy copyediting of any type of ms for a very reasonable, per-word rate."

STEELE EDITING

1928 Meandering Way, McKinney TX 75071. (972)984-8514. **E-mail:** frank@steele-editing.com. **Website:** www.steele-editing.com. **Contact:** Frank Steele, owner. Estab. 2011. Offers professional proofreading, copyediting, fact checking, and indexing at a reasonable price.

ADDITIONAL INFORMATION "I have more than 30 years experience in publishing. I specialize in general nonfiction, religious/spiritual material, coaching/self-help/motivational material, children's books, and I'm open to almost anything."

WILLIAM H. STEVENSON

11229 Suncrest Dr., Huntsville AL 35803. (256)823-9017; (256)541-0139. **E-mail:** whsteve3@gmail.com. **Contact:** William H. Stevenson.

ADDITIONAL INFORMATION Bill began his career as a scientist and ended as a freelance writer. A chemist by training, he worked for 25 years on a variety of projects in industry and as a government contractor, writing more than 20 scientific and technical publications. During this time he also published a number of freelance magazine articles on topics ranging from the chemistry of sunscreens to a profile of FBI undercover agent Robert Wittman, "the world's greatest art recovery detective." He is now a fulltime freelance writer and editor. See resume at www.the-efa.org/members/data/resumes/stevensonwh.pdf.

KRISTEN STIEFFEL

Orlando FL (407)928-7801. **E-mail:** kristen@kristen-stieffel.com.

ADDITIONAL INFORMATION Kristen Stieffel is a writer and writing coach specializing in line editing and copyediting. She works primarily in the Christian submarket but has also edited books for the general market. Primary expertise is in speculative fiction, but she also works in other genres. Her nonfiction areas of expertise include business, history, and Bible study.

CYNDI A. SUMMERS

2279 Yorkshire Road, Birmingham MI 48009. (586)945-8775. **E-mail:** cyndisummers@prodigy.net. **Website:** linkedin.com/pub/cyndi-summers/9/75/8bb. **Contact:** Cyndi A. Summers, publicist/editor. Estab. 1998. Offers publicity and/or editing services.

ADDITIONAL INFORMATION Specializes in socially and culturally progressive initiatives.

SUSAN D. BIELSKI, EDITOR/ PROOFREADER

20 Main St. #2240, Exeter NH 03833. (603)778-0902. **E-mail:** sue@sdb-editing.com. **Website:** sdb-editing.com. **Contact:** Sue Bielski, principal. Estab. 1997. Experienced J.D. edits nonfiction works for in-house use or for general publication. Specializes in contracts, legal memoranda, client correspondence, marketing and training materials, book mss, and articles/casenotes. Other services include statutory analysis, legal research, case briefing, and online fact checking.

SWANSON EDITORIAL SERVICES, INC.

2029 SE Cypress Ave., Portland OR 97214. (503)239-7194. **E-mail:** kris@swansoneditorial.com. **Contact:** Kristin Swanson, owner. "In business for the last 20 years as a consultant and freelance writer, developmental editor, andproject/production manager in the area of K-12 and college textbook educational materials publishing. Co-author of Nexos, an introductory college Spanish textbook program; Alianzas, an Intermediate College Spanish Program, all published by Cengage Learning."

ADDITIONAL INFORMATION Kristin Swanson has been a freelancer for 25 years working as a writer and editor in the areas of foreign language and ELL educational publishing, among other content areas. Fluent in Spanish and able to work in French and Italian (but not fluent in those languages). Also works as a project manager for editorial and production projects. Has working knowledge of html. Projects include interactive whiteboard activities, activities using .KMZ files, animation scripts, textbooks, workbooks, teacher materials, web activities, testing materials, and information packets such as author guidelines and FAQ sheets. Checks Spanish translations and translates from Spanish into English. She has been the managing editor of an educational journal and is familiar with conventions of scholarly publishing. See resume at www.the-efa.org/members/data/resumes/swansonk.pdf.

TASKMASTERS EDITING, WRITING, AND MARKETING SERVICES

30 Randall St., South Portland ME 04106. **E-mail:** murraylamont@yahoo.com. **Website:** www.taskmasters.webs.com. **Contact:** Lorraine C. Lamont, owner. Estab. 1995.

ADDITIONAL INFORMATION "For 2 decades, I've offered my freelance editing, copywriting, research, excerpting/rewrites, and localization/QA services for US and UK English. I enjoy a wonderful rapport with my ongoing international clients. When it comes to fine-tuning projects for the global market, Taskmasters excels!"

TEXABLE COMMUNICATIONS

P.O. Box 41023, Austin TX 78704. (512)522-4515. **E-mail:** contact@texable.com. **Website:** www.texable.com. **Contact:** Jeff Iezzi.

ADDITIONAL INFORMATION Years as freelancer: 8. "As an experienced author, editor, and translator, I have a proven track record of developing effective communication materials. During the last 15 years, I have worked on a wide variety of online and print publications—corporate websites, marketing brochures, product handbooks, and style guides. My native language is American English, and I speak, read, and write fluent German."

RUTH E. THALER-CARTER

2500 East Ave., Suite 7K, Rochester NY 14610. (585)248-8464 (home); (585)248-8464 (business). **Fax:** (585)248-3638. **E-mail:** ruth@writerruth.com. **Website:** www.writerruth.com. **Contact:** Ruth E. Thaler-Carter.

ADDITIONAL INFORMATION Ruth Thaler-Carter is an award-winning freelance writer, editor, proofreader, desktop publisher and speaker who has a business called "I can write about anything!" She specializes in articles for and about associations and nonprofits, and in all aspects of newsletters, from concept through publication, including training and critiques. She is a fast, effective, accurate writer, editor and proofreader with a lively writing voice, wide-ranging network of resources and sharp eye for details. She teaches freelancing, editing/prooofreading and website classes, both online and in person, for several professional organizations. She also holds an annual conference for freelancers through Communication Central (www.communication-central.com).

THE WRITE WORD

16 Tulsa Lane, Watsonville CA 95076. (831)724-7321. **Website:** tombentley.com. **Contact:** Tom Bentley, owner. Estab. 1996. Offers business copywriting and editing for B2B and B2C companies. Also available for fiction and nonfiction book editing, including developmental editing, line editing, and proofreading.

AMY THOMPSON EDITING

Council Bluffs IA (402)660-7109. **E-mail:** amy@amythompsonediting.com; amythompsonediting@gmail.com. **Website:** www.amythompsonediting.com. **Contact:** Amy Thompson, owner.
ADDITIONAL INFORMATION Years in field: 25. Years as a freelancer: 2. "All writing is storytelling and your favorite story is your own. I can help you write and polish that story so that it becomes someone else's favorite as well. With over 20 years of experience editing and proofreading everything from magazines and websites to marketing materials, grants and fiction/nonficiton mss, I can help you make your project shine."

TIGERXGLOBAL

Kansas City MO (270)302-0036. **E-mail:** maria@tigerxeditor.com. **Website:** www.tigerxglobal.com. **Contact:** Maria D'Marco.
ADDITIONAL INFORMATION "TigerXglobal offers experienced, knowledgeable, insightful editing services for every type of written work. Your ms receives personalized attention through every step of your edit with comprehensive reviews that bring your work to its fullest potential. TigerX edits ensure clarity, maximize your unique style, and reveal opportunities to strengthen your story, message, or concept. Query to determine which editing service, or blend of services, best suits your needs. Editing can be stand-alone or combined services, including proofreading, style/language edits, continuity reviews, fact-checking, and full developmental edits. An initial consult is performed free of charge to determine your specific needs. A proposal or quote will be supplied from the information gained in this preliminary consult." Maria D'Marco has been in the field for 20 years. Contact her using the form on her website.

THE TOBIN TOUCH, LLC

Arlington Heights IL (773)368-3079. **Fax:** (773)283-7852. **E-mail:** stacey.tobin@thetobintouch.com. **Website:** www.thetobintouch.com. **Contact:** Stacey C. Tobin, PhD., ELS. Estab. 2003.
ADDITIONAL INFORMATION Stacey Tobin is an "independent PhD medical and scientific writer and board-certified editor in the life sciences, with a background in cellular and molecular physiology research and 14-years' experience in writing, editing, formatting, and submitting peer-reviewed journal articles, invited reviews, editorials, and textbook chapters, as well as preparing abstracts and posters for presentation at professional conferences." She also reviews NIH and NSF grant applications for content organization, continuity, and formatting. Stacey has a B.Sc. (biology, chemistry minor); M.S. (molecular physiology); Ph.D. (neurobiology and physiology). Her subjects are: reproductive medicine, obstetrics and gynecology, oncology, cardiology, diabetes and metabolism, endocrinology, and HIV/AIDS. Stacey Tobin is the owner of The Tobin Touch, LLC, April 2003 - present. Recent assignments include writing and editing for the National Institutes of Health and National Cancer Institute grant applications, invited reviews, and peer-reviewed mss for publication in national journals and international meeting proceedings, as well as creating meeting abstracts and posters. See her resume at www.the-efa.org/members/data/resumes/tobins.pdf.

TO PRESS & BEYOND

825 E. Pedregosa St., Suite 2, Santa Barbara CA 93103. (805)898-2263. **E-mail:** info@topressandbeyond.com. **Website:** www.topressandbeyond.com. **Contact:** Gail M. Kearns, president. Estab. 1995.
ADDITIONAL INFORMATION "Gail M. Kearns and her team at To Press & Beyond are specialists in book publishing consulting and support services. With over 16 years of experience, they skillfully and successfully guide your print and/or e-book project from ms to finished book, educating and coaching every step of the way. Their comprehensive range of services include writing, developmental editing and copyediting, proofreading, design and layout, printing, distribution, sales and promotion, both in trade

and niche markets and on the web. Our books consistently win editorial and design awards."

TREEHOUSE PUBLISHING GROUP LLC

8734 Norcross Dr., St. Louis MO 63126. (314)363-4546. **E-mail:** authorservices@treehousepublishing-group.com. **Website:** treehousepublishinggroup.com. **Contact:** Kristina Makansi, managing partner. Estab. 2013. Treehouse Publishing Group offers a full menu of a la carte author services as well as assisted self-publishing under our Treehouse imprint.

ADDITIONAL INFORMATION "At TPG, we believe that every project is as unique as the author who created it. That's why we individually tailor each package—from developmental edits to book layouts to website design—to suit your specific goals."

TREEHOUSES AUTHOR SERVICES, LLC

3963 Flora Place, St. Louis MO 63110. **E-mail:** authorservices@treehouseauthorservices.com. **Website:** treehouseauthorservices.com. **Contact:** Kristina Makansi, partner/co-owner. Estab. 2013.

ADDITIONAL INFORMATION Offers developmental editing, line editing, copy editing, proofreading, cover design, print book and e-book formatting, publishing assistance.

TRITTIN EDITING

Oklahoma City OK **E-mail:** sheryl@trittinediting.com. **Website:** www.trittinediting.com. **Contact:** Sheryl Trittin. Estab. 2000.

ADDITIONAL INFORMATION Sheryl Trittin has over 15 years of experience in the field. Sheryl completed the Professional Sequence in Editing certificate program at UC Berkley in 2010. She also has a B.A. degree in literature and environmental science and has completed graduate-level courses in editing and nonfiction writing. She is currently enrolled in the Professional Sequence in Editing certificate program at UC Berkeley. Trittin Editing offers professional editing services, specializing in copyediting and proofreading.

T-SQUARE

4320 Volga Court, New Port Richey FL 34655. (727)505-9388. **E-mail:** timothy.duerksen@gmail.com. **Contact:** Timothy Duerksen, owner/editor. Estab. 2014.

ADDITIONAL INFORMATION Offers freelance editing and formatting. "I am also building a local/online writing community. Resources available on request."

VALERIE JOY TURNER

E-mail: vjt@valeriejoyturner.com. **Website:** http://valeriejoyturner.com. **Contact:** Valerie Turner.

ADDITIONAL INFORMATION Valerie Turner offers a variety of editing services from proofreading and light editing to substantive editing, writing, and reviewing translations. She specializes in works on Middle Eastern history, Islamic studies, and Arabic translations. She holds a Certificate in Editing from the University of Chicago, a Master of Arts in Middle Eastern Studies, and a Bachelor of Arts in Islamic History. She is a native English speaker, with advanced Arabic (reading, writing, and speaking), and familiarity with Persian and French. She is experienced using various Arabic transliteration systems. See Valerie's website for pay rates.

PHILIP TURNER BOOK PRODUCTIONS LLC

New York NY **E-mail:** philipsturner@gmail.com. **Website:** http://philipsturner.com. **Contact:** Philip Turner, editing, representation, consulting.

ADDITIONAL INFORMATION Offers line editing of proposals and mss for agents, authors, and publishers. Nonfiction and selected fiction. Services include proposal editing, book proposal development, and line-editing. Cost: Rates given upon review of material. Contact for rates. See http://philipsturner.com or www.publishersmarketplace.com for additional information.

TWA SOLUTIONS

P.O. Box 4481, Upper Marlboro MD 20775. (202)702-7120. **Fax:** (888)559-9693. **E-mail:** jessica@twasolutions.com. **Website:** www.twasolutions.com. **Contact:** Jessica Wright Tilles, owner/creative director. Estab. 2000.

ADDITIONAL INFORMATION Offers book cover design, interior design (typesetting), editing, web design.

TWO SONGBIRDS PRESS

(916)837-3017. **E-mail:** robin@twosongbirdspress.com. **Website:** www.twosongbirdspress.com. **Contact:** Robin Martin, founder/editor.

ADDITIONAL INFORMATION Robin Martin has spent 14 years in the field; 10 years as a freelancer. "During her tenure on the editing staff of an internationally-acclaimed literary magazine with a circulation of 160,000, Robin evaluated mss for publication and was a contest judge. She is currently the senior editor of a creative nonfiction literary magazine. With professionally trained writing skills and strong editorial judgment, she is able to identify the elements of a powerful and effective story and to articulate the strengths and weaknesses of a piece. She consults with and mentors novice and intermediate writers on craft. She performs substantive, line, and developmental edits, generates content, ghostwrites blog, newsletter, web content for professionals." MA English (Writing) California State University, Sacramento; BA English (Summa Cum Laude) Rutgers College.

BETTY ANN TYSON

87 Pierce Road, Watertown MA 02472. (617)924-7715. **E-mail:** ba_tyson@comcast.net. **Website:** bettyanntyson.com. **Contact:** Betty Ann Tyson.
ADDITIONAL INFORMATION Experienced editor/proofreader with book publishing experience. Elizabeth has been in the field for 40 years.

VERSATILE WRITING AND EDITING SERVICES

Tucson AZ (520)990-9582. **E-mail:** lmarkowitz@aol.com. **Website:** www.lauramarkowitz.com. **Contact:** Laura Markowitz. "Versatile, award-winning editor and writer with 28 years of experience."
ADDITIONAL INFORMATION "Visit my website for more information about my background and experience. Feel free to give me a call or email me to discuss your project. I'm versatile, deadline-driven and a good listener, and I look forward to helping you."

VERSATILITY

1490 W. Gurley St., Prescott AZ 86303. (928)458-9303. **Fax:** (928)202-4183. **E-mail:** tarafort@cableone.net. **Contact:** Tara Fort. Estab. 2009.
ADDITIONAL INFORMATION Has over 15 years' experience freelancing. Offers proofreading, editing, and copyediting.

BRANDY VICKERS

Cincinnati OH **E-mail:** brandyvickers@gmail.com. **Contact:** Brandy Vickers.
ADDITIONAL INFORMATION "Brandy Vickers is a versatile freelance editor with 18 years of experience in the book industry. Her editorial services include copyediting, proofreading, and substantive editing. A former in-house editor for a trade book

publisher, she is also experienced in writing catalog copy, cover copy, and reader's guide discussion questions for fiction and nonfiction works. She is familiar with Chicago Manual (CMS), Council of Science Editors (CSE), American Psychological Association (APA), and American Medical Association (AMA) style guidelines. Areas of interest: STEMM (Science, Technical, Engineering, Mathematics, and Medical) editing, cookbooks, fiction, and literary nonfiction. Electronic Editing Software: Microsoft Word, Adobe Acrobat, Adobe InDesign, Adobe InCopy, InMath, MathType."

VIRTUAL OFFICE TOOLS

P.O. Box 961204, Riverdale GA 30296. (678)532-1156. **E-mail:** mindyrogers.vot2013@gmail.com. **Website:** myvirtualofficetools.com. **Contact:** Mindy Rogers, owner/virtual assistant. Estab. 2013. Virtual Office Tools offers accounting and administrative services to other small businesses, including writers and authors.
ADDITIONAL INFORMATION Services available include: proofreading, editing, copywriting, blogging, public relations, advertising, event planning, making and returning phone calls, calendar management, website management, social media management, and much more.

ROBERT GABRIEL (GABE) WAGGONER

207 14th Place NE, Washington DC 20002. (202)569-8472. **E-mail:** gwaggoner@gmail.com. **Website:** www.nasw.org/users/rgwaggoner.
ADDITIONAL INFORMATION Robert Gabriel Waggoner is a full-time freelance science writer and editor who has been in the field for 13 years. His work consists primarily of editing biomedical text for journals, books, and monographs (BELS certified); "I am trained in the physical sciences and work with astronomy/astrophysics and quantum physics as well. I enjoy working both directly with authors and with publishers."

A WAY WITH WORDS

607-720 Wonderland Road N., London ON N6H 4Y8 Canada. (519)902-8428. **E-mail:** johnsonk@sympatico.ca. **Website:** mansuscriptcopyediting.blogspot.com. **Contact:** Kim Johnson. Estab. 1998.
ADDITIONAL INFORMATION Offers novel, ms, short story critiquing; plot direction assistance-structure, formulation, storyline configuration; ed-

iting and proofreading (grammar, spelling, punctuation).

WEIGHT OF THE WORD INDEXING SERVICE

7140 Simms St., Unit 106, Arvada CO 80004. (303)619-2332. **E-mail:** gina@weightoftheword.com. **Website:** www.weightoftheword.com. **Contact:** Gina Guilinger, owner/indexer. Estab. 2011.

ADDITIONAL INFORMATION "Weight of the Word specializes in back-of-book indexes in a wide variety of subjects."

ERIN WILHELM

62 Cedar St., #705, Seattle WA 98121. **E-mail:** wilhelm.erin@gmail.com. **Contact:** Erin Wilhelm. Estab. 2006.

ADDITIONAL INFORMATION Offers writing, editing, fact checking, and research services with specialization in healthcare and sciences.

MEAGAN WILSON

12 Pond View Heights, Rochester NY 14612. **E-mail:** meaganwilson@burngraphite.net. **Website:** www.burntgraphite.net. **Contact:** Meagan Wilson, owner. Estab. 2011.

ADDITIONAL INFORMATION "I offer line editing, proofreading, and ms critiques for commercial fiction and nonfiction."

WITHPENANDPAPER.COM

Santa Monica CA 90404. (310)828-8421. **E-mail:** withpenandpaper@verizon.net. **Website:** withpenandpaper.com. **Contact:** Heiga Schier, PhD. Estab. 1998.

ADDITIONAL INFORMATION "Unlock the potential of your ms! Professional editor and published author provides powerful and personalized editorial services to published, self-published, and not-yet published authors of fiction and nonfiction."

A WORD AFFAIR LLC

(201)404-0217. **E-mail:** trishpeters@msn.com; ppeters@awordaffair.com. **Website:** www.awordaffair.com. **Contact:** Patricia C. Peters. Estab. 2004.

ADDITIONAL INFORMATION A Word Affair LLC is a professional editorial services company established by Patricia Peters in 2004. The editorial services include ms critique, conceptual editing, line editing, copyediting, proofreading, and analysis of the submission package. Whether you are a publisher, literary agent, published or unpublished writer, A Word Affair's mission is to make your project shine. An editing professional for 16 years, Patricia has worked with various genres, editing projects for Random House, Simon & Schuster, McGraw-Hill, Bamboo Books, CDS Books, Gale, and private clients. Her projects include crime fiction, romance novels, young adult fiction, children's fiction, biography, memoir, health, spirituality, business books, essays, reference books, earth sciences, and social sciences. Patricia has been a guest editor and panelist at the Pacific Northwest Writers Association Conference and the Colorado Gold Conference. She holds a Ph.D. in English Literature from Drew University in Madison, New Jersey, and has taught courses in freshman composition, creative writing, and American literature.

WORD COLLABORATIVE

Atlanta GA (678)612-7463. **E-mail:** jennifer@wordcollaborative.com. **Website:** www.wordcollaborative.com. **Contact:** Jennifer Yankopolus, freelance editor.

ADDITIONAL INFORMATION "I work with writers of any experience level or background to make their first drafts or last drafts ready for publication, whether a book, memoir, novel, or essay. I specialize in working with first-time authors, providing sensitive feedback and guidance throughout the entire writing and editing process. Besides architecture and design, I have experience with business, general nonfiction, fiction, and history topics, as well as self-published titles."

WORDCRAFT EDITING & WRITING SERVICES

40 Genung Circle, Ithaca NY 14850. (607)277-3641; (607)592-7846. **E-mail:** wordcrft@twcny.rr.com. **Website:** www.wordcraftithaca.com. **Contact:** William E. Barnett, Ph.D. Estab. 1998.

ADDITIONAL INFORMATION Established by William Barnett, "WordCraft specializes in scholarly editing, research, and writing in all academic fields as well as in popular writing of every conceivable kind. Dr. Barnett has edited, proofread, or adapted for re-publication dozens of articles in the fields of hospitality management and marketing, real estate finance, and food and beverage management, along with hundreds of articles, dissertations, and books in many other academic fields including economics, psychology and other social sciences, several humanities disciplines, and science." He has worked in the field for 19 years, 16 years as a freelancer after 3 as the late Dr. Carl Sagan's personal editorial and research assistant.

WORDCRAFTER

Sea Cliff NY 11579. (516)674-0415. **E-mail:** wordcrafter47@yahoo.com. **Contact:** Joslyn Pine.

ADDITIONAL INFORMATION "As a seasoned publishing professional and full-time freelancer, my skills include writing and rewriting, line/substantive and developmental editing, copyediting and proofreading, as well as ms evaluation. Adult fiction is my specialty, while the mystery/crime/thriller genre is my subspecialty. My client list includes two publishers (ongoing) as well as a growing list of individual writers. Please refer to my project list and testimonials on the Editorial Freelancers Association website: http://www.the-efa.org."

WORDISWORTH

15500 Armsby Lane, Morgan Hill CA 95037. (408)779-2399. **E-mail:** info@wordisworth.com. **Website:** www.wordisworth.com. **Contact:** Alison Macmillan, co-owner. Estab. 2008.

ADDITIONAL INFORMATION "WordIsWorth is an independent information and publishing company run by a husband and wife team who offer publishing, editing, writing, and design services."

WORDSART NONFICTION BOOK EDITING

(914)376-6892. **E-mail:** editart@optonline.net. **Website:** www.dlamont.com. **Contact:** Daveda Lamont.

ADDITIONAL INFORMATION Services offered include comprehensive editing, line and copy editing, developmental editing, revisions, rewriting, and reorganization of nonfiction mss.

WORDSWORTH EDITORIAL SERVICES

59 Harvey Ct., Irvine CA 92617. (949)357-0941 for. **E-mail:** laura.a.long@cox.net. **Website:** www.wordswortheditorial.com. **Contact:** Laura Ann Long.

ADDITIONAL INFORMATION Editorial services, including copyediting, proofreading, fact checking, ms preparation for eBook publication, grant writing, copy writing. "Crystal clear written communication is our goal at Wordsworth Editorial Services. Well written ideas and expertly edited documents have maximum impact, gain your readers' trust, and win the results you seek. Wordsworth Editorial Services provides personalized copy writing, copy editing, and proofreading services for business and individuals. When it's worth saying right, Wordsworth Editorial Services is your personalized editorial partner."

THE WRITE HELP, LLC

Littleton CO **Website:** www.thewritehelp.net. **Contact:** Dianne Lorang, owner. Estab. 1996.

ADDITIONAL INFORMATION "The Write Help, LLC offers editing and writing services with an emphasis on nonfiction, including inspirational and creative nonfiction. Along with editing, from developmental to proofreading, we are experienced in writing book proposals and website content."

THE WRITE IDEA LLC

1545 NW 57th St., #613, Seattle WA 98107. (206)789-8049. **E-mail:** garden@thewriteidea.com. **Website:** www.thewriteidea.com. **Contact:** Jenny Garden, owner. Estab. 1990.

ADDITIONAL INFORMATION "The Write Idea LLC is a copyediting service that offers content editing and editorial consultation in addition to the expected mastery of English grammar, syntax, usage, and punctuation. The Write Idea promises superior results with delivery on or before deadline."

WRITE ON LLC

P.O. Box 10071, Fort Wayne IN 46850. (260)466-6218. **E-mail:** lauren@lcagg.com. **Website:** lcagg.com. **Contact:** Lauren Caggiano. Estab. 2006.

ADDITIONAL INFORMATION Offers copywriting, feature writing, French translation, editing/proofreading, social media management, SEO writing, public relations, and grantwriting.

WRITE PERSPECTIVES

2404 Central Road, Rolling Meadows IL 60008. (847)392-6861. **E-mail:** bvd6656@hotmail.com. **Website:** www.writeperspectives.com. **Contact:** Betsy van Die, owner/chief PR consultant. Estab. 2013.

ADDITIONAL INFORMATION Offers versatile writing/editing services, specializing in branding, writing, and digital content development strategies for clients in the medical/health, association, and not-for-profit sector. Services include blogs, clinical research/writing, copywriting, design, editing, feature articles, newsletters and brochures, press releases, project management, public awareness campaigns, scripts, speechwriting, social media, and web content development.

WRITERCHICK LLC

9179 Crouse Willison Road, Johnstown OH 43031. **E-mail:** writerchick.nancy@gmail.com. **Website:** www.linkedin.com/in/lafever. **Contact:** Nancy LaFever, owner/CEO. Estab. 2005.

ADDITIONAL INFORMATION "Full-time freelance writer/editor with 10 years experience crafting and publishing thousands of magazine articles, professional blog posts, web content, copywriting, and extensive editing services for clients in diverse industries."

THE WRITER'S ALLY

1325 Bedford Ave., #5800, Pikesville MD 21282. **Website:** www.thewritersally.com. **Contact:** Allyson E. Machate, owner/chief editor. Estab. 2004.

ADDITIONAL INFORMATION "We're on a mission to help bring better books to the world's readers by assisting, guiding, and supporting would-be authors on their publishing journey. Get our free e-book and check out our blog today."

WRITER'S RESOURCE

(866)212-9805. **E-mail:** consultant@writersresource.us. **Website:** www.writersresource.us. **Contact:** Laine Cunningham. Estab. 1994.

ADDITIONAL INFORMATION Writer's Resource works with authors, public speakers, thought leaders and small presses to ghostwrite, rewrite, and edit fiction and nonfiction; market books, speaking engagements and products; and branding at every step. One of the most important benefits is Laine's ability to convey the core message in a clear way. Every step stays focused on the client's short- and long-term goals.

WRITE TO SELL YOUR BOOK

16 W. 23rd St., 4th Floor, New York NY 10010. (866)821-4164. **E-mail:** diane@writetosellyourbook.com. **Website:** www.writetosellyourbook.com. **Contact:** Diane O'Connell, editorial director. Estab. 2008.

ADDITIONAL INFORMATION "With over 25 years publishing experience, including editor at Random House and author of 6 books, O'Connell specializes in working with first-time authors, and has helped numerous authors achieve publishing success, including some that have become bestsellers. She works in

fiction, nonfiction, and memoir. Her services include ms critiquing, developmental editing, copyediting, coaching, and production management."

WRITE WAY COPYEDITING LLC

Sun Prairie WI 53590. (608)837-8091. **E-mail:** diana.schramer@thewritewaycopyediting.com. **Website:** www.writewaycopyediting.com. **Contact:** Diana Schramer, owner. Estab. 2010.

ADDITIONAL INFORMATION "Three levels of copyediting—light, medium, and heavy—for book-length mss, e-books, blogs, essays, short stories, articles, newsletters, annual reports, and academic reports."

THE WRITE WORD

16 Tulsa Lane, Watsonville CA 95076. (831)824-7717. **E-mail:** bentguy@charter.net. **Website:** www.tombentley.com. **Contact:** Tom Bentley, owner. Estab. 1996.

ADDITIONAL INFORMATION Offers copywriting and editing services for businesses, including marketing collateral, web content, press releases, and case studies. Also offers editing of novels and nonfiction books, from developmental editing to proofreading.

WRITING AS A GHOST

310 W. 39th St., Vancouver WA 98660. (360)566-2781. **Fax:** (360)989-3980. **E-mail:** denise@writingmyownbook.com. **Website:** writingmyownbook.com. **Contact:** Denise Rutledge, account manager. Estab. 2006. Writing as a Ghost offers freelance design, coaching and editorial services as a package and as individual services.

ADDITIONAL INFORMATION Design services include layout and design and ms preparation for POD publishing, Kindle and Smashwords submission. Coaching services include research and ms development, including assistance with developing market competitive approach to topic. Editing services range from simple proof reading and copy editing to substantive editing. Denise Rutledge approaches the written word as a combination of crafted words and visual message.

WRITING FROM THE DEEPER SELF

484 Lake Park Ave., #537, Oakland CA 94610. (510)653-7673. **E-mail:** naomirosedeepwrite@yahoo.com. **Website:** www.essentialwriting.com. **Contact:** Naomi Rose. Estab. 1995.

ADDITIONAL INFORMATION "Our process, called 'Writing From the Deeper Self,' allows the writer to have a profoundly fulfilling experience in doing the writing. The premise is that within everyone is a creative spark that wants expression, even if the material is educational or factual."

X-HEIGHT STUDIO

83 High St., Milford MA 01757. (508)478-3897; (508)478-6077. **Fax:** (508)478-6077. **E-mail:** cecile@x-heightstudio.com. **Website:** www.x-heightstudio.com. **Contact:** Cecile Kaufman. Estab. 1999.

ADDITIONAL INFORMATION X-Height Studio was founded by Cecile Kaufman. She was educated at Massachusetts College of Art and the Univ. of California at Berkeley, and received her B.A. with honors in Comparative Literature. Cecile has 23 years' experience in publishing. She began as a freelance proofreader for HarperCollins in San Francisco. Later she worked as a book designer and production manager at Waite Group Press, an imprint of Macmillan Computer Publishing, where Cecile managed the process from copyediting mss to interacting with printers.

YAMSTER COMMUNICATIONS, LLC

P.O. Box 333, 6 Mill St., Harrington ME 04643-0333. **E-mail:** mmcsorley@maineline.net. **Website:** www.yamstercommunications.com. **Contact:** Mike McSorley, president. Estab. 2004.

ADDITIONAL INFORMATION Services offered include "first read" edit of mss and complete audio book production.

THE YP PUBLISHING

253-4025 Dorchester Road, Niagara Falls ON L2E7K8 Canada. (905) 341-0997. **E-mail:** info@theyppublishing.com. **Website:** www.theyppublishing.com. **Contact:** Yvonne Wu, media strategist, author/speaking assistant. Estab. 2008.

ADDITIONAL INFORMATION Services offered include virtual book tours, Amazon bestseller campaigns, online book promotion, websites, ms preparation, book proposals, ebook conversion, print coordination, and social media support.

FREELANCE
DESIGNERS

//

People really shouldn't judge a book by its cover, but one of the hard truths of publishing is that readers do, in fact, make purchasing decisions based off the covers of books. A poorly designed book cover can doom the best mss to obscurity. On the other hand, a well-designed cover can sometimes help less-than-worthy books enjoy wonderful sales. The smart self-publisher excels at every level. That includes working to put the best cover on the best ms possible.

Finding the right designer for your project can make the difference between success and failure. One knock against self-publishing that still persists is that self-published books are of lesser quality. By using freelance designers, you can work to overcome that specific hurdle in the self-publishing process by giving potential readers a beautiful cover and interior design to admire.

However, there are a variety of freelance design services available with different pricing structures. It's important to remember that sometimes you get what you pay for, and it's possible to pay (or overpay) for services you don't really need. The "How Much Should I Charge?" pay rate chart should help with determining an appropriate fee with your freelance designer.

Beyond determining a fair rate, self-publishers need to know what type of design assistance they need. For instance, do you just need someone to design a book cover? Do you need illustration or photography assistance? Could you use help with fonts and interior layout and formatting?

Each service may have a different fee and a different amount of time required to complete the work. In determining freelance rates, you'll need to know the hourly rate and time requirement to assign a fair fee that will result in quality work. Setting unfair expectations is bad for the freelancer, but it also puts your project at risk, because you're counting on the freelancers to give their best.

KEEP IN MIND

Starting locally will allow you to research each company carefully and learn about their past performance and make it easier to have face-to-face discussions about the design. Realize that any face-to-face time and time on the phone may be considered "billable hours" by your freelancer. Be sure to agree on all such fees and get it in writing before starting work. It will help ensure a more professional working relationship and provide both sides with more security.

Going local is not a requirement. In fact, you may find that going with another designer outside of your area is more affordable or provides you with a freelancer who has better qualifications. Always ask for previous experience and consider checking references, especially if you're investing a lot of money in the design process. After all, you want to make sure your money will be money well spent.

SHAILA ABDULLAH

8408 Dulac Dr., Austin TX 78729. (512)924-7674. E-mail: info@myhouseofdesign.com. **Website:** www.myhouseofdesign.com. **Contact:** Shaila Abdullah, owner. Estab. 1995. Offers web, multimedia, and print services.

ADDITIONAL INFORMATION Services for web & multimedia include websites, content management systems, Wordpress sites, landing pages, book launch campaigns, e-mail campaigns, e-newsletters, social media pages, web banners and ads, multimedia demos, presentations, and online courses. Services for print include book covers, book interiors, book design, e-book design, flyers and sell sheets, postcards, posters, business cards, stationery, ads, brand, and identity.

AMY THORNTON DESIGN

465 Winona Ct., Denver CO 80204. (303)915-7567. **E-mail:** AmyThorntonArtworks@gmail.com. **Website:** www.amythorntondesign.com. **Contact:** Amy Thornton, owner/designer. Estab. 1994. For over twenty years, AmyThorntonDesign.com has been creating award-winning publications that combine the harmonious integration of content and visual elements. With extensive experience in a variety of markets, AmyThorntonDesign.com delivers a wide range of publication design and production services. Platforms include: text-heavy scholarly journals, annual reports, magazine editorial layout, marketing brochures, media kits, and popular books on any subject.

CARISSA ANDREWS

21521 Rebel Road, Merrifield MN 56465. **E-mail:** carissa.andrews@pendomus.com. **Website:** www.carissaandrews.com. **Contact:** Carissa Andrews. Estab. 2006.

ADDITIONAL INFORMATION Offers ghostwriting, copywriting, content writing, book design, logo design, various graphic design, speaking and book events, marketing tips and tricks, and author platform help.

ART OF MELUSH

New York NY (347)536-1466. **E-mail:** info@artofmelush.com. **Website:** www.artofmelush.com. **Contact:** Melinda McCarthy, illustrator/fine artist. Estab. 2013. **ADDITIONAL INFORMATION** Offers b&w and full color illustratiion and cover design/artwork.

BELLE ETOILE STUDIOS

112 Reton Ct., Cary NC 27513. **E-mail:** michael@belleetoilestudios.com. **Website:** www.belleetoilestudios.com. **Contact:** Michael Trudeau, editorial manager/co-owner. Estab. 2009. Belle Etoile is a 2-person publishing services studio from principals Michael Trudeau and Jamie Kerry.

ADDITIONAL INFORMATION "We offer design, production, and editorial to book-publishing houses and self-publishing authors." Editorial services include developmental editing, substantive editing, copyediting, proofreading, fact-checking, editorial project management, copywriting, and ms review and consultation. Design and production services include typesetting/page layout, book cover design, book interior design, book production management, logo design, branding, general graphic design, and e-book creation. "We work primarily with literary fiction, genre fiction, general nonfiction, and poetry. Our genre fiction experience includes titles in crime, fantasy and science fiction, horror, mystery and suspense, romance, young adult, and more. Our trade nonfiction experience includes titles in autobiography and biography, cultural studies and social sciences, ecology, health, history, humor, memoir, politics, sports, the occult, and more."

JOE BIEL DESIGN

2752 N. Williams Ave., Portland OR 97227. (503)232-3666. **Fax:** (888)503-0599. **E-mail:** joe@microcosmpublishing.com. **Website:** microcosmpublishing.com. **Contact:** Joe Biel, designer. Estab. 1995. Specializes in one and two color design interiors and two and four color book covers.

ADDITIONAL INFORMATION "We've designed hundreds of books over the life of a teenager, and we'd be happy to consider designing your book. Rates are based on how much affinity we have for your job, your budget, and how much time is presently available but can be tailored to fit any reasonable budget."

JENNIFER BILLOCK CREATIVE SERVICES

12004 255th Ave., Trevor WI 53179. **E-mail:** jenniferjoanbillock@gmail.com. **Website:** www.jenniferbillock.com. **Contact:** Jennifer Billock, owner. Estab. 2012.

ADDITIONAL INFORMATION Jennifer Billock Creative Services offers editing, writing, and layout design services. Specialties include developmental and copy editing for self-publishing mss, travel material, recipe and cookbook writing and editing, book proposals, and magazine work of all types.

BOOK COMPLETION

2407 California St. SE, Huntsville AL 35801. **E-mail:** cara@bookcompletion.com. **Website:** bookcompletion.com. **Contact:** Cara Stein, owner. Estab. 2012. Services include weaving and melding content into a ms; editing and polishing mss; designing cover to match branding, attract readers, and convey the feel and message of book's content; designing an interior layout to go with the cover and help communicate the message; producing the book as a PDF e-book for sale or distribution on your website; producing the book as an e-book in Kindle and e-pub formats for sale on Amazon, Barnes & Noble, etc.; and producing the book for print.

ADDITIONAL INFORMATION "We do the whole process, from writing and editing to layout and design. The result will be an attractive, professional book that showcases your work. Let us be your one-stop shop to get your book finished and fabulous!"

THE BOOK DOCTOR IS IN

San Pedro CA 90732. (310)346-8852. **E-mail:** stacey@thebookdoctorisin.com. **Website:** thebookdoctorisin.com. **Contact:** Stacey Aaronson, fulfiller of publishing dreams and founder. Estab. 2011. Offers market analysis program, professional editing, artistic book cover design, standout book layout and design, writing services, superb e-book design, custom graphics creation, publishing facilitation, engaging promo materials, creative website design, attentive communication, and handholding from start to finish.

ADDITIONAL INFORMATION "I take you by the hand as a self-publishing author and transform your ms into the book you've dreamed of—from impeccable editing and proofreading to engaging, audience-targeted cover and professional interior design—rivaling or exceeding a traditional house publication."

TRISTAN BOWERSOX DESIGN

3538 N. Carefree Circle, Apartment E, Colorado Springs CO 80917. (913)369-5063. **E-mail:** tristan.bowersox@gmail.com. **Website:** tristanbowersox.com. **Contact:** Tristan Bowersox, designer. Estab. 2011.

ADDITIONAL INFORMATION Offers book cover design, web design, and HTML/CSS.

WYNNE BROWN LLC

2733 W. Hilltop Road, Portal AZ 85632. (520)558-1131. **E-mail:** wynnebrown@mac.com. **Website:** www.wynnebrown.com. **Contact:** Wynne Brown, owner. Estab. 2012. Wynne Brown has spent 35 years as a freelance graphic designer, writer, and editor. Design services include book design, presentations, brochures, newsletters, technical illustrations, logo development.

ADDITIONAL INFORMATION She also spent 6 years as a copy editor at a mid-sized daily newspaper and has edited books, magazine articles, and academic publications. She is comfortable with Associated Press, Chicago Manual of Style, and American Psychological Association stylebooks.

THE BUTTERFLY TYPEFACE

1303 Calla Circle, Fayetteville NC 28303. (501)251-8118. **E-mail:** butterflytypeface.imw@gmail.com. **Website:** www.thebutterflytypeface.com. **Contact:** Iris Williams McGee, owner. Estab. 2014.

ADDITIONAL INFORMATION Offers editing, writing, ms typeset and design.

CALLIGRAPHY BY MICHAEL NOYES

0 E. 4th St., #18, Richmond VA 23224. (804)943-1522. **E-mail:** michael@michaelnoyes.com. **Website:** www.michaelnoyes.com. **Contact:** Michael Noyes, owner. Estab. 1997. Primarily a graphic designer, specializing in text layout, typography, and calligraphy.

ADDITIONAL INFORMATION "I use Adobe Photoshop and Illustrator primarily in corporate branding, logos, brochures, and book covers. Wordpress is my preferred web authoring platform. My calligraphy designs may be seen online."

CAROUSEL PHOTOGRAPHY & DESIGN

95 Lloyd St., Lively ON P34 1C1 Canada. **E-mail:** christine@carouselphotodesign.com. **Website:** www.carouselphotodesign.com. **Contact:** Christine Lewis, owner. Estab. 2009.

ADDITIONAL INFORMATION Offers book/cover layout and design, websites, and marketing materials.

CECALLI BOOKS, ARTS & DESIGN

calle L #13, col UAPR, del. Coyoacan, Mexico City DF 04800 Mexico. **E-mail:** cecalli@gmail.com. **Website:** www.cecalli.com. **Contact:** Carlos Rodriguez. Estab. 2013.

ADDITIONAL INFORMATION Offers brading (logos, brochures, ID cards), graphic design (photo retouch, posters, illustration), editorial design (books, e-books, magazines), and web design (HTML, banners).

KERI CHRISTIAN

204 Falkirk Court, Fredericksburg VA 22046. (916)905-7074. **E-mail:** keric@kerichristian.com. **Website:** kerichristian.com. **Contact:** Keri Christian, designer. Estab. 2005.

ADDITIONAL INFORMATION "I offer a variety of services including web design/development, graphic design, hosting services, online marketing with Google AdWords, AdSense, PPC campaigns, and SEO."

GEORGE CLEMES DIRECT

220 McKendree Ave., Annapolis MD 21401. (410)280-2967. **E-mail:** george@georgeclemesdirect. com. **Website:** www.georgeclemesdirect.com. **Contact:** George Clemes, president. Estab. 2008.

ADDITIONAL INFORMATION George Clemes Direct specializes in web and print design for all applications, including books, book covers, annual reports, posters, logos, menus, corporate collateral and direct marketing collateral, such as self-mailers and component packages.

CREATIVELINK

P.O. Box 318, Hammondsport NY 14840. **E-mail:** info@creativelinkgraphics.com. **Website:** creativelinkgraphics.com. **Contact:** Anne Kiley, sole proprietor. Estab. 1995. Creativelink is a complete design service; check website for portfolio.

ADDITIONAL INFORMATION Offers innovative, production-oriented book design services for authors wanting to self-publish, but who want their books to look as individual as they are themselves. Also complete writing and editorial service.

CSINCLAIRE WRITE-DESIGN

3405 Old Chapel Hill Road, Unit B, Durham NC 27707. (919)260-0031. **E-mail:** info@cswritedesign. com. **Contact:** Charlotte Sinclaire, owner. Estab. 1992.

ADDITIONAL INFORMATION Offers services in both graphic design and editorial evaluation. Editorial is to the extent requested, anything from a simple read-through with comments to red-lining, rewriting, or even ghostwriting. Fiction or nonfiction welcome.

DADIVAN BOOKS

3104 E. Camelback Road #160, Phoenix AZ 85016. (347)291-1779. **Fax:** (928)268-9181. **E-mail:** dadivanbooks@gmail.com. **Website:** www.dadivanbooks. com. **Contact:** Bootsie Martinez, editor. Estab. 1989. "We are professional writers, editors, and publishers with over a century of combined experience in the publishing world."

ADDITIONAL INFORMATION Dadivan Books also offers complete self-publishing from soup-to-nuts, including economical subsidy publishing services. "We specialize in helping authors achieve their individual dreams, whether that dream is improving a ms through proofreading or editing, preparing a ms in e-publishing formats, preparing a ms in paperback layout, designing the perfect cover, or fulfilling another editorial need, including ghostwriting and book doctoring. All services are available a la carte or as part of an economical package."

DESIGNWRITE

12 Bourne Rise, Collingbourne Ducis, Marlborough Wiltshire SN8 3HG United Kingdom. **E-mail:** simon@designwrite.co.uk. **Website:** www.designwrite. co.uk. **Contact:** Simon Carreck. Estab. 1998.

ADDITIONAL INFORMATION Offers content/copy/line editing, ghostwriting, and audio/video scripting. Also, book/magazine/catalogue layout and page design.

DGA MEDICAL COMMUNICATIONS

2700 Maple Ave., Bristol PA 19007. (215)498-1859. **E-mail:** deb@dgamedcom.com. **Website:** www. dgamedcom.com. **Contact:** Debbie Anderson, medical writer/instructional designer. Estab. 2012.

ADDITIONAL INFORMATION Services offered include advisory board meetings, case studies, PowerPoint presentations, e-learning courses, sales training materials, annotated guides, brochures, company leave-behinds, video scripts and vignettes, call guides, webinars, video newsletters, e-books, newsletters, articles, briefs, advertisements, assessments, website content, abstracts, posters, reports, outlines, and more.

DOVE MEDIA GROUP INC.

6505 E. Central #301, Wichita KS 67206. **E-mail:** dovemedia@cox.net. **Website:** meetdmg.com. **Contact:** Laurie Dove, president. Estab. 1999.

ADDITIONAL INFORMATION Offers custom print and web design, full-service editorial.

LAURYL EDDLEMON GRAPHIC DESIGN

7404 Rockberry Cove, Austin TX 78750. **E-mail:** lauryl.eddlemon@gmail.com. **Website:** www.lauryleddlemon.com. **Contact:** Lauryl Eddlemon. Estab. 2004. Lauryl Eddlemon is an Austin-based freelance designer specializing in print design with a focus on publications.

ADDITIONAL INFORMATION Services include book design, magazine editorial design, corporate identity, annual reports, catalogs, point-of-sale pieces, brochures/flyers, newsletters, posters, and advertisements.

EDEN CREATIVE MARKETING

(972)979-8130. **Fax:** (866)365-2055. **E-mail:** edencreative@verizon.net. **Website:** www.edencreativemarketing.com. **Contact:** Jessica LaBeau, owner. Estab. 1994. Specializes in historical novels, city books, and memoirs.

ADDITIONAL INFORMATION Offers book design/production, brochures, author promotional sheets, business cards, advertising/branding messages.

EDITWRITEDESIGN

E-mail: editwritedesign@yahoo.com. **Website:** www.editwritedesign.com.

ADDITIONAL INFORMATION Editorial services include comprehensive editing. Other services include cover design and interior design and layout. Cost: Contact for quote. See website for additional information.

EMBREE LITERARY SERVICES

138 W. Alta Green, Port Hueneme CA 93041. (805)985-1113. **E-mail:** maryembree@gmail.com. **Website:** www.maryembree.com. **Contact:** Mary Embree, owner/manager. Estab. 1990. Mary Embree is an author, freelance editor, literary consultant, seminar and workshop presenter, and public speaker. Since 1990, she has helped writers with their book mss from first to final draft, guiding and editing their book projects according to professional book publishing standards. Her services include writing and editing book proposals, query letters to literary agents and book publishers, and preparing mss for presentation.

ADDITIONAL INFORMATION If authors choose to self-publish, she guides them through the entire process, such as registering their copyright and getting ISBNs, barcodes, and Library of Congress Control numbers. Embree and her associates design and type-

set interior pages of the book as well as eye-catching book covers, providing print-ready PDF files.

ERIAKO ASSOCIATES

(310)392-6537. **E-mail:** eriakoassociates@gmail.com. **Contact:** Erika Fabian, CEO. Estab. 1982. Offers design, editing, and overseeing entire publishing process. Erika Fabian of Eriako Associates is an international book designer as well as writer and editor. She has personally written 22 books, some published by the likes of Putnam, Ballantine, and Harlequin. Her books have also been translated and published in several languages.

ADDITIONAL INFORMATION "We cover essentially all phases of publishing for books, brochures, and advertising materials. We also do professional photography of authors, and for the material if it needs photo illustration."

FALL FOR THE BOOK

Fairfax VA (703)993-3986. **E-mail:** executivedirector@fallforthebook.org. **Website:** fallforthebook.org. **Contact:** William Miller, executive director. Estab. 1999.

ADDITIONAL INFORMATION "What began as a 2-day literary event, organized by George Mason University and the City of Fairfax, has expanded into a week-long, multiple-venue, regional festival that brings together people of all ages and interests, thanks to growing community interest and generous supporting partners."

FILAMENT CREATIVE

1024 SW Main St. #730, Portland OR 97205. (509)844-4251. **E-mail:** ryan@filament-creative.com. **Website:** www.filament-creative.com. **Contact:** Ryan Peinhardt, graphic designer. Estab. 2011.

ADDITIONAL INFORMATION Offers graphic design and book design.

CASSANDRA FREY

1421 Yale Dr., Holiday FL 34691. **E-mail:** cassf316@gmail.com. **Contact:** Cassandra Frey.

ADDITIONAL INFORMATION Offers proofreading, editing (books, advertisements, etc.), design assistance, ghost writing, assistance with speaking engagements, and more.

FRIDAY & FRIENDS

P.O. Box 370, Hot Springs MT 59845. (406)210-8701. **E-mail:** fridayandfriends@z9mail.com. **Contact:** Susan Campbell, principal. Estab. 2004.

ADDITIONAL INFORMATION Offers ms evaluation; comprehensive edit; rewrite and/or ghostwrite;

instruction in Chicago Manual of Style; book design, format, and conversion to pdf. Competitive rates.

GAL-FRIDAY PUBLICITY

308-1114 Howie Ave., Coquitlam BC V3J 1V1 Canada. (604)366-7846. **E-mail:** rachel@gal-fridaypublicity. com. **Website:** www.gal-fridaypublicity.com. **Contact:** Rachel Sentes, founder/publicist. Estab. 2009. Offers business and book publicity, e-book publicity/ publishing, media kit creation and design, editing, ms consultations, ghostwriting, Wordpress websites, copy editing, proposal writing, and literary agent and publishing consultations.

ADDITIONAL INFORMATION "We have worked in all aspects of the book industry behind and in front of the scenes."

TINA GARCIA

Riverview FL 33578. **E-mail:** tinagarcia100@gmail. com. **Website:** www.tina-garcia.com. **Contact:** Tina Garcia, graphic designer. Estab. 2003.

ADDITIONAL INFORMATION Offers e-book and cover design, brochure and flyer designer, logos and stationery, packaging design, audio and video editing, news infographics and interactives.

GEEKY GIRL, LLC

128 Wentworth Dr., Lansdale PA 19446. (215)393-8740. **E-mail:** rex@karinrex.com. **Website:** www.geekygirlonline.com. **Contact:** Karin Rex, president. Estab. 1989.

ADDITIONAL INFORMATION "Geeky Girl offers technical and professional writing services and instructional design."

GLYPHICS

3219 E. Camelback Road, #462, Phoenix AZ 85018. (602)670-3114. **E-mail:** terry@glyphicsdesign.com. **Website:** glyphicsdesign.com. **Contact:** Terry Duffy, owner. Estab. 1985.

ADDITIONAL INFORMATION "We do branding, book design, packaging, museum exhibit panel design, illustration."

GRATZER GRAPHICS LLC

Union Ridge Dr., Adamstown MD 21710. (301)874-3131. **E-mail:** design@gratzergraphics.com. **Website:** gratzergraphics.com. **Contact:** Colleen Gratzer, principal/graphic designer. Estab. 2003. Offers print, web, and logo design.

ADDITIONAL INFORMATION Services include print ads, annual reports, banner ads, book covers, book layout, brochures, circulation, direct mail, directories, HTML e-mails, logos/identity packages, magazines, media kits, print newsletters, postcards, posters, banners, rebranding, social media design, trade show/event displays, and websites.

GREYSIGHT STUDIOS

Syracuse NY 13206. (315)497-7278. **E-mail:** support@ greysightstudios.com. **Website:** greysightstudios.com. **Contact:** Willie Putmon Jr., owner. Estab. 1996.

ADDITIONAL INFORMATION Offers layout design, logo design, web design, video editing, mobile development, brochures, magazine design/layout, print ads, complete identity packages, flyers, posters, promotional materials, mail inserts, web promotions, image enhancement/corrections/manipulation, image background removal.

ANNABELLE HAVLICEK

932 S. 11th St., Milwaukee WI 53204. (414)241-0585. **E-mail:** ahavlicek@ntvbmedia.com. **Website:** www. smallscreensilversurfer.com. **Contact:** Annabelle Havlicek, owner/operator.

ADDITIONAL INFORMATION "I have over 30 years of desktop publishing experience in a Mac environment and can design your book from cover to cover. Call or e-mail me for a brainstorming session and a quote."

DARLENE HAWVER

E-mail: darlene@hawver.net. **Website:** darlenehawver. com. **Contact:** Darlene Hawver, graphic designer. Estab. 2009. Offers graphic design services.

ADDITIONAL INFORMATION Services include book covers, editorial design, publication design, logos, stationery, newsletters, posters, and more.

THE HELP

648 Rivenhurst St., Bremerton WA 98310. (360)440-5795. **E-mail:** admin@thehelpbyastrids.com. **Website:** www.thehelpbyastrids.com. **Contact:** Marie Astrid Stanek, owner/manager. Estab. 2008. The Help is a fast growing virtual assistance agency.

ADDITIONAL INFORMATION Services provided include administrative support, writing and translation, and multimedia and graphic design.

HIFI BRAND BOOST

P.O. Box 16568, Seattle WA 98116. **E-mail:** jessie@hifi-brandboost.com. **Website:** www.hifibrandboost.com. **Contact:** Jessie Russo, designer. Estab. 1996.

ADDITIONAL INFORMATION Offers print design, web design, logo and ID design, illustration, social media, blogging.

HISTORICAL EDITORIAL

6420 Toney Lane, Spotsylvania VA 22553. **E-mail:** jennyq@historicaleditorial.com. **Website:** historicaleditorial.com. **Contact:** Jennifer Quinlan, owner. Estab. 2010.

ADDITIONAL INFORMATION Offers developmental editing, copyediting, and cover design.

IDEAS TO IMAGES

5256 Aero Dr., Unit 3, Santa Rosa CA 95403. (707)542-4301. **E-mail:** ideas@sonic.net. **Website:** ideas-to-images.com/samples. **Contact:** Gary Palmatier, owner. Estab. 1984.

ADDITIONAL INFORMATION "I design, illustrate, compose, and manage cover-to-cover book projects from ms through printing. I work closely with authors/publishers to design a cover and interior suited to the target market. If desired, I also hire and supervise editorial freelancers (copyeditors, proofreaders, and indexers) and liaise with printers (delivering preflighted PDF files and reviewing proofs)."

INDIEMOBI

Website: indiemobi.wordpress.com. **Contact:** Rebecca Long, owner. Estab. 2012.

ADDITIONAL INFORMATION Solo/freelance company that offers formatting for e-books and Createspace. "Friendly and fast turnaround service with affordable prices."

INDIGO EDITING & PUBLICATIONS

917 SW Oak St., #302, Portland OR 97205. (503)629-9216. **E-mail:** info@indigoediting.com. **Website:** www.indigoediting.com. **Contact:** Ali McCart, senior editor. Estab. 2006.

ADDITIONAL INFORMATION "Indigo started as a firm of freelance editors. It's now grown to offer design, e-book conversion, and publishing project management services in addition to editing. With multiple publishing professionals on hand, authors can rest assured that their book will be professionally edited by an expert in their genre, designed with a keen eye toward readability, and produced with all the latest publishing trends in mind."

INNATE PRODUCTIONS

371 Barrie Road, P.O. Box 244, Pakenham ON K0A 2X0 Canada. (613)623-1029. **E-mail:** innateproductionsmail@gmail.com. **Website:** innateproductions. ca. **Contact:** Ellen Gable Hrkach, James Hrkach. Estab. 2005.

ADDITIONAL INFORMATION Offers self-publishing book coaching (assisting new authors to self-publish their own books, guiding them through the various steps), formatting for print, formatting for Kindle, cover design, and editorial (developmental editing for novels).

JBBD

942 1/2 North Havenhurst Dr., West Hollywood CA 90046. (323)650-1114. **E-mail:** jerry@jbbd.net. **Website:** jbbd.net. **Contact:** Jerry Brown, owner/creative director. Estab. 2001.

ADDITIONAL INFORMATION "JBBD is a full-service graphic and web design studio which offers special, discounted rates to both new and established authors."

JESSIE SK DESIGN

5264 Erskine Way SW, Seattle WA 98136. **E-mail:** jessiesk@gmail.com. **Website:** http://jessiesk.dunked. com. **Contact:** Jessie Summa-Kusiak, designer. Estab. 1996.

ADDITIONAL INFORMATION Offers print, web, logo & ID design, and illustrations.

JLMORENO EDITING, PRODUCTION & DESIGN

When Clarity Counts, (480)540-7637. **E-mail:** jlmoreno@whenclaritycounts.com. **Website:** www.whenclaritycounts.com. **Contact:** Jerryll L. Moreno, MA, Certified Scholary Editor.

ADDITIONAL INFORMATION JLMoreno is a freelance and academic editor providing production management, editing, proofing, and design that transform information into knowledge and connects content with scholars worldwide. Currently, Jerryll works closely with authors, typesetters, indexers, publishers, and acquisition managers to provide a wide variety of publishing expertise. As a publishing professional, she believes that negotiating best practices and competing interests is critical to successfully transform information into knowledge, create quality content, and build lasting relationships with authors and presses.

PAULA L. JOHNSON

P.O. Box 51096, Pasadena CA 91115. (626)577-5593. **E-mail:** paulajohnson@mac.com. **Website:** paulaljohnson.com. **Contact:** Paula Johnson, designer. Estab. 1984.

ADDITIONAL INFORMATION Services include preparing files for BookBaby, CreateSpace, Lightning Source, and Lulu, and advising on practical matters like ISBNs and pricing. In addition, she has created websites for more than a dozen professional writers.

AMBER JONES CONSULTING

6301 Stonewood Dr., Plano TX 75024. **E-mail:** amber@amberjonesconsulting.com. **Website:** www.amberjonesconsulting.com. **Contact:** Amber Jones, owner/freelance graphic designer. Estab. 2013.

ADDITIONAL INFORMATION "With 6+ years of experience in the marketing/digital space and 10 years as a graphic designer, I offer clients a 'one-stop shop' for all of their marketing needs, including graphic design, web design, online marketing strategy development, and copywriting."

ESTHER KEANE COMMUNICATIONS

834 Point Way, Virginia Beach VA 23462. (757)652-4874. **E-mail:** esther@estherkeane.com. **Website:** estherkeane.com. **Contact:** Esther Keane, editor. Estab. 2012.

ADDITIONAL INFORMATION Offers ms evaluation/line editing, copyediting/proofreading, fact check, book cover design, and writing (ghostwriting, back flap synopsis for book cover, press release, reviews, and more).

KELLEY & HALL BOOK PUBLICITY

5 Briar Lane, Marblehead MA 01945. (617)680-1976. **E-mail:** jocelyn@kelleyandhall.com. **Website:** www.kelleyandhall.com. **Contact:** Jocelyn Kelley, partner. Estab. 2004. Kelley & Hall is a literary publicity company that is dedicated to helping authors and publishers with their promotion, marketing, and media relations.

ADDITIONAL INFORMATION "We create effective book buzz as well as author recognition that will increase book sales. We help writers build their author brand. Book marketing and book promotion are the cornerstones of Kelley & Hall. We have recently partnered with an independent publishing company, Grey Swan Press (www.greyswanpress.com)."

LENTINI DESIGN

1626 Virginia Road, Los Angeles CA 90019. (323)766-8090. **E-mail:** info@lentinidesign.com. **Website:** www.lentinidesign.com. **Contact:** Hilary Lentini, owner. Estab. 1990.

ADDITIONAL INFORMATION Services include branding development, marketing pieces/deliverables, web development/deliverables, social media.

MAUREEN LILLA

77 State Road, Plymouth MA 02360. **E-mail:** mlilla777@aol.com. **Contact:** Maureen Lilla, principle. Estab. 1986. Offers developmental editing for authors, professionals, and business writers; development of query letters and book proposals; writing and ghostwriting; book doctoring; book and book cover design.

ADDITIONAL INFORMATION Client list available upon request.

LITTRELL DESIGN

Monroeville IN 46773. **E-mail:** carina.littrell@gmail.com. **Website:** www.be.net/carinalittrell. **Contact:** Carina Littrell, owner/graphic designer. Estab. 2012.

ADDITIONAL INFORMATION "I'm ready to meet your design needs. Give me an idea of what you are looking for and I will make it happen. I have a BA in graphic design and more than 5 years of working as a graphic/web designer in the printing business. I specialize in brochures, postcards, business cards, letterheads/envelopes, CMS web design and e-mail marketing."

MAJEAU DESIGNS

153 Somerside Rd. SE, Medicine Hat AB T1B 0N4 Canada. **E-mail:** corey_majeau@hotmail.com. **Website:** www.facebook.com/MajeauDesigns?ref=stream. **Contact:** Corey Majeau, freelance designer. Estab. 2003. Offers book cover designs (both e-book and paperback), e-book formatting, logo designs, website designs.

ADDITIONAL INFORMATION "I use the latest design software and vector imaging."

DICK MARGULIS CREATIVE SERVICES

284 W. Elm St., New Haven CT 06515. (203)389-4413. **E-mail:** dick@dmargulis.com. **Website:** www.dmargulis.com. **Contact:** Dick Margulis, owner. Estab. 2004. Offers high-quality printed and electronic books for discerning clients. Thoughtful editing, appropriate design, expert production, comprehensive project management, for publishers of all sizes and for all kinds of books.

ADDITIONAL INFORMATION "If you are an author, agent, publisher, or other organization considering a book project, I'd like the opportunity to quote on the services you need. I have been involved in both editing and typography in one way or another for over half a century; my experience is broad and deep."

NIC MCD LLC

1601 Highview Dr., Des Moines IA 50315. (319)621-8877. **E-mail:** nic@nicmcd.com. **Website:** nicmcd.com. **Contact:** Nic McDougal, illustrator/designer. Estab. 2011. Emerging artist and recent grad from the Minneapolis College of Art and Design.

ADDITIONAL INFORMATION "My business offers self-published authors the opportunity to bring their ideas to life! I offer cover artwork, interior layouts, and a variety of marketing collateral, including video book trailers and web design."

MEDIANEIGHBOURS.COM

20 Via del Vaquero, Santa Fe NM 87508. **Website:** www.medianeighbours.com. **Contact:** Mary Neighbour, owner/editor. Estab. 2009.

ADDITIONAL INFORMATION "At MediaNeighbours.com, we translate real-world challenges to e-world results. We help authors, artists, small businesses, and nonprofits who are looking for ways to represent themselves across the internet and promote their products and services."

BRIAN MIHOK DESIGN

31 Berkley Place #2, Buffalo NY 14209. **E-mail:** brian@brianmihok.com. **Website:** design.brianmihok.com. **Contact:** Brian Mihok, book designer. Estab. 2010. Offers complete book design services, which includes cover, wrap, and inside layouts.

ADDITIONAL INFORMATION "My design skills are flexible but my approach tends toward modern, clean, and striking. Prices for designs vary but are available for all budgets. I believe a design should be an extension of the ms itself, offering the tone and spirit of the book in visual form. Really, it should stop a book browser in her tracks! Bottom line is your book deserves a great design, and I'd love to make it for you."

MISSELAINEOUSART

2301 47th St., Lubbock TX 79412. (806)799-0077. **E-mail:** misc469art@gmail.com. **Contact:** Elaine Atkinson, owner. Estab. 1996. An illustrator and graphic designer interested, preferably, in children's books. "My experience has been to take the job from inception, talking to the customer about ideas to the finished product. This includes design, layout, illustration,

caligraphy, and anything else that needs to be completed. My latest children's book illustration is *Baxter Barret Brown's Cowboy Band* by Tim McKenzie.

MURPHY DESIGN

1216 Arch St., 2C, Philadelphia PA 19107. (215)977-7093. **Website:** www.murphydesign.net. Estab. 1985. Rosemary Murphy is an experienced graphic designer.

ADDITIONAL INFORMATION Murphy works in a collaborative style and would be interested in designing book covers, lettering, logos, graphic illustration for print or web and information graphics.

PAPER STAR EDITORIAL & DESIGN

33846 Fourteenth St., Union City CA 94587. (831)402-2074. **E-mail:** tomiko@paperstareditorial.com. **Website:** www.paperstareditorial.com. **Contact:** Tomiko Breland, owner. Estab. 2013.

ADDITIONAL INFORMATION "Paper Star Editorial & Design offers editing, graphic design, and ms review services. Based in the Bay Area in California, we believe that everyone deserves the opportunity to present the best version of themselves, and that sometimes it takes a little help (and professional expertise) to achieve that version."

LINDA AU PARKER

P.O. Box 133, New Brighton PA 15066. **E-mail:** linda@lindamaubooks.com. **Website:** www.lindamaubooks.com. **Contact:** Linda Au Parker, independent contractor. Estab. 2006.

ADDITIONAL INFORMATION "I have been proofreading professionally for more than 27 years. I have worked for various publishers, including F+W Publications, Crown & Covenant, Carroll & Graf, and more. Most of my work now is with independent authors who need help cleaning up their mss before submitting to agents or publishers or who need help polishing those final mss before self-publishing."

PICKWICK WRITING SERVICES

140 Lazy Willow Lane, Unit 102, Myrtle Beach SC 29588. (843)582-2197. **E-mail:** mdevlin30@gmail.com. **Website:** pickwickwritingservices.wordpress.com. **Contact:** Matthew Devlin, lead editor. Estab. 2008.

ADDITIONAL INFORMATION "The Pickwick Writing Team consists of 2 published, well-educated, professional writers. We are dedicated to providing our clients with quick and high quality services at reasonable rates. The services we offer include, but are not limited to, ms and website editing; creating dynamic written content for websites, brochures, marketing e-mails, etc.; ghost writing and co-writing."

SHEN PLUM ILLUSTRATION

70 Empire Ave., Toronto ON M4M 2L4 Canada. **E-mail:** shen.plum@gmail.com. **Website:** www.shen-plum.com. **Contact:** Shen Plum. Offers illustration, art, drawing, illustrative font/typeface, cover art.

PRO NOVEL EDITING SERVICES

3805 Burke, Cheyenne WY 82009. (307)772-1741. **Fax:** (501)325-0305. **E-mail:** proediting@earthlink.net. **Website:** www.pronovelediting.com. **Contact:** Michael McIrvin, founding writer and editor. Estab. 2003. Pro Novel Editing Services can provide the following for fiction writers of all skill levels: line editing, developmental (content) editing, novel ms critiques, and query letters.

ADDITIONAL INFORMATION Pro Novel Editing Services can also facillitate the following for self-publishers: book layout in the appropriate program files required by your POD company, book cover design, conversion to all digital formats, e-book layout and design, and website design.

QM DESIGN GROUP

19728 Elizabeth Way, Canyon Country CA 913151. (661)250-9914. **Fax:** (661)449-3838. **E-mail:** hillary@qmdesigngroup.com. **Website:** www.qmdesigngroup.com. **Contact:** Hillary Broadwater, president/creative director. Estab. 2007. "We're creative and casual with a corporate background. We get to know our clients and their businesses, so that we can create a Visual Voice, one that will stand out and be heard. We examine your business and goals and work together to uncover the story that will be the support behind your brand—one that will be heard every time.

"Whether creating an identity for a new company or broadening the scope of an existing one, we strive to create simple, efficient, and long-term solutions for our clients. From our corporate office in Santa Clarita, California, we service clients across the country and around the globe."

ADDITIONAL INFORMATION Services include: Sales and marketing collateral, stationary systems, sales kits, press kits, catalogs, brochures, magazines, direct mail, signage, package and label design, web design, and creative direction.

KATHLEEN M. REILLY

P.O. Box 574, Willow Spring NC 27592. **E-mail:** kate@kathleenreilly.com. **Website:** www.kathleenreilly.com. **Contact:** Kathleen Reilly, owner. Estab. 2001.

ADDITIONAL INFORMATION Offers e-book cover design and layout, infographics, and marketing collateral.

KIMBERLY RINKER

12A Kingery Quarter, Willowbrook IL 60527. (708)557-2790. **E-mail:** trotrink@aol.com. **Website:** www.kimberlyrinker.com. **Contact:** Kimberly Rinker, award-winning freelance journalist. Estab. 1984.

ADDITIONAL INFORMATION "Multiple-award winning journalist with 30+ years experience. Provides feature writing, copy editing, nonfiction journalism, ghostwriting, press releases, web design and content input. See my website for a list of clients and to view my recent projects."

JODY ROGINSON CREATIVE SERVICES

6444 E. Spring St. #312, Long Beach CA 90815. **Website:** jodyroginson.com. **Contact:** Jody Roginson, owner. Estab. 2000.

ADDITIONAL INFORMATION Offers graphic, cover and page design, page composition and illustration. Print coordination and e-publication formatting or consultation is available as well.

THERESA ROSENACKER DESIGN

2845 Minot Ave., Cincinnati OH 45209. (513)312-8992. **E-mail:** theresa@theresarosenacker.com. **Website:** www.theresarosenacker.com. **Contact:** Theresa Rosenacker, principal. Estab. 2013.

ADDITIONAL INFORMATION Offers print and digital design services, specializing in small business and non-profit.

RPARTEKO DESIGNS

740 Westview Dr., Apt. 47, Ossian IN 46777. (260)255-9544. **E-mail:** parteko.rachel@gmail.com. **Website:** facebook.com/RPartekoDesigns. **Contact:** Rachel Parteko, graphic artist. Estab. 2008.

ADDITIONAL INFORMATION Offers book cover design, book formatting and layout, business cards, flyers, brochures, banner and logo design, T-shirt design, hand-drawn pictures/illustrations, and Facebook cover page/marketing.

JULIE SCHROEDER DESIGNS

Summit NJ **E-mail:** julieschroeder@mac.com. **Website:** www.julieschroederdesigns.com. **Contact:** Julie Schroeder, owner/designer. Estab. 1997.

ADDITIONAL INFORMATION Offers book covers and interiors, promotional pieces for the web and print.

MAX SCRATCHMANN ILLUSTRATION

5/7 Lady Nairne Place, Edinburgh EH8 7LZ United Kingdom. **E-mail:** max.scratchmann@btinternet.com. **Website:** www.maxscratchmann.com. **Contact:** Max Scratchmann, illustrator/designer. Estab. 1984.

ADDITIONAL INFORMATION Offers freelance illustration and design. Illustrator with over 30 years experience. Book covers for traditional print, POD, or e-books. Book layouts for print or POD. Interior illustrations. No job too small and special rates for indie publishers and self-publishers.

SISTER MUSES

P.O. Box 14201, Irving TX 75014. **E-mail:** inquiries@sistermuses.com. **Website:** www.sistermuses.com. **Contact:** S.K. Valenzuela, lead editor. Estab. 2014.

ADDITIONAL INFORMATION SAs an independent publishing imprint, we offer authors a wide array of professional services, including ms proofreading, editing, and design, cover design, and story doctoring and analysis. "We offer a complimentary review of the first 10 pages of a ms in order to assist our clients in choosing the package that will provide the best results for the best value."

SOMATIC ARTS EDITING

9611 Rainier Ave. S., Seattle WA 98118. **E-mail:** leslie.eliel@gmail.com. **Website:** http://somatic-arts.weebly.com. **Contact:** Leslie Eliel, owner. Estab. 1988.

ADDITIONAL INFORMATION Offers book design and book production from idea to product for writers in the Somatic Arts and related fields—popular neuroscience; somatic psychology; mindfulness training; and body-based moralities for treating PTSD, trauma, nervous-system disregulation, anxiety, and chronic pain. Will work with trade books, booklets, and coffee table books.

JULES STEWART INDEPENDENT GRAPHIC DESIGN

4033 Louisiana #6, San Diego CA 92104. **E-mail:** juliannestewart@gmail.com. **Website:** julesstewart.carbonmade.com. **Contact:** Jules Stewart, designer. Estab. 2008. Modern but adaptable, clean design style.

ADDITIONAL INFORMATION Offers digital illustration and design of logos, promotional materials, posters, business cards, resumes, and more.

JEANNE STOCK DESIGN

Kempton PA 19529. **E-mail:** jeannestock@jstockdesign.com. **Website:** jstockdesign.com. **Contact:** Jeanne Stock, owner. Estab. 1980. Prior experience: publication art director/designer for regional and national publications and book designer.

ADDITIONAL INFORMATION Offers design services from concept through production for print projects; specializing in publication design and graphic logos. "I believe that a good outcome requires communication. Creative energy, attention to detail and hard work as well as good design. Every job is equally important and receives my complete attention from start to finish."

STUDIO A DESIGN

Fort Wayne IN 46804. (260)437-6658. **E-mail:** angelahudson@studio-a-design.com. **Website:** www.studio-a-design.com. **Contact:** Angela S. Hudson, graphic designer/marketing specialist. Estab. 2012.

ADDITIONAL INFORMATION Offers print design (letterhead, business cards, wine labels, book covers, T-shirts, brochures, posters, print advertisements, product packaging, music CDs, postcards, even programs, invitations, announcements, catalogs/schedules, signage, banners, book layout, graphics/illustrations), logos (company logos, product logos, event logos, corporate identity, branding), photography (people, product, event, artistic), marketing, consulting (strategic marketing plans, website referrals), and event planning (large corporate events, luncheons, conferences, galas).

SUNNY BAY ARTS

15 Simcoe Terrace SW, Calgary AB T3H 4S6 Canada. (403)252-0792. **E-mail:** info@sunnybayarts.ca. **Website:** www.sunnybayarts.ca. **Contact:** Barbori G. Streibl, co-owner. Estab. 2011. Sunny Bay Arts sells stock photography and artwork.

ADDITIONAL INFORMATION Please enquire about logo design and book cover design services.

STEPHEN TIANO

638 Fresh Pond Ave., #314, Calverton NY 11933. (631)284-3842. **E-mail:** steve@tianobookdesign.com. **Website:** www.tianobookdesign.com. **Contact:** Stephen Tiano, freelance book designer, page compositor and layout artist. Estab. 1992. Offers interior and cover book design and layout.

ADDITIONAL INFORMATION "I create sample interior pages (including all master pages and stylesheets). We discuss the sample pages to get a sense of what works and what might stand some improvement. Then, I make all adjustments and changes until you approve. Upon approval of sample pages, I finalize them into a template. Next, I resample any art (photos) that are less than 300 dpi and correct for color (balance/contrast of black & white), scale to size. Finally (for the interior), I make formatted, balanced interior pages from provided final text files imported into the approved template and place all art appropriately. I create and provide the final, cross-platform, printer-ready PDFs—during the work process, when I send pages to you for review, they will be PDFs to screen resolution for easy e-mailing—after accounting for any necessary specifications for PDFs your printer requires."

TO PRESS & BEYOND

825 E. Pedregosa St., Suite 2, Santa Barbara CA 93103. (805)898-2263. **E-mail:** info@topressandbeyond.com. **Website:** www.topressandbeyond.com. **Contact:** Gail M. Kearns, president. Estab. 1995.
ADDITIONAL INFORMATION "Gail M. Kearns and her team at To Press & Beyond are specialists in book publishing consulting and support services. With over 16 years of experience, they skillfully and successfully guide your print and/or e-book project from ms to finished book, educating and coaching every step of the way. Their comprehensive range of services include writing, developmental editing and copyediting, proofreading, design and layout, printing, distribution, sales and promotion, both in trade and niche markets and on the web. Our books consistently win editorial and design awards."

TREEHOUSE PUBLISHING GROUP LLC

8734 Norcross Dr., St. Louis MO 63126. (314)363-4546. **E-mail:** authorservices@treehousepublishinggroup.com. **Website:** treehousepublishinggroup.com. **Contact:** Kristina Makansi, managing partner. Estab. 2013. Treehouse Publishing Group offers a full menu of a la carte author services as well as assisted self-publishing under our Treehouse imprint.
ADDITIONAL INFORMATION "At TPG, we believe that every project is as unique as the author who created it. That's why we individually tailor each package—from developmental edits to book

layouts to website design—to suit your specific goals."

TREEHOUSES AUTHOR SERVICES, LLC

3963 Flora Place, St. Louis MO 63110. **E-mail:** authorservices@treehouseauthorservices.com. **Website:** treehouseauthorservices.com. **Contact:** Kristina Makansi, partner/co-owner. Estab. 2013.
ADDITIONAL INFORMATION Offers developmental editing, line editing, copy editing, proofreading, cover design, print book and e-book formatting, publishing assistance.

TURNING HEADS

73-1104 Nuuanu Place, G204, Kailua Kona HI 96740. (562)437-1443. **E-mail:** vic_warren@hotmail.com. **Website:** www.vicwarren.com. **Contact:** Vic Warren, owner. Estab. 1999. Portfolio available upon request.
ADDITIONAL INFORMATION "Sophisticated design and marketing concepts should be more than hot-off-the-desktop formulas using the latest typeface with plenty of bars and borders. They need to build on the unique strengths of a specific product strategy. And they must be responsive to sound business objectives such as sales schedules and budgets. Vic Warren has been solving communication problems for eyars, creating indelible images in words and pictures for an array of successful and smart clients. He's best known for creating the Eskimo corporate image for Alaska Airlines. Branding and corporate image are two of his strengths, and, since joining the writing profession, has designed award-winning book covers as well."

KAT TUSHIM

175 N. Harbor Dr., 2313, Chicago IL 60601. **Website:** hattushim.com. **Contact:** Kat Tushim. Estab. 2007.
ADDITIONAL INFORMATION "I offer 7 years of professional creative direction experience in marketing campaigns, package and identity design, and poster art. I have experience designing book covers for authors who have self-published their work."

TWA SOLUTIONS

P.O. Box 4481, Upper Marlboro MD 20775. (202)702-7120. **Fax:** (888)559-9693. **E-mail:** jessica@twasolutions.com. **Website:** www.twasolutions.com. **Contact:** Jessica Wright Tilles, owner/creative director. Estab. 2000.
ADDITIONAL INFORMATION Offers book cover design, interior design (typesetting), editing, web design.

2FACED DESIGN

Heritage Commons Office Park, 11 Middlesex Ave., Suite 10A, Wilmington MA 01887. **Website:** www.2faceddesign.com. **Contact:** Kristie Langone, director. Estab. 2008. Offers e-book covers, front cover design, full cover design, full jacket design, and ms and copyediting. "We're 2Faced. Not like Dr. Jekyll and Mr. Hyde. We're multifaceted with strengths in writing and design. We're wordsmiths who use concept and imagery to convey powerful emotions."

ADDITIONAL INFORMATION "Think of us as the set designers of your story, or the photographers at your book's school photo. We'll provide visual messages, concepts, and ideas; covers that trigger a strategic response to position your book in front of your audience. We give authors and publishers a suite of different options when it comes to their covers—from digital to print."

SUZANNE WESLEY FREELANCE WRITING & DESIGN

2964 Terri Lee Court, Terre Haute IN 47805. (812)877-4204. **E-mail:** suzanne@suzannewesley.com. **Website:** www.suzannewesley.com. **Contact:** Suzanne Wesley, owner/creative director. Estab. 2009.

ADDITIONAL INFORMATION Offers design and copy writing services for the creation of book covers (print or digital), business cards, flyers, postcards, one sheets, bookmarks, web ads, print advertisements, posters, Facebook or blog headers, newsletters, brochures, annual reports, e-mail, and more.

WORDISWORTH

15500 Armsby Lane, Morgan Hill CA 95037. (408)779-2399. **E-mail:** info@wordisworth.com. **Website:** www.wordisworth.com. **Contact:** Alison Macmillan, co-owner. Estab. 2008.

ADDITIONAL INFORMATION "WordIsWorth is an independent information and publishing company run by a husband and wife team who offer publishing, editing, writing, and design services."

WRITE PERSPECTIVES

2404 Central Road, Rolling Meadows IL 60008. (847)392-6861. **E-mail:** bvd6656@hotmail.com. **Website:** www.writeperspectives.com. **Contact:** Betsy van Die, owner/chief PR consultant. Estab. 2013.

ADDITIONAL INFORMATION Offers versatile writing/editing services, specializing in branding, writing, and digital content development strategies for clients in the medical/health, association, and not-for-profit sector. Services include blogs, clinical research/writing, copywriting, design, editing, feature articles, newsletters and brochures, press releases, project management, public awareness campaigns, scripts, speechwriting, social media, and web content development.

WRITING AS A GHOST

310 W. 39th St., Vancouver WA 98660. (360)566-2781. **Fax:** (360)989-3980. **E-mail:** denise@writingmyownbook.com. **Website:** writingmyownbook.com. **Contact:** Denise Rutledge, account manager. Estab. 2006. Writing as a Ghost offers freelance design, coaching and editorial services as a package and as individual services.

ADDITIONAL INFORMATION Design services include layout and design and ms preparation for POD publishing, Kindle and Smashwords submission. Coaching services include research and ms development, including assistance with developing market competitive approach to topic. Editing services range from simple proof reading and copy editing to substantive editing. Denise Rutledge approaches the written word as a combination of crafted words and visual message.

INDEPENDENT PUBLICISTS

One part of the self-publishing process is creating the product you plan to sell. In the case of self-publishing, that product is a book (either in print or digital form). Another part is raising awareness about your product and sharing how it will improve the lives of anyone who buys it.

One way to improve awareness is by working to get good publicity for yourself and your project. For some self-publishers, independent publicists help fill this need by using their media savvy and years of media experience and connections to land interviews for their clients.

Finding the right publicist for your project can enhance your book's chances of success. Since many traditional book retailers won't shelve self-published books, it's up to the self-publisher to find less traditional paths to raising book awareness.

However, all publicists are not created equal. Search for one that specializes in your subject area. Ask for references and find out if previous clients felt satisfied with their investment in independent publicists.

To help determine a fair rate, self-publishers need to know what type of publicity assistance they need and how rates will be determined. For instance, are you paying the publicist on a flat scale regardless of results? Are you paying for number of contacts they make? Or are you paying for actual interviews and reviews?

Know what rates you're paying and why you're paying them. Setting unfair expectations is bad for the freelancer, but it also puts your project at risk, because you're counting on the freelancers to give their best. At the same time, you want to make sure you're getting a fair return on your investment.

KEEP IN MIND

Starting locally will allow you to research each company carefully and learn about their past performance and make it easier to have face-to-face discussions about the project. Realize that any face-to-face time and time on the phone may be considered "billable hours" by your freelancer. Be sure to agree on all such fees and get it in writing before starting work. It will help ensure a more professional working relationship and provide both sides with more security.

Going local is not a requirement. In fact, it may be impossible to find an independent publicist in your state. That said, always ask for previous experience and consider checking references, especially if you're investing a lot of money in the publicity process. After all, you want to make sure your money will be money well spent.

ACCURATE WRITING & MORE

16 Barstow Lane, Hadley MA 01035. (413)586-2388. **E-mail:** shel@principledprofit.com. **Website:** www.frugalmarketing.com. **Contact:** Shel Horowitz, owner. Estab. 1982. Offers book marketing and book shepherding services.

ADDITIONAL INFORMATION For book marketing, develops marketing strategy and individualized marketing plans for authors, books, and book series. For book shepherding, helps make the decision to publish traditionally, self-publish, e-publish, or publish through a subsidy publisher and to implement the chosen strategy.

STEPHANIE BARKO, LITERARY PUBLICIST

16100 Crystal Hills, Austin TX 78737. **E-mail:** stephanie@stephaniebarko.com. **Website:** www.stephaniebarko.com. **Contact:** Stephanie Barko, founder. Estab. 2006.

ADDITIONAL INFORMATION Offers book promotion for professionally edited indie and traditionally published adult nonfiction and historical fiction within one year of release.

BOOKING AUTHORS INK

E-mail: lynda@bookingauthorsink.com. **Website:** bookingauthorsink.com. **Contact:** Lynda Bouchard, chief inspiration officer. Estab. 1999.

ADDITIONAL INFORMATION Offers a boutique public relations firm dedicated to authors. "I do publicity and marketing, editing, speech writing, guest blog posts, event planning, and concierge services for authors."

BOUTIQUE LITERARY CONSULTANCY

2932 B. Langhorne Rd., Lynchburg VA 24501-1734. (615)681-9977. **E-mail:** lspain@laboutiqueave.com. **Website:** www.laboutiqueave.com. **Contact:** John Gosslee, executive editor. Estab. 2012. Boutique is a literary consultant agency and editing house. "Our group of award-winning and widely-published authors provide personalized, nurturing support for your work. We pass work on to a number of literary agents and publishers. Boutique has placed mss with Big Six publishers like Random House, Simon & Schuster, and HarperCollins, as well as with Atlantic Grove, Farrar, Straus & Giroux, and Knopf, in addition to numerous mid-sized and small publishers nationwide. We've additionally placed short fiction, poems, essays, and other work with a long list of top literary magazines through our referrals. We also de-velop a sound approach to a range of career objectives, including university teaching placement, book touring, fellowship applications, author visibility, creating an extended readership around an author's work, and other specific career-building objectives."

B.Y. COMMUNICATIONS WORLDWIDE

1500 Fuente Ct., #206, Palm Beach Gardens FL 33410. (561)459-4729. **E-mail:** brigitte.yuille@bycomworldwide.com. **Website:** www.bycomworldwide.com. **Contact:** Brigitte Yuille, CEO/founder. Estab. 2011.

ADDITIONAL INFORMATION Offers copywriting and content marketing services, including blog writing, article writing, e-books, marketing videos, newsletters, social media marketing, speech writing, whitepapers, PR kits, video courses, and more.

COPY A LA CARTE

484 W. 43rd St., Apt. 24F, New York NY 10036-6341. (212)564-6343. **E-mail:** macle8@aol.com. **Contact:** Chris MacLeod. Estab. 1992.

ADDITIONAL INFORMATION Offers editing, writing, and customized copywriting services.

JULIA DRAKE PUBLIC RELATIONS

1186 Aztec, Topanga CA 90290. (323)304-2433. **E-mail:** info@juliadrakepr.com. **Website:** www.juliadrakepr.com. **Contact:** Julia Drake, CEO/founder. Estab. 2009. Julia Drake Public Relations is a boutique literary publicity company that has worked with over 100 clients from New York Times bestselling authors to first-time self-published authors.

ADDITIONAL INFORMATION Drake has appeared as a speaker on many industry panels, including the Independent Writers Association of California, UCLA, the Women's National Book Association, and the Lambda Literary Foundation.

GAL-FRIDAY PUBLICITY

308-1114 Howie Ave., Coquitlam BC V3J 1V1 Canada. (604)366-7846. **E-mail:** rachel@gal-fridaypublicity.com. **Website:** www.gal-fridaypublicity.com. **Contact:** Rachel Sentes, founder/publicist. Estab. 2009. Offers business and book publicity, e-book publicity/publishing, media kit creation and design, editing, manuscript consultations, ghostwriting, Wordpress websites, copy editing, proposal writing, and literary agent and publishing consultations.

ADDITIONAL INFORMATION "We have worked in all aspects of the book industry behind and in front of the scenes."

LINDA JAY EDITORIAL SERVICES

323 Post St., Petaluma CA 94952. (415)320-0083. E-mail: lindajay@aol.com. **Contact:** Linda Jay, copywriter/copyeditor. Estab. 2001. Offers promotional writing for self-published authors, including: Back jacket copy, flap copy, press releases, website text, brochures, newsletters, magazine profiles, feature stories, case studies, titles, and captions. Also copy edits book mss for self-published and traditionally published authors. Has edited more than 75 mss in past 3 years, including the following genres: business, memoir, fantasy, novels, spirituality, and women's issues.

JKSCOMMUNICATIONS

5008 Danby Dr., Nashville TN 37211. **E-mail:** julie@jkscommunications.com. **Website:** www.jkscommunications.com. **Contact:** Julie Schoerke, founder; Marissa Curnutte, managing director. Estab. 2000.

ADDITIONAL INFORMATION "JKSCommunications is a full-service literary publicity firm that represents some fo the finest publishers, authors, and books in the United States. Our team consists of professionals who specialize in media relations, new-model book tours, social networking, online visibility, book trailer production, and website development specifically for the book publishing industry."

KELLEY & HALL BOOK PUBLICITY

5 Briar Lane, Marblehead MA 01945. (617)680-1976. **E-mail:** jocelyn@kelleyandhall.com. **Website:** www.kelleyandhall.com. **Contact:** Jocelyn Kelley, partner. Estab. 2004. Kelley & Hall is a literary publicity company that is dedicated to helping authors and publishers with their promotion, marketing, and media relations.

ADDITIONAL INFORMATION "We create effective book buzz as well as author recognition that will increase book sales. We help writers build their author brand. Book marketing and book promotion are the cornerstones of Kelley & Hall. We have recently partnered with an independent publishing company, Grey Swan Press (www.greyswanpress.com)."

LAUNCH PUBLICITY

64 Rhinestone Terrace, San Rafael CA 94903. (415)686-0668. **E-mail:** steve@launchpublicity.com. **Website:** www.launchpublicity.com. **Contact:** Steve Keyser, publicist. Estab. 2006. Launch Publicity is a performance-based PR firm specializing in media relations.

ADDITIONAL INFORMATION "We don't bill by the hour or hide behind fat retainers. We're totally focused on bringing value to our clients by making them more visible and relevant in today's continually evolving media driven world."

PAULA MARGULIES COMMUNICATIONS

8145 Borzoi Way, San Diego CA 92129. (858)538-2047. **Fax:** (858)538-8445. **E-mail:** paula@paulamargulies.com. **Website:** www.paulamargulies.com. **Contact:** Paula Margulies, publicist/owner. Estab. 1992. Paula Margulies represents all kinds of authors and works on an hourly basis.

ADDITIONAL INFORMATION She writes press releases and places them on the newswires, creates media kits, sets up book tours and speaking appearances, schedules radio, television, print, and web interviews, sets up blog and social media tours, and handles all types of exposure opportunities related to book promotion.

MEDIANEIGHBOURS.COM

20 Via del Vaquero, Santa Fe NM 87508. **Website:** www.medianeighbours.com. **Contact:** Mary Neighbour, owner/editor. Estab. 2009.

ADDITIONAL INFORMATION "At MediaNeighbours.com, we translate real-world challenges to e-world results. We help authors, artists, small businesses, and nonprofits who are looking for ways to represent themselves across the internet and promote their products and services."

MOKA EXECUTIVE GROUP (M3G), LLC

21626 Stratford Ct., Oak Park MI 48237. **E-mail:** mokaexecgroup@gmail.com. **Website:** mokaexecutivegroup.wordpress.com. **Contact:** Megan McColla, media coordinator and copywriter. Estab. 2011. Moka Executive Group specializes in new media and brand publishing, with additional experience in public speaking. McColla brings deep understanding of brand management, internet marketing, events/promotional marketing, market research, and media relations. She works to spot emerging trends and issues, and understands their relevance to consumers. Promotes favorable image of clients through multimedia channels. Produces quality content with consistent style and structure: press releases, articles, blogs, speeches, etc. Pitches news stories, works alongside marketing teams to design ads. Develops campaigns to increase awareness, presence, and sales.

MYERS PRODUCTIONS

P.O. Box 4201, Scottsdale AZ 85261. **E-mail:** psmyers1@cox.net. **Contact:** Patricia Myers, president. Estab. 1985. Offers writing, editing, press releases, publicity, public relations.

ADDITIONAL INFORMATION Specializes in business and personality profiles, food, dining, nightlife, music, travel, books, and local history.

PR BY THE BOOK

2113 Nathan Dr., Round Rock TX 78683. (512)501-4399. **Fax:** (512)532-6170. **E-mail:** babs@prbythebook.com. **Website:** www.prbythebook.com. **Contact:** Babs Chandrasoma, Business Development Coordinator. Estab. 2002. PR by the Book is a small boutique publicity firm specializing in literary media relations campaigns, publishing consultation, small business publicity, and publicity tours for authors and experts. Headquartered in Austin with a Nashville office added in 2013, this team of seasoned publicists has worked on books in nearly every genre, and with dozens of major publishing houses and small presses.

ADDITIONAL INFORMATION Offers pre-publication publicity campaigns, full service branding publicity campaigns, blog tours, tour media pitching, and social media services.

PRHOLLYWOOD

1801 Century Park E., Suite 2400, Los Angeles CA 90067. (310)383-9502. **E-mail:** monica@prhollywood.com. **Website:** www.prhollywood.com. **Contact:** Monica Matulich, managing partner. Estab. 1991.

ADDITIONAL INFORMATION Offers strategic advice about how to promote, market and sell your book successfully in a crowded marketplace. Includes media strategy, author branding, book tours, book signing events, book reviews, video creation, website design, press releases, SEO, newsletters, etc. "We help you maximize traditional and online media for the best results!"

PUBLISIDE PERSONAL PUBLICITY

333 W. Brown Deer Rd., Milwaukee WI 53217. **Website:** publiside.com. **Contact:** Gail Sideman. Estab. 1998. Traditional and social media combined with creative promotion to provide authors the best opportunity to publicize their books to an attentive audience.

QUICK FAME SYSTEM

3 Anderson Dr., Olmstedville NY 12857. (518)532-9327. **E-mail:** edsmith@americasleadingmediapitch-coach.com. **Website:** americasleadingmediapitch-coach.com. **Contact:** Edward Smith, president. Estab. 1985. "Edward W. Smith is a publicity expert specializing in coach clients on how to pitch broadcast, print, and social media to obtain coverage for themselves, their product, or book. His experience in publicity coaching spans over 20 years and he has helped over 1,000 clients surpass their publicity goals. He works with individual clients, businesses, and non-profit organizations, from tech start-ups to charities and authors. He created the "quick fame system" to help clients pitch the media. The program is unique in that it includes coaching, so it can be tailored to work with any client's needs."

KIMBERLY RINKER

12A Kingery Quarter, Willowbrook IL 60527. (708)557-2790. **E-mail:** trotrink@aol.com. **Website:** www.kimberlyrinker.com. **Contact:** Kimberly Rinker, award-winning freelance journalist. Estab. 1984.

ADDITIONAL INFORMATION "Multiple-award winning journalist with 30+ years experience. Provides feature writing, copy editing, non-fiction journalism, ghostwriting, press releases, web design and content input. See my website for a list of clients and to view my recent projects."

LAUREN ROSENBERG PUBLIC RELATIONS

Santa Monica CA (310)393-9114. **E-mail:** lauren@lrpr.com. **Website:** lrpr.com. **Contact:** Lauren Rosenberg, publicist/owner. Estab. 1996. LRPR is a national marketing communications and public relations firm.

ADDITIONAL INFORMATION "We specialize in representing luxury consumer businesses, those appealing to a customer with a higher-income bracket, but we have also successfully represented businesses appealing to the general public. In addition, we represent authors and entertainers." Services include publicity, marketing, event planning, advertising/branding, image consulting, and personal publicity.

CYNDI A. SUMMERS

2279 Yorkshire Rd., Birmingham MI 48009. (586)945-8775. **E-mail:** cyndisummers@prodigy.net. **Website:** linkedin.com/pub/cyndi-summers/9/75/8bb. **Contact:** Cyndi A. Summers, publicist/editor. Estab. 1998. Offers publicity and/or editing services.

ADDITIONAL INFORMATION Specializes in socially and culturally progressive initiatives.

JOANNA SWANK CONSULTING

8 Crawford Dr., Sicklerville NJ 08081. **E-mail:** jswank@joannaswank.com. **Website:** www.joannaswank.com. **Contact:** Joanna Swank, consultant/owner. Estab. 1993.

ADDITIONAL INFORMATION "Joanna Swank Consulting is a one-woman show with the creative mind of a thousand. Joanna Swank is a multi-time self-published author, public speaker, lecturer and college instructor. The sole purpose and goal of Joanna Swank Consulting is to help guide and nurture aspiring authors through the murky waters of self-publishing. We offer a variety of programs to meet anyone's budget."

ELEANOR VAN NATTA PUBLICITY

906 N. 10th Way, Ridgefield WA 98642. **E-mail:** eleanor@eleanorvannatta.com. **Website:** www.eleanorvannatta.com. **Contact:** Eleanor Van Natta, publicist. Estab. 2009.

ADDITIONAL INFORMATION Offers author publicity, specializing in nonfiction adult books, especially health and wellness and psychology, but open to other genres. Strong focus on getting clients exposure on radio. Other services include press releases, book trailers, and assistance with websites and social media.

WELLS COMMUNICATIONS, INC.

5858 Kiyot Way, Los Angeles CA 90094. (310)745-1119. **Fax:** (310)745-1121. **E-mail:** awellsinla@aol.com. **Contact:** Alison Wells, owner. Estab. 1997. Offers general public relations services and unit film/television publicity. Experience as a personal publicist and freelance writer.

JESSICA WINN

Draper UT 84020. (281)889-5851. **E-mail:** jessica.winn@jollyfishpress.com. **Website:** winnoverhere.com. **Contact:** Jessica Winn, publicist. Estab. 2013.

ADDITIONAL INFORMATION Offers book publicity services: social media support, help developing a publishing plan, reviewer management, press release kit, book tour package, representation and branding.

XPRESS PRESS NEWS SERVICE

4741 Sarazen Dr., Hollywood FL 33021. (954)989-3338. **E-mail:** editorial@xpresspress.com. **Website:** www.xpresspress.com. **Contact:** Tina Koenig, owner. Estab. 1986. Offers press release writing, press release distribution, pitching, development of content and scheduling calendars for Twitter, Facebook, Pinterest and other social media outlets.

ADDITIONAL INFORMATION "We've always had a heavy focus on tech and can be a lifeline to authors who are not tech savvy and/or have no interest in handling this aspect of their PR and marketing."

CONFERENCES

Conferences provide self-publishers with a great opportunity to accomplish a few things. First, conferences are designed to help writers improve their craft and knowledge of the publishing business. In fact, some conferences are even designed to help self-publishers specifically.

Second, conferences are great networking opportunities. You may find freelance editors and designers here to help with your project. Or you may find bloggers who can help promote your book through guest posts, interviews, or reviews. And you might also find new readers that will buy copies on the spot.

Finally, conferences do one thing exceptionally well for writers of all skill levels and experience: They help give a jolt of excitement and energy. This enthusiasm should not be discounted, because it helps spur new ideas, innovation, and success.

KEEP IN MIND

Starting locally will allow you to save money on travel and other expenses (such as food, paying for a hotel, etc.). However, you may decide that paying more for your conference experience is worth it if you're receiving the type of instruction and/or making the connections you need the most. Keep in mind that your conference expenses may actually be considered a business expense and a tax deduction. Consult your accountant to confirm.

Once you decide upon a conference to attend, make a conference plan. This plan will include directions to the event, contact information for organizers (in case you can't find your way), a list of which panels and/or sessions you wish to attend (don't wait until the day of the event to figure this out), and any other tasks you'd like to accomplish.

Leave the door open to be spontaneous with your schedule and take advantage of unexpected opportunities, but having a plan will make sure you don't feel cheated out of an incredible experience after the event is over.

One more important note: Bring business cards to the event and keep them somewhere that's easy for you to dispense. Any person you speak with should receive your card, even the nice person who sat next to you at lunch, because you never know who will present you with your first or next lucky break.

ABROAD WRITERS CONFERENCES

17363 Sutter Creek Road, Sutter Creek CA 95685. (209)296-4050. **E-mail:** abroadwriters@yahoo. com. **Website:** www.abroad-crwf.com/index.html. "Abroad Writers Conferences are devoted to introducing our participants to world views here in the US and abroad. Throughout the world we invite several authors to come join us to give readings and to participate on a panel. Our discussion groups touch upon a wide range of topics from important issues of our times to publishing abroad and in the United States. Our objective is to broaden our cultural and scientific perspectives of the world through discourse and writing." Conferences are held throughout the year in various places worldwide. See website for scheduling details. Conference duration: 7-10 days. "Instead of being lost in a crowd at a large conference, Abroad Writers' Conference prides itself on holding small group meetings where participants have personal contact with everyone. Stimulating talks, interviews, readings, Q&A's, writing workshops, film screenings, private consultations and social gatherings all take place within a week to ten days. Abroad Writers' Conference promises you true networking opportunities and full detailed feedback on your writing."

COSTS Prices start at $2,750. Discounts and upgrades may apply. Particpants must apply to program no later than 3 months before departure. To secure a place you must send in a deposit of $1,000. Balance must be paid in full twelve weeks before departure. See website for pricing details.

ADDITIONAL INFORMATION Agents participate in conference. Application is online at website.

ALASKA WRITERS CONFERENCE

Alaska Writers Guild, PO Box 670014, Chugiak AK 99567. **E-mail:** bahartman@me.com; alaskawritersguild.awg@gmail.com. **Website:** alaskawritersguild. com. **Contact:** Brooke Hartman. Annual event held in the fall—usually September. Duration: 2 days. There are many workshops and instructional tracks of courses. This event sometimes teams up with SCB-WI and Alaska Pacific University to offer courses at the event. Several literary agents are in attendance each year to hear pitches and meet writers.

COSTS Up to $275, though discounts for different memberships brings down that number.

ACCOMMODATIONS Crowne Plaza Hotel in Anchorage. Conference room rates available. Several scholarships are available (see the website).

ALGONKIAN FIVE DAY NOVEL CAMP

2020 Pennsylvania Ave. NW, Suite 443, Washington DC 20006. **E-mail:** algonkian@webdelsol.com. **Website:** fwwriters.algonkianconferences.com. Conference duration: 5 days. Average attendance: 12 students maximum per workshop. "During 45+ hours of actual workshop time, students will engage in those rigorous narrative and complication/plot exercises necessary to produce a publishable ms. Genres we work with include general commercial fiction, literary fiction, serious and light women's fiction, mystery/cozy/thriller, SF/F, young adult, and memoir/narrative nonfiction. The three areas of workshop emphasis will be Premise, Platform, and Execution. Site: "The Algonkian Park is located 30 miles from Washington, D.C. It is 12 miles from Dulles International Airport (the perfect place to fly into—cab fares from Dulles to Algonkian are about $25.00). The cottages are fully furnished with TV, phones, linens, dishes, central air and heat. All cottages feature fireplaces, decks with grills, equipped kitchens, cathedral ceilings, and expansive riverside views of the Potomac. Participants each have their own room in the cottage. The address of the Algonkian Park Management headquarters is 47001 Fairway Drive, Sterling, Virginia, and their phone number is (703)450-4655. If you have any questions about the cottages or facilities, ask for Lawan, the manager."

AMERICAN CHRISTIAN WRITERS CONFERENCES

P.O. Box 110390, Nashville TN 37222-0390. (800)219-7483. **Fax:** (615)834-7736. **E-mail:** acwriters@aol.com. **Website:** www.acwriters.com. **Contact:** Reg Forder, director. Estab. 1981. ACW hosts dozens of annual two-day writers conferences and mentoring retreat across America taught by editors and professional freelance writers. These events provide excellent instruction, networking opportunities, and valuable one-on-one time with editors. Annual conferences promoting all forms of Christian writing (fiction, nonfiction, scriptwriting). Conferences are held between March and November during each year.

COSTS Costs vary based on conference. Prices also depend on whether it is a conference or a mentoring retreat.

ACCOMMODATIONS Special rates are available at the host hotel (usually a major chain like Holiday Inn). **ADDITIONAL INFORMATION** Send a SASE for conference brochures/guidelines.

ANNUAL SPRING POETRY FESTIVAL

City College, 160 Convent Ave., New York NY 10031. (212)650-6356. **Website:** www1.ccny.cuny.edu/prospective/humanities/poetry. Writer workshops geared to all levels. **Open to students.** Annual poetry festival. Festival held May 17, 2011. Registration limited to 325. Cost of workshops and festival: free. Write for more information. Site: Theater B of Aaron Davis Hall.

ANTIOCH WRITERS' WORKSHOP

c/o Antioch University Midwest, 900 Dayton St., Yellow Springs OH 45387. (937)769-1803. **E-mail:** info@antiochwritersworkshop.com. **Website:** www.antiochwritersworkshop.com. **Contact:** Sharon Short, director. Estab. 1986. Average attendance: 80. Programs are offered year-round; see the website for details. The dates of the 2014 conference are July 12-18. Workshop concentration: fiction, poetry, personal essay, memoir. Workshop located at Antioch University Midwest in the Village of Yellow Springs. 2014 summer program keynoter and Sunday morning craft class leader is Anre Dubus III. Faculty for morning classes and afternoon seminars through rest of the week include Hallie Ephron, Marly Youmans, Gayle Brandeis, Tara Ison, Mike Mullin, and many other authors as well as visiting literary agents. Writers of all levels (beginner to advanced) of fiction, memoir, personal essay, and poetry are warmly welcomed to discover their next steps on their writing paths— whether that's developing craft or preparing to submit for publication. An agent and an editor will be speaking and available for meetings with attendees. **COSTS** (registration fee plus tuition) Full week: $735, non-local, first time attendees; $675, alumni/locals; $575 for Ohio College/University students and faculty. Optional ms critique is $75[$85] for Full Week attendees. A la carte: $125 [$150], Saturday Seminar; $375, Morning Only classes; $375, Afternoon Only Focus on Form seminar. **ACCOMMODATIONS** Accommodations are available at local hotels and bed & breakfasts.

ART WORKSHOPS IN GUATEMALA

4758 Lyndale Ave. S, Minneapolis MN 55419-5304. (612)825-0747. **E-mail:** info@artguat.org. **Website:** www.artguat.org. **Contact:** Liza Fourre, director. Estab. 1995. Annual. Workshops held year-round. Maximim class size: 10 students per class. **COSTS** See website. ncludes tuition, lodging, breakfast, ground transportation. **ACCOMMODATIONS** All transportation and accommodations included in price of conference. **ADDITIONAL INFORMATION** Conference information available now. For brochure/guidelines visit website, e-mail or call. Accepts inquiries by e-mail, phone.

ASPEN SUMMER WORDS LITERARY FESTIVAL & WRITING RETREAT

Aspen Writers' Foundation, 110 E. Hallam St., #116, Aspen CO 81611. (970)925-3122. **Fax:** (970)925-5700. **E-mail:** info@aspenwriters.org. **Website:** www.aspenwriters.org. **Contact:** Natalie Lacy, programs coordinator. Estab. 1976. 2014 dates: June 14-18. ASW is one part laboratory and one part theater. It is comprised of two tracks—the Writing Retreat and the Literary Festival—which approach the written word from different, yet complementary angles. The Retreat features introductory and intensive workshops with some of the nation's most notable writing instructors and includes literature appreciation symposia and professional consultations with literary agents and editors. The Writing Retreat supports writers in developing their craft by providing a winning combination of inspiration, skills, community, and opportunity. The Literary Festival is a booklover's bliss, where the written word takes center stage. Since 2005, each edition of the Festival has celebrated a particular literary heritage and culture by honoring the stories and storytellers of a specific region. Annual conference held the fourth week of June. Conference duration: 5 days. Average attendance: 150 at writing retreat; 300+ at literary festival. **COSTS** Check website each year for updates. **ACCOMMODATIONS** Discount lodging at the conference site will be available. 2014 rates to be announced (see website). Free shuttle around town.

ATLANTA WRITERS CONFERENCE

E-mail: awconference@gmail.com. **E-mail:** gjweinstein@yahoo.com. **Website:** atlantawritersconference.com. **Contact:** George Weinstein. The Atlanta Writers Conference happens twice a year (every 6 months) and invites several agents, editors and authors each time. There are instructional sessions, and time to pitch professionals.

ACCOMMODATIONS Westin Airport Atlanta Hotel
ADDITIONAL INFORMATION There is a free shuttle that runs between the airport and the hotel.

ATLANTIC CENTER FOR THE ARTS

1414 Art Center Ave., New Smyrna Beach FL 32168. (386)427-6975. **Fax:** (386)427-5669. **E-mail:** program@atlanticcenterforthearts.org. **Website:** www.atlanticcenterforthearts.org. Internship and residency programs. A Florida artist-in-residence program in which artists of all disciplines work with current prominent artists in a supportive and creative environment.

ACCOMMODATIONS $850; $25 non-refundable application fee. Financial aid is availableParticipants responsible for all meals.Accommodations available on site. See website for application schedule and materials.

AUSTIN INTERNATIONAL POETRY FESTIVAL

P.O. Box 26455, Austin TX 78755. (512)777-1888. **E-mail:** lynn@aipf.org. **E-mail:** james@aipf.org. **Website:** www.aipf.org. **Contact:** Ashley S. Kim, festival director. Estab. 1993. Annual Austin Internatinal Poetry Festival (AIPF) April 11-14, is open to the public. This four-day citywide, all-inclusive celebration of poetry and poets has grown to become "the largest non-juried poetry festival in the U.S." The festival will include up to 20 live local readings, youth anthology read, 20 poetry workshops, 5 open mics, 5 music and poetry presentations, two anthology competions and complete readings, two poetry slams, an all-night open mic and a poetry panel symposium. API projects over 250 registered poets from the international, national, state, and local areas

ACCOMMODATIONS Includes anthology submission fee, program bio, scheduled reading at one of AIPF's 15 venues, participation in all events, 1 catered meal, workshop participation, and more.

ADDITIONAL INFORMATION Offers multiple poetry contests as part of festival. Guidelines available on website. Registration form available on website. "Largest non-juried poetry festival in the U.S.!"

BALTIMORE COMIC-CON

Baltimore Convention Center, One West Pratt St., Baltimore MD 21201. (410)526-7410. **E-mail:** general@baltimorecomiccon.com. **Website:** www.baltimore-comiccon.com. **Contact:** Marc Nathan. Estab. 1999. Annual. September 5-7, 2014. Conference "promoting the wonderful world of comics to as many people as possible." The Baltimore Comic-Con welcomes the return of The Harvey Awards: "The Harvey Awards are one of the comic book industry's oldest and most respected awards. The Harveys recognize outstanding achievements in over 20 categories, ranging from Best Artist to The Hero Initiative Lifetime Achievement Award. They are the only industry awards both nominated by and selected by the full body of comic book professionals."

ACCOMMODATIONS Does not offer overnight accommodations. Provides list of area hotels or lodging options.

ADDITIONAL INFORMATION For brochure, visit website.

BALTIMORE WRITERS' CONFERENCE

English Department, Liberal Arts Building, Towson University, 8000 York Road, Towson MD 21252. (410)704-3695. **E-mail:** prwr@towson.edu. **Website:** baltimorewritersconference.org. Estab. 1994. "Annual conference held in November at Towson University. Conference duration: 1 day. Average attendance: 150-200. Covers all areas of writing and getting published. Held at Towson University. Session topics include fiction, nonfiction, poetry, magazine and journals, agents and publishers. Sign up the day of the conference for quick critiques to improve your stories, essays, and poems."

COSTS $75-95 (includes all-day conference, lunch and reception). Student special rate of $35 before mid-October, $50 thereafter.

ACCOMMODATIONS Hotels are close by, if required.

ADDITIONAL INFORMATION Writers may register through the BWA website. Send inquiries via e-mail.

BAY TO OCEAN WRITERS' CONFERENCE

P.O. Box 544, St. Michaels MD 21663. (443)786-4536. **E-mail:** info@baytoocean.com. **Website:** www.baytoocean.com. Estab. 1998. Contacts include Diane Marquette, Mala Burt, Judy Reveal (coordinators).

COSTS Adults $155, students $55. A paid ms review is also available—details on website. Includes continental breakfast and networking lunch.

ADDITIONAL INFORMATION Mail-in registration form available on website in December prior to the conference. Pre-registration is required, no registration at door. Conference usually sells out one month in advance. Conference is for all levels of writers.

BIG SUR WRITING WORKSHOP

Henry Miller Library, Highway One, Big Sur CA 93920. (831)667-2574. **Website:** bigsurwriting.wordpress.com. Annual workshops focusing on children's and young adult writing (picture books, middle grade, and young adult). (2014 dates: both March 7-9 and Dec. 5-7.) Workshop held in Big Sur Lodge in Pfeiffer State Park. Cost of workshop: $770; included meals, lodging, workshop, Saturday evening reception; $600 if lodging not needed. www.henrymiller.org. This event is helmed by the literary agents of the Andrea Brown Literary Agency, which is the most successful agency nationwide in selling kids books. All attendees meet with at least 2 faculty members, so work is critiqued.

BLOCKBUSTER PLOT INTENSIVE WRITING WORKSHOPS (SANTA CRUZ)

Santa Cruz CA **E-mail:** contact@blockbusterplots.com. **Website:** www.blockbusterplots.com. **Contact:** Martha Alderson M.A. (also known as the Plot Whisperer), instructor. Estab. 2000. Held 4 times per year. Conference duration: 2 days. Average attendance: 20. Workshop is intended to help writers create an action, character, and thematic plotline for a screenplay, memoir, short story, novel, or creative nonfiction. Site: Conference hall.

COSTS $95 per day.

ACCOMMODATIONS Provides list of area hotels and lodging options.

ADDITIONAL INFORMATION Brochures available by e-mail or on website. Accepts inquiries by e-mail.

BLOODY WORDS MYSTERY CONFERENCE

E-mail: 2014.bloodywords.com/contact. **E-mail:** chair@bloodywords.com. **Website:** www.2014.bloodywords.com. **Contact:** Cheryl Freedman, chair. Estab. 1999. 2014 info: June 6-8 in Toronto. Theme: Theme: Danse Macabre: Historical Mysteries and the Dance of Death. "This is a conference for both readers and writers of mysteries, the only one of its kind in Canada. Programming includes presentations by experts in forensics, criminology, and publishing; panels with authors discussing a range of topics; workshops; Friday night special event; and more. See About Us on our website for details."

COSTS $190 Canadian (includes the opening reception, special event and banquet, all panels, readings, dealers' room, workshops, chance to meet with an agent, and more.

ACCOMMODATIONS Offers block of rooms at the Hyatt Regency on King. Check website for details.

ADDITIONAL INFORMATION Sponsors short mystery story contest (blind judging)—5,000 word limit; judges are experienced editors of anthologies; fee is $5 (entrants must be registered for conference). Also sponsors The Bony Blithe Award for light mysteries; see website for details. Conference information is available now on our website. Agents and editors participate in conference.

BLUE RIDGE CHRISTIAN "AUTUMN IN THE MOUNTAINS" NOVELISTS RETREAT

(800)588-7222. **E-mail:** ylehman@bellsouth.net. **Website:** www.lifeway.com/novelretreat. **Contact:** Yvonne Lehman, director. Estab. 2007. Annual retreat held in October at Ridgecrest/LifeWay Conference Center near Asheville NC. (2014 dates: October 19-22, 2014.) For beginning and advanced novelists. Site: LifeWay/Ridgecrest Conference Center, 20 miles east of Asheville, NC. Faculty: Yvonne Lehman (director, over 50 novels, editor Lighthouse Publishing of Carolinas), Lynette Eason (best-selling suspense, 20 books), Ann Tatlock (two-time Christy winner), Diana Flegal (Hartline Literary Agent), Edie Melson (novelist, social media expert), Ron & Janet Benrey (Mystery/suspense, Greenbrier publishers/editors).

COSTS Before April 1 tuition: $275. After April 1: $325. Lodging $69-$89 per night.

BOOKS-IN-PROGRESS CONFERENCE

Carnegie Center for Literacy and Learning, 251 West Second Street, Lexington KY 40507. (859)254-4175. **E-mail:** ccll1@carnegiecenterlex.org; lwhitaker@carnegiecenterlex.org. **Website:** carnegiecenterlex.org/events/books-in-progress-conference/. **Contact:** Laura Whitaker. Estab. 2010. This is an annual writing conference at the Carnegie Center for Literacy and Learning in Lexington, KY. "The conference will offer writing and publishing workshops and includes a keynote presentation." Literary agents are flown in to meet with writers and hear pitches. Website is updated several months prior to each annual event.

COSTS $175.

ACCOMMODATIONS Several area hotels are nearby.

BOOMING GROUND ONLINE WRITERS STUDIO

Buch E-462, 1866 Main Mall, UBC, Vancouver BC V6T 1Z1 Canada. **Fax:** (604)648-8848. **E-mail:** contact@boomingground.com. **Website:** www.boomingground.com. **Contact:** Robin Evans, director. Writer mentorships geared toward beginner, intermediate, and advanced levels in novel, short fiction, poetry, nonfiction, and children's writing, and more. **Open to students.** Online mentorship program—students work for 6 months with a mentor by e-mail, allowing up to 120-240 pages of material to be created. Program cost: $500 (Canadian). Site: online and by e-mail.

BREAD LOAF IN SICILY WRITERS' CONFERENCE

Middlebury College, Middlebury VT 05753. (802)443-5286. **Fax:** (802)443-2087. **E-mail:** ncargill@middlebury.edu; BLSICILY@middlebury.edu. **Website:** www.middlebury.edu/blwc/SICILY. **Contact:** Michael Collier, Director. Estab. 2011. Annual conference held in September. Conference duration: 7 days. Offers workshops for fiction, nonfiction, and poetry. Agents and editors will be in attendance. 2014 dates: Sept. 21-27. Average attendance: 32.

COSTS $2,790—includes tuition, housing.

ACCOMMODATIONS Hotel Villa San Giovanni in Erice, Sicily (western coast of the island).

BREAD LOAF ORION ENVIRONMENTAL WRITERS' CONFERENCE

Middlebury College, Middlebury VT 05753. (802)443-5286. **Fax:** (802)443-2087. **E-mail:** ncargill@middlebury.edu; BLORION@middlebury.edu. **Website:** www.middlebury.edu/blwc/BLOrion. **Contact:** Michael Collier, Director. Estab. 2014. Annual conference held in June. Conference duration: 7 days. Offers workshops for fiction, nonfiction, and poetry. Agents and editors will be in attendance. 2014 dates: June 9-15. Average attendance: 60.

COSTS $1,995—includes tuition, housing.

ACCOMMODATIONS mountain campus of Middlebury College.

BREAD LOAF WRITERS' CONFERENCE

Middlebury College, Middlebury College, Middlebury VT 05753. (802)443-5286. **Fax:** (802)443-2087. **E-mail:** ncargill@middlebury.edu. **E-mail:** blwc@middlebury.edu. **Website:** www.middlebury.edu/blwc. **Contact:** Michael Collier, Director. Estab. 1926. Annual conference held in late August. Conference duration: 10 days. Offers workshops for fiction, nonfiction, and poetry. Agents and editors will be in attendance.

COSTS $2,935 (includes tuition, housing).

ACCOMMODATIONS Bread Loaf Campus in Ripton, Vermont.

ADDITIONAL INFORMATION 2014 Conference Dates: August 13-23. Location: mountain campus of Middlebury College. Average attendance: 230.

THE BUSINESS OF PET WRITING CONFERENCE

The Pet Socialite, Prince Street Station, PO Box 398, New York NY 10012. (212)631-3648. **E-mail:** info@petwritingconference.com. **Website:** www.petwritingconference.com. **Contact:** Charlotte Reed, director. Estab. 2008. Conference duration: 1 day. Next workshop held spring 2014. Average attendance: 100. Annual conference caters to authors and journalists with interest in writing about animals. Offers seminars and workshops that "help pet writers increase their visibility with better blogging, column writing, and hosting internet radio shows; learning more about narrative and creative nonfiction; build their freelance portfolio with newspaper, magazine, and blog clips; and create successful book marketing campaigns. Offers opportunity to meet with two top agents and editors on an individualized basis. Also welcomes a variety of notable veterinarians and prominent representatives from the pet food industry who are eager to assist pet writers with their research, book and article ideas, contact information, additional educational opportunities, and access to materials (studies, reports, press releases, newsletters, etc). Featured agents have included Kate Epstein, Jeffrey Kleinman, and Meredith Hays.

COSTS Varies by year. 2014 costs not yet clear.

ADDITIONAL INFORMATION Brochures and guidelines available on website.

BUSINESS OF WRITING INTERNATIONAL SUMMIT

P.O. Box 4486, Louisville KY 40204. (502)303-7926. **E-mail:** larry@tbowt.com. **Website:** www.businessofwritingsummit.com. **Contact:** Larry DeKay or Peggy DeKay. Estab. 2012. Learn how to grow your book sales and build your author platform at this annual 2-day event for writers and authors. The summit brings together industry experts from around the world and features multiple programming tracks, including publishing, book promotion and marketing, e-books and social media, and the craft of writing. More than 2 dozen exciting sessions to choose from each year, great food, outstanding networking opportunities, and more.

COSTS $200-300 range

ACCOMMODATIONS An official hotel is designated each year for attendees that offers a special money-saving room rate and is within close proximity of the event. Details available online.

ADDITIONAL INFORMATION This is a fun, exciting and energy-filled event which allows unprecedented access to speakers and exhibitors. Event organizers Larry and Peggy DeKay pride themselves on creating a warm and hospitable environment where attendees feel welcome and have the opportunity to make new and lasting friendships and business relationships.

BYRDCLIFFE ARTS COLONY

34 Tinker St., Woodstock NY 12498. (845)679-2079. **Fax:** (845)679-4529. **E-mail:** info@woodstockguild. org. **Website:** www.woodstockguild.org. Estab. 1991. Offers 1-month residencies June-September. Open to composers, writers, and visual artists. Accommodates 15 at 1 time. Personal living quarters include single rooms, shared baths, and kitchen facilities. Offers separate private studio space. Composers must provide their own keyboard with headphone. Activities include open studio and readings for the Woodstock community at the end of each session. The Woodstock Guild, parent organization, offers music and dance performances and gallery exhibits.

COSTS $600/month; fellowships available. Residents are responsible for own meals and transportation.

ADDITIONAL INFORMATION Deadline: March 15. Online application; visit woodstockguild.org for submission guidelines. Download application fee and online payment from website.

BYRON BAY WRITERS FESTIVAL

Northern Rivers Writers' Centre, P.O. Box 1846, 69 Johnson St., Byron Bay NSW 2481 Australia. 040755-2441. **E-mail:** jeni@nrwc.org.au. **Website:** www.byronbaywritersfestival.com. **Contact:** Jeni Caffin, director. Estab. 1997. Annual festival held the first weekend in August at Byron's Bay Belongil Fields. Festival duration: 3 days. Celebrate and reflect with over 100 of the finest writers from Australia and overseas. Workshops, panel discussions, and literary breakfasts, lunches, and dinners will also be offered. The Byron Bay Writers Festival is organised by the staff and Committee of the Northern Rivers Writers' Centre, a member based organisation receiving core funding from Arts NSW.

COSTS See costs online under Tickets. Early bird, NRWC members and students, kids.

ADDITIONAL INFORMATION "2014 Festival dates are August 1-3 with workshops beginning July 28 and discounted Early Bird passes are on sale from April 4 at our website or 02 6685 6262. Full program on sale June 9.

CALIFORNIA CRIME WRITERS CONFERENCE

Co-sponsored by Sisters in Crime/Los Angeles and the Southern California Chapter of Mystery Writers of America, **E-mail:** sistersincrimela@gmail.com. **Website:** www.ccwconference.org. Estab. 1995. Biennial. Conference held in June. Average attendance: 200. Two-day conference on mystery and crime writing. Offers craft, forensic and career-buildings sessions, 2 keynote speakers, author, editor, and agent panels and book signings. Breakfast and lunch both days included.

ADDITIONAL INFORMATION Conference information is available at www.ccwconference.org.

CAPE COD WRITERS CENTER ANNUAL CONFERENCE

P.O. Box 408, Osterville MA 02655. **E-mail:** writers@capecodwriterscenter.org. **Website:** www.capecodwriterscenter.org. **Contact:** Nancy Rubin Stuart, executive director. Duration: 3 days; first week in August. Offers workshops in fiction, commercial fiction, nonfiction, poetry, writing for children, memoir, pitching your book, screenwriting, digital communications, getting published, ms evaluation, mentoring sessions with faculty. Held at Resort and Conference Center of Hyannis, Hyannis, MA.

COSTS Vary, depending on the number of courses selected.

CAPON SPRINGS WRITERS' WORKSHOP

2836 Westbrook Drive, Cincinnati OH 45211-0627. (513)481-9884. **E-mail:** beckcomm@fuse.net. Estab. 2000. No conference scheduled for 2014. There is a tentative 2015 event. Check the website often for updates. Conference duration: 3 days. Covers fiction, creative nonfiction, and publishing basics. Conference is held at Capon Springs and Farms Resort, a secluded 5,000-acre mountain resort in West Virginia.

COSTS Check in 2015.

ACCOMMODATIONS Facility has swimming, hiking, fishing, tennis, badminton, volleyball, basketball, ping pong, etc. A 9-hole golf course is available for an additional fee.

ADDITIONAL INFORMATION Brochures available for SASE. Inquire via e-mail.

CELEBRATION OF SOUTHERN LITERATURE

Southern Lit Alliance, 3069 S. Broad St., Suite 2, Chattanooga TN 37408-3056. (423)267-1218. **Fax:** (866)483-6831. **E-mail:** srobinson@southernlitalliance.org. **Website:** www.southernlitalliance.org. **Contact:** Susan Robinson. "The Celebration of Southern Literature stands out because of its unique collaboration with the Fellowship of Southern Writers, an organization founded by towering literary figures like Eudora Welty, Cleanth Brooks, Walker Percy, and Robert Penn Warren to recognize and encourage literature in the South. The 2015 celebration marked 26 years since the Fellowship selected Chattanooga for its headquarters and chose to collaborate with the Celebration of Southern Literature. More than 50 members of the Fellowship will participate in the 2015 event, discussing hot topics and reading from their latest works. The Fellowship will also award 11 literary prizes and induct new members, making this event the place to discover up-and-coming voices in Southern literature. The Southern Lit Alliance's Celebration of Southern Literature attracts more than 1,000 readers and writers from all over the U.S. It strives to maintain an informal atmosphere where conversations will thrive, inspired by a common passion for the written word. The Southern Lit Alliance (formerly The Arts & Education Council) started as 1 of 12 pilot agencies founded by a Ford Foundation grant in 1952. The Alliance is the only organization of the 12 still in existence. The Southern Lit Alliance celebrates southern writers and readers through community education and innovative literary arts experiences."

CHICAGO WRITERS CONFERENCE

E-mail: ines@chicagowritersconference.org; mare@chicagowritersconference.org. **E-mail:** ines@chicagowritersconference.org; ✉mare@chicagowritersconference.org. **Website:** chicagowritersconference.org. **Contact:** Mare Swallow. Estab. 2011. This conference happens every year in the fall. 2014 dates: Oct 24-26. Find them on Twitter at @ChiWritersConf. The conference brings together a variety of publishing professionals (agents, editors, authors) and brings together several Chicago literary, writing, and bookselling groups.

CLARION WEST WRITERS WORKSHOP

P.O. Box 31264, Seattle WA 98103-1264. (206)322-9083. **E-mail:** info@clarionwest.org. **Website:** www.clarionwest.org. "Contact us through our webform." **Contact:** Nelle Graham, workshop director. Clarion West is an intensive 6-week workshop for writers preparing for professional careers in science fiction and fantasy, held annually in Seattle WA. Usually goes from mid-June through end of July. Conference duration: 6 weeks. Average attendance: 18. Held near the University of Washington. Deadline for applications is March 1. Instructors are well-known writers and editors in the field.

COSTS $3,600 (for tuition, housing, most meals). Limited scholarships are available based on financial need.

ACCOMMODATIONS Workshop tuition, dormitory housing and most meals: $3,600. Students stay on-site in workshop housing at one of the University of Washington's sorority houses. "Students write their own stories every week while preparing critiques of all the other students' work for classroom sessions. This gives participants a more focused, professional approach to their writing. The core of the workshop remains speculative fiction, and short stories (not novels) are the focus." Conference information available in Fall. For brochure/guidelines send SASE, visit website, e-mail or call. Accepts inquiries by e-mail, phone, SASE. Limited scholarships are available, based on financial need. Students must submit 20-30 pages of ms with 4-page biography and $40 fee ($30 if received prior to February 10) for applications sent by mail or e-mail to qualify for admission.

ADDITIONAL INFORMATION This is a critique-based workshop. Students are encouraged to write a story every week; the critique of student material produced at the workshop forms the principal activity of the workshop. Students and instructors critique mss as a group. Conference guidelines are available for a SASE. Visit the website for updates and complete details.

CLARKSVILLE WRITERS CONFERENCE

1123 Madison St., Clarksville TN 37040. (931)551-8870. **E-mail:** artsandheritage@cdelightband.net;

burawac@apsu.edu. **E-mail:** artsandheritage@cde-lightband.net; burawac@apsu.edu. **Website:** www.artsandheritage.us/writers/. **Contact:** Ellen Kanervo. Annual conference held in the summer. The conference features a variety of presentations on fiction, nonfiction and more. Past attendees include: Darnell Arnoult, Earl S. Braggs, Christopher Burawa, Susan Gregg Gilmore, James & Lynda O'Connor, Katharine Sands, George Singleton, Bernis Terhune, p.m. terrell. Our presentations and workshops are valuable to writers and interesting to readers. This fun, affordable, and talent-laden conference is presented at Austin Peay State University and the Clarksville Country Club.

COSTS Costs available online; prices vary depending on how long attendees stay and if they attend the banquet dinner.

ADDITIONAL INFORMATION Multiple literary agents are flown in to the event every year to meet with writers and take pitches.

CONFERENCE FOR WRITERS & ILLUSTRATORS OF CHILDREN'S BOOKS

Book Passage, 51 Tamal Vista Blvd., Corte Madera CA 94925. (415)927-0960, ext. 239. **E-mail:** bpconferences@bookpassage.com. **Website:** www.bookpassage.com. Contact Kathryn Petrocelli, conference coordinator. Writer and illustrator conference geared toward beginner and intermediate levels. Sessions cover such topics as the nuts and bolts of writing and illustrating, publisher's spotlight, market trends, developing characters/finding voice in your writing, and the author/agent relationship. Four-day conference held each summer. Includes opening night dinner, 3 lunches and a closing reception.

CRESTED BUTTE WRITERS CONFERENCE

P.O. Box 1361, Crested Butte CO 81224. **E-mail:** coordinator@conf.crestedbuttewriters.org. **Website:** www.crestedbuttewriters.org/conf.php. **Contact:** Barbara Crawford or Theresa Rizzo, co-coordinators. Estab. 2006.

COSTS $330 nonmembers; $300 members; $297 Early Bird; The Sandy Writing Contest Finalist $280; and groups of 5 or more $280.

ACCOMMODATIONS The conference is held at The Elevation Hotel, located at the Crested Butte Mountain Resort at the base of the ski mountain (Mt. Crested Butte, CO). The quaint historic town lies nestled in a stunning mountain valley 3 short miles from the resort area of Mt. Crested Butte. A free bus runs frequently between the 2 towns. The closest airport is 30 miles away, in Gunnison CO. Our website lists 3 lodging options besides rooms at the Event Facility. All condos, motels and hotel options offer special conference rates. No special travel arrangements are made through the conference; however, information for car rental from Gunnison airport or the Alpine Express shuttle is listed on the conference FAQ page.

ADDITIONAL INFORMATION "Our conference workshops address a wide variety of writing craft and business. Our most popular workshop is Our First Pages Readings—with a twist. Agents and editors read opening pages volunteered by attendees-with a few best selling authors' openings mixed in. Think the A/E can identify the bestsellers? Not so much. Each year one of our attendees has been mistaken for a bestseller and obviously garnered requests from some on the panel. Agents attending: Carlie Webber—CK Webber Associates and TBDs. The agents will be speaking and available for meetings with attendees through our Pitch and Pages system. Editors attending: Christian Trimmer, senior editor at Disney Hyperion Books, and Jessica Williams of Harper Collins. Award-winning authors: Mark Coker, CEO of Smashwords; Kristen Lamb, social media guru, Kim Killion, book cover designer; Jennifer Jakes; Sandra Kerns; and Annette Elton. Writers may request additional information by e-mail."

DESERT DREAMS CONFERENCE: REALIZING THE DREAM

P.O. Box 27407, Tempe AZ 85285. **E-mail:** desertdreams@desertroserwa.org; desertdreamsconference@gmail.com. **Website:** www.desertroserwa.org. **Contact:** Conference coordinator. Estab. 1986. Last conference held April 2012. Next conference April 4-6, 2014. Average attendance: 250. Desert Dreams Writers' Conference provides authors of all skill levels, from beginner to multi-published, with the tools necessary to take their writing to the next level. Sessions will include general writing, career development, genre-specific, agent/publisher spotlights, as well as an agent/editor panel. There will also be one-on-one appointments with editors or agents, a book signing, and keynote addresses. Site: Tempe Mission Palms Resort & Hotel, Tempe, AZ.

COSTS Vary each year; approximately $200-235 for full conference.

ACCOMMODATIONS Hotels may vary for each conference; it is always a resort location in the Phoenix area.

ADDITIONAL INFORMATION Sponsors contest as part of conference, open to conference attendees only. For brochure, inquiries, contact by e-mail, phone, fax, mail or visit website. Agents and editors participate in conference.

DETROIT WORKING WRITERS ANNUAL WRITERS CONFERENCE

Detroit Working Writers, Box 82395, Rochester MI 48308. **E-mail:** conference@detworkingwriters.org. **Website:** dww-writers-conference.org/. Estab. 1961. 2014 dates: May 17. The theme in 2014 is "A Writer's Worth." Location is the main branch of the Clinton-Macomb Public Library in Clinton Twp, MI. Conference is one day, with breakfast, luncheon and keynote speaker, 4 breakout sessions, and three choices of workshop session. Much more info available online. Detroit Working Writers was founded on June 5, 1900, as the Detroit Press Club, The City of Detroit's first press club. Today, more than a century later, it is a 501 (c)(6) organization, and the State of Michigan's oldest writer's organization. In addition to the Conference, DWW hold quarterly workshops on craft-related topics such as the elements of poetry, finding the perfect agent, and memoir development.

COSTS $60-150, depending on early bird registration and membership status within the organization.

ERMA BOMBECK WRITERS WORKSHOP

University of Dayton, 300 College Park, Dayton OH 45469. **E-mail:** erma@udayton.edu. **Website:** humorwriters.org. **Contact:** Teri Rizvi. This is a specialized writing conference for writers of humor (books, articles, essays, film/TV). It happens every two years. The 2014 conference is from April 10-12. The Bombeck Workshop is the only one in the country devoted to both humor and human interest writing. Through the workshop, the University of Dayton and the Bombeck family honor one of America's most celebrated storytellers and humorists. Over the past decade, the workshop has attracted such household names as Dave Barry, Art Buchwald, Nancy Cartwright, Don Novello, Garrison Keillor, Gail Collins, Connie Schultz, Adriana Trigiani and Alan Zweibel. The workshop draws approximately 350 writers from around the country and typically sells out very quickly, so don't wait once registration opens.

FESTIVAL OF FAITH AND WRITING

Department of English, Calvin College, 1795 Knollcrest Circle SE, Grand Rapids MI 49546. (616)526-6770. **E-mail:** ffw@calvin.edu. **Website:** festival.calvin.edu. Estab. 1990. Biennial festival held in April. Conference duration: 3 days. The festival brings together writers, editors, publishers, musicians, artists, and readers to discuss and celebrate insightful writing that explores issues of faith. Focuses on fiction, nonfiction, memoir, poetry, drama, children's, young adult, academic, film, and songwriting. Past speakers have included Katherine Paterson, Wally Lamb, Eugene Patterson, Marilynne Robinson, Joyce Carol Oates, Salman Rushdie and Michael Chabon. Agents and editors attend the festival.

COSTS Consult festival website.

ACCOMMODATIONS Shuttles are available to and from local hotels. Shuttles are also available for overflow parking lots. A list of hotels with special rates for conference attendees is available on the festival website. High school and college students can arrange on-campus lodging by e-mail.

ADDITIONAL INFORMATION Online registration is open up to approx. 1 month before the event. (2014 online registration is open through March 14.) Accepts inquiries by e-mail and phone. Next festival is April 10-12, 2014.

FISHTRAP, INC.

400 Grant Street, P.O. Box 38, Enterprise OR 97828-0038. (541)426-3623. **E-mail:** director@fishtrap.org. **Website:** www.fishtrap.org. **Contact:** Barbara Dills, interim director. In 21 years, Fishtrap has hosted over 200 published poets, novelists, journalists, song writers, and nonfiction writers as teachers and presenters. Although workshops are kept small, thousands of writers, teachers, students and booklovers from around the west have participated in Fishtrap events on a first come first served basis. Writer workshops geared toward beginner, intermediate, advanced and professional levels. Open to students, scholarships available. A series of writing workshops and a writers' gathering is held each July. During the school year Fishtrap brings writers into local schools and offers workshops for teachers and writers of children's and young adult books. Other programs include writing and K-12 teaching residencies, writ-

ers' retreats, and lectures. College credit available for many workshops. See website for full program descriptions and to get on the e-mail and mail lists.

FLATHEAD RIVER WRITERS CONFERENCE

P.O. Box 7711, Kalispeil MT 59904-7711. (406)881-4066. **E-mail:** answers@authorsoftheflathead.org. **Website:** www.authorsoftheflathead.org/conference. asp. Estab. 1990. Two day conference packed with energizing speakers. After a focus on publishing the past two years, this year's focus is on writing, getting your mss honed and ready for your readers. Highlights include two literary agents who will review 12 mss one-on-one with the first 24 paid attendees requesting this opportunity, a synopsis writing workshop, a screenwriting workshop, poetry, and more.

COSTS Check teh website for updated cost information.

ACCOMMODATIONS Rooms are available at a discounted rate.

ADDITIONAL INFORMATION Watch website for additional speakers and other details. Register early as seating is limited.

FLORIDA CHRISTIAN WRITERS CONFERENCE

530 Lake Kathryn Circle, Casselberry FL 32707. (386)295-3902. **E-mail:** FloridaChristianWritersConf@gmail.com. **Website:** floridacwc.net. **Contact:** Eva Marie Everson, Mark Hancock. Estab. 1988. Annual conference held in February/March. Conference duration: 4 days. Average attendance: Limited to 250 people. "The Florida Christian Writers Conference 2014 meets under the stately oaks of Lake Yale Conference Center near Leesburg, Florida. The conference is designed to meet the needs of beginning writers to published authors. This is your opportunity to learn more about the publishing industry, to build your platform, and to follow God's leading to publish the message He has given you. We offer 90 one-hour workshops and 9 or more six-hour classes."

COSTS $675 (includes tuition, meals).

ACCOMMODATIONS We provide a shuttle from the Orlando airport. $725/double occupancy; $950/single occupancy.

ADDITIONAL INFORMATION "Each writer may submit 2 works for critique. We have specialists in every area of writing. Brochures/guidelines are available online or for a SASE."

FUN IN THE SUN

Florida Romance Writers, P.O. Box 550562, Fort Lauderdale FL 33355. **E-mail:** FRWfuninthesun@yahoo.com. **Website:** frwfuninthesunmain.blogspot.com. Estab. 1986. Biannual conference held in January/February on a cruise ship. (2015 details: Jan. 22-26, on the Liberty of the Seas by Royal Carribean.) Features intensive workshops on the craft of writing taught by an array of published authors; a marketing and publicity boot camp; an open-to-the-public book signing for all attending published authors; one-on-one editor/agent pitch sessions; and special events.

COSTS See website for updates, depending on membership status and registration date. Early bird discounts is before Feb. 14, 2014.

ADDITIONAL INFORMATION Ours is the longest-running conference of any RWA chapter. Brochures/registration are available online, by e-mail, or for a SASE.

GENEVA WRITERS CONFERENCE

Geneva Writers Group, Switzerland. **E-mail:** info@GenevaWritersGroup.org. **Website:** www.genevawritersgroup.org. Estab. 1993. Biennial conference (even years) held at Webster University in Bellevue/Geneva, Switzerland. (The 2014 dates were Jan. 31 - Feb. 2.) Conference duration: 2.5 days, welcoming more than 200 writers from around the world. Speakers and presenters have included Peter Ho Davies, Jane Alison, Russell Celyn Jones, Patricia Hampl, Robert Root, Brett Lott, Dinty W. Moore, Naomi Shihab Nye, Jo Shapcott, Wallis Wilde Menozzi, Susan Tiberghien, Jane Dystel, Laura Longrigg, and Colin Harrison.

GREAT LAKES WRITERS FESTIVAL

Lakeland College, P.O. Box 359, Sheboygan WI 53082-0359. **E-mail:** elderk@lakeland.edu. **Website:** www.greatlakeswritersfestival.org. Estab. 1991. Annual. Last conference held November 7-8, 2013. Conference duration: 2 days. "Festival celebrates the writing of poetry, fiction, and creative nonfiction." Site: "Lakeland College is a small, 4-year liberal arts college of 235 acres, a beautiful campus in a rural setting, founded in 1862." No themes or panels; just readings and workshops. 2013 faculty included Nick Lantz and Allyson Goldin Loomis.

COSTS Free and open to the public. Participants may purchase meals and must arrange for their own lodging.

ACCOMMODATIONS Does not offer overnight accommodations. Provides list of area hotels or lodging options.

ADDITIONAL INFORMATION All participants who would like to have their writing considered as an object for discussion during the festival workshops should submit it to Karl Elder electronically by October 15. Participants may submit material for workshops in 1 genre only (poetry, fiction, or creative nonfiction). Sponsors contest. Contest entries must contain the writer's name and address on a separate title page, typed, and be submitted as clear, hard copy on Friday at the festival registration table. Entries may be in each of 3 genres per participant, yet only 1 poem, 1 story, and/or 1nonfiction piece may be entered. There are 2 categories—high school students on 1 hand, all others on the other—of cash awards for first place in each of the 3 genres. The judges reserve the right to decline to award a prize in 1 or more of the genres. Judges will be the editorial staff of *Seems* (a.k.a. Word of Mouth Books), excluding the festival coordinator, Karl Elder. Information available in September. For brochure, visit website.

GREEN MOUNTAIN WRITERS CONFERENCE

47 Hazel St., Rutland VT 05701. (802)236-6133. **E-mail:** ydaley@sbcglobal.net. **E-mail:** yvonnedaley@me.com. **Website:** vermontwriters.com. **Contact:** Yvonne Daley, director. Estab. 1999. "Annual conference held in the summer. Covers fiction, creative nonfiction, poetry, journalism, nature writing, essay, memoir, personal narrative, and biography. Held at The Mountain Top Inn and Resort, a beautiful lakeside inn located in Chittenden, VT. Speakers have included Grace Paley, Ruth Stone, Howard Frank Mosher, Chris Bohjalian, Yvonne Daley, David Huddle, David Budbill, Jeffrey Lent, Verandah Porche, Tom Smith, and Chuck Clarino."

COSTS $500 before May 1; $550 and up after May 1. Partial scholarships are available.

ACCOMMODATIONS Dramatically reduced rates at The Mountain Top Inn and Resort for attendees. Close to other area hotels, b&bs in Rutland County, Vermont.

ADDITIONAL INFORMATION Participants' mss can be read and commented on at a cost. Sponsors contests. Conference publishes a literary magazine featuring work of participants. Brochures available on website or e-mail. "We offer the opportunity to learn from some of the nation's best writers at a small, supportive conference in a lakeside setting that allows one-to-one feedback. Participants often continue to correspond and share work after conferences."

GULF COAST WRITERS CONFERENCE

P.O. Box 35038, Panama City FL 32412. (850)628-6028. **E-mail:** PottersvillePress@mchsi.com. **Website:** www.gulfcoastwritersconference.com/. Estab. 1999. Annual conference held in September in Panama City, Fla. Conference duration: 2 days. Average attendance: 100+. This conference is deliberately small and writer-centric with an affordable attendance price. (The 2013 event was the first time the conference was completely free.) Speakers include writers, editors and agents. Cricket Freeman of the August Agency is often in attendance. A former keynote speaker was mystery writer Michael Connelly.

THE TYRONE GUTHRIE CENTRE

Annaghmakerrig, Newbliss, County Monaghan Ireland. **E-mail:** info@tyroneguthrie.ie. **Website:** www.tyroneguthrie.ie. Estab. 1981. Offers year-round residencies. Artists may stay for anything from 1 week to 3 months in the Big House, or for up to 6 months at a time in one of the 5 self-catering houses in the old farmyard. Open to artists of all disciplines. Accommodates 13 in the big house and up to 7 in the farmyard cottages. Personal living quarters include bedroom with bathroom en suite. Offers a variety of workspaces. There is a music room for composers and musicians with a Yamaha C3M-PE conservative grand piano, a performance studio with a Yamaha upright, a photographic darkroom and a number of studios for visual artists, one of which is wheelchair accessible. At certain times of the year it is possible, by special arrangement, to accommodate groups of artists, symposiums, master classes, workshops and other collaborations.

COSTS Irish and European artists: €300/week for the big house; €150 for self-catering cottages; others pay €600 per week, all found, for a residency in the Big House and €300 per week (plus gas and electricity costs) for one of the self-catering farmyard houses. To qualify for a residency, it is necessary to show evidence of a significant level of achievement in the relevant field.

ADDITIONAL INFORMATION Application forms and guidelines are available on the website. Only artists with a proven track record in their field of creativity may apply. i.e* you must be published by a recognised publisher, or You must have had a solo exibition in a recognised Art Gallery. There are other criteria for other Art forms, if in doubt, please e-mail info@tyroneguthrie.ie. Submit application form with CV to be reviewed by the selection committee of board members at quarterly meetings. Applications are considered on an ongoing basis and will be acknowledged on receipt. Applications go before a Selection Committee of the Board of the Centre, which meets quarterly. Successful applicants will be notified by letter usually within a few weeks of the Selection Committee's decision.

HAIKU NORTH AMERICA CONFERENCE

1275 Fourth St. PMB #365, Santa Rosa CA 95404. **E-mail:** welchm@aol.com. **Website:** www.haikunorthamerica.com. **Contact:** Michael Dylan Welch. Biannual conference held August 14-18 on board the historic Queen Mary ocean liner, permanently docked in Long Beach, California. Haiku North America (HNA) is the largest and oldest gathering of haiku poets in the United States and Canada. There are no membership fees and HNA provides breaking news and interaction at the HNA blog. All haiku poets and interested parties are welcome. It is a long weekend of papers, panels, workshops, readings, performances, book sales, and much socialization with fellow poets, translators, scholars, editors, and publishers. Both established and aspiring haiku poets are welcome. **ACCOMMODATIONS** Typically around $200, including a banquet and some additional meals. Accommodations at discounted hotels nearby are an additional cost. Information available on website as details are finalized closer to the conference date.

HAMPTON ROADS WRITERS CONFERENCE

P.O. Box 56228, Virginia Beach VA 23456. **E-mail:** hrwriters@cox.net. **Website:** hamptonroadswriters.org. Workshops cover fiction, nonfiction, screenplays, memoir, poetry, and the business of getting published. A bookshop, book signings, and many networking opportunities will be available. Multiple literary agents are in attendance each year to meet with writers. Much more information available on the website. **COSTS** Up to $255. Costs vary. There are discounts for members, for early bird registration, for students and more.

HEDGEBROOK

PO Box 1231, Freeland WA 98249-9911. (360)321-4786. **Fax:** (360)321-2171. **Website:** www.hedgebrook.org. **Contact:** Vito Zingarelli, residency director. Estab. 1988. "Hedgebrook is a retreat for women writers on Whidbey Island on 48 beautiful acres, near Seattle, where writers of diverse cultural backgrounds working in all genres, published or not, come from around the globe to write, rejuvenate, and be in community with each other. Located on beautiful Whidbey Island near Seattle, Hedgebrook offers one of the few residency programs in the world exclusively dedicated to supporting the creative process of women writers, and bringing their work to the world through innovative public programs." **ADDITIONAL INFORMATION** Go online for more information.

HIGHLAND SUMMER CONFERENCE

Box 7014, Radford University, Radford VA 24142-7014. (540)831-5366. **Fax:** (540)831-5951. **E-mail:** tburriss@radford.edu; rbderrick@radford.edu. **Website:** www.radford.edu/content/cehd/home/departments/appalachian-studies.html. **Contact:** Dr. Theresa Burriss, Ruth Derrick. Estab. 1978. The Highland Summer Writers' Conference is a one-week lecture-seminar workshop combination conducted by well-known guest writers. It offers the opportunity to study and practice creative and expository writing within the context of regional culture. The course is graded on Pass/Fail basis for undergraduates and letter grades for graduate students. It may be taken twice for credit. The class runs Monday through Friday 9 a.m.-noon and 1:30-4:30 p.m., with extended hours on Wednesday, and readings and receptions by resident teachers on Tuesday and Thursday evening in McConnell Library 7:30-9:30 p.m. The evening readings are free and open to the public. **ACCOMMODATIONS** "We do not have special rate arrangements with local hotels. We do offer accommodations on the Radford University campus in a recently refurbished residence hall." **ADDITIONAL INFORMATION** Conference leaders typically critique work done during the one-week conference, and because of the one-week format, students will be asked to bring preliminary work when they arrive at the conference, as well as submit a portfolio following the conference. Brochures/guidelines are available in March by request.

HOFSTRA UNIVERSITY SUMMER WRITING WORKSHOPS

University College for Continuing Education, 250 Hofstra University, Hempstead NY 11549-2500. (516)463-7200. **Fax:** (516)463-4833. **E-mail:** ce@hofstra.edu. **Website:** hofstra.edu/academics/ce. **Contact:** Colleen Slattery, Senior Associate Dean. Estab. 1972. Hofstra University's 2-week Summer Writers Program, a cooperative endeavor of the Creative Writing Program, the English Department, and Hofstra University Continuing Education (Hofstra CE), offers 8 classes which may be taken on a noncredit or credit basis, for both graduate and undergraduate students. Led by master writers, the Summer Writing Program operates on the principle that true writing talent can be developed, nurtured and encouraged by writer-in-residence mentors. Through instruction, discussion, criticism and free exchange among the program members, writers begin to find their voice and their style. The program provides group and individual sessions for each writer. The Summer Writing Program includes a banquet, guest speakers, and exposure to authors such as Oscar Hijuelos, Robert Olen Butler (both Pulitzer Prize winners), Maurice Sendak, Cynthia Ozick, Nora Sayre, and Denise Levertov. Often agents, editors, and publishers make presentations during the conference, and authors and students read from published work and works in progress. These presentations and the conference banquet offer additional opportunities to meet informally with participants, master writers and guest speakers. Average attendance: 65. Conference offers workshops in short fiction, nonfiction, poetry, and occasionally other genres such as screenplay writing or writing for children. Site is the university campus on Long Island, 25 miles from New York City.

COSTS Check website for current fees. Credit is available for undergraduate and graduate students. Choose one of 9 writing genres and spend two intensive weeks studying and writing in that genre.

ACCOMMODATIONS Free bus operates between Hempstead Train Station and campus for those commuting from New York City on the Long Island Rail Road. Dormitory rooms are available.

ADDITIONAL INFORMATION Students entering grades 9-12 can now be part of the Summer Writers Program with a special section for high school students. Through exercises and readings, students will learn how to use their creative impulses to improve their fiction, poetry and plays and learn how to create cleaner and clearer essays. During this intensive 2-week course, students will experiment with memoir, poetry, oral history, dramatic form and the short story, and study how to use character, plot, point of view and language.

HOLLYWOOD PITCH FESTIVAL

Fade In Magazine, P.O. Box 2699, Beverly Hills CA 90213. (800)646-3896. **E-mail:** inquiries@fadeinonline.com. **Website:** hollywoodpitchfestival.com/. Estab. 1996. 2014: August 1-3, Los Angeles. Register online or Call To Register (800) 646-3896. Conference duration: Three days. This is a pitch event that provides non-stop pitch meetings over a two-day period with 200 of Hollywood's top buyers/representatives under one roof. HPF only has one class - a pitch class taught by a professional A-list filmmaker on Saturday morning, and it is optional. Each attendee will received by e-mail a list of the companies/industry representatives attending, what each company is currently looking to produce (i.e., genre, budget), along with each company's credits. We also post a genre list at each event for cross-reference.

COSTS Our ticket prices are flat fees that cover each attendee's entire weekend (including food and drink). There are no other extra, added costs (i.e., no per pitch meeting fees) involved (unless you're adding hotel rooms).

HOUSTON WRITERS GUILD CONFERENCE

HOUSTON WRITERS GUILD CONFERENCE 31160, Houston TX 77231. (713)721-4773. **E-mail:** HoustonWritersGuild@Hotmail.com. **E-mail:** HoustonWritersGuild@Hotmail.com. **Website:** houstonwritersguild.org. 2014 date: Saturday, April 12. This annual conference, organized by the Houston Writers Guild, has concurrent sessions and tracks on the craft and business of writing. Each year, multiple agents are in attendance taking pitches from writers.

COSTS Costs are different for members and non-members. 2014 costs: $100 members, $125 non-members.

ADDITIONAL INFORMATION There is a writing contest at the event. There is also a for-pay pre-conference workshop the day before the conference.

HOW TO BE PUBLISHED WORKSHOPS

P.O. Box 100031, Irondale AL 35210-3006. **E-mail:** mike@writing2sell.com. **Website:** www.writing2sell.com. **Contact:** Michael Garrett. Estab. 1986. Workshops are offered continuously year-round at various locations. Conference duration: 1 session. Average attendance: 10-15. Workshops to "move writers of category fiction closer to publication." Focus is not on how to write, but how to get published. Site: Workshops held at college campuses and universities. Themes include marketing, idea development, characterization, and ms critique. Special critique is offered, but advance submission is not required. Workshop information available on website. Accepts inquiries by e-mail. **COSTS** $79-99.

INDIANA UNIVERSITY WRITERS' CONFERENCE

464 Ballantine Hall, 1020 E. Kirkwood Ave., Bloomington IN 47405-7103. (812)855-1877. **Fax:** (812)855-9535. **E-mail:** writecon@indiana.edu. **Website:** www. indiana.edu/~writecon. **Contact:** Bob Bledsoe, director. Estab. 1940. Annual. Conference/workshops held in May. Average attendance: 115. "The Indiana University Writers' Conference believes in a craft-based teaching of fiction writing. We emphasize an exploration of creativity through a variety of approaches, offering workshop-based craft discussions, classes focusing on technique, and talks about the careers and concerns of a writing life."
COSTS Workshop, $550/week; classes only, $300/week.
ACCOMMODATIONS Information on accommodations available on website.
ADDITIONAL INFORMATION Fiction workshop applicants must submit up to 25 pages of prose. Registration information available for SASE, by e-mail, or on website.

INTERNATIONAL CREATIVE WRITING CAMP

111-11th Ave.SW, Minot ND 58701-6081. (701)838-8472. **Fax:** (701)838-1351. **E-mail:** info@internationalmusiccamp.com. **Website:** www.internationalmusiccamp.com. **Contact:** Joseph Alme, interim director. Writer and illustrator workshops geared toward beginner, intermediate and advanced levels. **Open to students.** Sessions offered include those covering poems, plays, mystery stories, essays. Workshop held June 23-29. Registration limited to 40. The summer camp location at the International Peace Garden on the Border between Manitoba and North Dakota is an ideal site for creative thinking. Excellent food, housing, and recreation facilities are available.

COSTS Before May 1, $375; after May 1—$390. Write for more information.

INTERNATIONAL MUSIC CAMP CREATIVE WRITING WORKSHOP

111-11th Ave. SW, Minot ND 58701. (701)838-8472. **Fax:** (701)838-1351. **E-mail:** info@internationalmusiccamp.com. **Website:** www.internationalmusiccamp.com. **Contact:** Christine Baumann and Tim Baumann, camp directors. Estab. 1956. Annual. Conference held in June. Average attendance: 35. "The workshop offers students the opportunity to refine their skills in thinking, composing, and writing in an environment that is conducive to positive reinforcement. In addition to writing poems, essays, and stories, individuals are encouraged to work on their own area of interest with conferencing and feedback from the course instructor." Site: International Peace Garden on the border between the US and Canada. "Similar to a university campus, several dormitories, classrooms, lecture halls, and cafeteria provide the perfect site for such a workshop. The beautiful and picturesque International Peace Garden provides additional inspiration to creative thinking." Instructor: Melissa Cournia & Andrea Nell.
COSTS $395, includes tuition, room and board. Early bird registration (postmarked by May 1) $370.
ACCOMMODATIONS Airline and depot shuttles are available upon request. Housing is included in the fee.
ADDITIONAL INFORMATION Conference information is available on the website. Welcomes questions via e-mail.

INTERNATIONAL WOMEN'S FICTION FESTIVAL

Via Cappuccini 8E, Matera 75100 Italy. (39)0835-312044. **Fax:** (39)0835-312093. **E-mail:** e.jennings@womensfictionfestival.com. **Website:** www.womensfictionfestival.com/. **Contact:** Elizabeth Jennings. Estab. 2004. Annual conference usually held in September 2014 dates: Sept. 25-28, 2014. Conference duration: 3.5 days. Average attendance: 100. Sessions on fiction, nonfiction, screenwriting, writing for children, poetry, etc. International writers conference with a strong focus on fiction and a strong focus on marketing to international markets.
COSTS 220 euros.
ACCOMMODATIONS Le Monacelle, a restored 17th century convent. A paid shuttle is available from the Bari Airport to the hotel in Matera.

IOWA SUMMER WRITING FESTIVAL

The University of Iowa, C215 Seashore Hall, University of Iowa, Iowa City IA 52242. (319)335-4160. **Fax:** (319)335-4743. **E-mail:** iswfestival@uiowa.edu. **Website:** uiowa.edu/~iswfest. Estab. 1987. Annual festival held in June and July. Conference duration: Workshops are 1 week or a weekend. Average attendance: Limited to 12 people/class, with over 1,500 participants throughout the summer. "We offer courses across the genres: novel, short story, poetry, essay, memoir, humor, travel, playwriting, screenwriting, writing for children, and women's writing. Held at the University of Iowa campus." Speakers have included Marvin Bell, Lan Samantha Chang, John Dalton, Hope Edelman, Katie Ford, Patricia Foster, Bret Anthony Johnston, Barbara Robinette Moss, among others.

COSTS $590 for full week; $305 for weekend workshop. Housing and meals are separate.

ACCOMMODATIONS Accommodations available at area hotels. Information on overnight accommodations available by phone or on website.

ADDITIONAL INFORMATION Brochures are available in February. Inquire via e-mail or on website.

IWWG ANNUAL SUMMER CONFERENCE

International Women's Writing Guild "Remember the Magic" Annual Summer Conference, International Women's Writing Guild, P.O. Box 810, Gracie Station, New York NY 10028. (212)737-7536. **Fax:** (212)737-9469. **E-mail:** iwwgquestions@gmail.com. **Website:** www.iwwg.org. **Contact:** Hannelore Hahn, executive director. Writer and illustrator workshops geared toward all levels. Offers over 50 different workshops—some are for children's book writers and illustrators. Also sponsors other events throughout the U.S. Annual workshops. Workshops held every summer for a week. Length of each session: 90 minutes; sessions take place for an entire week. Registration limited to 500. Write for more information.

JACKSON HOLE WRITERS CONFERENCE

PO Box 1974, Jackson WY 83001. (307)413-3332. **E-mail:** nicole@jacksonholewritersconference.com. **Website:** jacksonholewritersconference.com. Estab. 1991. Annual conference held June 27-29. Conference duration: 4 days. Average attendance: 110. Covers fiction, creative nonfiction, and young adult and offers ms critiques from authors, agents, and editors. Agents in attendance will take pitches from writers. Paid ms critique programs are available.

COSTS $365 if registered by May 12. Accompanying teen writer: $175. Pre-Conference Writing Workshop: $150.

ADDITIONAL INFORMATION Held at the Center for the Arts in Jackson, Wyoming and online.

JAMES RIVER WRITERS CONFERENCE

ArtWorks Studios 136, 320 Hull St., #136, Richmond VA 23224. (804)433-3790. **Fax:** (804)291-1466. **E-mail:** info@jamesriverwriters.com; fallconference@jamesriverwriters.com. **Website:** www.jamesriverwriters.com. **Contact:** Katharine Herndon, exec. director. Estab. 2003.

COSTS The cost was up to $240, though less expensive options were available. See the website for all pricing options.

ACCOMMODATIONS Richmond is easily accessibly by air and train. Provides list of area hotels or lodging options. "Each year we arrange for special conference rates at an area hotel."

ADDITIONAL INFORMATION Workshop material is not required, however we have offered an option for submissions: the first pages critique session in which submissions are read before a panel of agents and editors who are seeing them for the first time and are asked to react on the spot. No additional fee. No guarantee that a particular submission will be read. Details posted on the website, www.jamesriverwriters.com. Information available in June. For brochure, visit website. Agents participate in conference. Editors participate in conference. Both meet with writers to take pitches. Previous agents in attendance include April Eberhardt, Deborah Grosvenor, Victoria Skurnick, and Paige Wheeler.

JOURNEY INTO THE IMAGINATION: A FIVE-DAY WRITING RETREAT

995 Chapman Road, Yorktown NY 10598. (914)962-4432. **E-mail:** emily@emilyhanlon.com. **Website:** www.thefictionwritersjourney.com/Spring_Writing_Retreat.html. **Contact:** Emily Hanlon. PO Box 536 Estab. 2004. Annual. 2014 dates: May 6-11. Average attendance: 8-12. "Purpose of workshop: fiction, memoir, short story, creativity, and the creative process." Site: Pendle Hill Retreat Center in Wallingford, PA (just north of Philadelphia). "Excellent food and lovely surroundings and accommodations. The core of this weekend's work is welcoming the unknown into your

writing. We will go on a magical mystery tour to find and embrace new characters and to deepen our relationship to characters who already may people our stories. Bring something on which you are already working or simply bring along your Inner Writer, pen and a journal, and let the magic unfold!"

COSTS 2014: 5 nights—$1150 if you register before March 1. $1250 after March 1. All rooms are private with shared bath.

ADDITIONAL INFORMATION For brochure, visit website.

KACHEMAK BAY WRITERS CONFERENCE

Kenai Peninsula College - Kachemak Bay Campus, 533 East Pioneer Ave., Homer AK 99603. **E-mail:** iy-conf@uaa.alaska.edu. **Website:** http://writersconfer-ence.uaa.alaska.edu. Annual writers conference held in the summer (usually June). 2014 dates: June 13-17; keynote speaker is Alice Sebold. Sponsored by Kache-mak Bay Campus - Kenai Peninsula College /UAA. This nationally recognized writing conference features workshops, readings and panel presentations in fiction, poetry, nonfiction, and the business of writing. There are "open mic" sessions for conference registrants; evening readings open to the public; agent / editor consultations, and more.

COSTS See the website. Some scholarships available; see the website.

ACCOMMODATIONS Homer is 225 miles south of Anchorage, Alaska on the southern tip of the Kenai Peninsula and the shores of Kachemak Bay. There are multiple hotels in the area.

KENTUCKY WOMEN WRITERS CONFERENCE

University of Kentucky College of Arts & Sciences, 232 E. Maxwell St., Lexington KY 40506. (859)257-2874. **E-mail:** kentuckywomenwriters@gmail.com. **Website:** womenwriters.as.uky.edu/. **Contact:** Ju-lie Wrinn, director. Estab. 1979. Conference held in second or third weekend of September. The 2014 dates are Sept. 12-13. The 2014 location is the Carn-egie Center for Literacy in Lexington, Ky. Confer-ence duration: 2 days. Average attendance: 150-200. Conference covers all genres: poetry, fiction, creative nonfiction, playwriting. Writing workshops, panels, and readings featuring contemporary women writers. The 2014 conference will feature Pulitzer Prize-winning poet Tracy K. Smith as its keynote speaker.

COSTS $175 early bird discount before Aug 1., $195 thereafter; $30 for undergraduates and younger; includes boxed lunch on Friday; $20 for Writers Reception. Other meals] and accommodations are not included.

ADDITIONAL INFORMATION Sponsors prizes in poetry ($200), fiction ($200), nonfiction ($200), playwriting ($500), and spoken word ($500). Winners also invited to read during the conference. Pre-registration opens May 1.

KENTUCKY WRITERS CONFERENCE

Western Kentucky University and the Southern Kentucky Book Fest, Western Kentucky University Libraries, 1906 College Heights Blvd., Bowling Green KY 42101. (270)745-4502. **E-mail:** kristie.lowry@wku.edu. **Website:** www.sokybookfest.org/KYWritersConf. **Contact:** Kristie Lowry. This event is entirely free to the public. (2014 dates: April 25-26.) Duration: 1 day. Precedes the Southern Kentucky Book Fest the next day. Authors who will be participating in the Book Fest on Saturday will give attendees at the Writers Conference the benefit of their wisdom on Friday. Free workshops on a variety of writing topics will be presented during this day-long event. Sessions run for 75 minutes and the day begins at 9:00am and ends at 3:30pm. The conference is open to anyone who would like to attend including high school students, college students, teachers, and the general public.

KENYON REVIEW WRITERS WORKSHOP

Kenyon College, Gambier OH 43022. (740)427-5207. **Fax:** (740)427-5417. **E-mail:** kenyonreview@kenyon.edu; writers@kenyonreview.org. **Website:** www.ke-nyonreview.org. **Contact:** Anna Duke Reach, director. Estab. 1990. Annual 8-day workshop held in June. Participants apply in poetry, fiction, creative nonfiction, literary hybrid/book arts or writing online, and then participate in intensive daily workshops which focus on the generation and revision of significant new work. Held on the campus of Kenyon College in the rural village of Gambier, Ohio. Workshop leaders have included David Baker, Ron Carlson, Rebecca McClanahan, Meghan O'Rourke, Linda Gregorson, Dinty Moore, Tara Ison, Jane Hamilton, Lee K. Abbott, and Nancy Zafris.

COSTS $1,995; includes tuition, room and board.

ACCOMMODATIONS The workshop operates a shuttle to and from Gambier and the airport in Columbus, Ohio. Offers overnight accommodations.

Participants are housed in Kenyon College student housing. The cost is covered in the tuition.

ADDITIONAL INFORMATION Application includes a writing sample. Admission decisions are made on a rolling basis. Workshop information is available online at www.kenyonreview.org/workshops in November. For brochure send e-mail, visit website, call, fax. Accepts inquiries by SASE, e-mail, phone, fax.

KEY WEST LITERARY SEMINAR

718 Love Lane, Key West FL 33040. (888)293-9291. **E-mail:** mail@kwls.org. **Website:** www.kwls.org. "The mission of KWLS is to promote the understanding and discussion of important literary works and their authors; to recognize and support new voices in American literature; and to preserve and promote Key West's literary heritage while providing resources that strengthen literary culture." The annual seminar and writers' workshop program are held in January. Scholarships are available to teachers, librarians, and students. Awards are given to emerging writers. See website for details.

COSTS $575/seminar; $450/writers' workshops.

ACCOMMODATIONS A list of nearby lodging establishments is made available.

KILLER NASHVILLE

P.O. Box 680759, Franklin TN 37068-0686. (615)599-4032. **E-mail:** contact@killernashville.com. **Website:** www.killernashville.com. Jaden Terrell, Exec. Dir. **Contact:** Clay Stafford, founder. Estab. 2006. Annual. Next events: Aug. 21-24, 2014. Conference duration: 3 days. Average attendance: 400+. Conference designed for writers and fans of mysteries and thrillers, including fiction and nonfiction authors, playwrights, and screenwriters. There are many opportunities for authors to sign books. Killer Nashville's 2014 writers conference will have over 60 sessions, 2 guests of honor, agent / editor / publisher roundtables, 5 distinct session tracks (general writing, genre specific writing, publishing, publicity & promotion, and forensics, breakout sessions for intense study, special sessions, ms critiques (fiction, nonfiction, short story, screenplay, marketing, query), realistic mock crime scene for guests to solve, networking with bestselling authors, agents, editors, publishers, attorneys, publicists, representatives from law and emergency services, mystery games, authors' bar, wine tasting event, two cocktail receptions, guest of honor dinner and awards program, prizes, free giveaways, free book signings, and more.

COSTS Early Bird Registration: $210 (February 15); Advanced Registration: $220 (April 30); $230 for three day full registration.

ACCOMMODATIONS The Hutton Hotel has all rooms available for the Killer Nashville Writers' Conference.

ADDITIONAL INFORMATION Additional information about registration is provided online.

KINDLING WORDS EAST

VT **Website:** www.kindlingwords.org. Annual retreat held in late January near Burlington, Vermont. A retreat with three strands: writer, illustrator and editor; professional level. Intensive workshops for each strand, and an open schedule for conversations and networking. Registration limited to approximately 70. Hosted by the 4-star Inn at Essex (room and board extra). Participants must be published by a CCBC listed publisher, or if in publishing, occupy a professional position. Registration opens August 1 or as posted on the website, and fills quickly. Check website to see if spaces are available, to sign up to be notified when registration opens each year, or for more information.

KINDLING WORDS WEST

Breckenridge CO **Website:** www.KindlingWords.org. Annual retreat held in late April/early May out west. 2014 location is the Mountain Thunder Lodge in Breckenridge, CO. KWW is an artist's colony-style week with workshops by gifted teachers followed by a working retreat. Participants gather just before dinner to have white-space discussions; evenings include fireside readings, star gazing and songs. $415 tuition; room/board extra. Participants must be published by CBC-recognized publisher.

KUNDIMAN POETRY RETREAT

P.O. Box 4248, Sunnyside NY 11104. **E-mail:** info@kundiman.org. **Website:** www.kundiman.org. **Contact:** June W. Choi, executive director. Held annualy June 19-23 at Fordham University's Rose Hill campus. "Opento Asian American poets. Renowned faculty will conduct workshops and provide one-on-one mentorship sessions with fellows. Readings and informal social gatherings will also be scheduled. Fellows selected based on sample of 6-8 poems and short essay answer. Applications should be received between December 15-February 1."

COSTS $350

ACCOMMODATIONS Room and board is free to accepted Fellows.

ADDITIONAL INFORMATION Additional information, guidelines, and online application available on website.

LA JOLLA WRITERS CONFERENCE

P.O. Box 178122, San Diego CA 92177. (858)467-1978. **E-mail:** akuritz@san.rr.com. **Website:** www.lajollawritersconference.com. **Contact:** Jared Kuritz, director. Estab. 2001. Annual conference held in October/November. Conference duration: 3 days. Average attendance: 200. The LJWC covers all genres and both fiction and nonfiction as well as the business of writing. We take particular pride in educating our attendees on the business aspect of the book industry and have agents, editors, publishers, publicists, and distributors teach classes. There is unprecedented access to faculty at the LJWC. Our conference offers lecture sessions that run for 50 minutes, and workshops that run for 110 minutes. Each block period is dedicated to either workshop or lecture-style classes, with 6-8 classes on various topics available each block. For most workshop classes, you are encouraged to bring written work for review. Literary agents from prestigious agencies such as The Andrea Brown Literary Agency, The Dijkstra Agency, The McBride Agency and Full Circle Literary Group, the Zimmerman Literary Agency, the Van Haitsma Literary Agency, the Farris Literary Agency and more have participated in the past, teaching workshops in which they are familiarized with attendee work. Late night and early bird sessions are also available.] The conference creates a strong sense of community, and it has seen many of its attendees successfully published.

COSTS Information available online at website.

LAS VEGAS WRITERS CONFERENCE

Henderson Writers' Group, 614 Mosswood Dr., Henderson NV 89015. (702)564-2488; or, toll-free, (866)869-7842. **E-mail:** marga614@mysticpublishers.com. **Website:** www.lasvegaswritersconference.com. Annual. Held in April. Conference duration: 3 days. Average attendance: 150 maximum. "Join writing professionals, agents, industry experts, and your colleagues for 3 days in Las Vegas as they share their knowledge on all aspects of the writer's craft. While there are formal pitch sessions, panels, workshops, and seminars, the faculty is also available throughout the conference for informal discussions and ad-

vice. Plus, you're bound to meet a few new friends, too. Workshops, seminars, and expert panels will take you through writing in many genres including fiction, creative nonfiction, screenwriting, journalism, and business and technical writing. There will be many Q&A panels for you to ask the experts all your questions." Site: Sam's Town Hotel and Gambling Hall in Las Vegas.

COSTS $425 until 1/14/14; $475 starting 1/15/14; $500 at door; $300 for one day.

ADDITIONAL INFORMATION Sponsors contest. Agents and editors participate in conference.

LAURA THOMAS JUNIOR WRITERS AUTHORS CONFERENCE

Laura Thomas Communications, Delta British Colombia V6X 2M9 Canada. (604)307-4971. **E-mail:** laura@laurathomascommunications.com. **Website:** http://laurathomascommunications.com/conference/. **Contact:** Laura Thomas. Estab. 2013. New conference held in the fall and spring each year. Conference duration: 1 day, 9-5. Covers poetry and writing for children and young adults, ages 9-21. Speakers have included Michelle Barker (author and editor), Deneka Michaud (journalist and communications professional), Lois Peterson (author), Darlene Foster (author), and George Opacic (author and publisher).

COSTS $89 single ticket and $79 sibling rate. Includes workshops and meals, scholarships are available.

ADDITIONAL INFORMATION Writers may request information by e-mail.

THE MACDOWELL COLONY

100 High St., Peterborough NH 03458. (603)924-3886. **Fax:** (603)924-9142. **E-mail:** admissions@macdowellcolony.org. **Website:** www.macdowellcolony.org. Estab. 1907. Open to writers, playwrights, composers, visual artists, film/video artists, interdisciplinary artists and architects. Applicants submit information and work samples for review by a panel of experts in each discipline. Application form submitted online at www.macdowellcolony.org/apply.html.

COSTS Travel reimbursement and stipends are available for participants of the residency, based on need. There are no residency fees.

MENDOCINO COAST WRITERS CONFERENCE

1211 Del Mar Dr., second address is P.O. Box 2087, Fort Bragg CA 95437. (707)485-4032. **E-mail:** info@mcwc.org. **Website:** www.mcwc.org. Estab. 1988. Annual conference held in July. Average attendance: 80. Provides workshops for fiction, nonfiction, and poetry. Held at a small community college campus on the northern Pacific Coast. Workshop leaders have included Kim Addonizio, Lynne Barrett, John Dufresne, John Lescroart, Ben Percy, Luis Rodriguez, Peter Orner, Judith Barrington and Ellen Sussman. Agents and publishers will be speaking and available for meetings with attendees.

COSTS $525+ (includes panels, meals, 2 socials with guest readers, 4 public events, 3 morning intensive workshops in 1 of 6 subjects, and a variety of afternoon panels and lectures).

ACCOMMODATIONS Information on overnight accommodations is made available.

ADDITIONAL INFORMATION Emphasis is on writers who are also good teachers. Registration opens March 15. Send inquiries via e-mail.

MIDWEST WRITERS WORKSHOP

Ball State University, Department of Journalism, Muncie IN 47306. (765)282-1055. **E-mail:** midwestwriters@yahoo.com. **Website:** www.midwestwriters.org. **Contact:** Jama Kehoe Bigger, director. Annual workshop held in late July in eastern Indiana. Writer workshops geared toward writers of all levels. Topics include most genres. Faculty/speakers have included Joyce Carol Oates, George Plimpton, Clive Cussler, Haven Kimmel, James Alexander Thom, Wiliam Zinsser, Phillip Gulley, Lee Martin, and numerous bestselling mystery, literary fiction, young adult, and children's authors. Workshop also includes agent pitch sessions ms evaluation and a writing contest. Registration tentatively limited to 200.

COSTS $150-375. Most meals included.

ADDITIONAL INFORMATION Offers scholarships. See website for more information.

MISSOURI WRITERS' GUILD CONFERENCE

St. Louis MO **E-mail:** mwgconferenceinfo@gmail.com. **Website:** www.missouriwritersguild.org. **Contact:** Tricia Sanders, vice president/conference chairman. Writer and illustrator workshops geared to all levels. **Open to students.** Annual conference held early April or early May each year. Annual conference "gives writers the opportunity to hear outstanding speakers and to receive information on marketing, research, and writing techniques." Agents, editors, and published authors in attendance.

ACCOMMODATIONS 2014: Ramada Plaza Hotel downtown.

ADDITIONAL INFORMATION The primary contact individual changes every year, because the conference chair changes every year. See the website for contact info.

MONTEVALLO LITERARY FESTIVAL

Sta. 6420, University of Montevallo, Montevallo AL 35115. (205)665-6420. **Fax:** (205)665-6422. **E-mail:** murphyj@montevallo.edu. **Website:** www.montevallo.edu/english. **Contact:** Dr. Jim Murphy, director. Estab. 2003. Takes place annually, April 12.

COSTS Readings are free. Readings, plus lunch, reception, and dinner is $20. Master Class only is $30. Master Class with everything else is $50.

ACCOMMODATIONS Offers overnight accommodations at Ramsay Conference Center on campus. Call (205)665-6280 for reservations. Free on-campus parking. Additional information available at www.montevallo.edu/cont_ed/ramsay.shtm.

ADDITIONAL INFORMATION To enroll in a fiction workshop, contact Bryn Chancellor (bchancellor@montevallo.edu). Information for upcoming festival available in February For brochure, visit website. Accepts inquiries by mail (with SASE), e-mail, phone, and fax. Editors participate in conference. "This is a friendly, relaxed festival dedicated to bringing literary writers and readers together on a personal scale." Poetry workshop participants submit up to 5 pages of poetry; e-mail as Word doc to Jim Murphy (murphyj@montevallo.edu) at least 2 weeks prior to festival.

MONTROSE CHRISTIAN WRITERS' CONFERENCE

218 Locust St., Montrose PA 18801. (570)278-1001 or (800)598-5030. **Fax:** (570)278-3061. **E-mail:** mbc@montrosebible.org. **Website:** montrosebible.org. Estab. 1990. "Annual conference held in July. Offers workshops, editorial appointments, and professional critiques. We try to meet a cross-section of writing needs, for beginners and advanced, covering fiction, poetry, and writing for children. It is small enough to allow personal interaction between attendees and faculty. Speakers have included William Petersen, Mona Hodgson, Jim Fletcher, and Terri Gibbs." Held in Montrose, from July 20-25, 2014.

COSTS Tuition is $180.

ACCOMMODATIONS Will meet planes in Binghamton, NY and Scranton, PA. On-site accommodations: room and board $325-370/conference; $75-80/day including food (2014 rates). RV court available.

ADDITIONAL INFORMATION "Writers can send work ahead of time and have it critiqued for a small fee." The attendees are usually church related. The writing has a Christian emphasis. Conference information available in April. For brochure, visit website, e-mail or call. Accepts inquiries by phone or e-mail.

JENNY MCKEAN MOORE COMMUNITY WORKSHOPS

English Department, George Washingtion University, 801 22nd St. NW, Rome Hall, Suite 760, Washington DC 20052. (202) 994-6180. **Fax:** (202) 994-7915. **E-mail:** lpageinc@aol.com. **Website:** www.gwu.edu/~english/creative_jennymckeanmoore.html. **Contact:** Lisa Page, Acting Director of creative writing. Estab. 1976. Workshop held each semester at the university. Average attendance: 15. Concentration varies depending on professor—usually fiction or poetry. The Creative Writing department brings an established poet or novelist to campus each year to teach a writing workshop for GW students and a free community workshop for adults in the larger Washington community. Details posted on website in June, with an application deadline at the end of August or in early September.

ADDITIONAL INFORMATION Admission is competitive and by ms.

MOUNT HERMON CHRISTIAN WRITERS CONFERENCE

PO Box 413, Mount Hermon CA 95041. **E-mail:** info@mounthermon.org. **Website:** mounthermon.org. Estab. 1970. Annual professional conference (always held over the Palm Sunday weekend, Friday noon through Tuesday noon). Average attendance: 450. Sponsored by and held at the 440-acre Mount Hermon Christian Conference Center near San Jose, California in the heart of the coastal redwoods, we are a broad-ranging conference for all areas of Christian writing, including fiction, nonfiction, fantasy, children's, teen, young adult, poetry, magazines, inspirational and devotional writing. This is a working, how-to conference, with Major Morning tracks in all genres (including a track especially for teen writers), and as many as 20 optional workshops each afternoon. Faculty-to-student ratio is about 1 to 6. The bulk of our more than 70 faculty members are editors and publisher representatives from major Christian publishing houses nationwide. Speakers have included

T. Davis Bunn, Debbie Macomber, Jerry Jenkins, Bill Butterworth, Dick Foth and others.

COSTS Registration fees include tuition, all major morning sessions, keynote sessions, and refreshment breaks. Room and board varies depending on choice of housing options. Costs vary from $617 to $1,565 based on housing rates.

ACCOMMODATIONS Registrants stay in hotel-style accommodations. Meals are buffet style, with faculty joining registrants. See website for cost updates.

ADDITIONAL INFORMATION "The residential nature of our conference makes this a unique setting for one-on-one interaction with faculty/staff. There is also a decided inspirational flavor to the conference, and general sessions with well-known speakers are a highlight. Registrants may submit 2 works for critique in advance of the conference, then have personal interviews with critiquers during the conference. All conference information is online by December 1 of each year. Send inquiries via e-mail. Tapes of past conferences are also available online."

MUSE AND THE MARKETPLACE

Grub Street, 160 Boylston St., 4th Floor, Boston MA 02116. (617)695.0075. **E-mail:** info@grubstreet.org. **Website:** grubstreet.org/. The conferences are held in the late spring, such as early May. (2014 dates are May 2-4.) Conference duration: 3 days. Average attendance: 400. Dozens of agents are in attendance to meet writers and take pitches. Previous keynote speakers include Jonathan Franzen. The conferences has workshops on all aspects of writing.

COSTS Varies, depending on if you're a Member or Non-Member (includes 6 workshop sessions and 2 Hour of Power sessions with options for the Ms Mart and a Five-Star lunch with authors, editors and agents). Other passes are available for Saturday-only and Sunday-only guests.

NAPA VALLEY WRITERS' CONFERENCE

Napa Valley College, 1088 College Ave., St. Helena CA 94574. (707)967-2900, x1611. **E-mail:** writecon@napavalley.edu. **Website:** www.napawritersconference.org. **Contact:** John Leggett and Anne Evans, program directors. Estab. 1981. Established 1981. Annual weeklong event, 2014 dates: July 27 - Aug. 1. Location: Upper Valley Campus in the historic town of St. Helena, 25 miles north of Napa in the heart of the valley's wine growing community. Excellent cuisine provided by Napa Valley Cooking School. Average attendance:

48 in poetry and 48 in fiction. "Serious writers of all backgrounds and experience are welcome to apply." Offers poets workshops, lectures, faculty readings, ms critiques, and meetings with editors. "Poetry session provides the opportunity to work both on generating new poems and on revising previously written ones." **COSTS** Total participation fee is $900. More cost info (including financial assistance info) is online.

ADDITIONAL INFORMATION The conference is held at the Upper Valley Campus of Napa Valley College, located in the heart of California's Wine Country. During the conference week, attendees' meals are provided by the Napa Valley Cooking School, which offers high quality, intensive training for aspiring chefs. The goal of the program is to provide each student with hands-on, quality, culinary and pastry skills required for a career in a fine-dining establishment. The disciplined and professional learning environment, availability of global externships, low student teacher ratio and focus on sustainability make the Napa Valley Cooking School unique.

NASHVILLE SCREENWRITERS CONFERENCE

(615)254-2049. **E-mail:** info@nashscreen.com. **Website:** www.nashscreen.com/. 2014 dates: May 30 - June 1. The entire lineup of speakers and panelists is online. This is a three-day conference dedicated to those who write for the screen. Nashville is a city that celebrates its writers and its creative community, and every writer wants to have a choice of avenues to increase their potential for success. In this memorable weekend, conference participants will have the opportunity to attend various writing panels led by working professionals and participate in several special events.

NATCHEZ LITERARY AND CINEMA CELEBRATION

P.O. Box 1307, Natchez MS 39121-1307. (601)446-1208. **Fax:** (601)446-1214. **E-mail:** carolyn.smith@colin.edu. **Website:** www.colin.edu/nlcc. Estab. 1990. Annual conference held in February. Conference duration: 5 days. Conference focuses on all literature, including film scripts. Each year's conference deals with some general aspect of Southern history. Speakers have included Eudora Welty, Margaret Walker Alexander, William Styron, Willie Morris, Ellen Douglas, Ernest Gaines, Elizabeth Spencer, Nikki Giovanni, Myrlie Evers-Williams, and Maya Angelou.

NATIONAL WRITERS ASSOCIATION FOUNDATION CONFERENCE

10940 S. Parker Road, #508, Parker CO 80138. (303)841-0246. **E-mail:** natlwritersassn@hotmail.com. **Website:** www.nationalwriters.com. **Contact:** Sandy Whelchel, executive director. Estab. 1926. Annual conference held the second week of June in Denver. Conference duration: 1 day. Average attendance: 100. Focuses on general writing and marketing. **COSTS** Approximately $100.

ADDITIONAL INFORMATION Awards for previous contests will be presented at the conference. Brochures/guidelines are online, or send an SASE.

NETWO WRITERS CONFERENCE

Northeast Texas Writers Organization, P.O. Box 411, Winfield TX 75493. (469)867-2624 or Paul at (903)573-6084. **E-mail:** jimcallan@winnsboro.com. **Website:** www.netwo.org. Estab. 1987. Annual conference held in April. (2014 dates are April 25-26.) Conference duration: 2 days. Presenters include agents, writers, editors, and publishers. Agents in attendance will take pitches from writers. The conference features a writing contest, pitch sessions, critiques from professionals, as well as dozens of workshops and presentations. **COSTS** $60+ (discount offered for early registration).

ACCOMMODATIONS Online, we have posted information on lodging - motels and hotels. As the conference has moved to the Mount Pleasant Civic Center, we no longer have the "dorm accommodations" available in 2011 and before. The NETWO Writers Conference is at the Mount Pleasant Civic Center, in Mt. Pleasant, Texas. Located on U.S. Business 271 just one block south of Interstate 30, it is easily accessible from north, south, east and west. It offers excellent facilities: climate control, large rooms, excellent sound systems, ability to handle Power Point presentations, ample room for the on-site lunch which is part of the conference, improved restroom facilities, and private rooms for the one-on-one interviews with agents, editor and publisher. There is ample parking available. Several motels are within two blocks.

ADDITIONAL INFORMATION Conference is co-sponsored by the Texas Commission on the Arts. See website for current updates.

NEW JERSEY ROMANCE WRITERS PUT YOUR HEART IN A BOOK CONFERENCE

P.O. Box 513, Plainsboro NJ 08536. **E-mail:** dmcomfort@aol.com. **Website:** www.njromancewriters.org.

Estab. 1984. Annual conference held in October. Average attendance: 500. Workshops are offered on various topics for all writers of romance, from beginner to multi-published. Speakers have included Nora Roberts, Kathleen Woodiwiss, Patricia Gaffney, Jill Barnett and Kay Hooper. Appointments are offered with editors/agents.

ACCOMMODATIONS Special rate available for conference attendees at the Sheraton at Renaissance Woodbridge Hotel in Iselin, New Jersey.

ADDITIONAL INFORMATION Conference brochures, guidelines, and membership information are available for SASE. Massive book fair is open to the public with authors signing copies of their books.

THE NEW LETTERS WEEKEND WRITERS CONFERENCE

University of Missouri-Kansas City, 5101 Rockhill Road, Kansas City MO 64110-2499. (816)235-1168. **Fax:** (816)235-2611. **E-mail:** newletters@umkc.edu. **Website:** http://cas.umkc.edu/ce/. **Contact:** Robert Stewart, director. Estab. 1970s (as The Longboat Key Writers Conference). Annual conference held in late June. Conference duration: 3 days. Average attendance: 75. The conference brings together talented writers in many genres for seminars, readings, workshops, and individual conferences. The emphasis is on craft and the creative process in poetry, fiction, screenwriting, playwriting, and journalism, but the program also deals with matters of psychology, publications, and marketing. The conference is appropriate for both advanced and beginning writers. The conference meets at the university's beautiful Diastole Conference Center. Two- and 3-credit hour options are available by special permission from the director, Robert Stewart.

COSTS Participants may choose to attend as a noncredit student or they may attend for 1 hour of college credit from the University of Missouri-Kansas City. Conference registration includes Friday evening reception and keynote speaker, Saturday and Sunday continental breakfast and lunch.

ACCOMMODATIONS Registrants are responsible for their own transportation, but information on area accommodations is available.

ADDITIONAL INFORMATION Those registering for college credit are required to submit a ms in advance. Ms reading and critique are included in the credit fee. Those attending the conference for noncredit also have the option of having their ms critiqued for an additional fee. Brochures are available for a SASE after March. Accepts inquiries by e-mail and fax.

NIMROD ANNUAL WRITERS' WORKSHOP

800 S. Tucker Dr., Tulsa OK 74104. (918)631-3080. **E-mail:** nimrod@utulsa.edu. **Website:** www.utulsa.edu/nimrod. **Contact:** Eilis O'Neal, editor-in-chief. Estab. 1978. Annual conference held in October. Conference duration: 1 day. Offers one-on-one editing sessions, readings, panel discussions, and master classes in fiction, poetry, nonfiction, memoir, and fantasy writing. Speakers have included Ted Kooser, Colum McCann, Molly Peacock, Peter S. Beagle, Aimee Nezhukumatathil, Philip Levine, and Linda Pastan. Full conference details are online in August.

COSTS Approximately $50. Lunch provided. Scholarships available for students.

ADDITIONAL INFORMATION *Nimrod International Journal* sponsors *Nimrod* Literary Awards: The Katherine Anne Porter Prize for fiction and The Pablo Neruda Prize for poetry. Poetry and fiction prizes: $2,000 each and publication (1st prize); $1,000 each and publication (2nd prize). Deadline: must be postmarked no later than April 30.

NORTH CAROLINA WRITERS' NETWORK FALL CONFERENCE

P.O. Box 21591, Winston-Salem NC 27120. (336)293-8844. **E-mail:** mail@ncwriters.org. **Website:** www.ncwriters.org. Estab. 1985. Annual conference held in November in different NC venues. Average attendance: 250. This organization hosts 2 conferences: 1 in the spring and 1 in the fall. Each conference is a weekend full of workshops, panels, book signings, and readings (including open mic). There will be a keynote speaker, a variety of sessions on the craft and business of writing, and opportunities to meet with agents and editors.

COSTS Approximately $250 (includes 4 meals).

ACCOMMODATIONS Special rates are usually available at the Conference Hotel, but conferees must make their own reservations.

ADDITIONAL INFORMATION Available at www.ncwriters.org.

NORTHERN COLORADO WRITERS CONFERENCE

108 East Monroe Dr., Fort Collins CO 80525. (970)556-0908. **E-mail:** kerrie@northerncoloradowriters.com. **Website:** www.northerncoloradowriters.com. Estab. 2006. Annual conference held in the

spring (usually March or April) in Colorado. Conference duration: 2-3 days. The conference features a variety of speakers, agents and editors. There are workshops and presentations on fiction, nonfiction, screenwriting, children's books, staying inspired, and more. Previous agents who have attended and taken pitches from writers include Jessica Regel, Kristen Nelson, Rachelle Gardner, Andrea Brown, Ken Sherman Jessica Faust, Jon Sternfeld, and Jeffrey McGraw. Each conference features more than 30 workshops from which to choose from. Previous keynotes include Chuck Sambuchino. Andrew McCarthy and Stephen J. Cannell.

COSTS $295-445, depending on what package the attendee selects, and whether you're a member or nonmember.

ACCOMMODATIONS The conference is hosted at the Fort Collins Hilton, where rooms are available at a special rate.

ODYSSEY FANTASY WRITING WORKSHOP

P.O. Box 75, Mont Vernon NH 03057. **E-mail:** jcavelos@sff.net. **Website:** www.odysseyworkshop.org. Saint Anselm College 100 Saint Anselm Drive, Manchester, New Hampshire, 03102. Estab. 1996. Annual workshop held in June (through July). Conference duration: 6 weeks. Average attendance: 15. A workshop for fantasy, science fiction, and horror writers that combines an intensive learning and writing experience with in-depth feedback on students' mss. Held on the campus of Saint Anselm College in Manchester, New Hampshire. Speakers have included George R.R. Martin, Elizabeth Hand, Jane Yolen, Harlan Ellison, Melissa Scott and Dan Simmons.

COSTS In 2014: $1,965 tuition, $812 housing (double room), $1,624 (single room); $35 application fee, $450-600 food (approximate), $550 processing fee to receive college credit.

ADDITIONAL INFORMATION Students must apply and include a writing sample. Application deadline April 8. Students' works are critiqued throughout the 6 weeks. Workshop information available in October. For brochure/guidelines, send SASE, e-mail, visit website, or call. Accepts inquiries by SASE, e-mail, phone.

OKLAHOMA WRITERS' FEDERATION, INC. ANNUAL CONFERENCE

3800 Bonaire Place, Edmond OK 73013. **Website:** www.owfi.org. **Contact:** Christine Jarmola, president. Annual conference held just outside Oklahoma City. Held first weekend in May each year. Writer workshops geared toward all levels. Oklahoma Writers Federation, Inc. is open and welcoming to writers of all genres and all skill levels. Our goal is to help writers become better and to help beginning writers understand and master the craft of writing.Editorial Comments The theme of our conference is to create good stories with strong bones. We will be exploring cultural writing and cultural sensitivity in writing. This year we will also be looking at the cutting edge of publishing and the options it is producing.

COSTS $175 before April; $200 after April. Cost includes awards banquet and famous author banquet. Three extra sessions are available for an extra fee. Visit our website for a complete faculty list and conference information.

OREGON CHRISTIAN WRITERS SUMMER CONFERENCE

Red Lion Hotel on the River, 909 N. Hayden Island Dr., Portland OR 97217-8118. **E-mail:** summerconf@oregonchristianwriters.org. **Website:** www.oregonchristianwriters.org. **Contact:** Lindy Jacobs, OCW Summer Conference Director. Estab. 1989. Held annually in August at the Red Lion Hotel on the River, a full-service hotel. Conference duration: 4 days. 2015 dates: August 10-13. Average attendance: 225 (175 writers, 50 faculty). Top national editors, agents, and authors in the field of Christian publishing teach 12 intensive coaching classes and 30 workshops plus critique sessions. Published authors as well as emerging writers have opportunities to improve their craft, get feedback through ms reviews, meet one-on-one with editors and agents, and have half-hour mentoring appointments with published authors. Classes include fiction, nonfiction, memoir, young adult, poetry, magazine articles, devotional writing, children's books, and marketing. Daily general sessions include worship and an inspirational keynote address. Each year contacts made during the OCW summer conference lead to publishing contracts. 2014 conference theme will be "Writing with God: Take Heart," based on Psalm 27:14. 2014 Keynote speakers: Allen Arnold and Dan Walsh. Agents: Chip MacGregor, Mary Sue Seymour, Sue Brower, Bill Jensen, and Sandra Bishop. Other speakers/teachers: Susan May Warren, James Rubart, Randy Ingermanson, Jeff Gerke, Mary DeMuth, Jill Williamson, Leslie Gould, Susan Meissner, Joanna Echols, and Susan King. Past speakers have included: Liz Curtis Higgs, Francine Rivers, Bill Myers, Jeff Gerke, Angella Hunt, James L. Rubart, Susan May Warren, and James Scott Bell.

COSTS $475 for OCW members, $495 for nonmembers. Registration fee includes all classes, workshops, and 2 lunches and 3 dinners. Lodging additional. Full-time registered conferees may also pre-submit three proposals for review by an editor through the conference, plus sign up for a half-hour mentoring appointment with an author.

ACCOMMODATIONS Conference is held at the Red Lion on the River Hotel. Conferees wishing to stay at the hotel must make a reservation through the hotel. Some conferees commute. A block of rooms has been reserved at the hotel at a special rate for conferees and held until mid-July. The hotel reservation link will be posted on the website in late spring. Shuttle bus transportation will be provided by the hotel for conferees from Portland Airport (PDX) to the hotel, which is 20 minutes away.

ADDITIONAL INFORMATION Conference details will be posted online beginning in January. All conferees are welcome to attend the Cascade Awards ceremony, which takes place Wednesday evening during the conference. For more information about the Cascade Writing Contest, please check the website.

OUTDOOR WRITERS ASSOCIATION OF AMERICA ANNUAL CONFERENCE

615 Oak St., Suite 201, Missoula MT 59801. (406)728-7434. **E-mail:** info@owaa.org. **Website:** http://owaa.org. **Contact:** Jessica Pollett, conference and membership coordinator. Outdoor communicator workshops geared toward all levels. Annual three-day conference. Craft improvement seminars; newsmaker sessions. 2014 conference to be held in McAllen, TX. Cost of workshop: $425-449; includes attendance at all workshops and most meals. Visit owaa.org/2014conference for additional information.

OZARK CREATIVE WRITERS, INC. CONFERENCE

P.O. Box 424, Eureka Springs AR 72632. **E-mail:** ozarkcreativewriters@gmail.com. **Website:** www.ozarkcreativewriters.org. Open to professional and amateur writers, workshops are geared to all levels and all forms of the creative process and literary arts. Sessions sometimes include songwriting, with presentations by best-selling authors, editors, and agents. The OCW Conference promotes writing by offering competition in all genres. The annual event is held in October at the Inn of the Ozarks, in the resort town of Eureka Springs, Arkansas. Approximately 200 attend each year; many also enter the creative writing competitions.

PACIFIC COAST CHILDREN'S WRITERS WHOLE-NOVEL WORKSHOP: FOR ADULTS AND TEENS

P.O. Box 244, Aptos CA 95001. (831)684-2042. **Website:** www.childrenswritersworkshop.com. Estab. 2003. 2014 dates: Oct. 17-19. "Our seminar offers semi-advanced through published adult writers an editor and/or agent critique on their full novel or 15-30 page partial. (Mid-book and synopsis critique may be included with the partial.) A concurrent workshop is open to students age 13 and up, who give adults target-reader feedback. Focus on craft as a marketing tool. Team-taught master classes (open clinics for ms critiques) explore such topics as "Story Architecture and Arcs." Continuous close contact with faculty, who have included Andrea Brown, agent, and Simon Boughton, VP/executive editor at 3 Macmillan imprints. **Past seminars:** Oct. 10-12, 2013. Registration limited to 16 adults and 10 teens. For the most critique options, submit sample chapters and synopsis with e-application by mid May; open until filled. **Content:** Character-driven novels with protagonists ages 11 and older. Collegial format; 90 percent hands-on. Our pre-workshop anthology of peer mss maximizes learning and networking. Several enrollees have landed contracts as a direct result of our seminar. **Details:** visit our website and e-mail Director Nancy Sondel via the contact form."

PACIFIC NORTHWEST WRITER ASSN. SUMMER WRITER'S CONFERENCE

PMB 2717, 1420 NW Gilman Blvd., Ste. 2, Issaquah WA 98027. (425)673-2665. **E-mail:** pnwa@pnwa.org. **Website:** www.pnwa.org. Writer conference geared toward beginner, intermediate, advanced and professional levels. Meet agents and editors. Learn craft from renowned authors. Uncover new marketing secrets. PNWA's 59th Annual Conference will be held July 17-20, 2014, at the Hilton Seattle Airport & Conference Center, at the Hyatt Regency, Bellevue, WA 98004. This event usually has 10-20 literary agents in attendance taking pitches from writers.

PENNWRITERS CONFERENCE

RR #2, Box 241, Middlebury Center PA 16935. **Website:** www.pennwriters.org/prod/. Estab. 1987. The

Mission of Pennwriters Inc. is to help writers of all levels, from the novice to the award-winning and multi-published, improve and succeed in their craft. The annual Pennwriters conference is held every year in May in Pennsylvania, switching between locations—Lancaster in even years and Pittsburgh in odd years. 2014 event: May 16-18 at Eden Resort in Lancaster.

ACCOMMODATIONS See website for current information.

ADDITIONAL INFORMATION Sponsors contest. Published authors judge fiction in various categories. Agent/editor appointments are available on a first-come, first serve basis.

PHILADELPHIA WRITERS' CONFERENCE

P.O. Box 7171, Elkins Park PA 19027-0171. (215) 619-7422. **E-mail:** info@pwcwriters.org. **E-mail:** info@pwcwriters.org. **Website:** pwcwriters.org. Estab. 1949. Annual. Conference held in June. Average attendance: 160-200. Conference covers many forms of writing: novel, short story, genre fiction, nonfiction book, magazine writing, blogging, juvenile, poetry.

ACCOMMODATIONS Wyndham Hotel (formerly the Holiday Inn), Independence Mall, Fourth and Arch Streets, Philadelphia, PA 19106-2170. "Hotel offers discount for early registration."

ADDITIONAL INFORMATION Accepts inquiries by e-mail. Agents and editors attend conference. Visit us on the web for further agent and speaker details. Many questions are answered online.

PHOTOGRAPHERS' FORMULARY

P.O. Box 950, 7079 Hwy 83 N, Condon MT 59826-0950. (800)922-5255. **Fax:** (406)754-2896. **E-mail:** lynnw@blackfoot.net; formulary@blackfoot.net. **Website:** www.photoformulary.com; www.workshopsinmt.com. **Contact:** Lynn Wilson, workshop program director. Photographers' Formulary workshops include a wide variety of alternative processes, and many focus on the traditional darkroom. Located in Montana's Swan Valley, some of the best wilderness lands in the Rocky Mountains. See website for details on costs and lodging. Open to all skill levels. Workshops held frequently throughout the year. See website for listing of dates and registration.

PIKES PEAK WRITERS CONFERENCE

Pikes Peak Writers, PO Box 64273, Colorado Springs CO 80962. (719)244-6220. **E-mail:** info@pikespeakwriters.com. **Website:** www.pikespeakwriters.com.

Estab. 1993. Annual conference held in April Conference duration: 3 days. Average attendance: 300. Workshops, presentations, and panels focus on writing and publishing mainstream and genre fiction (romance, science fiction/fantasy, suspense/thrillers, action/adventure, mysteries, children's, young adult). Agents and editors are available for meetings with attendees on Saturday.

COSTS $300-500 (includes all meals).

ACCOMMODATIONS Marriott Colorado Springs holds a block of rooms at a special rate for attendees until late March.

ADDITIONAL INFORMATION Readings with critiques are available on Friday afternoon. Also offers a contest for unpublished mss; entrants need not attend the conference. Deadline: November 1. Registration and contest entry forms are online; brochures are available in January. Send inquiries via e-mail.

PIMA WRITERS' WORKSHOP

Pima College, 2202 W. Anklam Road, Tucson AZ 85709. (520)206-6084. **Fax:** (520)206-6020. **E-mail:** mfiles@pima.edu. **Contact:** Meg Files, director. Writer conference geared toward beginner, intermediate and advanced levels. **Open to students.** The conference features presentations and writing exercises on writing and publishing stories for children and young adults, among other genres. Annual conference. Workshop held in May. Cost: $100 (can include ms critique). Participants may attend for college credit. Meals and accommodations not included. Features a dozen authors, editors, and agents talking about writing and publishing fiction, nonfiction, poetry, and stories for children. Write for more information.

POETRY WEEKEND INTENSIVES

40 Post Ave., Hawthorne NJ 07506. (973)423-2921. **Fax:** (973)523-6085. **E-mail:** mariagillan@verizon.net. **Website:** www.mariagillan.com; www.mariagillan.blogspot.com. **Contact:** Maria Mazziotti Gillan, executive director. Estab. 1997. Usually held 2 times/year in June and December. Average attendance: 26.

COSTS $425, including meals. Offers a $25 early bird discount. Housing in on-site facilities included in the $425 price.

ACCOMMODATIONS Location: generally at St. Marguerite's Retreat House, Mendham, NJ; also several other convents and monasteries.

ADDITIONAL INFORMATION Individual poetry critiques available. Poets should bring poems to weekend. Registration form available for SASE or by fax or e-mail. Maria Mazziotti Gillan is the director of the Creative Writing Program of Binghamton University-State University of New York, exec. director of the Poetry Center at Passaic County Community College, and edits Paterson Literary Review. Laura Boss is the editor of *Lips* magazine. Fifteen professional development credits are available for each weekend.

ROCKY MOUNTAIN FICTION WRITERS COLORADO GOLD

Rocky Mountain Fiction Writers, P.O. Box 735, Confier CO 80433. **E-mail:** conference@rmfw.org. **Website:** www.rmfw.org. Estab. 1982. Annual conference held in September. Conference duration: 3 days. Average attendance: 350. Themes include general novel-length fiction, genre fiction, contemporary romance, mystery, science fiction/fantasy, mainstream, young adult, screenwriting, short stories, and historical fiction. Speakers have included Margaret George, Jodi Thomas, Bernard Cornwell, Terry Brooks, Dorothy Cannell, Patricia Gardner Evans, Diane Mott Davidson, Constance O'Day, Connie Willis, Clarissa Pinkola Estes, Michael Palmer, Jennifer Unter, Margaret Marr, Ashley Krass, and Andren Barzvi. Approximately 8 editors and 5 agents attend annually. **COSTS** Available online.

ACCOMMODATIONS Special rates will be available at conference hotel.

ADDITIONAL INFORMATION Editor-conducted workshops are limited to 8 participants for critique, with auditing available. Pitch appointments available at no charge. Friday morning master classes available. Craft workshops include beginner through professional levels. New as of 2013: Writers' retreat available immediately following conference; space is limited.

ROMANCE WRITERS OF AMERICA NATIONAL CONFERENCE

14615 Benfer Road, Houston TX 77069. (832)717-5200. **Fax:** (832)717-5201. **E-mail:** info@rwa.org. **Website:** www.rwa.org/conference. Estab. 1981. Annual conference held in July. (2014 conference: July 23-26 in San Antonio.) Average attendance: 2,000. More than 100 workshops on writing, researching, and the business side of being a working writer. Publishing professionals attend and accept appointments. The keynote speaker is a renowned romance writer. "Romance Writers of America (RWA) is a nonprofit trade association, with a membership of more than 10,000

romance writers and related industry professionals, whose mission is to advance the professional interests of career-focused romance writers through networking and advocacy."

COSTS $385-610 depending on your membership status as well as when you register.

ADDITIONAL INFORMATION Annual RTA awards are presented for romance authors. Annual Golden Heart awards are presented for unpublished writers. Numerous literary agents are in attendance to meet with writers and hear book pitches.

RT BOOKLOVERS CONVENTION

55 Bergen St., Brooklyn NY 11201. (718)237-1097 or (800)989-8816, ext. 12. **Fax:** (718)624-2526. **E-mail:** jocarol@rtconvention.com. **E-mail:** nancy@rt-bookreviews.com. **Website:** rtconvention.com. Annual conference held May 13-18. 2014 Convention will be in New Orleans a the Marriott Center on Canal Street. Features 125 workshops, agent and editor appointments, a book fair, and more.

COSTS See website for pricing and other information.

ACCOMMODATIONS Rooms available nearby.

SALT CAY WRITERS RETREAT

Salt Cay Bahamas. (732)267-6449. **E-mail:** admin@saltcaywritersretreat.com. **Website:** www.saltcaywritersretreat.com. **Contact:** Karen Dionne and Christopher Graham. 5-day retreat held in the Bahamas in October. "The Salt Cay Writers Retreat is particularly suited for novelists (especially those writing literary, upmarket commercial fiction, or genre novelists wanting to write a break-out book), memoirists and narrative nonfiction writers. However, any author (published or not-yet-published) who wishes to take their writing to the next level is welcome to apply." Speakers have included or will include Editors Chuck Adams (Algonquin Books), Amy Einhorn (Amy Einhorn Books); Agents Jeff Kleinman, Michelle Brower, Erin Niumata, Erin Harris (Folio Literary Management); authors Robert Goolrick, Jacquelyn Mitchard.

COSTS $2,450 through May 1; $2,950 after.

ACCOMMODATIONS Comfort Suites, Paradise Island, Nassau, Bahamas.

SAN DIEGO STATE UNIVERSITY WRITERS' CONFERENCE

SDSU College of Extended Studies, 5250 Campanile Dr., San Diego State University, San Diego CA 92182-1920. (619)594-2517. **Fax:** (619)594-8566. **E-mail:** sdsuwritersconference@mail.sdsu.edu. **Website:** ces.

sdsu.edu/writers. Estab. 1984. Annual conference held in January/February. Conference duration: 2.5 days. Average attendance: 350. Covers fiction, nonfiction, scriptwriting and e-books. Held at the Doubletree Hotel in Mission Valley. Each year the conference offers a variety of workshops for the beginner and advanced writers. This conference allows the individual writer to choose which workshop best suits his/her needs. In addition to the workshops, editor reading appointments and agent/editor consultation appointments are provided so attendees may meet with editors and agents one-on-one to discuss specific questions. A reception is offered Saturday immediately following the workshops, offering attendees the opportunity to socialize with the faculty in a relaxed atmosphere. Last year, approximately 60 faculty members attended.

COSTS Approximately $399-435.

ACCOMMODATIONS Attendees must make their own travel arrangements. A conference rate for attendees is available at the Doubletree Hotel.

SAN FRANCISCO WRITERS CONFERENCE

1029 Jones St., San Francisco CA 94109. (415)673-0939. **Fax:** (415)673-0367. **E-mail:** Barbara@sfwriters.org. **Website:** sfwriters.org. **Contact:** Barbara Santos, marketing director. Estab. 2003. "Annual conference held President's Day weekend in February. Average attendance: 400+. Top authors, respected literary agents, and major publishing houses are at the event so attendees can make face-to-face contact with all the right people. Writers of nonfiction, fiction, poetry, and specialty writing (children's books, cookbooks, travel, etc.) will all benefit from the event. There are important sessions on marketing, self-publishing, technology, and trends in the publishing industry. Plus, there's an optional 4-hour session called Speed Dating for Agents where attendees can meet with 20+ agents. Speakers have included Jennifer Crusie, Richard Paul Evans, Jamie Raab, Mary Roach, Jane Smiley, Debbie Macomber, Firoozeh Dumas, Zilpha Keatley Snyder, Steve Berry, Jacquelyn Mitchard. More than 20 agents and editors participate each year, many of whom will be available for meetings with attendees."

COSTS Check the website for pricing on later dates. 2014 pricing was $650-795 depending on when you signed up and early bird registration, etc.

ACCOMMODATIONS The Intercontinental Mark Hopkins Hotel is a historic landmark at the top of Nob Hill in San Francisco. The hotel is located so that everyone arriving at the Oakland or San Francisco airport can take BART to either the Embarcadero or Powell Street exits, then walk or take a cable car or taxi directly to the hotel.

ADDITIONAL INFORMATION "Present yourself in a professional manner and the contact you will make will be invaluable to your writing career. Brochures and registration are online."

SAN FRANCISCO WRITING FOR CHANGE CONFERENCE

1029 Jones St., San Francisco CA 94109. (415)673-0939. **E-mail:** Barbara@sfwriters.org. **Website:** SFWritingforChange.org. **Contact:** Barbara Santos, marketing director; Michael Larsen, co-director. Estab. 2004. Annual conference to be held September 6, 2014 at Unitarian Universalist Center in San Francisco. Average attendance: 100. Early discounts available. Includes panels, workshops, keynote address, editor, and agent consultations.

COSTS Costs to be announced. Please visit the website.

ACCOMMODATIONS Check website for event details, accommodations, directions, and parking.

ADDITIONAL INFORMATION "The limited number of attendees (150 or fewer) and excellent presenter-to-attendee ratio make this a highly effective and productive conference. The presenters are major names in the publishing business, but take personal interest in the projects discovered at this event each year." Guidelines available on website [sfwritingforchange.org].

SANTA BARBARA WRITERS CONFERENCE

27 W. Anapamu St., Suite 305, Santa Barbara CA 93101. (805)568-1516. **E-mail:** info@sbwriters.com. **Website:** www.sbwriters.com. Estab. 1972. Annual conference held June 8-13. Average attendance: 200. Covers fiction, nonfiction, journalism, memoir, poetry, playwriting, screenwriting, travel writing, young adult, children's literature, humor, and marketing. Speakers have included Ray Bradbury, William Styron, Eudora Welty, James Michener, Sue Grafton, Charles M. Schulz, Clive Cussler, Fannie Flagg, Elmore Leonard, and T.C. Boyle. Agents will appear on a panel; in addition, there will be an agents and editors day that allows writers to pitch their projects in one-on-one meetings.

COSTS Conference registration is $550 on or before March 16 and $625 after March 16.

ACCOMMODATIONS Hyatt Santa Barbara.

ADDITIONAL INFORMATION Register online or contact for brochure and registration forms.

SASKATCHEWAN FESTIVAL OF WORDS

217 Main St. N., Moose Jaw SK S6J 0W1 Canada. **Website:** www.festivalofwords.com. Estab. 1997. Annual 4-day event, third week of July (2014 dates: July 17-20). Location: Moose Jaw Library/Art Museum complex in Crescent Park. Average attendance: about 4,000 admissions. "Canadian authors up close and personal for readers and writers of all ages in mystery, poetry, memoir, fantasy, graphic novels, history, and novel. Each summer festival includes more than 60 events within 2 blocks of historic Main Street. Audience favorite activities include workshops for writers, audience readings, drama,performance poetry, concerts, panels, and music."

ACCOMMODATIONS Information available at www.templegardens.sk.ca, campgrounds, and bed and breakfast establishments. Complete information about festival presenters, events, costs, and schedule also available on website.

SCBWI—CANADA EAST

Canada. **E-mail:** canadaeast@scbwi.org. **Website:** www.canadaeast.scbwi.org. **Contact:** Lizann Flatt, regional advisor. Writer and illustrator events geared toward all levels. Usually offers one event in spring and another in the fall. Check website Events pages for updated information.

SCBWI COLORADO/WYOMING (ROCKY MOUNTAIN); EVENTS

E-mail: denise@rmcscbwi.org; todd.tuell@rmc-scbwi.org. **Website:** www.rmc.scbwi.org. **Contact:** Todd Tuell and Denise Vega, co-regional advisors. SCBWI Rocky Mountain chapter (CO/WY) offers special events, schmoozes, meetings, and conferences throughout the year. Major events: Fall Conference (annually, September); Summer Retreat, "Big Sur in the Rockies" (bi- and triannually). More info on website.

SCBWI EASTERN NEW YORK FALLING LEAVES MASTER CLASS RETREAT

Silver Bay NY **E-mail:** ntcastaldo@taconic.net. **Website:** http://easternny.scbwi.org; http://scbwi-easternny.org. **Contact:** Nancy Castaldo, regional advisor. One of 2 annual events hosted by the SCBWI Eastern New York (along with the Mid-Hudson Valley Conference in Poughkeepsie), this retreat is held in Silver Bay on Lake George in the late fall. Holds ms and portfolio critiques, Q&A and speaker sessions, intensives, and more, with respected authors, editors, literary agents, and publishers.

SCBWI—MIDATLANTIC; ANNUAL FALL CONFERENCE

P.O. Box 3215, Reston VA 20195. **E-mail:** teaganek@hotmail.com; valopttrsn@verizon.net. **Website:** midatlantic.scbwi.org/. **Contact:** Erin Teagan and Valerie Patterson, conference co-chairs; Ellen R. Braff, advisor. For updates and details visit website. Registration limited to 275. Conference fills quickly. Cost: $145 for SCBWI members; $175 for nonmembers. Includes continental breakfast and boxed lunch. Optional craft-focused workshops and individual consultations with conference faculty are available for additional fees.

SCBWI NEW ENGLAND WHISPERING PINES WRITER'S RETREAT

West Greenwich RI **E-mail:** lyndamullalyhunt@yahoo.com; momeraths@verizon.net. **Website:** http://lyndamullalyhunt.com. **Contact:** Lynda Mullaly Hunt, co-director; Mary Pierce, co-director. Three day/overnight retreat that offers the opportunity to work intimately with professionals in an idyllic setting. Attendees will work with others who are committed to quality children's literature in small groups and will benefit from a 30 minute one-on-one critique with a mentor. Also includes mentors' presentations and an intimate after dinner Q&A session, Team Kid Lit Jeopardy with prizes, and more. Retreat limited to 32 full time participants. Held annually in late March.

SCBWI—VENTURA/SANTA BARBARA; FALL CONFERENCE

Simi Valley CA 93094-1389. **E-mail:** maryafraser@gmail.com. **Website:** http://cencal.scbwi.org. **Contact:** Mary Ann Fraser, regional advisor. Estab. 1971. Writers' conference geared toward all levels. Speakers include editors, authors, illustrators and agents. Fiction and nonfiction picture books, middle grade and YA novels, and magazine submissions addressed. Annual writing contest in all genres plus illustration display. Conference held in October. For fees and other information, e-mail or visit website.

SCBWI WINTER CONFERENCE ON WRITING AND ILLUSTRATING FOR CHILDREN

8271 Beverly Blvd., Los Angeles CA 90048. (323)782-1010. **Fax:** (323)782-1892. **E-mail:** scbwi@scbwi.org. **Website:** www.scbwi.org. **Contact:** Stephen Mooser. Estab. 2000. (formerly SCBWI Midyear Conference), Society of Children's book Writers and Illustrators. Annual. Conference held in February. Average attendance: 1,000. Conference is to promote writing and illustrating for children: picture books; fiction; nonfiction; middle grade and young adult; network with professionals; financial planning for writers; marketing your book; art exhibition; etc. Site: Manhattan.

COSTS See website for current cost and conference information.

ADDITIONAL INFORMATION SCBWI also holds an annual summer conference in August in Los Angeles. See the listing in the West section or visit website for details.

THE SCHOOL FOR WRITERS FALL WORKSHOP

The Humber School for Writers, Humber Institute of Technology & Advanced Learning, 3199 Lake Shore Blvd. W., Toronto ON M8V 1K8 Canada. (416)675-6622. **E-mail:** antanas.sileika@humber.ca; hilary.higgins@humber.ca. **Website:** www.humber.ca/scapa/programs/school-writers. The School for Writers Workshop has moved to the fall with the International Festival of Authors. The workshop runs during the last week in October. Conference duration: 1 week. Average attendance: 60. New writers from around the world gather to study with faculty members to work on their novels, short stories, poetry, or creative nonfiction. Agents and editors participate in the conference. Include a work-in-progress with your registration. Faculty has included Martin Amis, David Mitchell, Kevin Barry, Rachel Kuschner, Peter Carey, Roddy Doyle, Tim O'Brien, Andrea Levy, Barry Unsworth, Edward Albee, Ha Jin, Julia Glass, Mavis Gallant, Bruce Jay Friedman, Isabel Huggan, Alistair MacLeod, Lisa Moore, Kim Moritsugu, Francine Prose, Paul Quarrington, Olive Senior, and D.M. Thomas, Annabel Lyon, Mary Gaitskill, M. G. Vassanji.

COSTS around $850 (in 2014). Some limited scholarships are available.

ADDITIONAL INFORMATION Accepts inquiries by e-mail, phone, and fax.

SCHOOL OF THE ARTS AT RHINELANDER UW-MADISON CONTINUING STUDIES

21 N Park St., 7th Floor, Madison WI 53715-1218. (608)262-7389. **E-mail:** lkaufman@dcs.wisc.edu. **Website:** continuingstudies.wisc.edu/lsa/soa/. Estab. 1964. "Each summer for 50 years, more than 250 people gather in northern Wisconsin for a week of study, performance, exhibits, and other creative activities. More than 50 workshops in writing, body/mind/spirit; food and fitness; art and folk art; music; and digital media are offered. Participants can choose from any and all 1-, 2-, 3- and 5-day classes to craft their own mix for creative exploration and renewal." Dates: July 19-23, 2014e. Location: James Williams Middle School and Rhinelander High School, Rhinelander, WI. Average attendance: 250.

COSTS Ranges from $20-$300 based on workshops.

ACCOMMODATIONS Informational available from Rhinelander Chamber of Commerce.

SEWANEE WRITERS' CONFERENCE

735 University Ave., 119 Gailor Hall, Stamler Center, Sewanee TN 37383-1000. (931) 598-1654. **E-mail:** allatham@sewanee.edu. **Website:** www.sewaneewriters.org. **Contact:** Adam Latham. Estab. 1990. Annual conference. 2014 dates: July 22 - Aug. 3. Average attendance: 150. "The University of the South will host the 25th session of the Sewanee Writers' Conference. Thanks to the generosity of the Walter E. Dakin Memorial Fund, supported by the estate of the late Tennessee Williams, the Conference will gather a distinguished faculty to provide instruction and criticism through workshops and craft lectures in poetry, fiction, and playwriting. During an intense twelve-day period, participants will read and critique each other's mss under the leadership of some of our country's finest fiction writers, poets, and playwrights. All faculty members and fellows give scheduled readings; senior faculty members offer craft lectures; open-mic readings accommodate many others. Additional writers, along with a host of writing professionals, visit to give readings, participate in panel discussions, and entertain questions from the audience. Receptions and mealtimes offer opportunities for informal exchange. This year's faculty includes fiction writers John Casey, Tony Earley, Adrianne Harun, Randall Kenan, Margot Livesey, Jill McCorkle, Alice McDermott, Christine Schutt, Allen Wier, and Steve Yarbrough; and poets Claudia Emerson, B.H. Fairchild,

Debora Greger, William Logan, Maurice Manning, Charles Martin, Mary Jo Salter, and A.E. Stallings. Daisy Foote and Dan O'Brien will lead the playwriting workshop. Diane Johnson and Wyatt Prunty will read from their work. The Conference will offer its customary Walter E. Dakin Fellowships and Tennessee Williams Scholarships, as well as awards in memory of Stanley Elkin, Horton Foote, Barry Hannah, John Hollander, Donald Justice, Romulus Linney, Howard Nemerov, Father William Ralston, Peter Taylor, Mona Van Duyn, and John N. Wall. Additional scholarships have been made possible by Georges and Anne Borchardt and Gail Hochman. Every participant – whether contributor, scholar, or fellow – receives assistance. The Conference fee reflects but two-thirds of the actual cost to attend. Additional funding is awarded to fellows and scholars."

COSTS $1,000 for tuition and $800 for room, board, and activity costs.

ACCOMMODATIONS Participants are housed in single rooms in university dormitories. Bathrooms are shared by small groups.

SOCIETY OF CHILDREN'S BOOK WRITERS & ILLUSTRATORS ANNUAL SUMMER CONFERENCE ON WRITING AND ILLUSTRATING FOR CHILDREN

8271 Beverly Blvd., Los Angeles CA 90048-4515. (323)782-1010. **Fax:** (323)782-1892. **E-mail:** scbwi@scbwi.org. **Website:** www.scbwi.org. Estab. 1972. Annual conference held in early August. Conference duration: 4 days. Average attendance: 1,000. Held at the Century Plaza Hotel in Los Angeles. Speakers have included Andrea Brown, Steven Malk, Ashley Bryan, Bruce Coville, Karen Hesse, Harry Mazer, Lucia Monfried, and Russell Freedman. Agents will be speaking and sometimes participate in ms critiques.

COSTS Approximately $450 (does not include hotel room).

ACCOMMODATIONS Information on overnight accommodations is made available.

ADDITIONAL INFORMATION Ms and illustration critiques are available. Brochure/guidelines are available in June online or for SASE.

THE SOUTHAMPTON WRITERS CONFERENCE

239 Montauk Highway, Southampton NY 11968. **Website:** www.stonybrook.edu/writers. Estab. 1975.

COSTS Application fee: $25; tuition, room and board: $2,445; tuition only: $1,775 (includes breakfast and lunch).

ACCOMMODATIONS On-campus housing-doubles and small singles additional cost for singles with shared baths-is modest but comfortable. Housing assignment is by lottery. Supplies list of lodging alternatives.

ADDITIONAL INFORMATION Applicants must complete an application form and submit a writing sample of unpublished, original work up to 20 pages (15 pages for poetry). See website for details. Brochures available in January by fax, phone, e-mail and on website. Accepts inquiries by SASE, e-mail, phone and fax.

SOUTH CAROLINA WRITERS WORKSHOP

4840 Forest Drive, Suite 6B: PMB 189, Columbia SC 29206. **E-mail:** scwwliaison@gmail.com; scww2013@gmail.com. **Website:** www.myscww.org/. Estab. 1991. Conference in October held at the Hilton Myrtle Beach Resort in Myrtle Beach, SC. Held almost every year. (2014 dates: Oct. 24-26.) Conference duration: 3 days. The conference features critique sessions, open mic readings, presentations from agents and editors and more. The conference features more than 50 different workshops for writers to choose from, dealing with all subjects of writing craft, writing business, getting an agent and more. Agents will be in attendance.

ACCOMMODATIONS Hilton Myrtle Beach Resort.

SOUTH COAST WRITERS CONFERENCE

Southwestern Oregon Community College, P.O. Box 590, 29392 Ellensburg Ave., Gold Beach OR 97444. (541)247-2741. **Fax:** (541)247-6247. **E-mail:** scwc@socc.edu. **Website:** www.socc.edu/scwriters. Estab. 1996. Annual conference held Presidents Day weekend in February. Conference duration: 2 days. Covers fiction, poetry, children's, nature, songwriting, and marketing. Melissa Hart is the next scheduled keynote speaker, and presenters include Robert Arellano, Bill Cameron, Tanya Chernov, Heidi Connolly, Kelly Davio, Tawna Fenske, Kim Cooper Findling, Stefanie Freele, and songwriter Chuck Pyle.

ADDITIONAL INFORMATION See website for cost and additional details.

SOUTHEASTERN WRITERS ASSOCIATION—ANNUAL WRITERS WORKSHOP

161 Woodstone, Athens GA 30605. **E-mail:** purple@southeasternwriters.org. **Website:** www.southeast-

ernwriters.com. **Contact:** Amy Munnell & Sheila Hudson, presidents. Estab. 1975. **Open to all writers.** (2014 dates: June 13-17.) Contests with cash prizes. Instruction offered for novel and short fiction, nonfiction, writing for children, humor, inspirational writing, and poetry. Ms deadline April 1st, includes free evaluation conference(s) with instructor(s). Agent in residence. Annual 4-day workshop held in June. Cost of workshop: $445 for 4 days or lower prices for daily tuition. (See online.) Accommodations: Offers overnight accommodations on workshop site. Visit website for more information and cost of overnight accommodations. E-mail or send SASE for brochure.

ACCOMMODATIONS Multiple hotels available in St. Simon's Island, GA.

SPACE COAST WRITERS GUILD ANNUAL CONFERENCE

No public address available, (321)956-7193. **E-mail:** scwg-jm@cfl.rr.com; stilley@scwg.org. **Website:** www.scwg.org/conference.asp. Annual conference held last weekend of January along the east coast of central Florida. Conference duration: 2 days. Average attendance: 150+. This conference is hosted each winter in Florida and features a variety of presenters on all topics writing. Critiques are available for a price, and agents in attendance will take pitches from writers. Previous presenters have included Debra Dixon, Davis Bunn (writer), Ellen Pepus (agent), Jennifer Crusie, Chuck Sambuchino, Madeline Smoot, Mike Resnick, Christina York, Ben Bova, Elizabeth Sinclair.

COSTS $180-220. Agent and editor appointments cost more.

ACCOMMODATIONS The conference is hosted on a beachside hotel, with special room rates available.

ADDITIONAL INFORMATION Agents are in attendance taking pitches every year.

SPACE (SMALL PRESS AND ALTERNATIVE COMICS EXPO)

Back Porch Comics, P.O. Box 20550, Columbus OH 43220. **E-mail:** bpc13@earthlink.net. **Website:** www.backporchcomics.com/space.htm. Next conference/trade show to be held April 12-13, 2014. Conference duration: 2 days. "The Midwest's largest exhibition of small press, alternative, and creator-owned comics." Site: Held at Ramada Plaza Hotel and Conference Center, 4900 Sinclair Road, Columbus, OH 43229. Over 150 small press artists, writers, and publishers.

COSTS Admission: $5 per day or $8 for weekend.

ADDITIONAL INFORMATION For brochure, visit website. Editors participate in conference.

SQUAW VALLEY COMMUNITY OF WRITERS

P.O. Box 1416, Nevada City CA 95959-1416. (530)470-8440. **E-mail:** info@squawvalleywriters.org. **Website:** www.squawvalleywriters.org. **Contact:** Brett Hall Jones, executive director. Estab. 1969.

COSTS Tuition is $995, which includes 6 dinners.

ACCOMMODATIONS The Community of Writers rents houses and condominiums in the Valley for participants to live in during the week of the conference. Single room (1 participant): $700/week. Double room (twin beds, room shared by conference participant of the same sex): $465/week. Multiple room (bunk beds, room shared with 2 or more participants of the same sex): $295/week. All rooms subject to availability; early requests are recommended. Can arrange airport shuttle pick-ups for a fee.

ADDITIONAL INFORMATION Admissions are based on submitted ms (unpublished fiction, 1 or 2 stories or novel chapters); requires $35 reading fee. Submit ms to Brett Hall Jones, Squaw Valley Community of Writers, P.O. Box 1416, Nevada City, CA 95959. Brochures are available online or for a SASE in February. Send inquiries viae-mail. Accepts inquiries by SASE, e-mail, phone. Agents and editors attend/participate in conferences.

STEAMBOAT SPRINGS WRITERS CONFERENCE

Steamboat Springs Arts Council, Eleanor Bliss Center for the Arts at the Depot, 1001 13th St., Steamboat Springs CO 80487. (970)879-9008. **Fax:** (970)879-8138. **E-mail:** info@steamboatwriters.com. **Website:** www.steamboatwriters.com. **Contact:** Susan de Wardt. Estab. 1982. Annual conference held in mid-July. Conference duration: 1 day. Average attendance: approximately 35. Attendance is limited. Featured areas of instruction change each year. Held at the restored train Depot. Speakers have included Carl Brandt, Jim Fergus, Avi, Robert Greer, Renate Wood, Connie Willis, Margaret Coel, and Kent Nelson.

COSTS Tuition: $50 early registration, $65 after May 4.

ADDITIONAL INFORMATION Brochures are available in April for a SASE. Send inquiries via e-mail.

STORY WEAVERS CONFERENCE

Oklahoma Writer's Federation, (405)682-6000. E-mail: president@owfi.org. **Website:** www.OWFI.org. **Contact:** Linda Apple, president. Oklahoma Writer's Federation, Inc. is open and welcoming to writers of all genres and all skill levels. Our goal is to help writers become better and to help beginning writers understand and master the craft of writing.

COSTS Cost is $150 before April. $175 after April. Cost includes awards banquet and famous author banquet. Three extra sessions are available for an extra fee: How to Self-Publish Your Novel on Kindle, Nook, and iPad (and make more money than being published by New York), with Dan Case; When Polar Bear Wishes Came True: Understanding and Creating Meaningful Stories, with Jack Dalton; How to Create Three-Dimensional Characters, with Steven James.

ACCOMMODATIONS The site is at the Embassy Suite using their meeting halls. There are very few stairs and the rooms are close together for easy access.

ADDITIONAL INFORMATION "We have 20 speakers, five agents, and nine publisher/editors for a full list and bios; please see website."

SUMMER WRITING PROGRAM

Naropa University, 2130 Arapahoe Ave., Boulder CO 80302. (303)245-4862. **Fax:** (303)546-5287. **E-mail:** swpr@naropa.edu. **Website:** www.naropa.edu/swp. **Contact:** Kyle Pivarnik, special projects manager. Estab. 1974. Annual. 2014 Workshops held June 1-28. Workshop duration: 4 weeks. Average attendance: 250. Offers college credit. Accepts inquiries by e-mail, phone. With 13 workshops to choose from each of the 4 weeks of the program, students may study poetry, prose, hybrid/cross-genre writing, small press printing, or book arts. Site: All workshops, panels, lectures and readings are hosted on the Naropa University main campus. Located in downtown Boulder, the campus is within easy walking distance of restaurants, shopping, and the scenic Pearl Street Mall.

COSTS $500/week, $2,000 for all 4 weeks (non-credit students).

ACCOMMODATIONS Housing is available at Snow Lion Apartments. Additional info is available on the housing website: naropa.edu/student-life/housing/.

ADDITIONAL INFORMATION Writers can elect to take the Summer Writing Program for noncredit, graduate, or undergraduate credit. The registration procedure varies, so consider whether or not you'll be taking the SWP for academic credit. All participants can elect to take any combination of the first, second, third, and/or fourth weeks. To request a catalog of upcoming program or to find additional information, visit naropa.edu/swp. Naropa University als welcomes participants with disabilities. Contact Andrea Rexilius at (303)546-5296 or arexilius@naropa.edu before May 15 to inquire about accessibility and disability accommodations needed to participate fully in this event.

SURREY INTERNATIONAL WRITERS' CONFERENCE

SIWC, P.O. Box 42023 RPO Guildford, Surrey BC V3R 1S5 Canada. **E-mail:** kathychung@siwc.ca. **Website:** www.siwc.ca. **Contact:** Kathy Chung, proposals contact and conference coordinator. Annual writing conference outside Vancouver, CA, held every October. Writing workshops geared toward beginner, intermediate, and advanced levels. More than 70 workshops and panels, on all topics and genres. Blue Pencil and Agent/Editor Pitch sessions included. Different conference price packages available. Check our website for more information. This event has many literary agents in attendance taking pitches.

TAOS SUMMER WRITERS' CONFERENCE

Department of English Language and Literature, MSC 03 2170, 1 University of New Mexico, Albuquerque NM 87131-0001. (505)277-5572. **Fax:** (505)277-2950. **E-mail:** taosconf@unm.edu. **Website:** www.unm.edu/~taosconf. **Contact:** Sharon Oard Warner. Estab. 1999. Annual conference held in July. Offers workshops and master classes in the novel, short story, poetry, creative nonfiction, memoir, prose style, screenwriting, humor writing, yoga and writing, literary translation, book proposal, the query letter and revision.Participants may also schedule a consultation with a visiting agent/editor.

COSTS Weeklong workshop registration $650, weekend workshop registration $350, master classes between $1,250 and $1,525.

ACCOMMODATIONS Held at the Sagebrush Inn and Conference Center.

TEXAS CHRISTIAN WRITERS' CONFERENCE

7401 Katy Freeway, Houston TX 77092. (713)686-7209. **E-mail:** dannywoodall@yahoo.com. Martha Rogers **Contact:** Danny Woodall. Estab. 1990. Open conference for all interested writers, held the first Saturday in August. "Focus on all genres." Sponsors a contest for short fiction; categories include articles, devotionals, poetry, short story, book proposals, drama. Fees: $8-15. Conference information available with SASE or e-mail to Danny Woodall. Agents participate in conference. Senior discounts available.

COSTS $65 for members of IWA, $80 nonmembers, discounts for seniors (60+) and couples, meal at noon, continental breakfast and breaks.

ACCOMMODATIONS Offers list of area hotels or lodging options.

ADDITIONAL INFORMATION Open conference for all interested writers. Sponsors a contest for short fiction; categories include articles, devotionals, poetry, short story, book proposals, drama. Fees: $8-15. Conference information available with SASE or e-mail to Danny Woodall, danny.woodall@. Agents participate in conference. (For contest information contact patav@aol.com.)

TEXAS WRITING RETREAT

Grimes County TX **E-mail:** PaulTCuclis@gmail.com. **E-mail:** PaulTCuclis@gmail.com. **Website:** www.texaswritingretreat.com. **Contact:** Paul Cuclis, coordinator. Estab. 2013. The Texas Writing Retreat is an intimate event with a limited number of attendees. Held on a private residence ranch an hour outside of Houston, it has an agent and editor in attendance teaching. All attendees get to pitch the attending agent. Meals and excursions and amenities included. This is a unique event that combines craft sessions, business sessions, time for writing, relaxation, and more.

COSTS Costs vary per year. Check the website for latest updates. There are different pricing options for those staying onsite vs. commuters.

ACCOMMODATIONS Private ranch residence in Texas.

THRILLERFEST

P.O. Box 311, Eureka CA 95502. **E-mail:** infocentral@thrillerwriters.org. **Website:** www.thrillerfest.com. **Contact:** Kimberley Howe, executive director. Grand Hyatt New York, 109 E. 42nd St., New York, NY 10017. Estab. 2006. Annual. 2014: July 8-12 in Manhattan. Conference duration: 5 days. Average attendance: 900. Workshop/conference/festival. "A great place to learn the craft of writing the thriller. Classes taught by NYT best-selling authors. A fabulous event for fans/readers to meet and spend a few days with their favorite authors and packed with terrific programming."

Speakers have included David Morrell, James Patterson, Sandra Brown, Ken Follett, Eric Van Lustbader, David Baldacci, Brad Meltzer, Steve Martini, R.L. Stine, Steve Berry, Kathleen Antrim, Douglas Preston, Gayle Lynds, Harlan Coben, Lee Child, Lisa Scottolini, Katherine Neville, Robin Cook, Andrew Gross, Kathy Reichs, Brad Thor, Clive Cussler, Donald Maass, M.J. Rose, and AlZuckerman. Two days of the conference are CraftFest, where the focus is on the craft of writing, and 2 days are ThrillerFest, which showcase the author-fan relationship. Also featured: AgentFest—a unique event where authors can pitch their work face-to-face to 50 top literary agents, and the International Thriller Awards and Banquet.

COSTS Price will vary from $300-1,100, depending on which events are selected. Various package deals are available offering savings, and Early Bird pricing is offered beginning September of each year.

ACCOMMODATIONS Grand Hyatt in New York City.

TMCC WRITERS' CONFERENCE

Truckee Meadows Community College, 5270 Neil Road, Reno NV 89502. (775)829-9010. **Fax:** (775)829-9032. **E-mail:** wdce@tmcc.edu. **Website:** wdce.tmcc.edu. Estab. 1991. Annual conference held April 27. Average attendance: 150. Conference focuses on strengthening mainstream/literary fiction and nonfiction works and how to market them to agents and publishers. Site: Truckee Meadows Community College in Reno, Nevada. "There is always an array of speakers and presenters with impressive literary credentials, including agents and editors." Speakers have included Chuck Sambuchino, Sheree Bykofsky, Andrea Brown, Dorothy Allison, Karen Joy Fowler, James D. Houston, James N. Frey, Gary Short, Jane Hirschfield, Dorrianne Laux, and Kim Addonizio

COSTS $119 for a full-day seminar; $32 for a 10-minute one-on-one appointment with an agent or editor.

ACCOMMODATIONS Contact the conference manager to learn about accommodation discounts.

ADDITIONAL INFORMATION "The conference is open to all writers, regardless of their level of experience. Brochures are available online and mailed in January. Send inquiries via e-mail."

TONY HILLERMAN WRITER'S CONFERENCE

1063 Willow Way, Santa FE NM 87505. (505)471-1565. **E-mail:** wordharvest@wordharvest.com. **Website:**

www.wordharvest.com. **Contact:** Jean Schaumberg, co-director. Estab. 2004. Annual event held in November. Conference duration: 3 days. Average attendance: 100. Site: Hilton Santa Fe Historic Plaza. First day: Pre-Conference Workshops, hands-on and interactive, taught by published authors who are also wonderful teachers. Second day: The New Book/New Author Breakfast where author attendees have a chance to talk about their new books. A full day of presentations on the craft of writing. We honor the winner of the $10,000 Tony Hillerman Prize for best first mystery at the Hillerman luncheon. A flash critique session - Writing With the Stars - is open to any interested attendee and adds to the fun and information. Third day: A full day of presentations on the business of writing. A book signing/reception is followed by the keynote dinner.

COSTS Previous year's costs: $395 per-registration.

ACCOMMODATIONS Hilton Santa Fe Historic Plaza offers $119 single or double occupancy. November 6-10. Book online with the hotel.

ADDITIONAL INFORMATION Sponsors a $10,000 first mystery novel contest with St. Martin's Press. Submission deadline for the Hillerman Mystery Competition is June 1. Visit the website for more guidelines.

UMKC WRITING CONFERENCE

5300 Rockhill Road, Kansas City MO 64110. (816)235-2736. **Fax:** (816)235-5279. **E-mail:** wittfeldk@umkc.edu. **Website:** http://www.newletters.org/writers-wanted/nl-weekend-writing-conference. **Contact:** Kathi Wittfeld. New Letters Weekend Writing Conference will be held June 27-29, 2014 at Diastole. New Letters Writer's Conference is geared toward all levels—beginner, intermediate, advanced and professional levels. Conferenvce open to students and community. Annual workshops. Workshops held in Summer. Cost of workshop varies. Write for more information. Mark Twain Writers Workshop will not be held in 2014.

UNICORN WRITERS CONFERENCE

P.O. Box 176, Redding CT 06876. (203)938-7405. **E-mail:** bookings@unicornwritersconference.com; unicornwritersconference@gmail.com. **E-mail:** bookings@unicornwritersconference.com; unicornwritersconference@gmail.com. **Website:** www.unicornwritersconference.com. This writers conference draws upon its close proximity to New York City and pulls in many literary agents and editors to pitch each year.

There are sessions, tracks, pitch gatherings, query/ms review sessions, and more.

ACCOMMODATIONS Held at Saint Clements Castle in Connecticut. Directions available on event website.

UNIVERSITY OF NORTH DAKOTA WRITERS CONFERENCE

Department of English, 110 Merrifield Hall, 276 Centennial Drive, Stop 7209, Grand Forks ND 58202. (701)777-2393. **Fax:** (701)777-2373. **E-mail:** crystal.alberts@email.und.edu. **Website:** http://und.edu/orgs/writers-conference/. **Contact:** Crystal Alberts, director. Estab. 1970. Annual conference. 2014 dates: April 2-4. Offers panels, readings, and films focused around a specific theme. Almost all events take place in the UND Memorial Union, which has a variety of small rooms and a 1,000-seat main hall. Past speakers include Art Spiegelman, Truman Capote, Sir Salman Rushdie, Allen Ginsberg, Alice Walker, and Louise Erdrich.

COSTS All events are free and open to the public. Donations accepted.

ACCOMMODATIONS All events are free and open to the public. Accommodations available at area hotels. Information on overnight accommodations available on website.

ADDITIONAL INFORMATION Schedule and other information available on website.

UW-MADISON WRITERS' INSTITUTE

21 North Park St., Room 7331, Madison WI 53715. (608)265-3972. **Fax:** (608)265-2475. **E-mail:** lscheer@dcs.wisc.edu. **Website:** www.uwwritersinstitute.org. **Contact:** Laurie Scheer. Estab. 1989. Annual. Conference usually held in April. Site: Madison Concourse Hotel, downtown Madison. Average attendance: 350-500. Conference speakers provide workshops and consultations. For information, send e-mail, visit website, call, fax. Accepts inquiries by SASE, e-mail, phone, fax. Agents and editors participate in conference.

COSTS $160-260; includes materials, breaks.

ACCOMMODATIONS Provides a list of area hotels or lodging options.

ADDITIONAL INFORMATION Sponsors contest.

VENTANA SIERRA WRITING WORKSHOPS

900 N. Roop St., Carson City NV 89701. **Website:** http://ventanasierraworkshops.com. Ventana Sierra offers intensive craft sessions taught by some of the finest authors, poets, memoirists, professors, and

writing coaches in the U.S., plus state of the industry talks, editor and agent panels, peer group critiques, and optional one-on-one ms reviews by high-level industry professionals. Offers 3 tracks of workshops: fiction, creative nonfiction/memoir, and poetry. Each of these 3 tracts takes place for 2 days in June. Also offers an add-on (for $100) One Day Intensive Workshop that includes 2 3-hour sessions, designed to take writing to another level with advanced techniques from experts. Authors can also register for optional ms ms critique ($75), where they can have up to 15 pages plus a synopsis critiqued by a top-level industry professional. A full schedule and list of speakers is available online.

COSTS $300 early bird fee; $350 fee after May 1

VERMONT STUDIO CENTER

P.O. Box 613, 80 Pearl Street, Johnson VT 05656. (802)635-2727. **Fax:** (802)635-2730. **E-mail:** info@ vermontstudiocenter.org. **Website:** www.vermont-studiocenter.org. **Contact:** Gary Clark, Writing Program Director. Estab. 1984. Founded by artists in 1984, the Vermont Studio Center is the largest international artists' and writers' Residency Program in the United States, hosting 50 visual artists and writers each month from across the country and around the world. The Studio Center provides 4-12 week studio residencies on an historic 30-building campus along the Gihon River in Johnson, Vermont, a village in the heart of the northern Green Mountains.

ACCOMMODATIONS "The cost of a 4-week residency is $3,750. Generous fellowship and grant assistance available. "Accommodations available on site. "Residents live in single rooms in ten modest, comfortable houses adjacent to the Red Mill Building. Rooms are simply furnished and have shared baths. Complete linen service is provided. The Studio Center is unable to accommodate guests at meals, overnight guests, spouses, children or pets."

ADDITIONAL INFORMATION Fellowships application deadlines are February 15, June 15 and October 1. Writers encouraged to visit website for more information. May also e-mail, call, fax.

VIRGINIA CENTER FOR THE CREATIVE ARTS

154 San Angelo Dr., Amherst VA 24521. (434)946-7236. **Fax:** (434)946-7239. **E-mail:** vcca@vcca.com. **Website:** www.vcca.com. Estab. 1971. Offers residencies year-round, typical residency lasts 2 weeks to 2

months. Open to originating artists: composers, writers, and visual artists. Accommodates 25 at one time. Personal living quarters include 22 single rooms, 2 double rooms, bathrooms shared with one other person. All meals are served. Kitchens for fellows' use available at studios and residence. The VCCA van goes into town twice a week. Fellows share their work regularly. Four studios have pianos. No transportation costs are covered. "Artists are accepted into the VCCA without regard for their ability to contribute financially to their residency. Daily cost is $180 per fellow. We ask fellows to contribute according to their ability."

COSTS Application fee: $30. Deadline: May 15 for October-January residency; September 15 for February-May residency; January 15 for June-September residency. Send SASE for application form or download from website. Applications are reviewed by panelists.

WESLEYAN WRITERS CONFERENCE

Wesleyan University, 294 High St., Room 207, Middletown CT 06459. (860)685-3604. **Fax:** (860)685-2441. **E-mail:** agreene@wesleyan.edu. **Website:** www.wesleyan.edu/writing/conference. Estab. 1956. Annual conference held June 12-16. Average attendance: 100. Focuses on the novel, fiction techniques, short stories, poetry, screenwriting, nonfiction, literary journalism, memoir, mixed media work and publishing. The conference is held on the campus of Wesleyan University, in the hills overlooking the Connecticut River. Features a faculty of award-winning writers, seminars and readings of new fiction, poetry, nonfiction and mixed media forms - as well as guest lectures on a range of topics including publishing. Both new and experienced writers are welcome. Participants may attend seminars in all genres. Speakers have included Esmond Harmsworth (Zachary Schuster Agency), Daniel Mandel (Sanford J. Greenburger Associates), Dorian Karchmar, Amy Williams (ICM and Collins McCormick), Mary Sue Rucci (Simon & Schuster), Denise Roy (Simon & Schuster), John Kulka (Harvard University Press), Julie Barer (Barer Literary) and many others. Agents will be speaking and available for meetings with attendees. Participants are often successful in finding agents and publishers for their mss. Wesleyan participants are also frequently featured in the anthology *Best New American Voices*.

ACCOMMODATIONS Meals are provided on campus. Lodging is available on campus or in town.

ADDITIONAL INFORMATION Ms critiques are available, but not required. Scholarships and teaching fellowships are available, including the Joan Jakobson Awards for fiction writers and poets; and the Jon Davidoff Scholarships for nonfiction writers and journalists. Inquire via e-mail, fax, or phone.

WESTERN RESERVE WRITERS & FREELANCE CONFERENCE

7700 Clocktower Dr., Kirtland OH 44094. (440) 525-7812. **E-mail:** deencr@aol.com. **Website:** www.deannaadams.com. **Contact:** Deanna Adams, director/conference coordinator. Estab. 1983. Biannual. Last conference held September 28, 2013. Conference duration: 1 day or half-day. Average attendance: 120. "The Western Reserve Writers Conferences are designed for all writers, aspiring and professional, and offer presentations in all genres—nonfiction, fiction, poetry, essays, creative nonfiction, and the business of writing, including Web writing and successful freelance writing." Site: "Located in the main building of Lakeland Community College, the conference is easy to find and just off the I-90 freeway. The Fall 2013 conference featured top-notch presenters from newspapers and magazines, along with published authors, freelance writers, and professional editors. Presentations included developing issues in today's publishing and publishing options, turning writing into a lifelong vocation, as well as workshops on plotting, creating credible characters, writing mysteries, romance writing, and tips on submissions, getting books into stores, and storytelling for both fiction and nonfiction writers. Included throughout the day are one-on-one editing consults, Q&A panel, and book sale/author signings."

COSTS Fall all-day conference includes lunch: $95. Spring half-day conference, no lunch: $69.

ADDITIONAL INFORMATION Brochures for the conferences are available by January (for spring conference) and July (for fall). Also accepts inquiries by e-mail and phone. Check Deanna Adams' website for all updates. Editors and agents often attend the conferences.

WHIDBEY ISLAND WRITERS' CONFERENCE

P.O. Box 1289, Langley WA 98260. **E-mail:** admin@nila.edu; wiwc@nila.edu. **Website:** www.nila.edu/wiwc/. This is an annual writing conference in the Pacific Northwest. There are a variety of sessions on topics such as fiction, craft, poetry, platform, agents, screenwriting, and much more. Topics are varied, and there is something for all writers. Multiple agents and editors are in attendance. The schedule and faculty change every year, and those changes are reflected online.

WILDACRES WRITERS WORKSHOP

233 S. Elm St., Greensboro NC 27401. (336)255-8210. **E-mail:** judihill78@yahoo.com. **Website:** www.wildacreswriters.com. **Contact:** Judi Hill, Director. Estab. 1985. Annual residential workshop held July 6-13. Conference duration: 1 week. Average attendance: 100. Workshop focuses on novel, short story, flash fiction, poetry, and nonfiction. 10 on faculty include Ron Rash, Carrie Brown, Dr. Janice Fuller, Phillip Gerard, Luke Whisnant, Dr. Joe Clark, John Gregory Brown, Dr. Phebe Davidson, Lee Zacharias, and Vicki Lane.

COSTS The total price for seven days is $690. This price includes workshop fees, one ms critique, programs, parties, room, and meals.

ADDITIONAL INFORMATION Include a 1-page writing sample with your registration. See the website for information.

WILLAMETTE WRITERS CONFERENCE

2108 Buck St., West Linn OR 97068. (503)305-6729. **Fax:** (503)344-6174. **Website:** www.willamettewriters.com/wwc/3/. Estab. 1981. Annual conference held in August. (2014 dates: Aug. 1-3.) Conference duration: 3 days. Average attendance: 600. "Willamette Writers is open to all writers, and we plan our conference accordingly. We offer workshops on all aspects of fiction, nonfiction, marketing, the creative process, screenwriting, etc. Also, we invite top-notch inspirational speakers for keynote addresses. We always include at least 1 agent or editor panel and offer a variety of topics of interest to both fiction and nonfiction writers and screenwriters." Agents will be speaking and available for meetings with attendees.

COSTS Pricing schedule available online.

ACCOMMODATIONS If necessary, arrangements can be made on an individual basis through the conference hotel. Special rates may be available. 2014 location is the Lloyd Center DoubleTree Hotel.

ADDITIONAL INFORMATION Brochure/guidelines are available for a catalog-sized SASE.

WINCHESTER WRITERS' CONFERENCE, FESTIVAL AND BOOKFAIR, AND IN-DEPTH WRITING WORKSHOPS

University of Winchester, Winchester Hampshire WA S022 4NR United Kingdom. 44 (0) 1962 827238. **E-mail:** judith.heneghan@winchester.ac.uk. **Website:** www.writersfestival.co.uk. The 34th Winchester Writers' Festival will be held on June 20-22 at the University of Winchester, Winchester, Hampshire S022 4NR. Joanne Harris, internationally acclaimed author of *Chocolat*, will give the Keynote Address and will lead an outstanding team of 60 best-selling authors, commissioning editors and literary agents offering day-long workshops, 40 short talks and 500 one-to-one appointments to help writers harness their creative ideas, turn them into marketable work and pitch to publishing professionals. Participate by entering some of the 12 writing competitions, even if you can't attend. Over 120 writers have now reported major publishing successes as a direct result of their attendance at past conferences. This leading international literary event offers a magnificent source of support, advice, inspiration and networking opportunities for new and published writers working in all genres. Enjoy a creative writing holiday in Winchester, the oldest city in England and only one hour from London.To view Festival programme, including all the competition details please go to: www.writersfestival.co.uk.

WINTER POETRY & PROSE GETAWAY

18 N. Richards Ave., Ventnor NJ 08406. (888)887-2105. **E-mail:** info@wintergetaway.com. **Website:** www.wintergetaway.com. **Contact:** Peter Murphy. Estab. 1994. Annual January conference at the Jersey Shore. "This is not your typical writers' conference. Advance your craft and energize your writing at the Winter Getaway. Enjoy challenging and supportive workshops, insightful feedback, and encouraging community. Choose from small, intensive workshops in memoir, novel, YA, nonfiction, and poetry."

ACCOMMODATIONS See website or call for current fee information.

ADDITIONAL INFORMATION Previous faculty has included Julianna Baggott, Christian Bauman, Laure-Anne Bosselaar, Kurt Brown, Mark Doty (National Book Award winner), Stephen Dunn (Pulitzer Prize winner), Dorianne Laux, Carol Plum-Ucci, James Richardson, Mimi Schwartz, Terese Svoboda, and more.

WISCONSIN BOOK FESTIVAL

Madison Public Library, 201 W. Mifflin St., Madison WI 53703. (608)266-6300. **E-mail:** bookfest@mplfoundation.org. **Website:** www.wisconsinbookfestival.org. Estab. 2002. Annual festival held in October. Conference duration: 5 days. The festival features readings, lectures, book discussions, writing workshops, live interviews, children's events, and more. Speakers have included Isabel Allende, Jonathan Alter, Paul Auster, Michael Chabon, Billy Collins, Phillip Gourevitch, Ian Frazier, Tim O'Brien, Elizabeth Strout.

COSTS All festival events are free.

WOMEN WRITERS WINTER RETREAT

Homestead House B&B, 38111 West Spaulding, Willoughby OH 44094. (440)946-1902. **E-mail:** deencr@aol.com. **Website:** www.deannaadams.com. Estab. 2007. Annual—always happens the last weekend in February. Conference duration: 3 days. Average attendance: 35-40. Retreat. "The Women Writers' Winter Retreat was designed for aspiring and professional women writers who cannot seem to find enough time to devote to honing their craft. Each retreat offers class time and workshops facilitated by successful women writers, as well as allows time to do some actual writing, alone or in a group. A Friday night dinner and keynote kick-starts the weekend, followed by Saturday workshops, free time, meals, and an open mic to read your works. Sunday wraps up with 1 more workshop and fellowship. All genres welcome. Choice of overnight stay or commuting." Site: Located in the heart of downtown Willoughby, this warm and attractive bed and breakfast is easy to find, around the corner from the main street, Erie Street, and behind a popular Arabica coffee house. Door prizes and book sale/author signings throughout the weekend.

COSTS Single room: $315; shared room: $235 (includes complete weekend package, with B&B stay and all meals and workshops); weekend commute: $165; Saturday only: $125 (prices include lunch and dinner).

ADDITIONAL INFORMATION Brochures for the writers retreat are available by December. Accepts inquiries and reservations by e-mail or phone. See Deanna's website for additional information and updates.

WOMEN WRITING THE WEST

8547 E. Araphoe Road, Box J-541, Greenwood Village CO 80112-1436. **E-mail:** conference@womenwritingthewest.org. **Website:** www.womenwritingthewest. org. 2014 dates: Oct 16-20 in Denver, Colo. "Women Writing the West is a nonprofit association of writers, editors, publishers, agents, booksellers, and other professionals writing and promoting the women's West. As such, women writing their stories in the American West in a way that illuminates them authentically. In addition, the organization provides support, encouragement, and inspiration to all women writing about any facet of the American West. Membership is open to all interested persons worldwide. Open to students. Cost of membership: Annual membership dues $65. Publisher dues are $65. International dues are $70. In addition to the annual dues, there is an option to become a sustaining member for $100. Sustaining members receive a WWW enamel logo pin, prominent listing in WWW publications, and the knowledge that they are assisting the organization. Members actively exchange ideas on a list e-bulletin board. WWW membership also allows the choice of participation in our marketing marvel, the annual WWW Catalog of Author's Books. An annual conference is held every fall. Our blog, Facebook and ListServ publish current WWW activities; features market research, and experience articles of interest pertaining to American West literature and member news. Sponsors annual WILLA Literary Award, which is given in several categories for outstanding literature featuring women's stories, set in the West. The winner of a WILLA literary Award receives a cash award and a trophy at the annual conference. Contest open to non-members. Annual conference held in third weekend in October. Covers research, writing techniques, multiple genres, marketing/promotion, and more. Agents and editors will be speaking and available for one-on-one meetings with attendees. Conference location changes each year."

COSTS See website. Discounts available for members, and for specific days only.

ACCOMMODATIONS See website for location and accommodation details.

WORDS & MUSIC

624 Pirate's Alley, New Orleans LA 70116. (504)586-1609. **Fax:** (504)522-9725. **E-mail:** info@wordsandmusic.org. **Website:** www.wordsandmusic.org. Estab. 1997. Annual conference held in November. 2014 conference: 20-24. Conference duration: 5 days. Average attendance: 300. Presenters include authors, agents,

editors and publishers. Past speakers included agents Deborah Grosvenor, Judith Weber, Stuart Bernstein, Nat Sobel, Jeff Kleinman, Emma Sweeney, Liza Dawson and Michael Murphy; editors Lauren Marino, Webster Younce, Ann Patty, Will Murphy, Jofie Ferrari-Adler, Elizabeth Stein; critics Marie Arana, Jonathan Yardley, and Michael Dirda; fiction writers Oscar Hijuelos, Robert Olen Butler, Shirley Ann Grau, Mayra Montero, Ana Castillo, H.G. Carrillo. Agents and editors critique mss in advance; meet with them one-on-one during the conference.

COSTS See website for a costs and additional information on accommodations. Website will update closer to date of conference.

ACCOMMODATIONS Hotel Monteleone in New Orleans.

WRITE-BY-THE-LAKE WRITER'S WORKSHOP & RETREAT

21 N. Park St., 7th Floor, Madison WI 53715. (608)262-3447. **E-mail:** cdesmet@dcs.wisc.edu. **Website:** www.dcs.wisc.edu/lsa/writing. **Contact:** Christine DeSmet, director. Open to all writers and students; 12 workshops for all levels. Includes 2 Master Classes for full-novel critique. Held the third week of June on UW-Madison campus. Registration limited to 15; fewer in Master Classes. Writing facilities available; computer labs, wi-fi in all buildings and on the outdoor lakeside terrace.

COSTS $365 before May 20; $415 after May 20. Additional cost for Master Classes and college credits. Cost includes instruction, welcome luncheon, and pastry/coffee each day.

ADDITIONAL INFORMATION E-mail for more information. "Registration opens every December for following June. See web pages online."

WRITE CANADA

The Word Guild, P.O. Box 1243, Trenton ON K8V 5R9 Canada. **E-mail:** info@thewordguild.com. **E-mail:** writecanada@rogers.com. **Website:** www.writecanada.org. Conference duration: 3 days. Annual conference. 2014 dates: June 12-14 in Guelph, Ontario for writers who are Christian of all types and at all stages. Offers solid instruction, stimulating interaction, exciting challenges, and worshipful community.

WRITE IT OUT

P.O. Box 704, Sarasota FL 34230-0704. (941)359-3824. **E-mail:** rmillerwio@aol.com. **Website:** www.writeitout.com. **Contact:** Ronni Miller, director. Estab. 1997. Workshops held 2-3 times/year in March, June, July and August. Conference duration: 5-10 days. Average attendance: 4-10. Workshops retreats on "expressive writing and painting, fiction, poetry, memoirs. We also offer intimate, motivational, in-depth free private conferences with instructors." Past facilitators included Arturo Vivante, novelist. Acquisitions:

ADDITIONAL INFORMATION "Critiques on work are given at the workshops." Conference information available year round. For brochures/guidelines e-mail, call, or visit website. Accepts inquiries by phone, e-mail. Workshops have "small groups, option to spend time writing and not attend classes, with personal appointments with instructors."

WRITERS@WORK CONFERENCE

P.O. Box 711191, Salt Lake City UT 84171-1191. (801)996-3313. **E-mail:** jennifer@writersatwork.org. **Website:** www.writersatwork.org. Estab. 1985. Annual conference held in June. (The 2014 conference is June 4-8.) Conference duration: 5 days. Average attendance: 250. Morning workshops (3-hours/day) focus on novel, advanced fiction, generative fiction, nonfiction, poetry, and young adult fiction. Afternoon sessions will include craft lectures, discussions, and directed interviews with authors, agents, and editors. In addition to the traditional, one-on-one ms consultations, there will be many opportunities to mingle informally with agents/editors. Held at the Alta Lodge in Alta Lodge, Utah. Speakers have included Steve Almond, Bret Lott, Shannon Hale, Emily Forland (Wendy Weil Agency), Julie Culver (Folio Literary Management, Chuck Adams (Algonquin Press), and Mark A. Taylor (Juniper Press).

COSTS $690-1,005, based on housing type and consultations.

ACCOMMODATIONS Onsite housing available. Additional lodging and meal information is on the website.

WRITER'S DIGEST CONFERENCES

F+W Media, Inc., 10151 Carver Road, Suite 200, Blue Ash OH 45242. **E-mail:** jill.ruesch@fwmedia.com. **E-mail:** phil.sexton@fwmedia.com. **Website:** www.writersdigestconference.com. Estab. 1995. The Writer's Digest conferences feature an amazing line up of speakers to help writers with the craft and business of writing. Each calendar year typically features multiple conferences around the country. In 2014, the New York conference will be Aug. 1-3, while the Los Angeles conference will be Aug. 15-17. The most popular feature of the east coast conference is the agent pitch slam, in which potential authors are given the ability to pitch their books directly to agents. For the 2014 conference, there will be more than 50 agents in attendance. For more details, see the website.

COSTS Cost varies by location and year. There are typically different pricing options for those who wish to stay for the entire event vs. daylong passes.

ACCOMMODATIONS A block of rooms at the event hotel is reserved for guests.

WRITERS' LEAGUE OF TEXAS AGENTS CONFERENCE

Writers' League of Texas, 611 S. Congress Ave., Suite 200 A-3, Austin TX 78704. (512)499-8914. **Fax:** (512)499-0441. **E-mail:** conference@writersleague.org. **E-mail:** jennifer@writersleague.org. **Website:** www.writersleague.org. Estab. 1982. Established in 1981, the Writers' League of Texas is a nonprofit professional organization whose primary purpose is to provide a forum for information, support, and sharing among writers, to help members improve and market their writing skills, and to promote the interests of writers and the writing community. The Writers' League of Texas Agents & Editors Conference is for writers at every stage of their career. Beginners can learn more about this mystifying industry and prepare themselves for the journey ahead. Those with completed mss can pitch to agents and get feedback on their mss from professional editors. Published writers can learn about market trends and network with rising stars in the world of writing. No matter what your market, genre, or level, our conference can benefit you.

COSTS Rates vary based on membership and the date of registration. The starting rate (registration through January 15) is $309 for members and $369 for non-members. Rate increases by through later dates. See website for updates.

ACCOMMODATIONS Check online for new information.

ADDITIONAL INFORMATION Event held from June 27-29, 2014. Contests and awards programs are offered separately. Brochures are available upon request.

WRITERS OMI AT LEDIG HOUSE

55 Fifth Ave., 15th Floor, New York NY 10003. (212)206-6114. **E-mail:** writers@artomi.org. **Web-**

site: www.artomi.org. Residency duration: 2 weeks to 2 months. Average attendance and site: "Up to 20 writers per session—10 at a given time—live and write on the stunning 300 acre grounds and sculpture park that overlooks the Catskill Mountains." Deadline: October 20.

ACCOMMODATIONS Residents provide their own transportation. Offers overnight accommodations.

ADDITIONAL INFORMATION "Agents and editors from the New York publishing community are invited for dinner and discussion. Bicycles, a swimming pool, and nearby tennis court are available for use."

WRITERS WEEKEND AT THE BEACH

P.O. Box 877, Ocean Park WA 98640. (360)262-0160. **E-mail:** pelkeyjc@hotmail.com. **E-mail:** bobtracie@hotmail.com; pelkeyjc@hotmail.com. **Contact:** John Pelkey. Estab. 1992. Annual conference held in April. Conference duration: 2 days. Average attendance: 45. A retreat for writers with an emphasis on poetry, fiction, and nonfiction. Held at the Ocean Park Methodist Retreat Center & Camp. Speakers have included Miralee Ferrell, Leslie Gould, Linda Clare, Birdie Etchison, Colette Tennant, Gail Dunham, and Marion Duckworth.

COSTS $200 for full registration before March 1 and $215 after March 1.

ACCOMMODATIONS Offers on-site overnight lodging.

WRITE ON THE RIVER

8941 Kelsey Lane, Knoxville TN 37922. **E-mail:** bob@bobmayer.org. **Website:** www.bobmayer.org. **Contact:** Bob Mayer. Estab. 2002. Held several times a year. Conference duration: 2 days. Held at a private residence.

COSTS Varies; depends on venue. Please see website for any updates.

ADDITIONAL INFORMATION Limited to 4 participants, and focused on their novel and marketability.

THE WRITERS' WORKSHOP

387 Beaucatcher Road, Asheville NC 28805. (828)254-8111. **E-mail:** writersw@gmail.com. **Website:** www.twwoa.org. Estab. 1984. Biannual writing retreat at Folly Beach, SC. 2014 dates: May 15-18. Kurt Vonnegut said: "God bless The Writers' Workshop of Asheville!" He and Don De Lillo, Peter Matthiessen, E.L. Doctorow, Eudora Welty, John le Carre and many other distinguished authors have given benefit readings for us. We offer classes, contests, retreats, and

other events. Workshops in all genres of writing, for beginning or experienced writers, are held in Asheville and Charlotte, NC. Our in-house Renbourne Editorial Agency offers the highest quality editing and revising services for writes of all genres.

COSTS Vary. Financial assistance available to low-income writers. Information on overnight accommodations is made available.

ADDITIONAL INFORMATION We also sponsor these contests, open to all writers: Annual Poetry Contest, Prizes from $100-300 (Deadline: Feb. 28); Hard Times Writing Contest, Prizes from $100-300, (Deadline: May 30); Fiction Contest, Prizes from $150-350 (Deadline: Aug. 30); Annual Memoirs Competition, Prizes from $150-350 (Deadline: Nov. 30). Contests for young writers are posted at our website.

WRITE-TO-PUBLISH CONFERENCE

WordPro Communication Services, 9118 W. Elmwood Dr., Suite 1G, Niles IL 60714-5820. (847)296-3964. **Fax:** (847)296-0754. **E-mail:** lin@writetopublish.com. **Website:** www.writetopublish.com. **Contact:** Lin Johnson, director. Estab. 1971. Annual. Conference held June 4-7, 2014. Average attendance: 200. Conference is focused for the Christian market and includes classes on writing for children. Writer workshops geared toward all levels. Open to students. Site: Wheaton College, Wheaton, IL (Chicago).

COSTS approximately $475; includes conference and banquet.

ACCOMMODATIONS In campus residence halls. Cost is approximately $280-360.

ADDITIONAL INFORMATION Optional ms evaluation available. College credit available. Conference information available in January. For details, visit website, or e-mail brochure@writetopublish.com. Accepts inquiries by e-mail, fax, phone.

WRITING AND ILLUSTRATING FOR YOUNG READERS CONFERENCE

1480 East 9400 South, Sandy UT 84093. **E-mail:** staff@wifyr.com. **Website:** www.wifyr.com. Estab. 2000. Annual workshop held in June 2014. Conference duration: 5 days. Average attendance: 100+. Learn how to write, illustrate, and publish in the children's and young adult markets. Beginning and advanced writers and illustrators are tutored in a small-group workshop setting by published authors and artists and receive instruction from and network with editors, major publishing house representatives, and literary agents. Afternoon attendees get to hear practical writing and publishing tips from published authors, literary agents, and editors. Held at the Waterford School in Sandy, UT. Speakers have included John Cusick, Stephen Fraser, Alyson Heller, and Ruth Katcher.

COSTS Costs available online.

ACCOMMODATIONS A block of rooms are available at the Best Western Cotton Tree Inn in Sandy, UT at a discounted rate. This rate is good as long as there are available rooms.

WRITING WORKSHOP AT CASTLE HILL

1 Depot Road, P.O. Box 756, Truro MA 02666-0756. **E-mail:** cherie@castlehill.org. **Website:** www.castle-hill.org. Poetry, Fiction, Memoir workshops geared toward intermediate and advanced levels. **Open to students.** Workshops by Keith Althaus: Poetry; Anne Bernays: Elements of Fiction; Elizabeth Bradfield: Poetry in Plein Air & Broadsides and Beyond: Poetry as Public Art; Melanie Braverman: In Pursuit of Exactitude: Poetry; Josephine Del Deo: Preoccupation in Poetry; Martin Espada: Barbaric Yamp: A Poetry Workshop; Judy Huge: Finding the Me in Memoir; Justin Kaplan: Autobiography. See website under Summer 2011 Writers for dates and more information.

THE HELENE WURLITZER FOUNDATION

P.O. Box 1891, Taos NM 87571. (575)758-2413. **Fax:** (575)758-2559. **E-mail:** hwf@taosnet.com. **Website:** www.wurlitzerfoundation.org. **Contact:** Michael A. Knight, executive director. Estab. 1953.

ACCOMMODATIONS "Provides individual housing in fully furnished studio/houses (casitas), rent and utility free. Artists are responsible for transportation to and from Taos, their meals and materials for their work. Bicycles are provided upon request."

WYOMING WRITERS CONFERENCE

Sheridan WY **E-mail:** pfrolander@rangeweb.net. **Website:** wyowriters.org. **Contact:** Patricia Frolander. This is a statewide writing conference for writers of Wyoming and neighboring states. Next conference: June 6-8, 2014 in Sheridan, WY. Each year, multiple published authors, editors and literary agents are in attendance.

BOOK FAIRS

Book fairs and festivals provide self-publishers with a great opportunity to accomplish a few things. First, conferences are designed to help writers improve their craft and knowledge of the publishing business. In fact, some conferences are even designed to help self-publishers specifically.

Second, conferences are great networking opportunities. You may find freelance editors and designers here to help with your project. Or you may find bloggers who can help promote your book through guest posts, interviews, or reviews. And you might also find new readers that will buy copies on the spot.

Finally, conferences do one thing exceptionally well for writers of all skill levels and experience: They help give a jolt of excitement and energy. This enthusiasm should not be discounted, because it helps spur new ideas, innovation, and success.

KEEP IN MIND

Starting locally will allow you to save money on travel and other expenses (such as food, paying for a hotel, etc.). However, you may decide that paying more for your confernce experience is worth it if you're receiving the type of instruction and/or making the connections you need the most. Keep in mind that your conference expenses may actually be considered a business expense and a tax deduction. Consult your account to confirm.

Once you decide upon a conference to attend, make a conference plan. This plan will include directions to the event, contact information for organizers (in case you can't find your way), a list of which panels and/or sessions you wish to attend (don't wait until the day of the event to figure this out), and any other tasks you'd like to accomplish.

Leave the door open to be spontaneous with your schedule and take advantage of unexpected opportunities, but having a plan will make sure you don't feel cheated out of an incredible experience after the event is over.

One more important note: Bring business cards to the event and keep them somewhere that's easy for you to dispense. Any person you speak with should receive your card, even the nice person who sat next to you at lunch, because you never know who will present you with your first or next lucky break.

ALABAMA BOOK FESTIVAL

301 Columbus St., Montgomery AL 36104. (888)240-1850. **E-mail:** alabamabookfestival@gmail.com. **Website:** www.alabamabookfestival.org.

ADDITIONAL INFORMATION "This free public event is the state's premier book festival, with some 5,000 people from around the state and the southeast converging in the capital to meet with and hear their favorite authors and scholars. A children's activity area is sure to make this a day of fun for the entire family."

ARKANSAS LITERARY FESTIVAL

100 Rock St., Little Rock AR 72205. **Website:** www.arkansasliteraryfestival.org.

ADDITIONAL INFORMATION "The Arkansas Literary Festival, the premier gathering of readers and writers in Arkansas, takes place at the Central Arkansas Library System's Main Library campus and other venues in the River Market and Argenta Arts districts. The festival is a stimulating mix of sessions, panels, special events, performances, workshops, presentations, opportunities to meet authors, book sales, and book signings." Most events are free and open to the public.

BALTIMORE BOOK FESTIVAL

Baltimore MD (410)752-8632. **E-mail:** baltimorebookfestival@promotionandarts.org. **Website:** www.baltimorebookfestival.com.

ADDITIONAL INFORMATION "The Baltimore Book Festival features hundreds of author appearances and book signings, 100+ exhibitors and booksellers, non-stop readings on multiple stages, cooking demos by celebrity chefs, poetry readings and workshops, panel discussions, walking tours, storytellers and hands-on projects for kids, street theater, live music, and a delicious variety of food, beer, and wine."

BETHESDA LITERARY FESTIVAL

7700 Old Georgetown Road, Bethesda MD 20814. (301)215-6660. **Fax:** (301)215-6664. **E-mail:** info@bethesda.org. **Website:** www.bethesda.org/specialevents/litfest/litfest.htm.

ADDITIONAL INFORMATION "The Bethesda Literary Festival hosts an array of local and national authors, journalists and poets, as well as writing contests and poetry contests."

BOOKS BY THE BANKS

Cincinnati OH **E-mail:** contact@booksbythebanks.org. **Website:** booksbythebanks.org.

ADDITIONAL INFORMATION "Books by the Banks vision is to encourage literacy among the Southwest Ohio/Northern Kentucky communities by promoting an annual festival showcasing organizations, and individuals, in support of fostering education and the love of reading."

BORDER BOOK FESTIVAL

314 S. Tornillo St., Las Cruces NM 88001. (575)523-3988. **Website:** www.borderbookfestival.org/bbf/.

ADDITIONAL INFORMATION Annual book festival in Las Cruces, New Mexico.

BOSTON BOOK FESTIVAL

1100 Massachusetts Ave., Suite 300B, Cambridge MA 02138. (617)945-9552. **Fax:** (617)576-1300. **E-mail:** info@bostonbookfest.org. **Website:** www.bostonbookfest.org.

ADDITIONAL INFORMATION "The Boston Book Festival celebrates the power of words to stimulate, agitate, unite, delight, and inspire by holding year-round events culminating in an annual, free festival that promotes a culture of reading and ideas and enhances the vibrancy of our city."

BROOKLYN BOOK FESTIVAL

249 Smith St., PMB #106, Brooklyn NY 11231. (570)362-6657. **E-mail:** lkoch@brooklynbookfestival.org. **Website:** www.brooklynbookfestival.org. **Contact:** Liz Koch.

ADDITIONAL INFORMATION "The Brooklyn Book Festival is the largest free literary event in New York City, presenting an array of national and international literary stars and emerging authors. One of America's premier book festivals, this hip, smart diverse gathering attracts thousands of book lovers of all ages to enjoy authors and the festivals lively literary marketplace."

BUCKEYE BOOK FAIR

205 W. Liberty St., Wooster OH 44691. (330)262-3244. **Fax:** (330)264-9852. **E-mail:** bbfmgr@woosterbook.com. **Website:** www.buckeyebookfair.com. **Contact:** Julia Wiesenberg.

ADDITIONAL INFORMATION "The annual Buckeye Book Fair is a full-day event featuring nearly 100 Ohio authors and illustrators who meet with readers and autograph copies of their latest works. Thousands of attendees from all over Ohio come to mingle, shop for books, and celebrate the joys of reading and writing."

CHILDREN'S LITERATURE FESTIVAL

2444 James C. Kirkpatrick Library, University of Central Missouri, Warrensburg MO 64093. (660)543-4306. **E-mail:** clfreg@ucmo.edu. **Website:** guides.library.ucmo.edu/clf. **Contact:** Naomi Williamson.
ADDITIONAL INFORMATION Annual 3-day festival sponsored by James C. Kirkpatrick Library.

COLLINGSWOOD BOOK FESTIVAL

P.O. Box 284, Collingswood NJ 08108. **Website:** www.collingswoodbookfestival.com.
ADDITIONAL INFORMATION "Festival-goers have an opportunity to stroll more than 6 blocks of Haddon Avenue filled with nationally recognized authors/speakers for adults and children, as well as booksellers, storytellers, poetry readings, workshops, exhibitors, kid-friendly activities, and entertainment for all ages. This award-winning festival is the longest running, largest literary event in the Delaware Valley. Remember, all events are free!"

CONNECTICUT CHILDREN'S BOOK FAIR

CT (860)486-1307. **E-mail:** suzy.staubach@uconn.edu. **Website:** bookfair.uconn.edu. **Contact:** Suzanne Staubach, co-chair.
ADDITIONAL INFORMATION "The Connecticut Children's Book Fair brings together prominent children's authors and illustrators and the general public in an annual event designed to foster the enjoyment of children's literature."

DAHLONEGA LITERARY FESTIVAL

Dahlonega GA **E-mail:** ariennewallace@windstream.net. **Website:** dahlonegaliteraryfestival.wordpress.com. **Contact:** Arienne Wallace.
ADDITIONAL INFORMATION "The Dahlonega Literary Festival is an annual celebration of books that takes place in March. Situated in Historic Downtown Dahlonega, the festival continues to grow and become more delightful as the years go on. We promise that it will interest anyone who is a lover of books and reading. All festival events are free and open to the public unless otherwise noted."

DECATUR BOOK FESTIVAL

Decatur GA (404)471-5769. **Website:** www.decaturbookfestival.com.

ADDITIONAL INFORMATION "The AJC Decatur Book Festival is the largest independent book festival in the country and one of the five largest overall. Since its launch, more than 1,000 world-class authors and hundreds of thousands of festival-goers have crowded the historic downtown Decatur square to enjoy book signings, author readings, panel discussions, an interactive children's area, live music, parades, cooking demonstrations, poetry slams, writing workshops, and more."

GAITHERSBURG BOOK FESTIVAL

506 S. Frederick Ave., Gaithersburg MD 20877. (301)258-6350. **Website:** gaithersburgbookfestival.org. **Contact:** Carolyn Crosby, senior program supervisor. Estab. 2010.
ADDITIONAL INFORMATION "The Gaithersburg Book Festival is a celebration of the written word and its power to enrich the human experience. Our mission is to foster an interest in reading, writing, and literary conversation."

GEORGIA LITERARY FESTIVAL

215 Sycamore St., Decatur GA 30030. (404)370-8450, ext. 2285. **Fax:** (404)370-8469. **Website:** www.georgiacenterforthebook.org/georgia-literary-festival. **Contact:** Joe Davich.
ADDITIONAL INFORMATION Annual multi-day book festival in Georgia.

THE GREAT VALLEY BOOKFEST

Monteca CA (209)824-3080. **E-mail:** toni@raymushomes.com. **Website:** greatvalleybookfest.org. **Contact:** Toni Raymus.
ADDITIONAL INFORMATION "At the Great Valley Bookfest, you can mingle with your favorite authors, discover new ones, or pick up that book you have been dying to read. For children, a book festival is a great place to develop a love for reading."

KENTUCKY BOOK FAIR

P.O. Box 715, Frankfort KY 40602. (502)229-2542. **E-mail:** kybookfair@ky.gov. **Website:** kybookfair.blogspot.com. **Contact:** Connie Crow, KBF manager. Estab. 1981.
ADDITIONAL INFORMATION "The Kentucky Book Fair has 3 key goals: To honor the profession of writing in the form of a 1-day celebration; to provide a format for authors to meet their reading public; and to raise money through the sale of books and donate all

profits to mostly school and public libraries throughout Kentucky."

LOS ANGELES TIMES FESTIVAL OF BOOKS

Los Angeles CA **E-mail:** eventinfo@latimes.com. **Website:** events.latimes.com/festivalofbooks. Estab. 1996.

ADDITIONAL INFORMATION This festival began "with a simple goal: to bring together the people who create books with the people who love to read them. The festival was an immediate success and has evolved to include live bands, poetry readings, chef demos, cultural entertainment and artists creating their work onsite."

LOUISIANA BOOK FESTIVAL

701 N. Fourth St., Baton Rouge LA 70802. (225)219-9503. **Fax:** (225)219-9840. **E-mail:** lbf@state.lib.la.us. **Website:** www.louisianabookfestival.org. **Contact:** Robert Wilson, assistant director.

ADDITIONAL INFORMATION "The Louisiana Book Festival is jam-packed with outstanding literary events. Whatever book genre is your favorite, you're sure to find something you'll enjoy!"

MIAMI BOOK FAIR INTERNATIONAL

401 NE Second Ave., Suite 4102, Miami FL 33132. (305)237-3258. **Fax:** (305)237-3978. **E-mail:** wbookfair@mcd.edu. **Website:** www.miamibookfair.com.

ADDITIONAL INFORMATION "The books are coming. And the readers and writers will follow, as they do by the hundreds of thousands every year for the Miami Book Fair International, an 8-day literary party in November."

NATIONAL BOOK FESTIVAL

Library of Congress, 101 Independence Ave. S.E., Washington DC 20540. (888)714-4696. **E-mail:** bookfest@loc.gov. **Website:** www.loc.gov/bookfest.

ADDITIONAL INFORMATION "This year's festival will feature authors, poets and illustrators in several pavillions. Festival-goers can meet and hear firsthand from their favorite poets and authors, get books signed, hear special entertainment, have photos taken with storybook characters and participate in a variety of activities."

ORANGE COUNTY CHILDREN'S BOOK FESTIVAL

CA (949)455-9096. **E-mail:** oconn71@gmail.com. **Website:** kidsbookfestival.com. **Contact:** Sandy O'Connor, exhibitor and vendor coordinator.

ADDITIONAL INFORMATION "Each year the OC Children's Book Festival gets better and better and this year promises to be the best one yet! There is something for everyone who loves books. We invite you to join other families that know reading is the secret to a happy and successful life."

ROCHESTER CHILDREN'S BOOK FESTIVAL

Rochester NY **Website:** www.rochesterchildrensbookfestival.com.

ADDITIONAL INFORMATION "Our mission is to promote reading to and by children, benefit Monroe County libraries, and forge connections between the community and children's authors and illustrators."

SAVANNAH BOOK FESTIVAL

One Diamond Causeway, Suite 21-331, Savannah GA 31406. (912)598-4040. **Fax:** (912)598-9214. **E-mail:** info@savannahbookfestival.org. **Website:** www.savannahbookfestival.org.

ADDITIONAL INFORMATION "The Savannah Book Festival is an annual event. Free and open to the public, it's a celebration of the written word and its role in improving the human experience. Our mission is to promote reading, writing, and civil conversation."

SOUTH CAROLINA BOOK FESTIVAL

P.O. Box 5287, Columbia SC 29250. (803)771-2477. **Fax:** (803)771-2487. **Website:** www.scbookfestival.org. Estab. 1997.

ADDITIONAL INFORMATION "The South Carolina Book Festival has grown progressively in size and consequence, becoming the nationally recognized and regionally dominant book festival that it is today."

SOUTH DAKOTA FESTIVAL OF BOOKS

1215 Trail Ridge Road, Suite A, Brookings SD 57006. (605)688-6113. **Fax:** (605)688-4531. **E-mail:** info@sdhumanities.org. **Website:** www.sdhumanities.org/programs_festival.htm.

ADDITIONAL INFORMATION "Each year thousands of people converge on the annual South Dakota Festival of Books, a weekend-long event that features more than 40 well-known authors participating in book signings, presentations, panel discussions, and readings. Author presentations are separated into six tracks: fiction, nonfiction, poetry, children's/young adult, history/tribal, and writer's support."

SOUTHERN KENTUCKY BOOK FEST

WKU Libraries, Cravens 106, 1906 College Heights Blvd., Bowling Green KY 42101. (270)745-4502. **Web-**

site: www.sokybookfest.org. **Contact:** Kristie Lowry, literary outreach coordinator.

ADDITIONAL INFORMATION "The Southern Kentucky Book Fest is one of the state's largest literary events and is presented by WKU Libraries, Warren County Public Library, and Barnes and Noble Booksellers. Held annually in April, the Book Fest draws thousands or readers of all ages who welcome the occasion to meet their favorite authors and purchase signed copies of their books."

SOUTHWEST FLORIDA READING FESTIVAL

FL (239)337-7323. **E-mail:** readingfestival@leegov.com. **Website:** www.readfest.org.

ADDITIONAL INFORMATION "This free annual festival incites a passion for reading. Renew your interest in reading as the festival authors are announced. Hear an author speak at the festival and get inspired to borrow or buy the book, maybe even write one of your own!"

TEXAS BOOK FESTIVAL

610 Brazos, Suite 200, Austin TX 78701. (512)477-4055. **Fax:** (512)322-0722. **E-mail:** bookfest@texasbookfestival.org. **Website:** www.texasbookfestival.org. Estab. 1995.

ADDITIONAL INFORMATION "The Texas Book Festival was established in 1995 by Laura Bush, a former librarian and an ardent advocate of literacy. The signature event has evolved into one of the premier literary events in the country and takes place in and around the State Capitol in Austin, hosting about 250 authors each year. More than 40,000 book lovers of all ages attend the festival annually, enjoying author readings and presentations, panel discussions, book signings, cooking demonstrations, live music, local food, YA authors, children's activities, and exhibiting vendors from across the state."

TUCSON FESTIVAL OF BOOKS

UA BookStores, Bldg. 19, 1209 E. University, Tucson AZ 85721. **E-mail:** executivedirector@tucsonfestivalofbooks.org. **Website:** tucsonfestivalofbooks.org. **Contact:** Marcy Euler, executive director. Estab. 2009.

ADDITIONAL INFORMATION Held on the UA campus, this festival regularly attracts 100,000+ people.

UTAH HUMANITIES BOOK FESTIVAL

202 West 300 North, Salt Lake City UT 84103. (801)359-9670. **Fax:** (801)531-7869. **E-mail:** buckingham@utahhumanities.org. **Website:** www.utahhumanities.org/bookfestival.htm. **Contact:** Cynthia Buckingham, executive director.

ADDITIONAL INFORMATION "The Utah Humanities Book Festival is Utah's oldest and only statewide book festival and has become Utah's signature literary event. The festival is a chance for book lovers of all types to enjoy some great, free-of-charge literary events at locations throughout Utah." The festival is statewide, free, and runs 6 weeks.

VIRGINIA FESTIVAL OF THE BOOK

145 Ednam Dr., Charlottesville VA 22903. (434)924-7548. **Fax:** (434)296-4714. **E-mail:** vabook@virginia.edu. **Website:** www.vabook.org. **Contact:** Nancy Damon, program director.

ADDITIONAL INFORMATION "The mission of the Virginia Festival of the Book is to bring together writers and readers and to promote and celebrate books, reading, literacy, and literary culture."

WEST HOLLYWOOD BOOK FAIR

West Hollywood CA (323)848-6511. **Website:** www.westhollywoodbookfair.org. **Contact:** Chris Worland.

ADDITIONAL INFORMATION "A total of 12 outdoor stages and indoor venues, throughout West Hollywood Park and West Hollywood Library, will host literary and arts programming that will appeal to a broad audience of all ages and interests."

TENNESSEE WILLIAMS/NEW ORLEANS LITERARY FESTIVAL

938 Lafayette St., Suite 514, New Orleans LA 70113. (504)581-1144. **E-mail:** info@tennesseewilliams.net. **Website:** www.tennesseewilliams.net.

ADDITIONAL INFORMATION "The festival's mission is threefold: to serve the community through educational, theatrical, literary, and musical programs; to nurture, support, and showcase regional, national, and international writers, actors, musicians, and other artists; and to honor the creative genius of Tennessee Williams, who considered this city his spiritual home."

YOUR 2014–2015 SELF-PUBLISHING CALENDAR

The best way for writers to achieve success is by setting goals. Goals are usually met by writers who give themselves deadlines. Something about having an actual date to hit helps create a sense of urgency in most writers (and editors for that matter). This writing calendar is a great place to keep your important deadlines.

Also, this writing calendar is a good tool for recording upcoming writing events you'd like to attend or contests you'd like to enter. Or use this calendar to block out valuable time for yourself—to just write.

Of course, you can use this calendar to record other special events, especially if you have a habit of remembering to write but of forgetting birthdays or anniversaries. After all, this calendar is now yours. Do with it what you will.

AUGUST 2014

SUN	MON	TUE	WED	THURS	FRI	SAT
					1	2
3	4	5	6	7	8	9
10	11	12	13	14	15	16
17	18	19	20	21	22	23
24	25	26	27	28	29	30
31						

Think big. Establish ambitious long-term goals.

SEPTEMBER 2014

SUN	MON	TUE	WED	THU	FRI	SAT
	1	2	3	4	5	6
7	8	9	10	11	12	13
14	15	16	17	18	19	20
21	22	23	24	25	26	27
28	29	30				

Break down what small steps are needed to take to accomplish these long-term goals.

OCTOBER 2014

SUN	MON	TUE	WED	THU	FRI	SAT
			1	2	3	4
5	6	7	8	9	10	11
12	13	14	15	16	17	18
19	20	21	22	23	24	25
26	27	28	29	30	31	

Set monthly writing goals for things such as word count or guest posts to submit.

NOVEMBER 2014

SUN	MON	TUE	WED	THU	FRI	SAT
						1
2	3	4	5	6	7	8
9	10	11	12	13	14	15
16	17	18	19	20	21	22
23	24	25	26	27	28	29
30						

Write a novel during November as part of NaNoWriMo!

DECEMBER 2014

SUN	MON	TUE	WED	THU	FRI	SAT
	1	2	3	4	5	6
7	8	9	10	11	12	13
14	15	16	17	18	19	20
21	22	23	24	25	26	27
28	29	30	31			

Revise your novel, or get your manuscript ready to self-publish.

JANUARY 2015

SUN	MON	TUE	WED	THU	FRI	SAT
				1	2	3
4	5	6	7	8	9	10
11	12	13	14	15	16	17
18	19	20	21	22	23	24
25	26	27	28	29	30	31

Evaluate your 2014 accomplishments and make 2015 goals.

FEBRUARY 2015

SUN	MON	TUE	WED	THU	FRI	SAT
1	2	3	4	5	6	7
8	9	10	11	12	13	14
15	16	17	18	19	20	21
22	23	24	25	26	27	28

Make an effort to find writing friends and peers who can help you edit and/or share your work.

MARCH 2015

SUN	MON	TUE	WED	THU	FRI	SAT
1	2	3	4	5	6	7
8	9	10	11	12	13	14
15	16	17	18	19	20	21
22	23	24	25	26	27	28
29	30	31				

Join a writing organization or small, local writing group.

SUN	MON	TUE	WED	THU	FRI	SAT
			1	2	3	4
5	6	7	8	9	10	11
12	13	14	15	16	17	18
19	20	21	22	23	24	25
26	27	28	29	30		

Try writing or self-publishing poetry for National Poetry Month.

MAY 2015

SUN	MON	TUE	WED	THU	FRI	SAT
					1	2
3	4	5	6	7	8	9
10	11	12	13	14	15	16
17	18	19	20	21	22	23
24	25	26	27	28	29	30
31						

Plan to attend a writing conference this summer. Have work(s) ready to sell.

JUNE 2015

SUN	MON	TUE	WED	THU	FRI	SAT
	1	2	3	4	5	6
7	8	9	10	11	12	13
14	15	16	17	18	19	20
21	22	23	24	25	26	27
28	29	30				

Before your book is self-published, start pitching guest posts to top blogs.

JULY 2015

SUN	MON	TUE	WED	THU	FRI	SAT
			1	2	3	4
5	6	7	8	9	10	11
12	13	14	15	16	17	18
19	20	21	22	23	24	25
26	27	28	29	30	31	

Spend time considering the best cover possible. Think about what pulls you in to a great cover.

AUGUST 2015

SUN	MON	TUE	WED	THU	FRI	SAT
						.1
2	3	4	5	6	7	8
9	10	11	12	13	14	15
16	17	18	19	20	21	22
23	24	25	26	27	28	29
30	31					

Get involved in social media. Set goals. Start a blog now, and join Twitter next month.

SEPTEMBER 2015

SUN	MON	TUE	WED	THU	FRI	SAT
		1	2	3	4	5
6	7	8	9	10	11	12
13	14	15	16	17	18	19
20	21	22	23	24	25	26
27	28	29	30			

Keep a comprehensive file of all your writing ideas, from book concepts to character quirks.

OCTOBER 2015

SUN	MON	TUE	WED	THU	FRI	SAT
				1	2	3
4	5	6	7	8	9	10
11	12	13	14	15	16	17
18	19	20	21	22	23	24
25	26	27	28	29	30	31

Remember to back up all your writing.

NOVEMBER 2015

SUN	MON	TUE	WED	THU	FRI	SAT
1	2	3	4	5	6	7
8	9	10	11	12	13	14
15	16	17	18	19	20	21
22	23	24	25	26	27	28
29	30					

Good writers read. Set a goal of reading at least two books a month.

DECEMBER 2015

SUN	MON	TUE	WED	THU	FRI	SAT
		1	2	3	4	5
6	7	8	9	10	11	12
13	14	15	16	17	18	19
20	21	22	23	24	25	26
27	28	29	30	31		

Reward yourself for good work. Celebrate successes, big and small.

PROFESSIONAL ORGANIZATIONS

//

AGENTS' ORGANIZATIONS

ASSOCIATION OF AUTHORS' AGENTS (AAA), 5-8 Lower John Street, Golden Square, London W1F 9HA . E-mail: anthonygoff@davidhigham.co.uk. Website: www.agentsassoc.co.uk.

ASSOCIATION OF AUTHORS' REPRESENTATIVES (AAR). E-mail: info@aar-online.org. Website: www.aar-online.org.

ASSOCIATION OF TALENT AGENTS (ATA), 9255 Sunset Blvd., Suite 930, Los Angeles CA 90069. (310)274-0628. E-mail: shellie@agentassociation.com. Website: www.agentassociation.com.

WRITERS' ORGANIZATIONS

ACADEMY OF AMERICAN POETS 584 Broadway, Suite 604, New York NY 10012-5243. (212)274-0343. Fax: (212)274-9427. E-mail: academy@poets.org. Website: www.poets.org.

AMERICAN CRIME WRITERS LEAGUE (ACWL), 17367 Hilltop Ridge Dr., Eureka MO 63205. Website: www.acwl.org.

AMERICAN INDEPENDENT WRITERS (AIW), 1001 Connecticut Ave. NW, Suite 701, Washington DC 20036. E-mail: info@aiwriters.org. Website: www.americanindependentwriters.org.

AMERICAN MEDICAL WRITERS ASSOCIATION (AMWA), 30 West Gude Drive, Suite 525, Rockville MD 20850-4347. (301)294-5303. Fax: (301)294-9006. E-mail: amwa@amwa.org. Website: www.amwa.org.

AMERICAN SCREENWRITERS ASSOCIATION (ASA), 269 S. Beverly Dr., Suite 2600, Beverly Hills CA 90212-3807. (866)265-9091. E-mail: asa@goasa.com. Website: www.asascreenwriters.com.

AMERICAN TRANSLATORS ASSOCIATION (ATA), 225 Reinekers Lane, Suite 590, Alexandria VA 22314. (703)683-6100. Fax: (703)683-6122. E-mail: ata@atanet.org. Website: www.atanet.org.

EDUCATION WRITERS ASSOCIATION (EWA), 2122 P St., NW Suite 201, Washington DC 20037. (202)452-9830. Fax: (202)452-9837. E-mail: ewa@ewa.org. Website: www.ewa.org.

HORROR WRITERS ASSOCIATION (HWA), 244 5th Ave., Suite 2767, New York NY 10001. E-mail: hwa@horror.org. Website: www.horror.org.

THE INTERNATIONAL WOMEN'S WRITING GUILD (IWWG),P.O. Box 810, Gracie Station, New York NY 10028-0082. (212)737-7536. Fax: (212)737-9469. E-mail: dirhahn@aol.org. Website: www.iwwg.com.

MYSTERY WRITERS OF AMERICA (MWA), 1140 Broadway, Suite 1507, New York NY 10001. (212)888-8171. Fax: (212)888-8107. E-mail: mwa@mysterywriters.org. Website: www.mys-terywriters.org.

NATIONAL ASSOCIATION OF SCIENCE WRITERS (NASW), P.O. Box 7905, Berkeley, CA 94707. (510)647-9500. E-mail: LFriedmann@nasw.org. website: www.nasw.org.

NATIONAL ASSOCIATION OF WOMEN WRITERS (NAWW), 24165 IH-10 W., Suite 217-637, San Antonio TX 78257. Phone/Fax: (866)821-5829. Website: www.naww.org.

ORGANIZATION OF BLACK SCREENWRITERS (OBS). Golden State Mutual Life Insurance Bldg., 1999 West Adams Blvd., Rm. Mezzanine Los Angeles, CA 90018. Website: www.obswriter.com.

OUTDOOR WRITERS ASSOCIATION OF AMERICA (OWAA), 121 Hickory St., Suite 1, Missoula MT 59801. (406)728-7434. E-mail: krhoades@owaa.org. Website: www.owaa.org.

POETRY SOCIETY OF AMERICA (PSA), 15 Gramercy Park, New York NY 10003. (212)254-9628. website: www.poetrysociety.org. Poets & Writers, 90 Broad St., Suite 2100, New York NY 10004. (212)226-3586. Fax: (212)226-3963. Website: www.pw.org.

ROMANCE WRITERS OF AMERICA (RWA), 114615 Benfer Road, Houston TX 77069. (832)717-5200. Fax: (832)717-5201. E-mail: info@rwanational.org. Website: www.rwanational.org.

SCIENCE FICTION AND FANTASY WRITERS OF AMERICA (SFWA), P.O. Box 877, Chestertown MD 21620. E-mail: execdir@sfwa.org. Website: www.sfwa.org.

SOCIETY OF AMERICAN BUSINESS EDITORS & WRITERS (SABEW), University of Missouri, School of Journalism, 30 Neff Annex, Columbia MO 65211. (602) 496-7862. E-mail: sabew@sabew. org. Website: www.sabew.org.

SOCIETY OF AMERICAN TRAVEL WRITERS (SATW), 7044 S. 13 St., Oak Creek WI 53154. (414)908-4949. Fax: (414)768-8001. E-mail: satw@satw.org. Website: www.satw.org.

SOCIETY OF CHILDREN'S BOOK WRITERS & ILLUSTRATORS (SCBWI), 8271 Beverly Blvd., Los Angeles CA 90048. (323)782-1010. E-mail: scbwi@scbwi.org. Website: www.scbwi.org.

WESTERN WRITERS OF AMERICA (WWA). E-mail: spiritfire@kc.rr.com. Website: www.westernwriters.org.

INDUSTRY ORGANIZATIONS

AMERICAN BOOKSELLERS ASSOCIATION (ABA), 200 White Plains Rd., Suite 600, Tarrytown NY 10591. (914)591-2665. E-mail: info@bookweb.org. Website: www.bookweb.org.

AMERICAN SOCIETY OF JOURNALISTS & AUTHORS (ASJA), 1501 Broadway, Suite 302, New York NY 10036. (212)997-0947. E-mail: director@asja.org. Website: www.asja.org.

ASSOCIATION FOR WOMEN IN COMMUNICATIONS (AWC), 3337 Duke St., Alexandria VA 22314. (703)370-7436. E-mail: info@womcom.org. Website: www.womcom.org.

ASSOCIATION OF AMERICAN PUBLISHERS (AAP), 71 5th Ave., 2nd Floor, New York NY 10003. Or, 50 F St. NW, Suite 400, Washington DC 20001. Website: www.publishers.org.

THE ASSOCIATION OF WRITERS & WRITING PROGRAMS (AWP), Mail Stop 1E3, George Mason University, Fairfax VA 22030. (703)993-4301. Fax: (703)993-4302. E-mail: services@awpwriter. org. website: www.awpwriter.org.

THE AUTHORS GUILD, INC., 31 E. 32nd St., 7th Floor, New York NY 10016. (212)563-5904. Fax: (212)564-5363. E-mail: staff@authorsguild.org. website: www.authorsguild.org.

CANADIAN AUTHORS ASSOCIATION (CAA), P.O. Box 581, Stn. Main Orilla ON L3V 6K5 Canada. (705)653-0323. E-mail: admin@canauthors.org. Website: www.canauthors.org.

CHRISTIAN BOOKSELLERS ASSOCIATION (CBA), P.O. Box 62000, Colorado Springs CO 80962-2000. (800)252-1950. Fax: (719)272-3510. E-mail: info@cbaonline.org. website: www.cbaonline.org.

THE DRAMATISTS GUILD OF AMERICA, 1501 Broadway, Suite 701, New York NY 10036. (212)398-9366. Fax: (212)944-0420. Website: www.dramatistsguild.com.

NATIONAL LEAGUE OF AMERICAN PEN WOMEN (NLAPW), 1300 17th St. NW, Washington DC 20036-1973. (202)785-1997. E-mail: nlapw1@verizon.net. Website: www.americanpen-women.org.

NATIONAL WRITERS ASSOCIATION (NWA), 10940 S. Parker Rd., #508, Parker CO 80134. (303)841-0246. Fax: (303)841-2607. E-mail: natlwritersassn@hotmail.com. Website: www.nationalwriters.com

NATIONAL WRITERS UNION (NWU), 256 West 38th Street, Suite 703, New York, NY 10018. (212)254-0279. Fax: (212)254-0673. E-mail: nwu@nwu.org. Website: www.nwu.org.

PEN AMERICAN CENTER, 588 Broadway, Suite 303, New York NY 10012-3225. (212)334-1660. Fax: (212)334-2181. E-mail: pen@pen.org. Website: www.pen.org.

THE PLAYWRIGHTS GUILD OF CANADA (PGC), 215 Spadina Ave., Suite #210, Toronto ON M5T 2C7 Canada. (416)703-0201. Fax: (416)703-0059. E-mail: info@playwrightsguild.ca. Website: www.playwrightsguild.com.

VOLUNTEER LAWYERS FOR THE ARTS (VLA), One E. 53rd St., 6th Floor, New York NY 10022. (212)319-2787. Fax: (212)752-6575. Website: www.vlany.org.

WOMEN IN FILM (WIF), 6100 Wilshire Blvd., Suite 710, Los Angeles CA 90048. (323)935-2211. Fax: (323)935-2212. E-mail: info@wif.org. Website: www.wif.org.

WOMEN'S NATIONAL BOOK ASSOCIATION (WNBA), P.O. Box 237, FDR Station, New York NY 10150. (212)208-4629. Fax: (212)208-4629. E-mail: publicity@bookbuzz.com. Website: www.wnba-books.org.

WRITERS GUILD OF ALBERTA (WGA), 11759 Groat Rd., Edmonton AB T5M 3K6 Canada. (780)422-8174. Fax: (780)422-2663. E-mail: mail@writersguild.ab.ca. Website: writersguild.ab.ca.

WRITERS GUILD OF AMERICA-EAST (WGA), 555 W. 57th St., Suite 1230, New York NY 10019. (212)767-7800. Fax: (212)582-1909. e-mail: info@wgaeast.org. Website: www.wgaeast.org.

WRITERS GUILD OF AMERICA-WEST (WGA), 7000 W. Third St., Los Angeles CA 90048. (323)951-4000. Fax: (323)782-4800. Website: www.wga.org.

WRITERS UNION OF CANADA (TWUC), 90 Richmond St. E., Suite 200, Toronto ON M5C 1P1 Canada. (416)703-8982. E-mail: info@writersunion.ca. Website: www.writersunion.ca.

GLOSSARY

#10 ENVELOPE. A standard, business-size envelope.

ADVANCE. A sum of money a publisher pays a writer prior to the publication of a book. It is usually paid in installments, such as one-half on signing contract; one-half on delivery of complete and satisfactory manuscript.

AGENT. A liaison between a writer and editor or publisher. An agent shops a manuscript around, receiving a commission when the manuscript is accepted. Agents usually take a 10-15% fee from the advance and royalties.

ARC. Advance reader copy.

ASSIGNMENT. Editor asks a writer to produce a specific article for an agreed-upon fee.

AUCTION. Publishers sometimes bid for the acquisition of a book manuscript that has excellent sales prospects. The bids are for the amount of the author's advance, advertising and promotional expenses, royalty percentage, etc. Auctions are conducted by agents.

AVANT-GARDE. Writing that is innovative in form, style, or subject.

BACKLIST. A publisher's list of its books that were not published during the current season, but that are still in print.

BIMONTHLY. Every two months.

BIO. A sentence or brief paragraph about the writer; can include education and work experience.

BIWEEKLY. Every two weeks.

BLOG. Short for weblog. Used by writers to build platform by posting regular commentary, observations, poems, tips, etc.

BLURB. The copy on paperback book covers or hard cover book dust jackets, either promoting the book and the author or featuring testimonials from book reviewers or well-known people in the book's field. Also called flap copy or jacket copy.

BOILERPLATE. A standardized contract.

BOUND GALLEYS. Prepublication edition of book, usually photocopies of final galley proofs; also known as "bound proofs."

BYLINE. Name of the author appearing with the published piece.

CATEGORY FICTION. A term used to include all types of fiction.

CHAPBOOK. A small booklet usually paperback of poetry, ballads or tales.

CIRCULATION. The number of subscribers to a magazine.

CLIPS. Samples, usually from newspapers or magazines, of a writer's published work.

COFFEE-TABLE BOOK. An heavily illustrated oversize book.

COMMERCIAL NOVELS. Novels designed to appeal to a broad audience. These are often broken down into categories such as western, mystery and romance. See also genre.

CONTRIBUTOR'S COPIES. Copies of the issues of magazines sent to the author in which the author's work appears.

CO-PUBLISHING. Arrangement where author and publisher share publications costs and profits of a book. Also known as cooperative publishing.

COPYEDITING. Editing a manuscript for grammar, punctuation, printing style and factual accuracy.

COPYRIGHT. A means to protect an author's work.

COVER LETTER. A brief letter that accompanies the manuscript being sent to and agent or editor.

CREATIVE NONFICTION. Nonfictional writing that uses an innovative approach to the subject and creative language.

CRITIQUING SERVICE. Am editing service in which writers pay a fee for comments on the salability or other qualities of their manuscript. Fees vary, as do the quality of the critiques.

CV. Curriculum vita. A brief listing of qualifications and career accomplishments.

ELECTRONIC RIGHTS. Secondary or subsidiary rights dealing with electronic/multimedia formats (i.e., the Internet, CD-ROMs, electronic magazines).

ELECTRONIC SUBMISSION. A submission made by modem or on computer disk.

EROTICA. Fiction that is sexually oriented.

EVALUATION FEES. Fees an agent may charge to evaluate material. The extent and quality of this evaluation varies, but comments usually concern salability of the manuscript.

FAIR USE. A provision of the copyright law that says short passages from copyrighted material may be used without infringing on the owner's rights.

FEATURE. An article giving the reader information of human interest rather than news.

FILLER. A short item used by an editor to "fill" out a newspaper column or magazine page. It could be a joke, an anecdote, etc.

FILM RIGHTS. Rights sold or optioned by the agent/author to a person in the film industry, enabling the book to be made into a movie.

FOREIGN RIGHTS. Translation or reprint rights to be sold abroad.

FRONTLIST. A publisher's list of books that are new to the current season.

GALLEYS. First typeset version of manuscript that has not yet been divided into pages.

GENRE. Refers either to a general classification of writing, such as the novel or the poem, or to the categories within those classifications, such as the problem novel or the sonnet.

GHOSTWRITER. Writer who puts into literary form article, speech, story or book based on another person's ideas or knowledge.

GRAPHIC NOVEL. A story in graphic form, long comic strip, or heavily illustrated story; of 40 pages or more.

HI-LO. A type of fiction that offers a high level of interest for readers at a low reading level.

HIGH CONCEPT. A story idea easily expressed in a quick, one-line description.

HONORARIUM. Token payment.

HOOK. Aspect of the work that sets it apart from others and draws in the reader/viewer.

HOW-TO. Books and magazine articles offering a combination of information and advice in describing how something can be accomplished.

IMPRINT. Name applied to a publisher's specific line of books.

JOINT CONTRACT. A legal agreement between a publisher and two or more authors, establishing provisions for the division of royalties the book generates.

KILL FEE. Fee for a complete article that was assigned and then cancelled.

LEAD TIME. The time between the acquisition of a manuscript by an editor and its actual publication.

LITERARY FICTION. The general category of serious, non-formulaic, intelligent fiction.

MAINSTREAM FICTION. Fiction that transcends popular novel categories such as mystery, romance and science fiction.

MARKETING FEE. Fee charged by some agents to cover marketing expenses. It may be used to cover postage, telephone calls, faxes, photocopying or any other expense incurred in marketing a manuscript.

MASS MARKET. Non-specialized books of wide appeal directed toward a large audience.

MEMOIR. A narrative recounting a writer's (or fictional narrator's) personal or family history; specifics may be altered, though essentially considered nonfiction.

MIDDLE GRADE OR MID-GRADE. The general classification of books written for readers approximately ages 9-11. Also called middle readers.

MIDLIST. Those titles on a publisher's list that are not expected to be big sellers, but are expected to have limited/modest sales.

MODEL RELEASE. A paper signed by the subject of a photograph giving the photographer permission to use the photograph.

MULTIPLE CONTRACT. Book contract with an agreement for a future book(s).

MULTIPLE SUBMISSIONS. Sending more than one book or article idea to a publisher at the same time.

NARRATIVE NONFICTION. A narrative presentation of actual events.

NET ROYALTY. A royalty payment based on the amount of money a book publisher receives on the sale of a book after booksellers' discounts, special sales discounts and returns.

NOVELLA. A short novel, or a long short story; approximately 7,000 to 15,000 words.

ON SPEC. An editor expresses an interest in a proposed article idea and agrees to consider the finished piece for publication "on speculation." The editor is under no obligation to buy the finished manuscript.

ONE-TIME RIGHTS. Rights allowing a manuscript to be published one time. The work can be sold again by the writer without violating the contract.

OPTION CLAUSE. A contract clause giving a publisher the right to publish an author's next book.

PAYMENT ON ACCEPTANCE. The editor sends you a check for your article, story or poem as soon as he decides to publish it.

PAYMENT ON PUBLICATION. The editor doesn't send you a check for your material until it is published.

PEN NAME. The use of a name other than your legal name on articles, stories or books. Also called a pseudonym.

PHOTO FEATURE. Feature in which the emphasis is on the photographs rather than on accompanying written material.

PICTURE BOOK. A type of book aimed at preschoolers to 8-year-olds that tells a story using a combination of text and artwork, or artwork only.

PLATFORM. A writer's speaking experience, interview skills, website and other abilities which help form a following of potential buyers for that author's book.

POD. Print on demand.

PROOFREADING. Close reading and correction of a manuscript's typographical errors.

PROPOSAL. A summary of a proposed book submitted to a publisher, particularly used for nonfiction manuscripts. A proposal often contains an individualized cover letter, one-page overview of the book, marketing information, competitive books, author information, chapter-by-chapter outline, and two to three sample chapters.

QUERY. A letter that sells an idea to an editor or agent. Usually a query is brief (no more than one page) and uses attention-getting prose.

REMAINDERS. Copies of a book that are slow to sell and can be purchased from the publisher at a reduced price.

REPORTING TIME. The time it takes for an editor to report to the author on his/her query or manuscript.

REPRINT RIGHTS. The rights to republish a book after its initial printing.

ROYALTIES, STANDARD HARDCOVER BOOK. 10 percent of the retail price on the first 5,000 copies sold; 12½ percent on the next 5,000; 15 percent thereafter.

ROYALTIES, STANDARD MASS PAPERBACK BOOK. 4-8 percent of the retail price on the first 150,000 copies sold.

ROYALTIES, STANDARD TRADE PAPERBACK BOOK. No less than 6 percent of list price on the first 20,000 copies; 7½ percent thereafter.

SASE. Self-addressed, stamped envelope; should be included with all correspondence.

SELF-PUBLISHING. In this arrangement the author pays for manufacturing, production and marketing of his book and keeps all income derived from the book sales.

SEMIMONTHLY. Twice per month.

SEMIWEEKLY. Twice per week.

SERIAL. Published periodically, such as a newspaper or magazine.

SERIAL FICTION. Fiction published in a magazine in installments, often broken off at a suspenseful spot.

SERIAL RIGHTS. The right for a newspaper or magazine to publish sections of a manuscript.

SHORT-SHORT. A complete short story of 1,500 words.

SIDEBAR. A feature presented as a companion to a straight news report (or main magazine article) giving sidelights on human-interest aspects or sometimes elucidating just one aspect of the story.

SIMULTANEOUS SUBMISSIONS. Sending the same article, story or poem to several publishers at the same time. Some publishers refuse to consider such submissions.

SLANT. The approach or style of a story or article that will appeal to readers of a specific magazine.

SLICE-OF-LIFE VIGNETTE. A short fiction piece intended to realistically depict an interesting moment of everyday living.

SLUSH PILE. The stack of unsolicited or misdirected manuscripts received by an editor or book publisher.

SOCIAL NETWORKS. Websites that connect users: sometimes generally, other times around specific interests. Four popular ones at the moment are MySpace, Facebook, Twitter and LinkedIn.

SUBAGENT. An agent handling certain subsidiary rights, usually working in conjuction with the agent who handled the book rights. The percentage paid the book agent is increased to pay the subagent.

SUBSIDIARY RIGHTS. All right other than book publishing rights included in a book publishing contract, such as paperback rights, book club rights and movie rights. Part of an agent's job is to negotiate those rights and advise you on which to sell and which to keep.

SUBSIDY PUBLISHER. A book publisher who charges the author for the cost to typeset and print his book, the jacket, etc., as opposed to a royalty publisher who pays the author.

SYNOPSIS. A brief summary of a story, novel or play. As part of a book proposal, it is a comprehensive summary condensed in a page or page and a half, single-spaced.

TABLOID. Newspaper format publication on about half the size of the regular newspaper page.

TEARSHEET. Page from a magazine or newspaper containing your printed story, article, poem or ad.

TOC. Table of Contents.

TRADE BOOK. Either a hardcover or softcover book; subject matter frequently concerns a special interest for a general audience; sold mainly in bookstores.

TRADE PAPERBACK. A soft-bound volume published and designed for the general public; available mainly in bookstores.

TRANSLATION RIGHTS. Sold to a foreign agent or foreign publisher.

UNSOLICITED MANUSCRIPT. A story, article, poem or book that an editor did not specifically ask to see.

YA. Young adult books

GEOGRAPHIC INDEX

GENERAL INDEX